BETTER HOMES AND GARDENS® BOOKS
Des Moines, Iowa

Better Homes and Gardens® Books
An Imprint of Meredith® Books
President, Book Group: Joseph J. Ward
Vice President and Editorial Director: Elizabeth P. Rice
Executive Editor: Nancy N. Green
Managing Editor: Christopher Cavanaugh
Art Director: Ernest Shelton

Cross-Stitcher's Big Book of Alphabets & Borders
Project Manager/Editor: Shelli McConnell
Associate Art Director: Tom Wegner
Text Copy Editor: Jennifer Speer Ramundt
Photographer: Perry Struse
Prop Stylist: Jill Abeloe Mead
Contributing Illustrator: Lyne Neymeyer
Production Manager: Doug Johnston
Prepress Production Manager: Randall Yontz
Graphic Production Coordinator: Paula Forest

Co-Produced by BANAR DESIGNS, Inc.
BANAR DESIGNS, Inc. Principals: Barbara Finwall, Nancy Javier, Arleen Bennett
Design Directors: Barbara Finwall, Nancy Javier
Editorial Director: Jan Mollett Evans, MORE THAN WORDS
Designers: Marina Anderson, Bette Ashley, Emie Bishop, Liz Turner Diehl, Gael Efron, Barbara Finwall, Nancy Javier, Wade Rollins, Barbara Vassler, Holly Witt
Computer Graphics: Amparo Orozco, Wade Rollins, Holly Witt
Chart Coordinator: Wade Rollins
Stitch Coordinators: Marita Dionisio, Nemie Torres
Stitchers: Arleen Bennett, Marita Dionisio, Melissa Dixon, Alice Hawkins, Hatsue Honey, Beth Kolb, Betty Kolb, Holly Kolb, Yoshiko Lehman, Patty Probst, Lina Rio, Kathi Schmierer, Nemie Torres
Seamstresses and Finishers: Nicki Birkett, Pat Parsons
Framing: Michael's, Oceanside, California; Fuhriman's, Logan, Utah; Lorie Cross Wall Decor, Eugene, Oregon
Proofreaders: Marita Dionisio, Nemie Torres, Holly Witt
Staff: Yoshiko Ball, Cecil Ekrut, Jean Jarrell, Liz Keogh, Danny Lapointe, Mateo Nicolas, Ayako Secola

First Edition. Printing Number and Year: 5 4 3 2 1 98 97 96 95 94
Library of Congress Catalog Card Number: 93-86595
ISBN: 0-696-00034-2

WE CARE!

The Crafts Department at Better Homes and Gardens® Books assembled this collection of projects for your crafting pleasure. Our staff is committed to providing you with clear and concise instructions so that you can complete each project. We guarantee your satisfaction with this book for as long as you own it. We welcome your comments and suggestions. Please address your correspondence to Better Homes and Gardens® Books Crafts Department, RW-240, 1716 Locust St., Des Moines, IA 50309-3023.

If you would like to order additional copies of any of our books, call 1-800-678-2803 or check with your local bookstore.

While a picture may be worth a thousand words, sometimes just a picture is not enough. Cross-stitchers have long known the value of including both words and pictures in their work. In the nineteenth century, young stitchers practiced their technique on samplers that included the alphabet, representations of their home or surroundings, and decorative motifs and borders. Later, young women of that era may have stitched monogrammed lingerie and linens for their hope chests.

In ever-increasing numbers, today's cross-stitchers are returning to the eloquent combination of words and pictures. These modern expressions are as varied as the stitchers themselves: adaptations of classic samplers, bordered sayings and poems, personalized wearables, and monogrammed home decorating items. A stitched piece becomes the ultimate gift when it is personalized with the recipient's name or features an especially meaningful phrase.

Unfortunately, it is often difficult to find in one project the combination of words and pictures that express your feelings. This book should make it easy to find the right mix for your next project. It is an inspiring reference work with many cross-stitched projects that use both visual elements and lettering. Each chapter has a distinctive theme. Choose from antique, Victorian, country, and elegant styles; there are alphabets for special occasions and holidays, whimsical designs for children and babies, and letters featuring floral and animal motifs. We hope this book will not only allow you to complete projects like the ones shown, but encourage you to branch out, combining the 100 alphabets and dozens of borders into creations that are uniquely your own.

Don't be afraid to improvise! If you feel that adding glass beads or metallic threads to a project would enhance it, give it a try. If you want to stitch a design on Aida fabric rather than linen, go ahead. If you want to substitute one border for another, do it. There are no right or wrong answers, only what does or does not please you.

If you need additional help, refer to the instructions in Cross-stitch Basics and Using Charted Alphabets in the back of the book. This information is designed to give you the confidence to use materials and techniques you may have never tried before. Remember, there is no secret to combining words and pictures; just get out your graph paper, and start designing your next project.

Kids Alphabets
by Wade Rollins

Animal Alphabets
by Bette Ashley

Special Occasion Alphabets
by Nancy Javier

Holiday Alphabets
by Barbara Vassler

Valentine's Day

Easter

Halloween

Thanksgiving

Christmas

Cross-Stitch Basics

General Project Instructions

Designer Profiles

To achieve diversity in designs for this book, we worked with 10 designers from very different backgrounds. They are female and male, represent three generations of stitchers, are college educated and self-taught, and have backgrounds in music, advertising, computer design, retailing, and art. Each designer contributed an entire chapter to the book; each chapter includes 10 alphabets and a number of borders. We are sure the distinct variety of styles will inspire your cross-stitching projects.

Marina Anderson

Marina Anderson has illustrated and designed in the fabric, needlework, and crafts fields for more than 17 years. Her sweet, whimsical style is recognizable and can be found in publications and kits by BANAR DESIGNS, Inc., and in many other craft and needlework publications. Her widely varied techniques include stitched and no-sew quilting and children's wearables.

Marina's studio is located in the beautiful mountain resort community of Bend, Oregon. She also travels regularly to Portland to work with the design staff at the manufacturer of her newest creation—an infant bedding line called Toy Time.

The Anderson family includes her husband, Jeff, and children Danya, age 17, Nick, 13, Scott, 8, and Max, 2. When time can be found, Marina enjoys skiing, gardening, and antiquing.

Marina would like to dedicate the designs in the Baby chapter to her youngest child, Maxwell David Anderson.

Bette Ashley

Bette Ashley has 18 years experience in needlework design and publication. She has designed, published, and marketed her own designs as well as published the work of other designers. Her innovative approach to design has brought her recognition in her field; in 1985, she was awarded the coveted Ginnie award for excellence and creativity in cross-stitch design. She is a member of The Society of Craft Designers and the Charted Designers of America.

In addition to cross-stitch, Bette has designed and published a series of appliqué and decorative painting patterns. She has also designed many craft and needlework books, leaflets, and kits for other well-known publishers. Needlepoint is another of her talents, and she has taught hundreds of students and judged several prestigious needlework shows.

After high school, Bette worked in the display department of a women's specialty store and soon was drawing their fashion ads for the newspaper. She attended the Art Museum School in Portland, Oregon, and the University of Oregon, while working in sales promotion, doing display work, commentating fashion shows, and modeling for a department store. Since that time, her varied career has included working for printers, owning needlework stores, and designing craft and fashion accessories.

Bette and her husband, Don, live with their five spoiled cats in northern California. Her clever designs are included in the Animals chapter of this book.

Emie Bishop

Emie Bishop didn't start out as a needle artist, but rather as a high school history and English teacher. The Logan, Utah, native married her high school sweetheart, Mike Bishop, after she graduated from Utah State University and taught while he completed his medical training. After Mike's graduation, the Bishops settled in Cache Valley, a small mountain community in northern Utah. Mike developed his medical practice, and together they raised five children: Marion, Eric, Matthew, Mark, and Scott.

It was during those busy years rearing her children that Emie cultivated her interest in needle art and frequently enrolled in art classes. Twelve years ago she began to share her love of needlework with other cross-stitchers when she established her own publishing company, Cross 'N Patch. Emie since has published more than 90 books and leaflets featuring her award-winning style, which incorporates a variety of historic and elegant stitches. An enthusiastic teacher, Emie finds special pleasure in helping others expand their knowledge of needlework.

A beautiful sampler created by Emie is featured in the Antique chapter of this book. It is typical of her designs with luscious, muted shades and a variety of stitches.

Liz Turner Diehl

Liz Turner Diehl is the owner of Designs by Liz Turner Diehl, Inc., a needlework manufacturing and publishing company established in 1980 in Eugene, Oregon. Creativity comes naturally to Liz, and designing seems to be hereditary. Her great-grandfather, an architect, designed 15 courthouses in Kansas. Her grandmother and mother were involved with needle art and painting. Liz has a degree in music, and she feels her love for music and color go hand in hand.

Liz has published numerous needlework books and kits. Her Tapestries and Tassels book won the Ginnie award in 1989 for creativity and excellence in charted design. She has also won the Best Display Award presented by The National Needlework Association for visual merchandising. As Director of Design for Madeira Marketing Ltd., Liz shares her expertise and enthusiasm in the use of fancy fibers.

While she travels extensively to educate consumers and attend trade shows, Liz finds her home state of Oregon to be a great spot for creativity. Going to the beach and mountains are her favorite activities. Demands on her time keep Liz on a tight schedule. Effective use of time is important because in addition to her business, she has two school-age children, Stuart and Spencer. Liz shares her exquisite designs with us in the Elegant chapter.

(continued)

Designer Profiles

(continued)

Gael Efron

Gael Efron is a well-known California artist from Palo Alto. She attended the Academy of Art in San Francisco and the Academia de Belle Arti in Rome, Italy. Her exceptional paintings have been displayed in several California galleries.

Drawing on her art background, Gael has expanded into other, related areas. Her exclusive, hand-painted tiles are used by many Bay area interior designers in homes of distinction. In the past three years, she has also designed several popular cross-stitch books for BANAR DESIGNS.

When she is not involved in her artistic pursuits, Gael enjoys reading, interior design, films, and, especially, spending time with her son, Miles, a student at Occidental College.

Gael's love of the outdoors and gardening inspired her to design the beautiful floral alphabet for this book. You may see a hint of the hand-painted tile look in her work in the Floral chapter.

Barbara Finwall

Barbara Finwall studied art at the highly regarded Chouinard Art Institute in Los Angeles. She also attended the Art Center School of Design in Los Angeles.

Barbara initially pursued an advertising career and received many advertising and design awards from the Los Angeles Advertising Women's Association and the Art Directors Club of Los Angeles. In 1971, she left the advertising world to start BANAR DESIGNS with her mother, Arleen Bennett, and sister, Nancy Javier. Barbara serves as the design director at BANAR, developing successful kits, books, and craft products.

For business and pleasure, Barbara enjoys traveling to Latin America, Europe, China, and all over the United States. When she's not busy designing and supervising their talented staff, she enjoys reading, rescuing stray animals, and decorating her country home. Barbara's flair for decorating is reflected in her designs for the Country chapter.

Nancy Javier

Nancy Javier is currently president of BANAR DESIGNS, where she is responsible for management and product development of the wholesale needlework and craft company. In addition, she oversees the sales and marketing at BANAR. A founder of the company—along with sister, Barbara, and mother, Arleen—Nancy has been involved in every phase of its growth. She displays a special flair for recognizing design trends in home decorating and clothing and for bringing exciting new products to the consumer.

Nancy graduated in 1974 from California State University at Los Angeles with a degree in anthropology. In conjunction with her studies, she was involved in an archeological dig in Peru for three months. Other travels have included business and product research trips to China and England and many miles of crisscrossing the United States to attend trade shows.

She lives in picturesque Fallbrook, California, with her daughter, Megan, who recently left for college in Boston to study film. Nancy shares a lifetime of celebration with us in the Special Occasion chapter.

Wade Rollins

Wade Rollins is a graphic designer in the San Diego area. He earned his degree in communications and art from Cal State Fullerton.

Wade currently resides on an avocado ranch. His rural lifestyle allows him to enjoy his favorite pastimes: hiking, camping, and photography. Wade's computer graphics career led him to BANAR DESIGNS, where he has worked for the last five years. He has also done free-lance work for other craft companies and magazines.

With an avid interest in designing, Wade has developed a broad range of designs for everything from iron-on wearables to tie-dyes. He shows a special aptitude for children's designs and crafts and currently heads the Children's Division at BANAR. You'll find Wade's colorful designs in the Kids chapter.

Barbara Vassler

Barbara Vassler has been an artist, sewing enthusiast, and needleworker since her school days. She combined all of these interests and started her own company, LITTLE BROWN HOUSE PATTERNS, 11 years ago.

Her line of patterns includes those for quilting and appliqué. She recently created delightful seasonal designs that can be created with no sewing at all. One of Barbara's more innovative products is a kit that includes the necessary fabric, lace, and other embellishments for covering bandboxes. She travels throughout the United States to various quilt shows where she displays and sells her unique patterns and products.

When not designing patterns or otherwise tending to business, Barbara enjoys hobbies that are quite far removed from her career with fabrics; wood carving and furniture building. She and her husband, Peter, love to explore the beautiful Pacific Northwest from their home base in Banks, Oregon.

Look in the Holidays chapter for Barbara's clever designs for Valentine's Day, Easter, Halloween, Thanksgiving, and Christmas.

Holly Witt

Holly Witt lives in the seaside community of Carlsbad, California. A graphic design major, she graduated from Iowa State University with a fine arts degree. While in college, she received many awards for her artwork.

Holly, who credits her mother for her avid interest in crafts, began her career in the fashion field, working in the art department of a nationwide retail chain. She gained further experience in graphic design after moving to California and working in a design studio. Holly has been immersed in the craft and needlework industry for the past two years as the newest addition to the BANAR DESIGNS creative staff. In addition, she has done free-lance designing for other major craft companies and publishers.

Combining her experience in fashion with her graphic design talents, Holly's greatest interest and expertise lies in the wearable arts field. Her love for working with ribbons, laces, antique buttons, and charms inspired her many lovely projects for the Victorian chapter.

When Holly is not designing, she enjoys rock climbing, scuba diving, and playing the piano.

Floral Alphabets

A green thumb isn't needed to make this garden grow. All you need instead is our impressive Floral Alphabet. The versatile flower motifs can be stitched alone or with letters to personalize your gifts. We've used it in widely varied projects; you are sure to think of many more.

Who plants
a seed
beneath the
sod
and waits to
see
believes in
God

Floral Afghan

USE FLORAL ALPHABET ON PAGES 17–29

Materials

Anne cloth: Taupe, 1¼ yard piece (Leisure Arts #11633), 18 count

Stitch

Follow the instructions for cross-stitching over two threads given in Cross-Stitch Basics. See General Afghan Instructions in Cross-Stitch Basics.

Finish

After cross-stitching the design, machine-stitch 3 inches away from the decorative bars at the edge of the design. Cut evenly about 4 inches beyond this stitched line. Fringe all four sides to the stitching line. Gather together every eight threads and tie in a knot.

Tissue Box Cover

USE FLORAL ALPHABET ON PAGES 17–29

Materials

Tissue holder: 14 count, ecru (Crafter's Pride)

Stitch

Follow the instructions for cross-stitching given in Cross-Stitch Basics. Start cross-stitching at the bottom center of the design about 1 inch up from the bottom of the premade tissue holder.

Finishing

Tissue holder is prefinished; no finishing is necessary. You may, however, want to add a ribbon in a color to match the design.

Pillow

USE FLORAL ALPHABET ON PAGES 17–29

Materials

Pillow: Premade with 7-count even-weave front, 11 inches square plus 2½ inch gathered chintz ruffle (Adam Originals)
Pillow form: 11 inches square
Tapestry needle: Size #20
(We used blue floss for the R on our pillow. Use the color of your choice.)

Stitch

Unzip the premade pillow and reach inside to cross-stitch the design. Follow the instructions for cross-stitching given in Cross-Stitch Basics. Use six strands of floss for cross-stitching and two strands for outlining.

Finish

The premade pillow requires no finishing. When finished stitching, insert pillow form.

Vest

USE SWEET PEA DESIGN FROM LETTER S IN FLORAL ALPHABET ON PAGES 17–29 (DO NOT USE LETTER UNLESS DESIRED)

Materials

Vest: Peach (Hirschberg/ Schutz, Inc.)
Waste canvas: 8.5 count, 7x7 inches

Stitch and Finish

Follow the instructions for cross-stitching and finishing with waste canvas given in Cross-Stitch Basics. The vest is premade; no sewing is necessary.

Floss: For the letter A

Symbol	Color name	DMC#	Anchor#
••	Ecru	Ecru	387
∧	Light peach	3713	1020
△	Medium peach	760	1022
▲	Dark peach***	3328	1024
/	Light green	966	214
◺	Medium green	320	215
◢	Dark green	987	210
×	Light rust	355	1014
✳	Dark rust	221	897
	Dark gray*	413	401
	Dark dark green**	319	218

*Backstitch inside the flowers in dark gray (two strands).
**Backstitch stamen in dark dark green (two strands).
***Backstitch the outside edge of the flowers in dark peach (two strands).

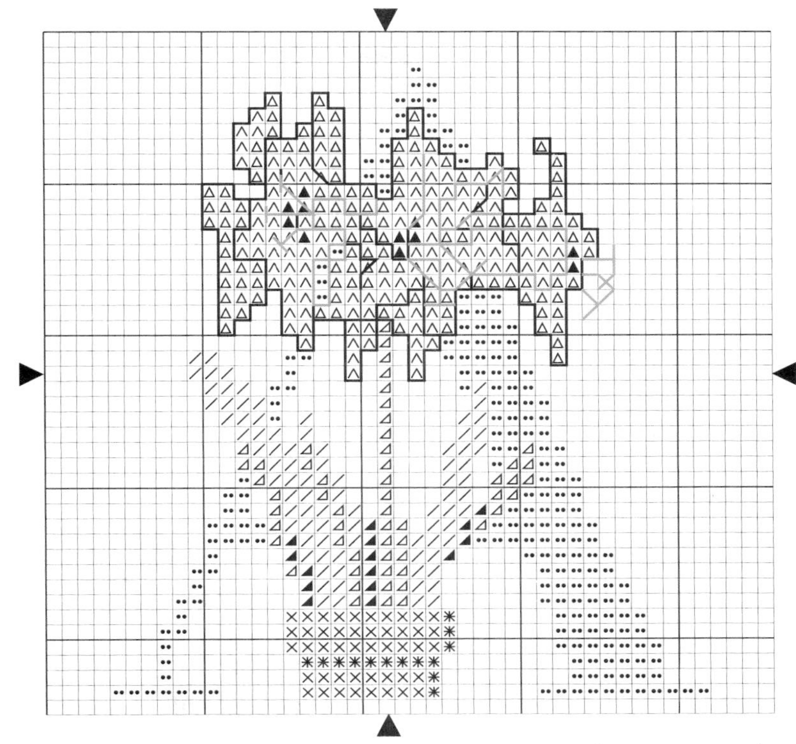

Floral Alphabet Stitch Count: 38 x 42

Stitching Tip

When using this alphabet for stitching an afghan, find the vertical center of each afghan square. Count up four rows (or two stitches) from the bottom of the square and start stitching the center bottom of the design here. When stitching anything else, use the center marks on your chart.

Floss: For the letter B

Symbol	Color name	DMC#	Anchor#
••	Ecru	Ecru	387
•	Light pink	3689	49
/	Light green	966	214
◺	Medium green	320	215
⊙	Light pink French knots		
	Dark dark green*	319	218
	Dark pink**	3350	59

*Backstitch vines in dark dark green (two strands).
**Backstitch flowers in dark pink (two strands).

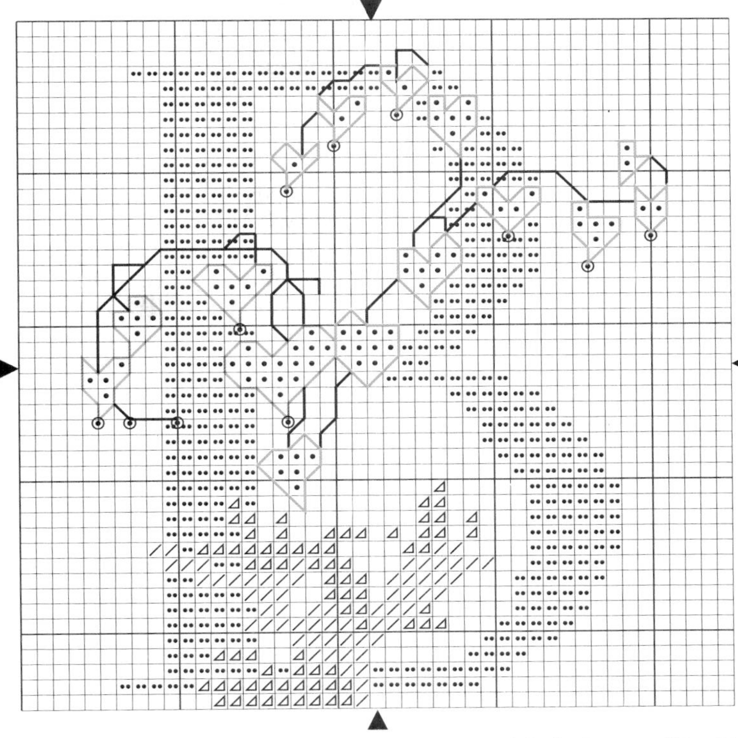

Floral Alphabet Stitch Count: 37 x 43

(continued)

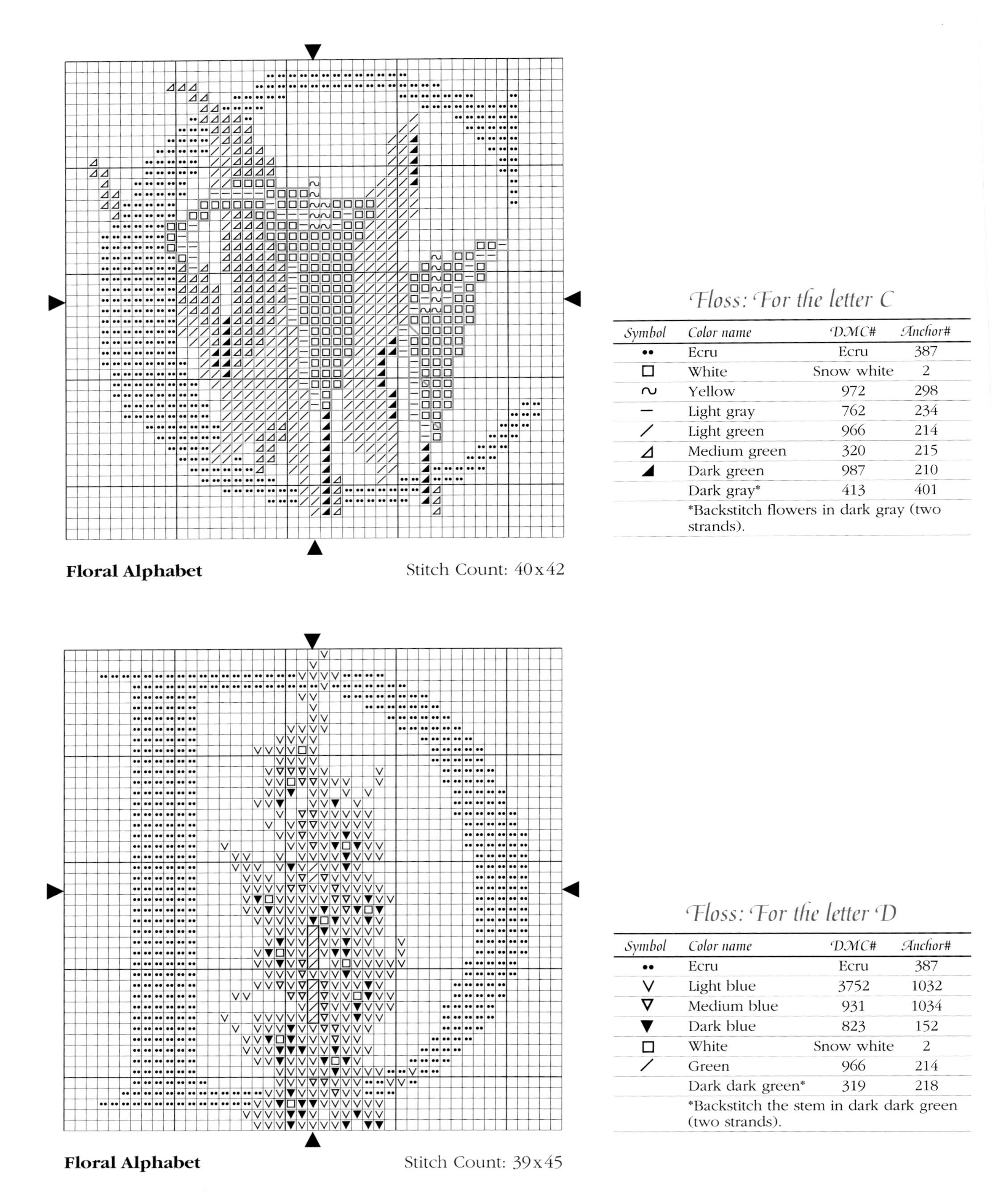

Floral Alphabet Stitch Count: 40x42

Floss: For the letter C

Symbol	Color name	DMC#	Anchor#
••	Ecru	Ecru	387
□	White	Snow white	2
∾	Yellow	972	298
—	Light gray	762	234
⁄	Light green	966	214
◺	Medium green	320	215
◢	Dark green	987	210
	Dark gray*	413	401

*Backstitch flowers in dark gray (two strands).

Floral Alphabet Stitch Count: 39x45

Floss: For the letter D

Symbol	Color name	DMC#	Anchor#
••	Ecru	Ecru	387
V	Light blue	3752	1032
▽	Medium blue	931	1034
▼	Dark blue	823	152
□	White	Snow white	2
⁄	Green	966	214
	Dark dark green*	319	218

*Backstitch the stem in dark dark green (two strands).

Floss: For the letter E

Symbol	Color name	DMC#	Anchor#
••	Ecru	Ecru	387
□	White	Snow white	2
—	Light gray	762	234
/	Light green	966	214
◿	Medium green	320	215
	Dark gray*	413	401
	*Backstitch flowers in dark gray (two strands).		

Floss: For the letter F

Symbol	Color name	DMC#	Anchor#
••	Ecru	Ecru	387
V	Light blue	334	977
▼	Dark blue	824	164
◑	Orange	722	324
/	Light green	966	214
◿	Medium green	320	215
◢	Dark green	987	210
⊙	Light blue french knots		
	Dark dark green*	319	218
	*Backstitch leaves, vines, and stems in dark dark green (two strands).		

(continued)

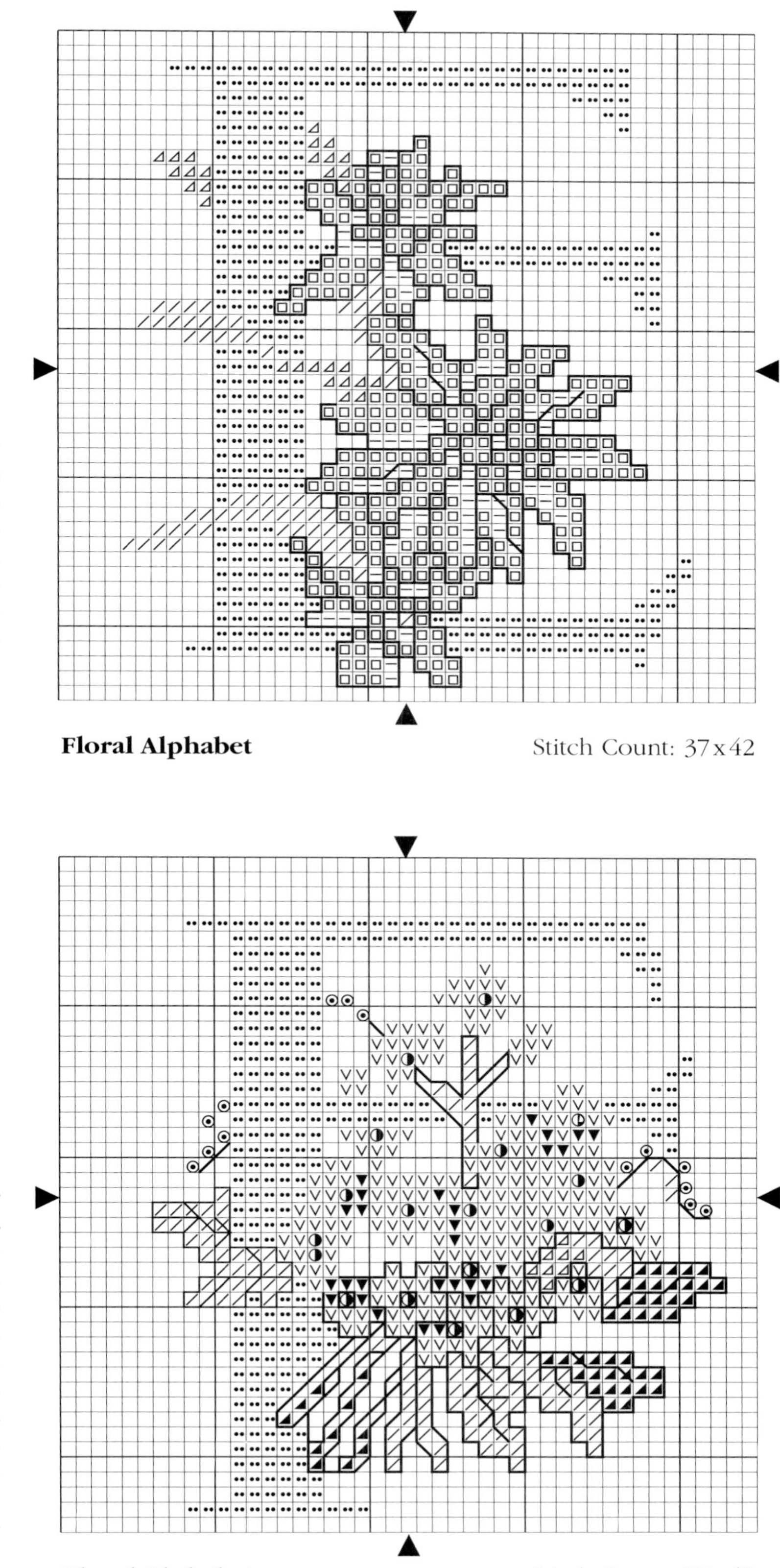

Floral Alphabet Stitch Count: 37 x 42

Floral Alphabet Stitch Count: 37 x 40

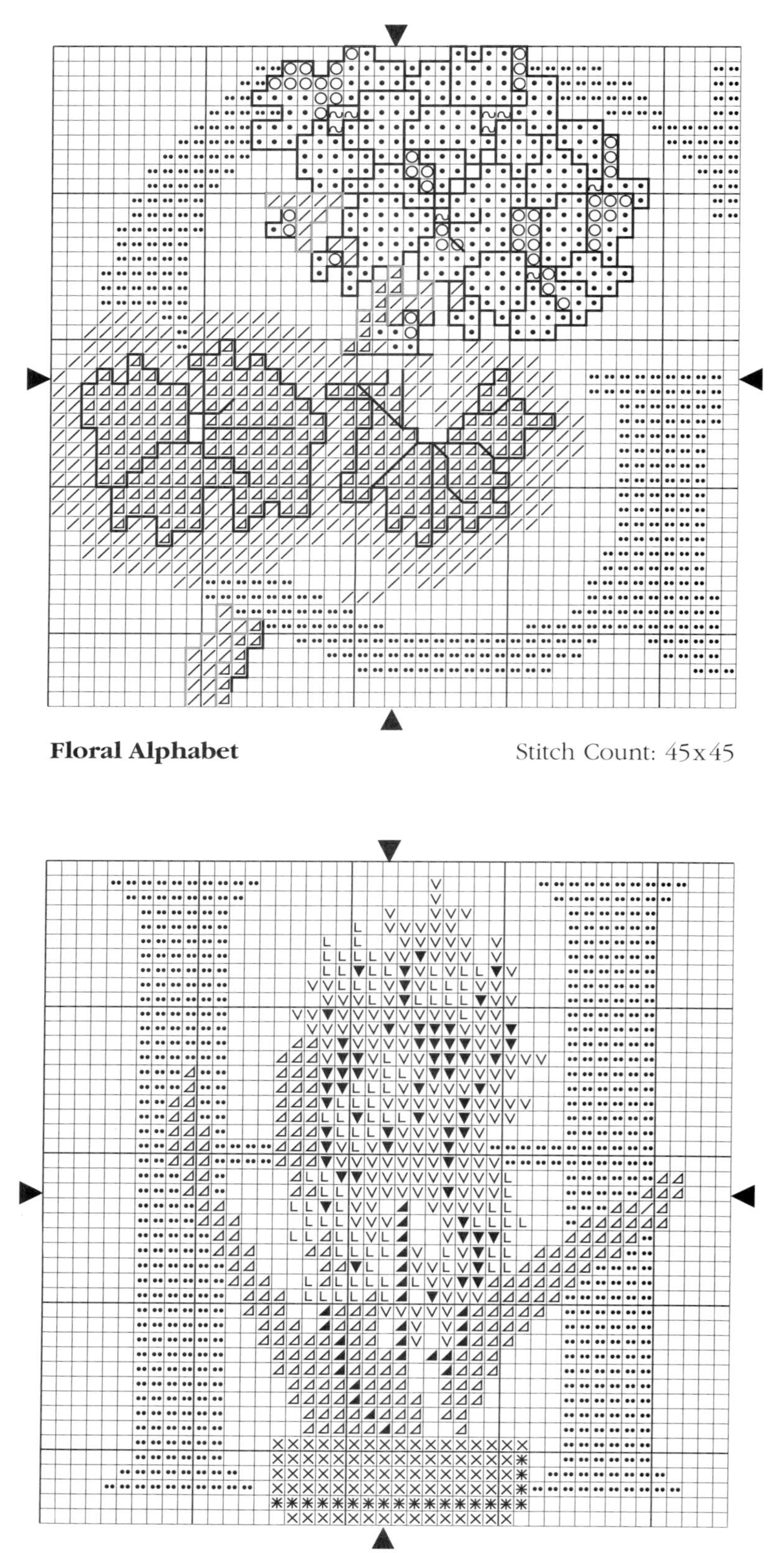

Floral Alphabet Stitch Count: 45x45

Floss: For the letter G

Symbol	Color name	DMC#	Anchor#
••	Ecru	Ecru	387
•	Light pink	818	48
○	Medium pink	3688	66
/	Light green	966	214
◿	Medium green	320	215
∾	Yellow	726	295
	Dark pink*	3687	68
	Dark dark green**	319	218

*Backstitch flowers in dark pink (two strands).
**Backstitch stems and veins of leaves in dark dark green (two strands).

Floral Alphabet Stitch Count: 38x42

Floss: For the letter H

Symbol	Color name	DMC#	Anchor#
••	Ecru	Ecru	387
V	Periwinkle	340	118
▼	Dark periwinkle	792	941
L	Lavender	211	342
◿	Medium green	320	215
◢	Dark green	987	210
×	Light rust	355	1014
✳	Dark rust	221	897

Floss: For the letter I

Symbol	Color name	DMC#	Anchor#
••	Ecru	Ecru	387
L	Light lavender	210	108
◣	Dark lavender	208	110
∾	Yellow	726	295
╱	Light green	966	214
◿	Medium green	320	215
◢	Dark green	987	210

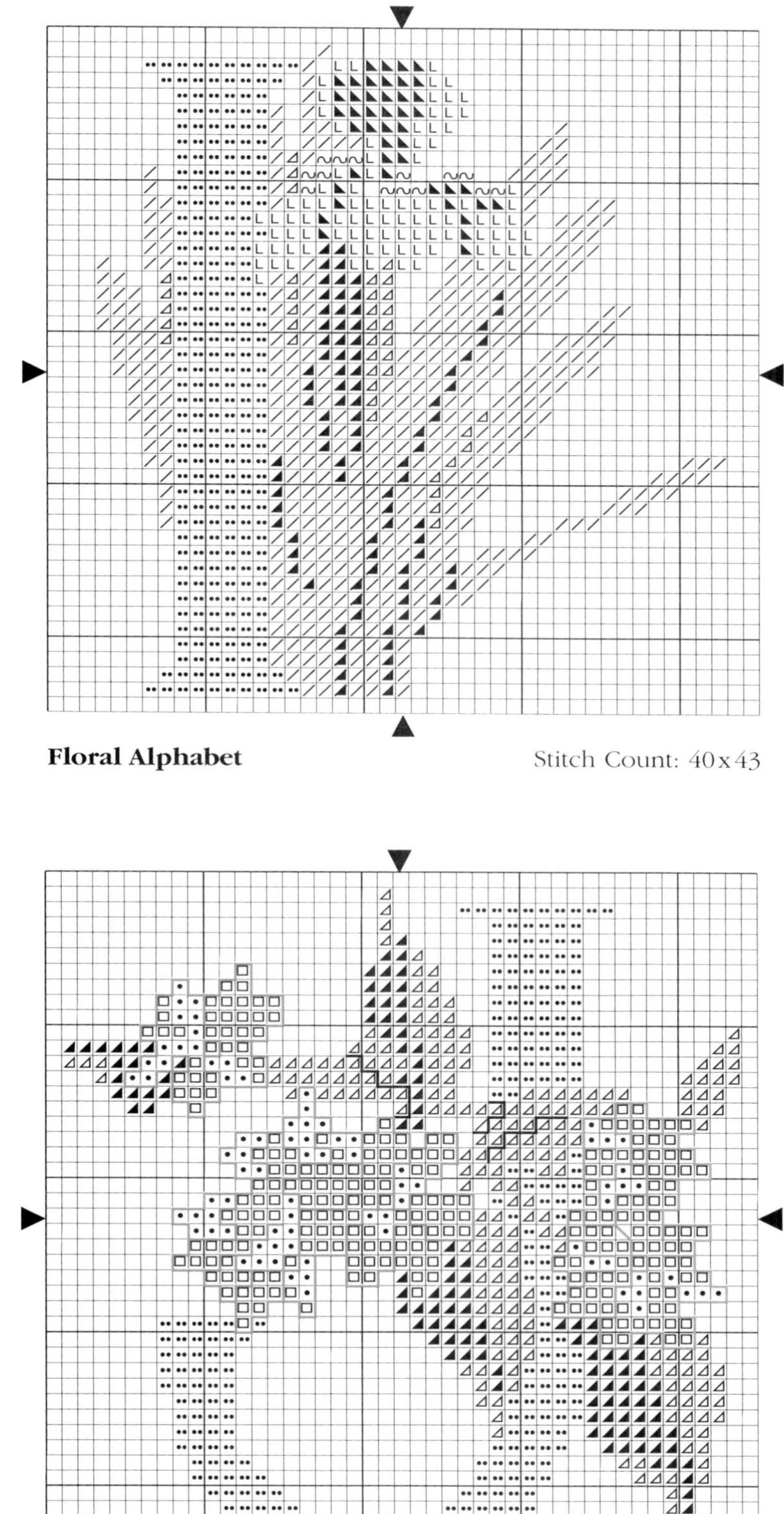

Floral Alphabet Stitch Count: 40x43

Floss: For the letter J

Symbol	Color name	DMC#	Anchor#
••	Ecru	Ecru	387
□	White	Snow white	2
•	Pink	818	23
◿	Medium green	320	215
◢	Dark green	987	210
	Dark dark green*	319	218
	Dark gray**	413	401
	*Backstitch leaves in dark dark green (two strands). **Backstitch flowers in dark gray (two strands).		

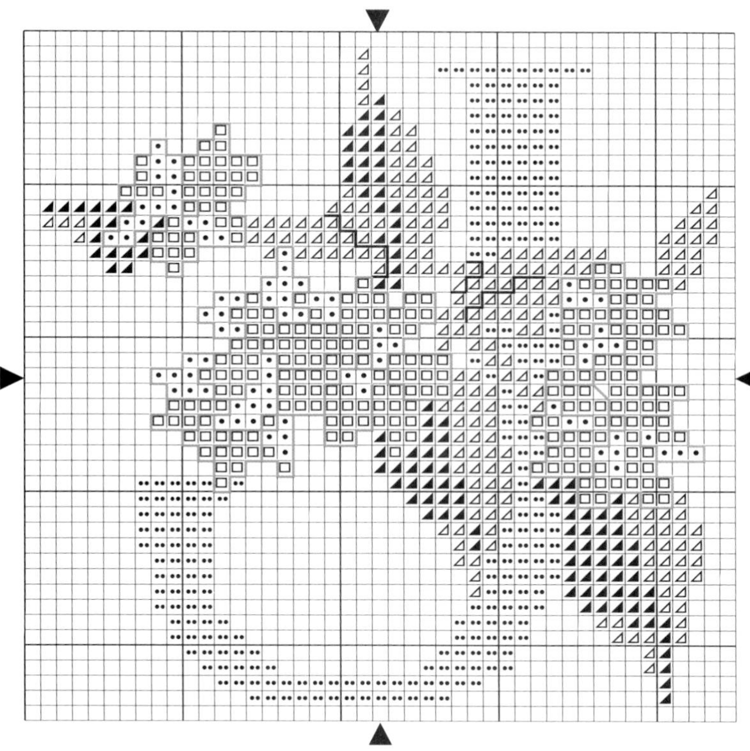

Floral Alphabet Stitch Count: 43x43

(continued)

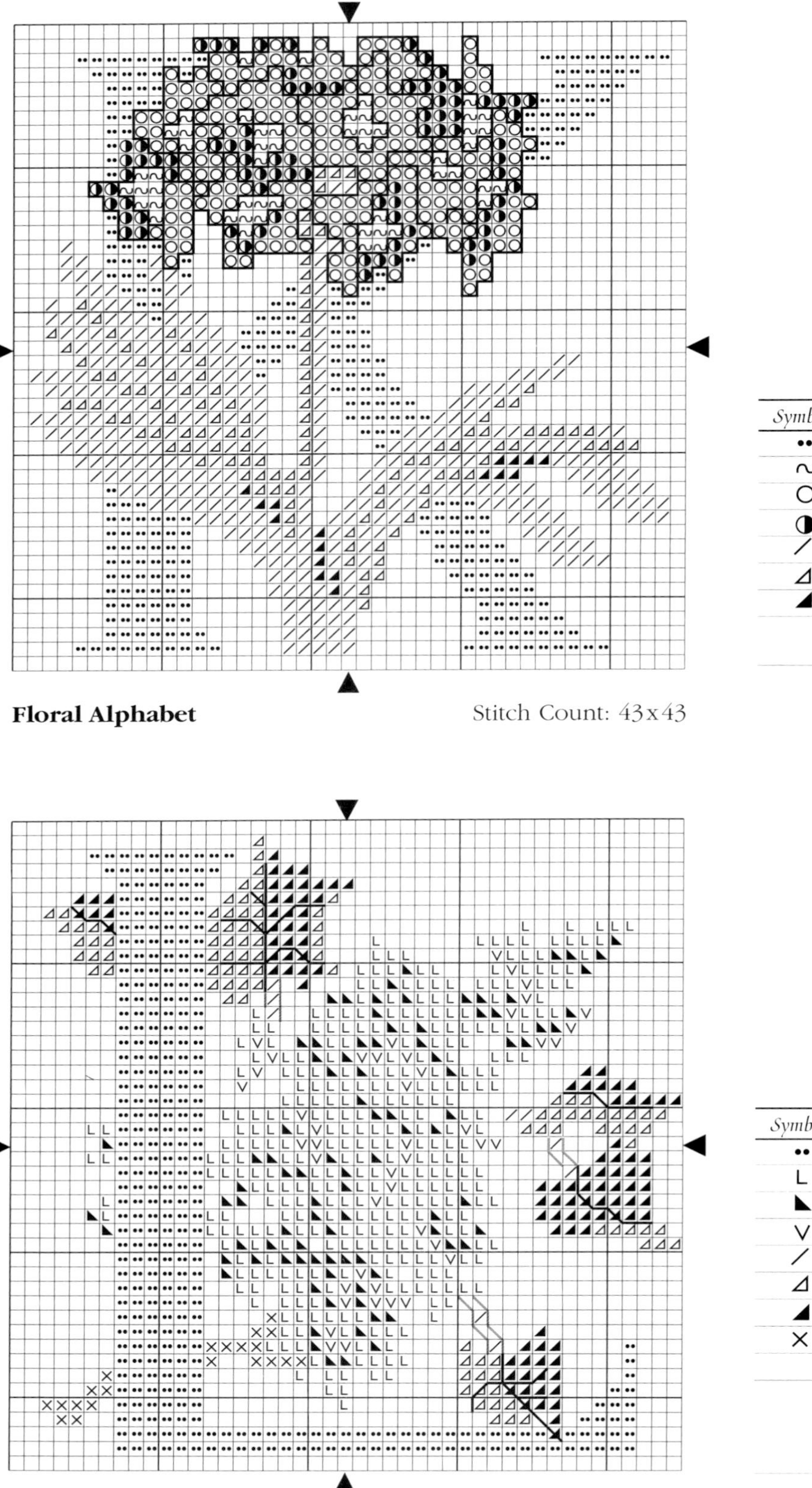

Floral Alphabet Stitch Count: 43x43

Floss: For the letter K

Symbol	Color name	DMC#	Anchor#
••	Ecru	Ecru	387
∾	Yellow	3078	292
○	Orange	722	323
◑	Dark orange*	921	1004
╱	Light green	966	214
◿	Medium green	320	215
◢	Dark green	987	210
	*Backstitch flower in dark orange (two strands).		

Floral Alphabet Stitch Count: 43x43

Floss: For the letter L

Symbol	Color name	DMC#	Anchor#
••	Ecru	Ecru	387
L	Light lavender	211	342
◣	Dark lavender	209	109
V	Periwinkle	340	118
╱	Light green**	966	214
◿	Medium green	320	215
◢	Dark green	987	210
X	Brown	300	352
	Dark dark green*	319	218
	*Backstitch veins in dark dark green (two strands). **Backstitch stems in light green (two strands).		

Floss: For the letter M

Symbol	Color name	DMC#	Anchor#
••	Ecru	Ecru	387
V	Light blue	932	1033
▼	Dark blue	931	1034
•	Light pink	818	23
○	Medium pink***	3688	66
♡	Dark pink	3687	68
/	Light green	966	214
◢	Medium green****	320	215
	Dark dark green*	319	218
	Dark dark blue**	3750	1035

*Backstitch tendrils and veins in leaves in dark dark green (two strands).
**Backstitch veins in flowers in dark dark blue (two strands).
***Backstitch flower shown in blue in medium pink (two strands).
****Backstitch stems where shown in medium green (two strands).

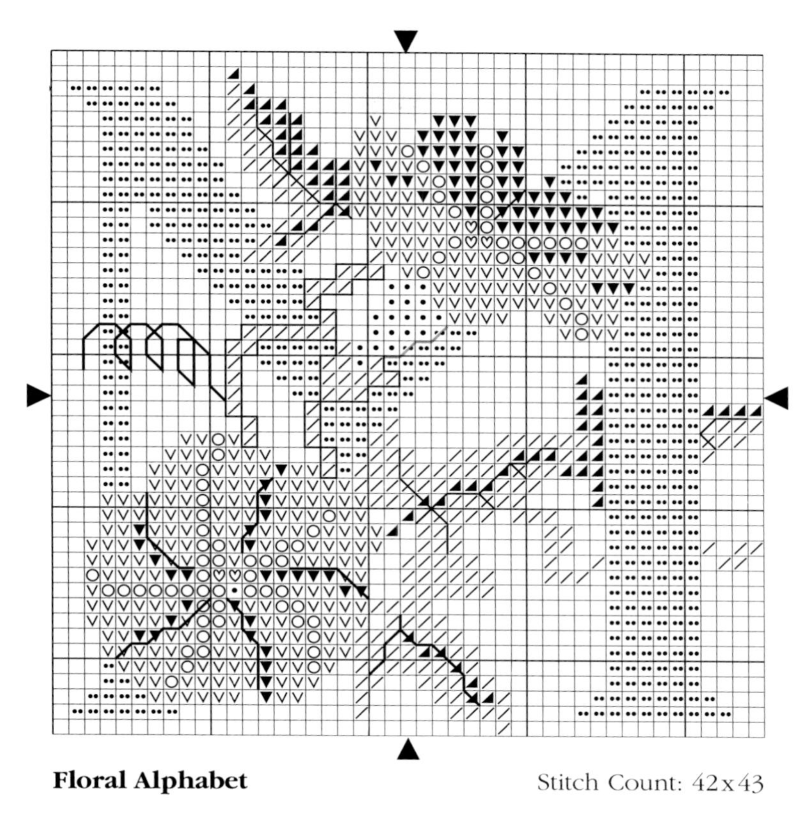

Floral Alphabet Stitch Count: 42x43

Floss: For the letter N

Symbol	Color name	DMC#	Anchor#
••	Ecru	Ecru	387
∾	Yellow	3078	292
◑	Light orange	722	323
+	Dark orange*	921	1004
×	Rust	221	897
/	Light green	966	214
◿	Medium green	320	215
	Dark dark green**	319	218

*Backstitch flowers in dark orange (two strands).
**Backstitch veins in leaves in dark dark green (two strands).

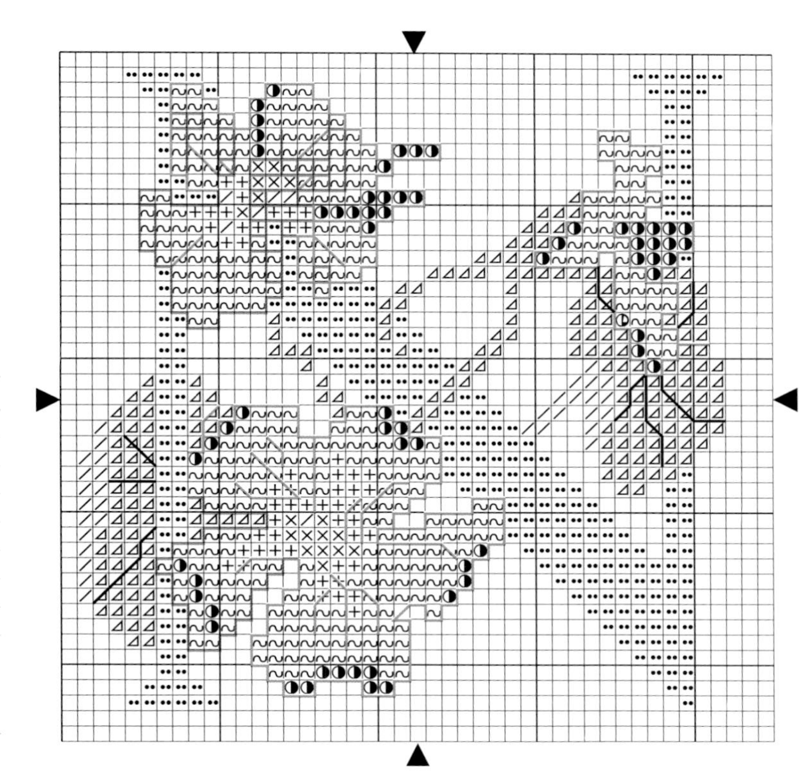

Floral Alphabet Stitch Count: 41x42

(continued)

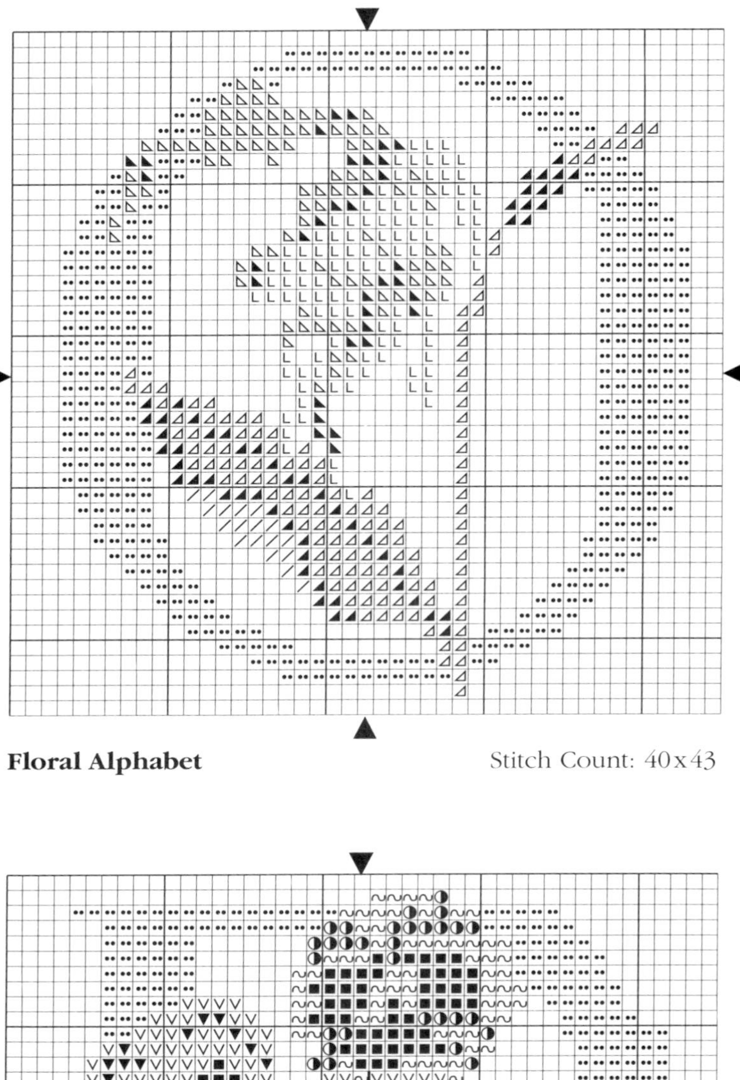

Floral Alphabet Stitch Count: 40x43

Floss: For the letter O

Symbol	Color name	DMC#	Anchor#
••	Ecru	Ecru	387
L	Light lavender	210	108
◺	Medium lavender	209	109
◣	Dark lavender	208	110
/	Light green	966	214
◿	Medium green	320	215
◢	Dark green	987	210

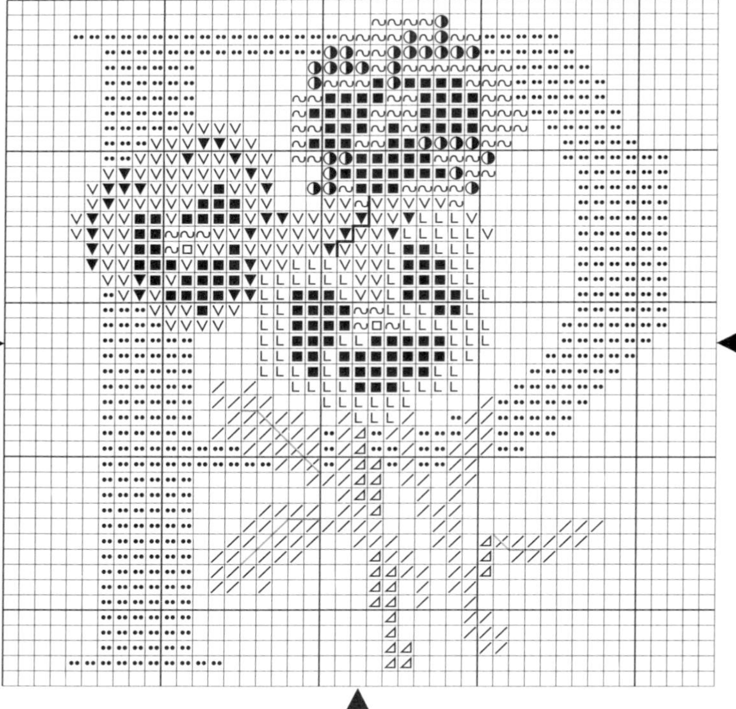

Floral Alphabet Stitch Count: 38x43

Floss: For the letter P

Symbol	Color name	DMC#	Anchor#
••	Ecru	Ecru	387
V	Light blue	3325	129
▼	Dark blue	334	977
□	White	Snow white	2
∿	Yellow	3078	292
◑	Orange	722	323
L	Lavender	209	109
/	Light green	966	214
◿	Medium green	320	215
■	Black**	310	403
	Dark dark green*	319	218

*Backstitch veins in leaves in dark dark green (two strands).
**Backstitch flowers in black where indicated (two strands).

Floss: For the letter Q

Symbol	Color name	DMC#	Anchor#
••	Ecru	Ecru	387
□	White	Snow white	2
=	Light gray	762	234
◿	Medium green	320	215
⊙	White french knots		
	Dark gray*	413	401
	Dark dark green**	319	218

*Outline flowers in dark gray (two strands).
**Outline stems in dark dark green (two strands).

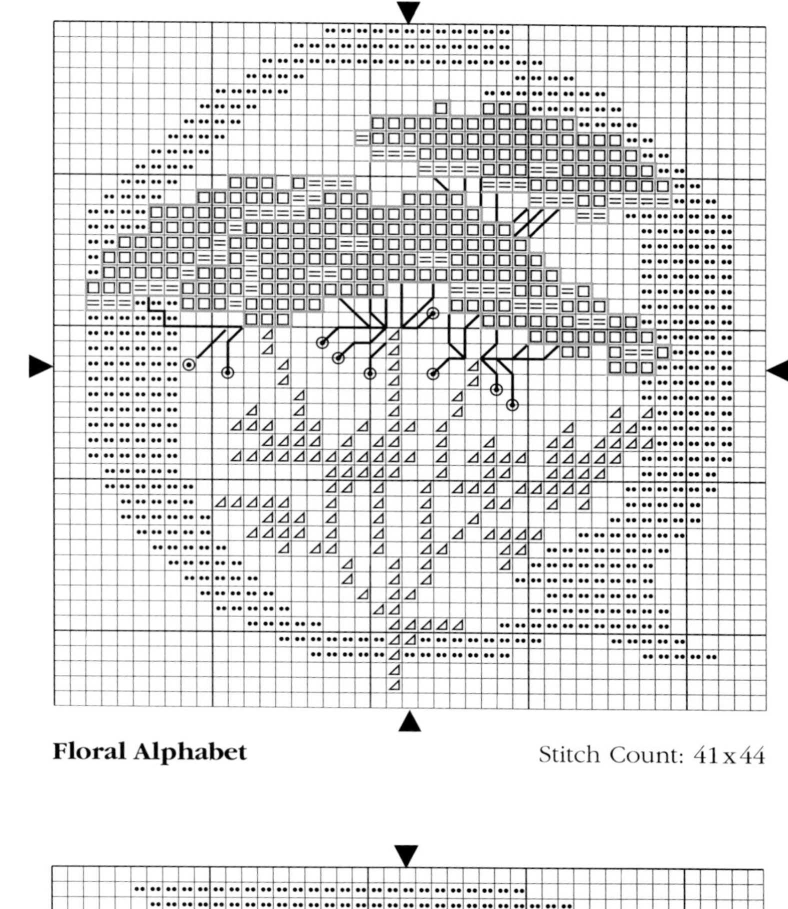

Floral Alphabet Stitch Count: 41 x 44

Floss: For the letter R

Symbol	Color name	DMC#	Anchor#
••	Ecru	Ecru	387
•	Light pink	818	48
●	Medium pink	3688	66
╱	Light green	966	214
◿	Medium green	320	215
	Dark dark green*	319	218
	Dark pink**	3687	68

*Backstitch stems in dark dark green (two strands).
**Backstitch flower in dark pink (two strands).

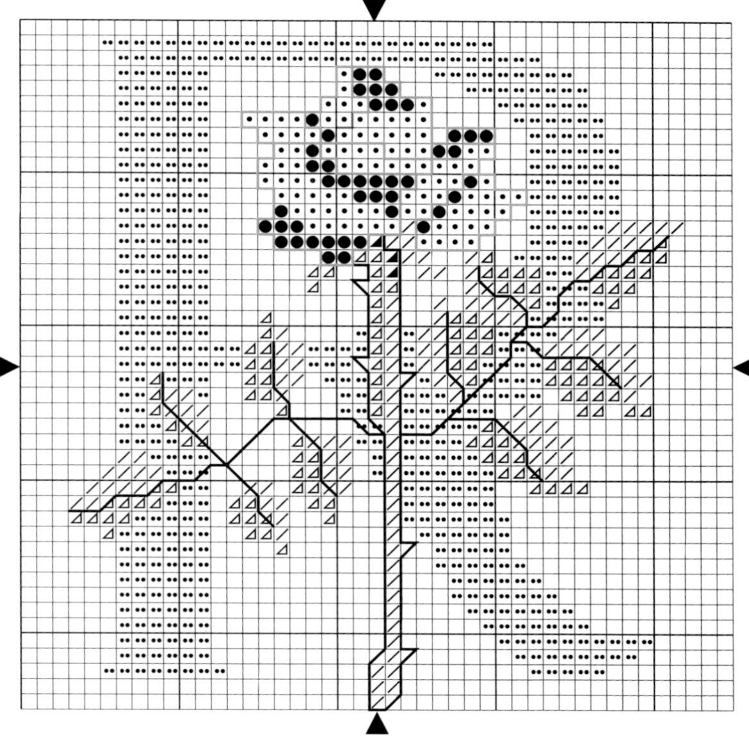

Floral Alphabet Stitch Count: 39 x 44

(continued)

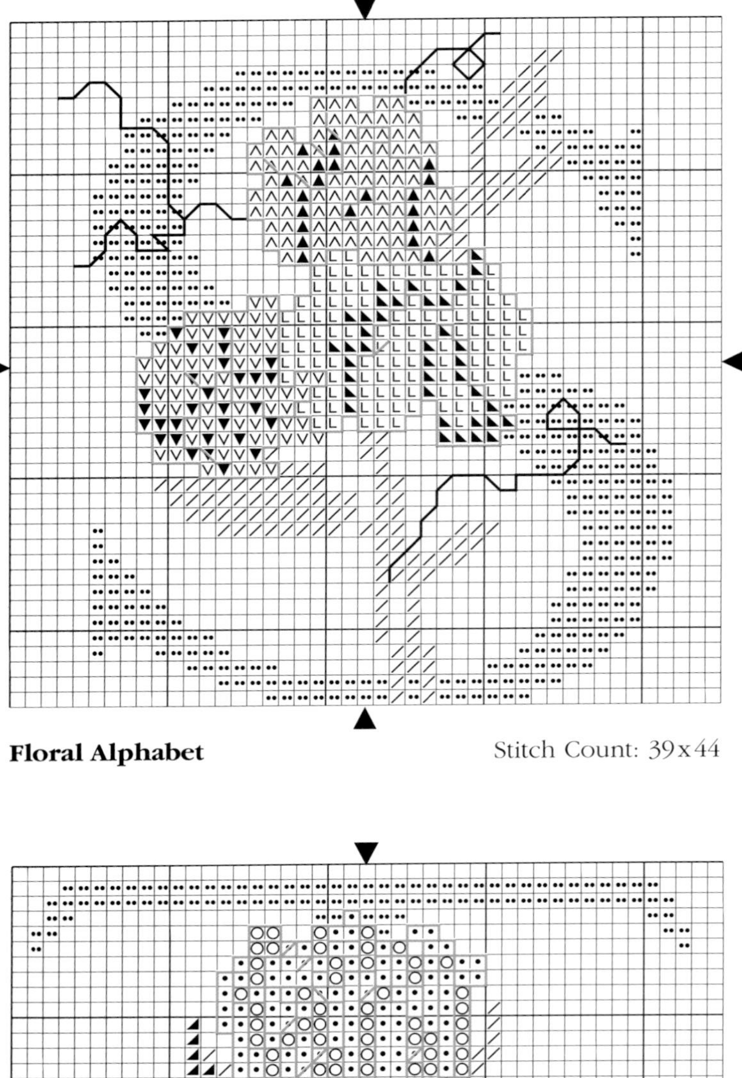

Floral Alphabet Stitch Count: 39x44

Floss: For the letter S

Symbol	Color name	DMC#	Anchor#
••	Ecru	Ecru	387
∧	Light peach	761	1021
▲	Dark peach	760	1022
	Dark dark peach*	3328	1025
L	Light lavender	211	342
◣	Dark lavender	209	109
	Dark dark lavender**	552	111
V	Light blue	3325	129
▼	Dark blue***	334	977
/	Light green	966	214
	Dark dark green****	319	218

*Backstitch peach flower in dark dark peach (two strands).
**Backstitch lavender flower in dark dark lavender (two strands).
***Backstitch blue flower in dark blue (two strands).
****Backstitch tendrils in dark dark green (two strands).

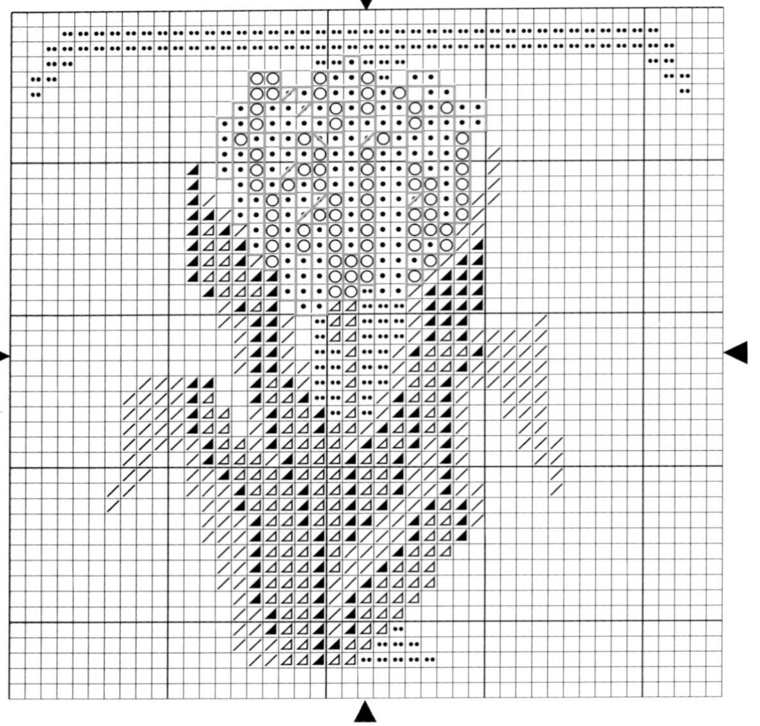

Floral Alphabet Stitch Count: 42x42

Floss: For the letter T

Symbol	Color name	DMC#	Anchor#
••	Ecru	Ecru	387
•	Light pink	818	48
○	Medium pink	3688	66
/	Light green	966	214
◿	Medium green	320	215
◢	Dark green	987	210
	Dark pink*	3687	68

*Backstitch flower in dark pink (two strands).

Floss: For the letter U

Symbol	Color name	DMC#	Anchor#
••	Ecru	Ecru	387
•	Light pink	818	23
○	Light peach	754	1012
L	Periwinkle	341	117
|	Light beige	950	4146
+	Dark beige	407	914
/	Light green	966	214
◿	Medium green	320	215
◢	Dark green***	987	210
	Dark peach*	3712	1023
	Dark dark green**	319	218

*Backstitch flower in dark peach where indicated with colored lines (two strands).
**Backstitch leaves in dark dark green where indicated with colored lines (two strands).
***Backstitch leaves in dark green where indicated with black lines (two strands).

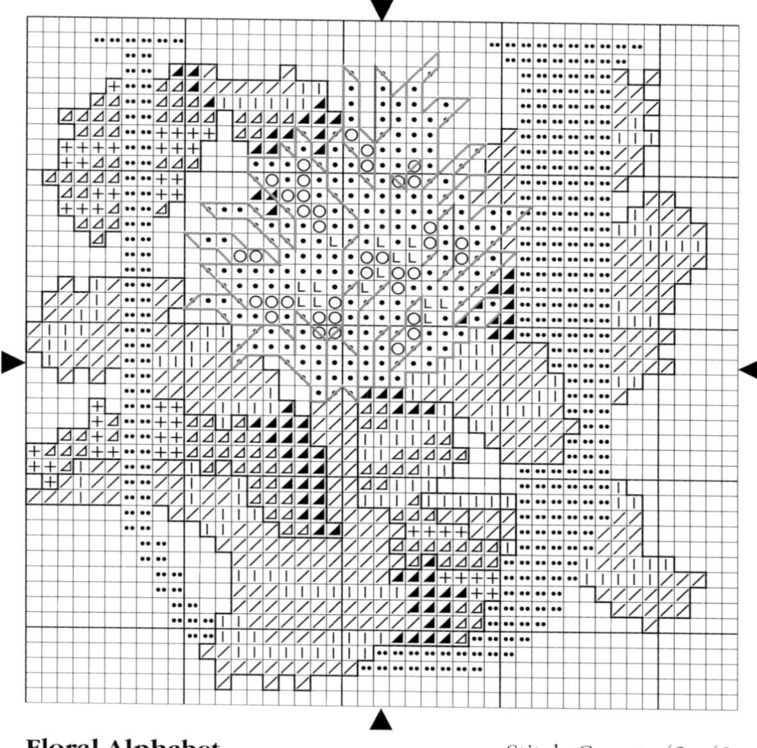

Floral Alphabet Stitch Count: 43x43

Floss: For the letter V

Symbol	Color name	DMC#	Anchor#
••	Ecru	Ecru	387
L	Light lavender	210	108
◣	Dark lavender*	209	109
•	Light pink	818	23
○	Medium pink	3688	66
/	Light green	966	214
◿	Medium green	320	215
◢	Dark green	987	210
∾	Yellow	3078	292
	Dark pink**	3350	59
	Dark dark green***	319	218

*Backstitch flowers in dark lavender where indicated with colored lines (two strands).
**Backstitch bow in dark pink (two strands).
***Backstitch stems in dark dark green (two strands).

Floral Alphabet Stitch Count: 42x45

(continued)

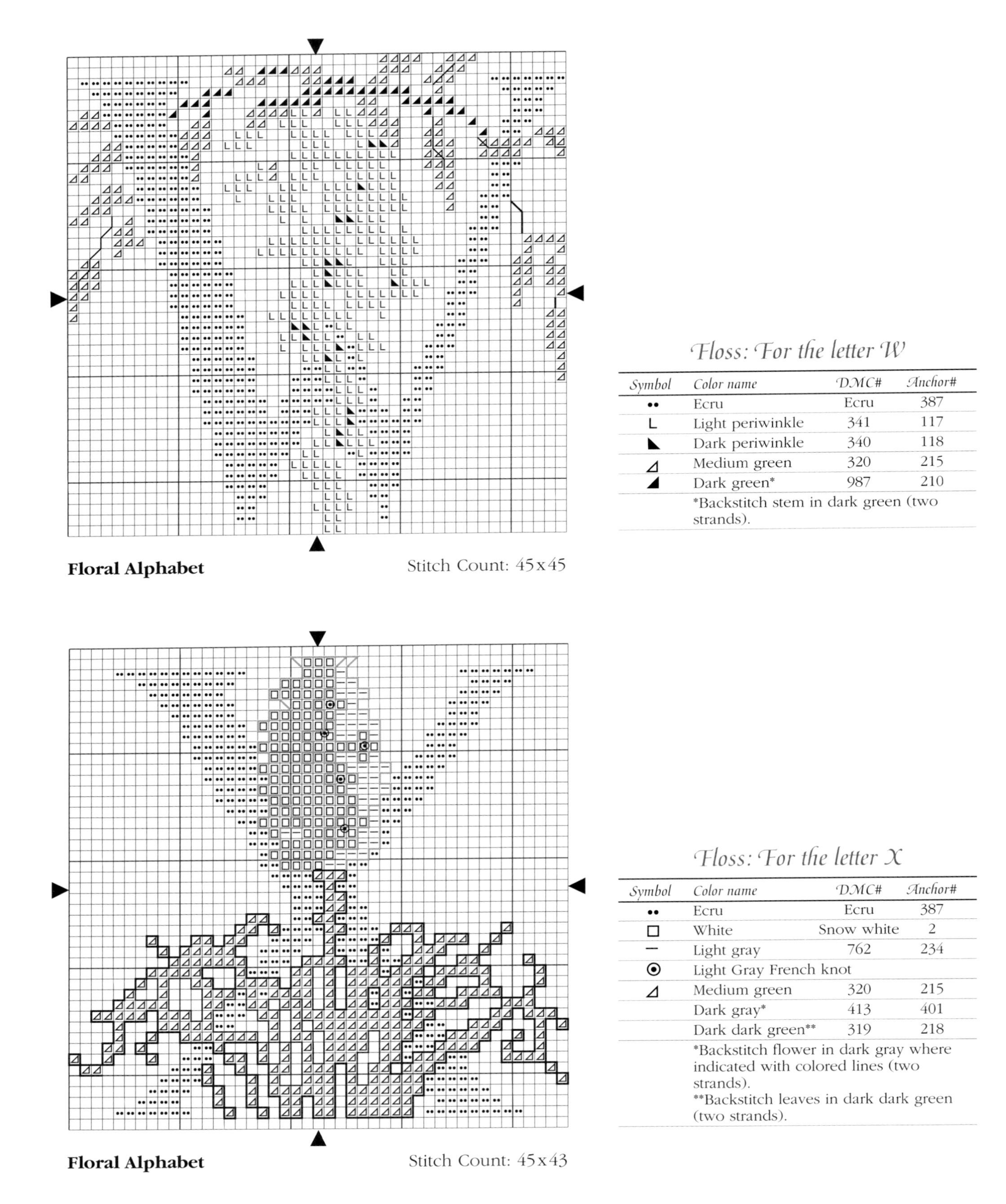

Floral Alphabet

Stitch Count: 45x45

Floss: For the letter W

Symbol	Color name	DMC#	Anchor#
••	Ecru	Ecru	387
L	Light periwinkle	341	117
◣	Dark periwinkle	340	118
◿	Medium green	320	215
◢	Dark green*	987	210
	*Backstitch stem in dark green (two strands).		

Floral Alphabet

Stitch Count: 45x43

Floss: For the letter X

Symbol	Color name	DMC#	Anchor#
••	Ecru	Ecru	387
□	White	Snow white	2
—	Light gray	762	234
⊙	Light Gray French knot		
◿	Medium green	320	215
	Dark gray*	413	401
	Dark dark green**	319	218
	*Backstitch flower in dark gray where indicated with colored lines (two strands). **Backstitch leaves in dark dark green (two strands).		

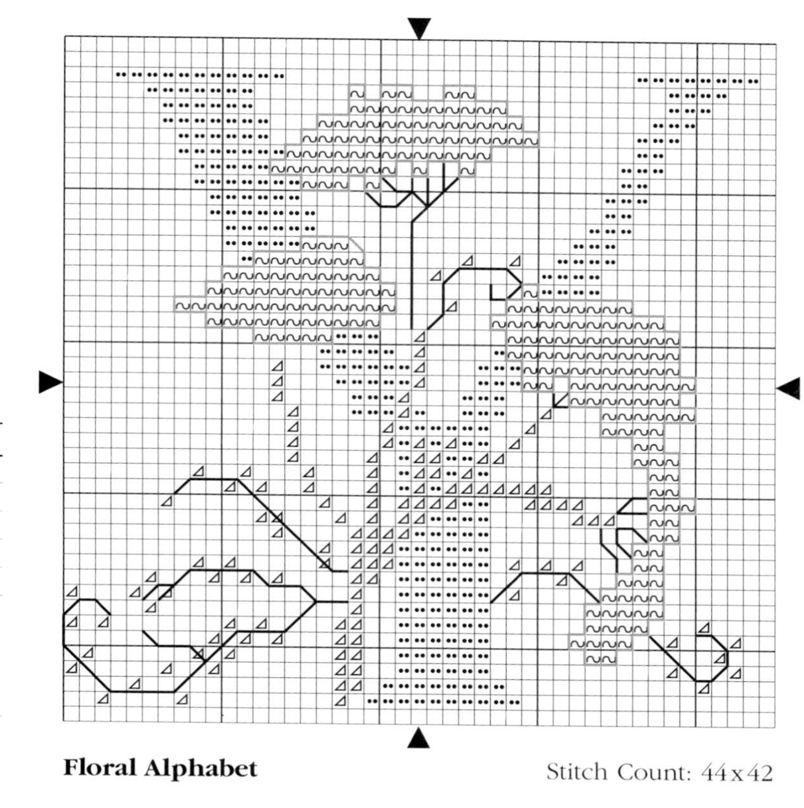

Floral Alphabet Stitch Count: 44x42

Floss: For the letter Y

Symbol	Color name	DMC#	Anchor#
••	Ecru	Ecru	387
∾	Yellow	3078	292
◿	Medium green	320	215
	Dark gray*	413	401
	Dark dark green**	319	218

*Backstitch flowers in dark gray where indicated with colored lines (two strands).
**Backstitch stems in dark dark green (two strands).

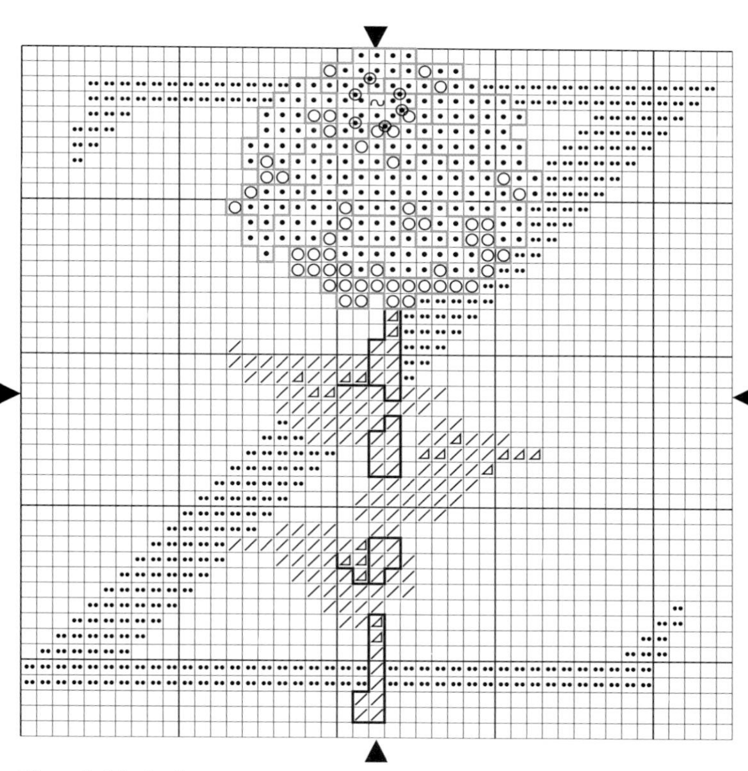

Floral Alphabet Stitch Count: 44x44

Floss: For the letter Z

Symbol	Color name	DMC#	Anchor#
••	Ecru	Ecru	387
•	Light pink	3733	75
○	Medium pink	335	38
⁄	Light green	966	214
◿	Medium green	320	215
∾	Yellow	3078	292
⊙	Yellow French knots		
	Dark pink*	309	42

*Backstitch flower shown in blue in dark pink (two strands).

Flower and Name
See page 17 for the floss colors for the chart at right. Use the appropriate flower from the Alphabet on pages 17–29 with the flower name on these two pages.

Flower and Name

Flower Names Chart

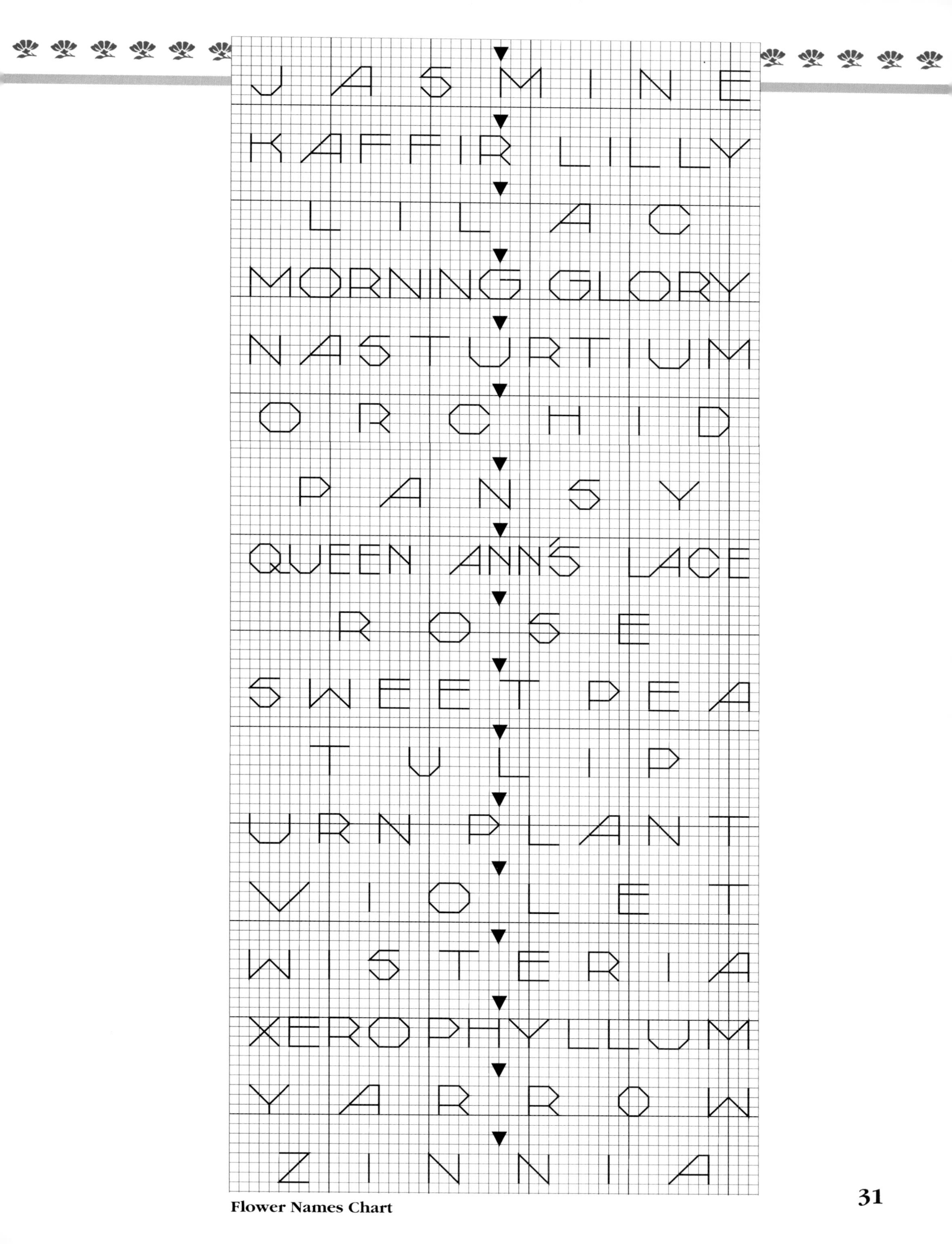

Flower Names Chart

Framed picture: "Who Plants a Seed"

Materials

Floba fabric: 14 count (Zweigart®), Article #3998, Color #53 Oatmeal 15x20 inches

Stitch

Follow the instructions for cross-stitching given in Cross-Stitch Basics.

Finish

We had this piece professionally framed. The framer cut a special mat to coordinate with the curve of the design.

Floss

Symbol	Color name	DMC#	Anchor#
•	Light pink ‡	818	23
●	Medium pink ‡	3688	66
	Dark pink*	3687	68
	Dark brown**	3371	382
⁄	Light green ‡	966	214
◿	Medium green	320	215
◢	Dark green***	319	218

*Backstitch border in dark pink (two strands).
**Backstitch letters in dark brown (two strands).
***Backstitch stems, leaves, and vines in dark green (one strand).
‡ Do lazy daisy stitches for leaves in light green and flowers in light pink and medium pink (two strands).

"Who Plants a Seed" Chart

Stitch Count: 98x142

(continued)

Floral Script Alphabet (uppercase)

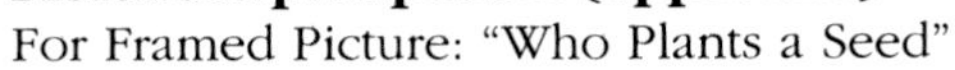

For Framed Picture: "Who Plants a Seed"

Do stitching and lazy daisy stitches in the colors of your choice. Stitch a French knot in center of each flower.

Floral Script Alphabet (uppercase)
For Framed Picture: "Who Plants a Seed"

Do stitching and lazy daisy stitches in the colors of your choice.

(continued)

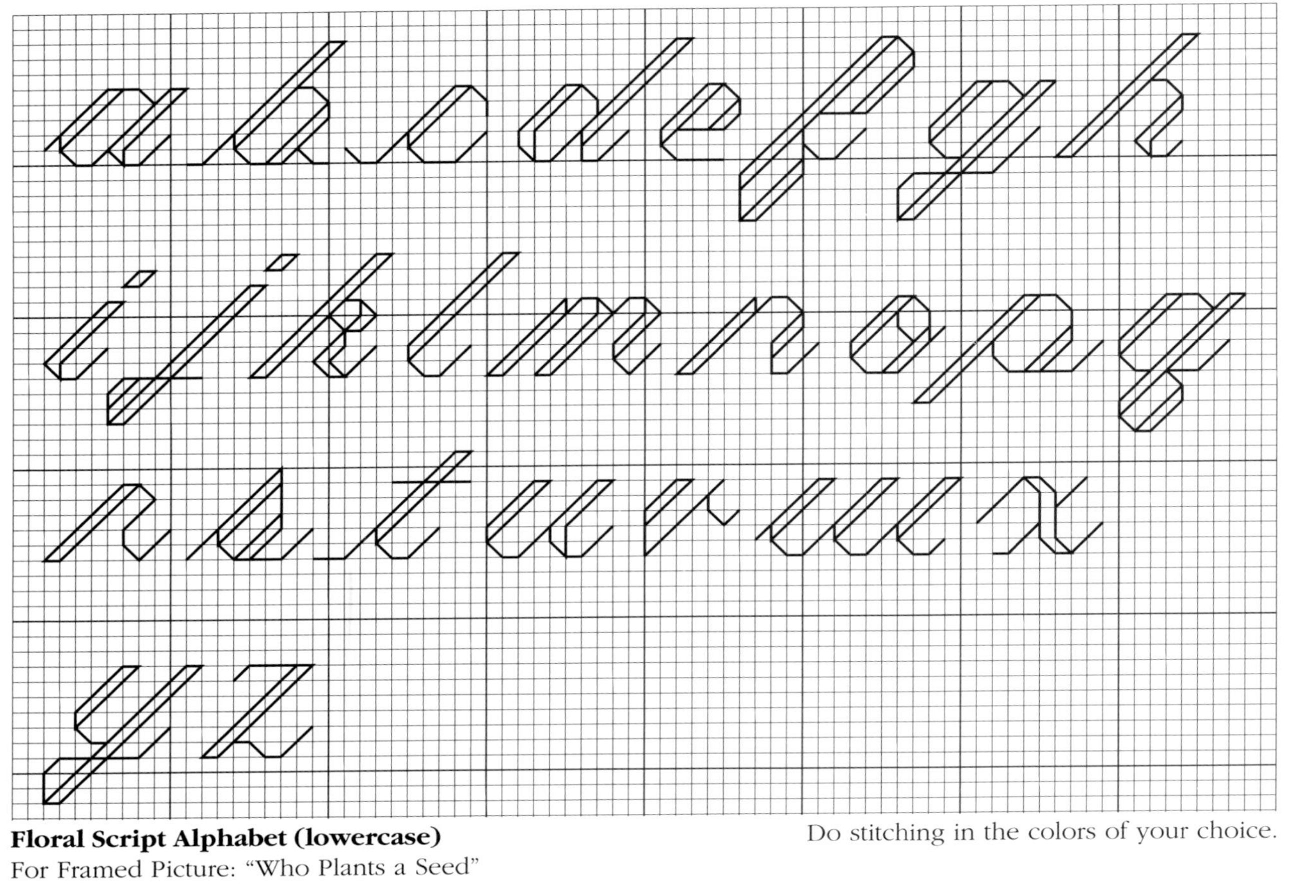

Floral Script Alphabet (lowercase)
For Framed Picture: "Who Plants a Seed"

Do stitching in the colors of your choice.

Locket

USE ELEMENTS OF ROSEBUD BORDER ON PAGE 39 (ONE TURNED UPSIDE DOWN)

Materials

Gold locket: (Thomas Collectibles)
Linen: Ivory, 36 count, 3x3 inches
Hot glue gun

Stitch

Follow the instructions for cross-stitching over two threads given in Cross-Stitch Basics.

Finish

Cut out a thin piece of cardboard following the pattern, right. Hold stitched fabric up to light over cardboard to center design. Cut fabric ¼ inch bigger than cardboard. Place thin piece of batting on back of fabric, and place cardboard over batting. Press into front part of locket. Snap locket together to close. With a hot glue gun, glue decorative screw into top of locket.

Barrette

USE FLOWER GARDEN ALPHABET ON PAGE 38 AND ROSE SURROUND BORDER ON PAGE 39

Materials

Barrette: (Wimpole Street)
Aida fabric: 14 count, ivory (Charles Craft), 3x5 inches

Stitch

Follow the instructions for cross-stitching in Cross-Stitch Basics. Lengthen the Rose Surround Border, if necessary, to fit a larger initial. To lengthen, just add more stitches to the dark green.

Finish

Follow manufacturer's instructions.

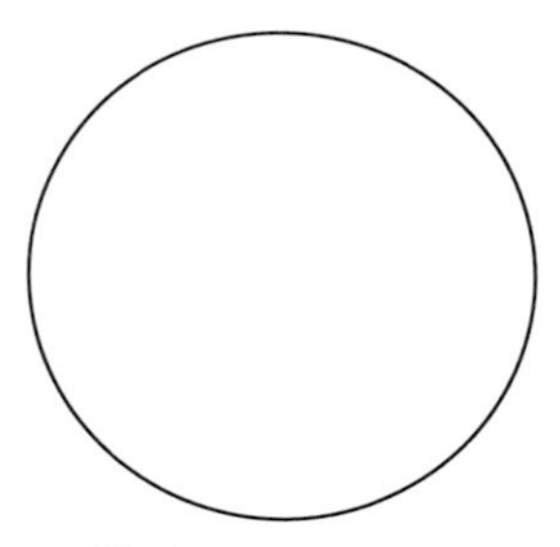

Full-Size Pattern For Locket

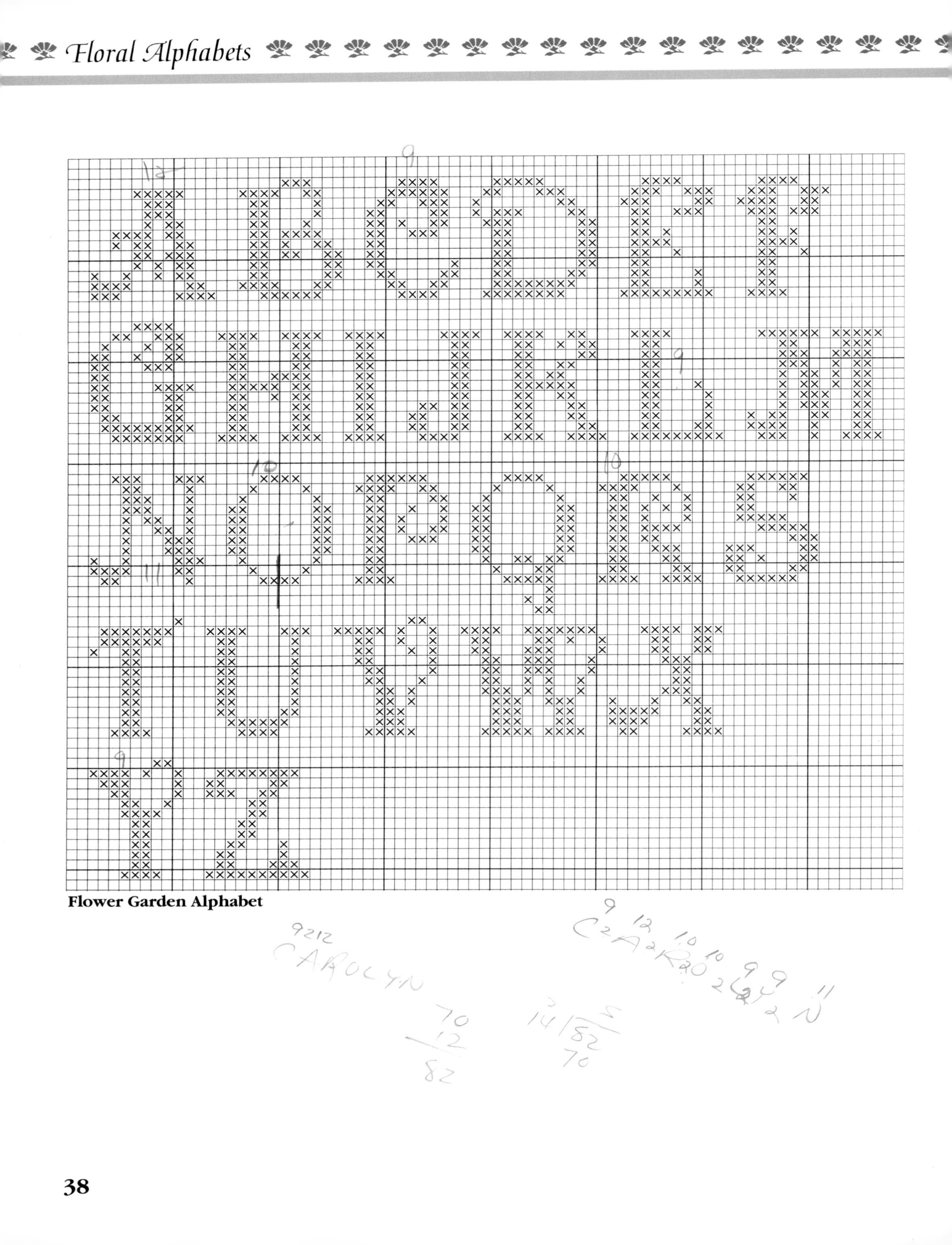

Flower Garden Alphabet

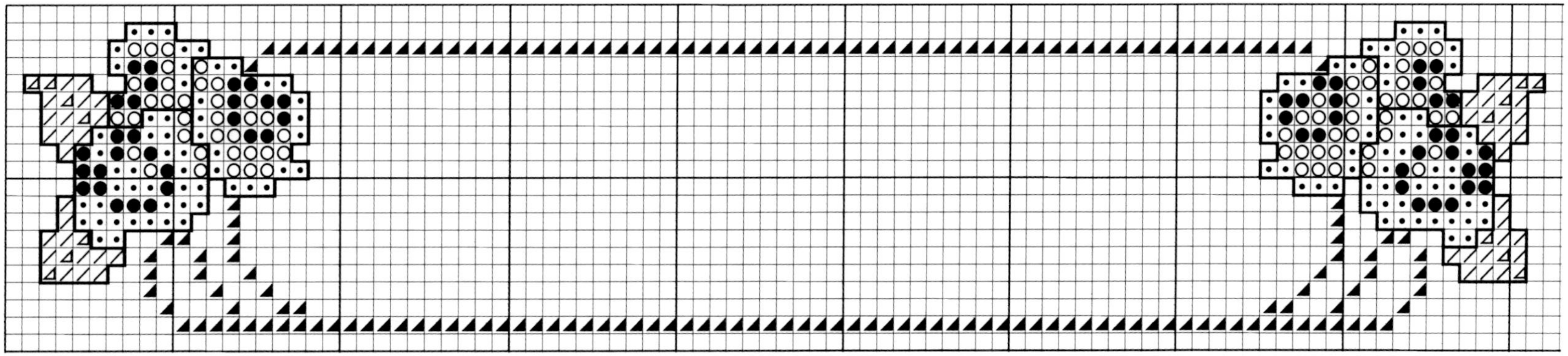

Rose Surround Border

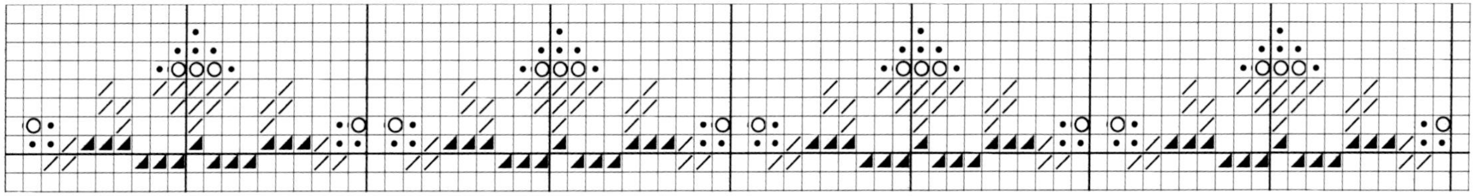

Rosebud Border

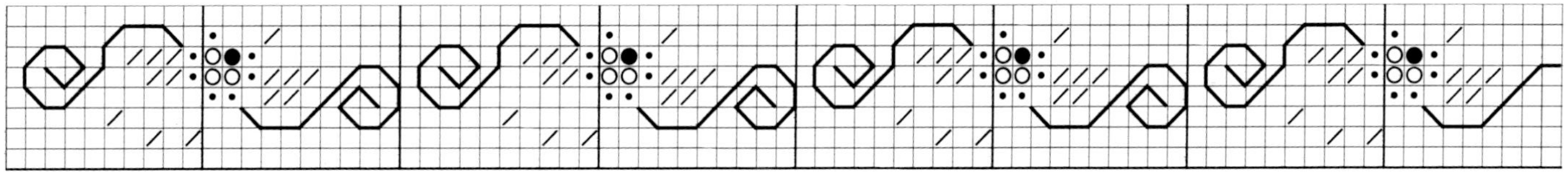

Trailing Rose Border

Floss for Floral Borders

Symbol	Color name	DMC#	Anchor#
•	Light pink	818	23
○	Medium pink	3688	66
●	Dark pink	3687	68
L	Lavender	211	342
/	Light green	966	214
◿	Medium green	320	215
◢	Dark green*	319	218
V	Light blue	932	1032
▼	Dark blue	930	1034
	*Backstitch stems in dark green (two strands).		

(continued)

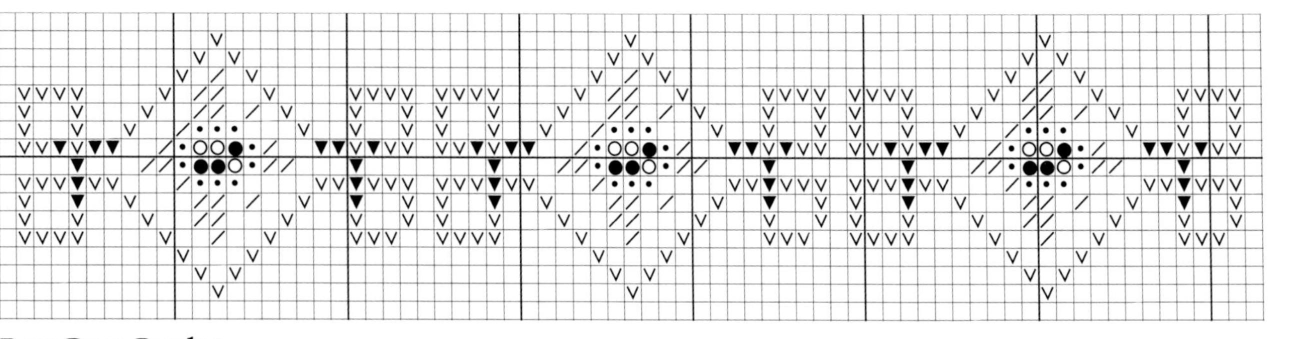

Rose Deco Border

Posey Border

Floss for Floral Borders

Symbol	Color name	DMC#	Anchor#
•	Light pink	818	23
○	Medium pink	3688	66
●	Dark pink	3687	68
L	Lavender	211	342
/	Light green	966	214
◢	Dark green*	319	218
V	Light blue	932	1032
▼	Dark blue	930	1034
	*Backstitch stems in dark green (two strands).		

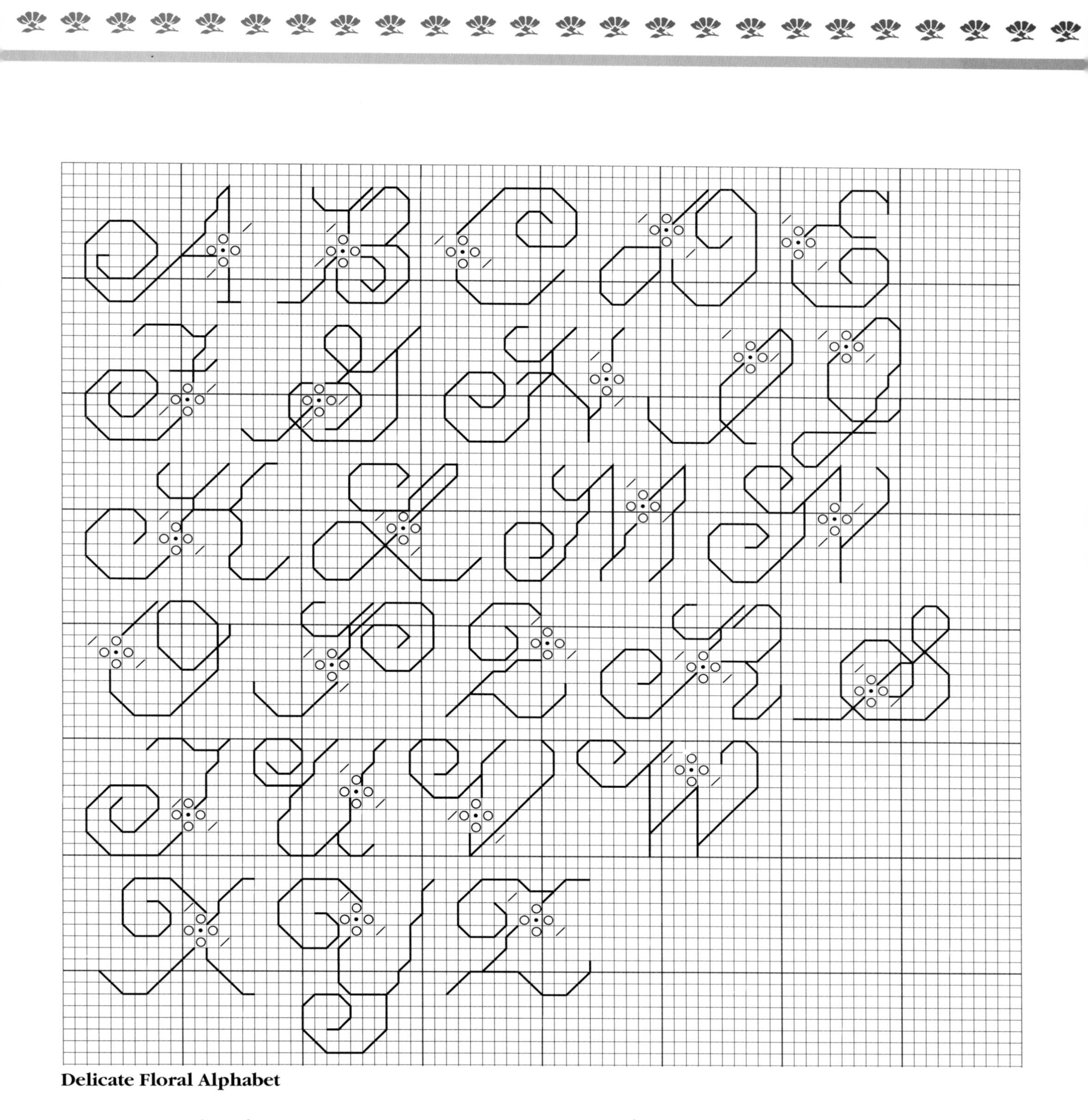

Delicate Floral Alphabet

Ideas for Use

These letters would be pretty stitched as initials on a linen handkerchief.

Floss

Symbol	Color name	DMC#	Anchor#
•	Light pink	818	23
O	Medium pink	3688	66
/	Green	966	214

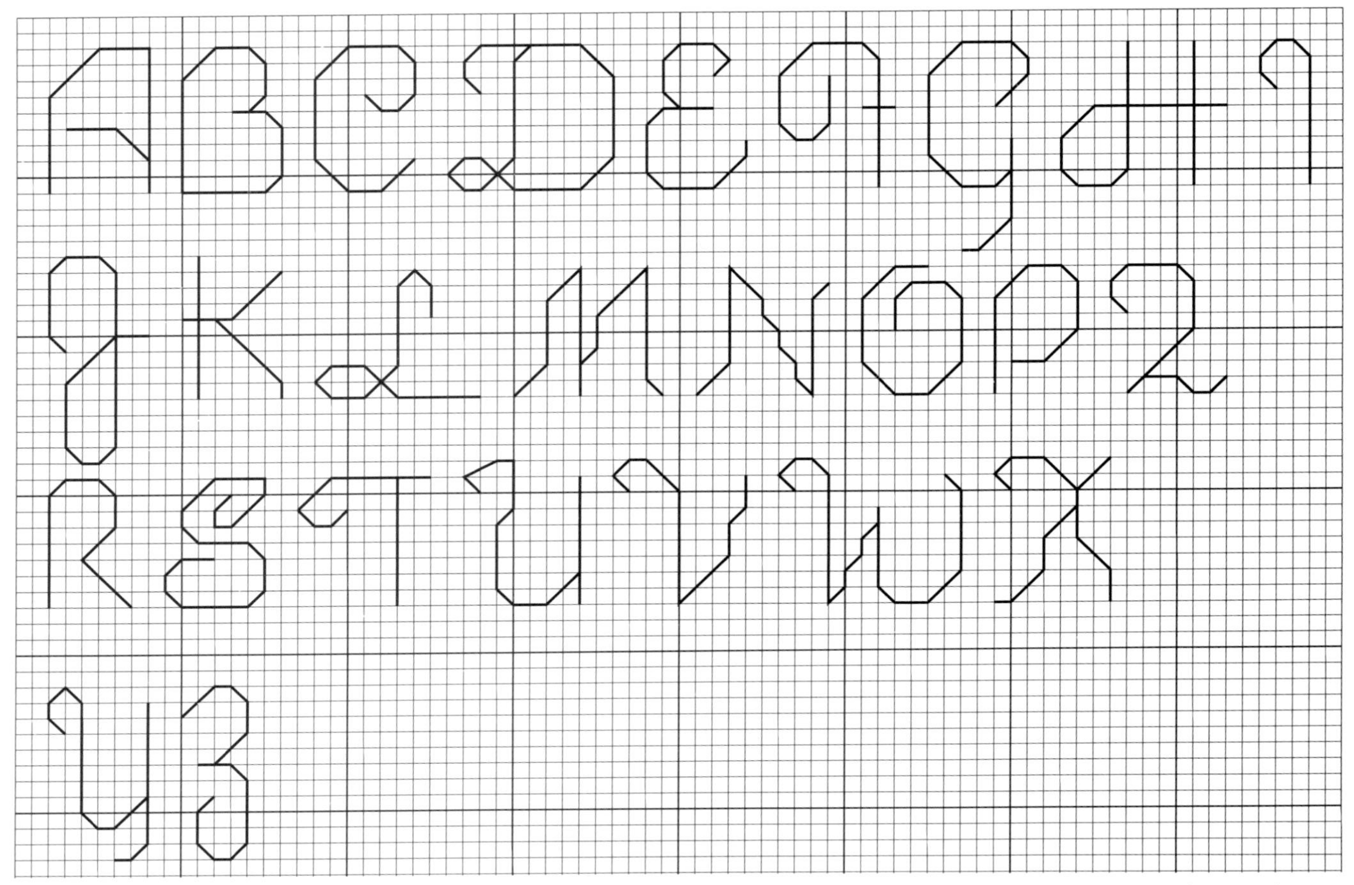

Versatile Floral Alphabet

Use floss colors of your choice.

Ideas for Use

This alphabet would be excellent for a simple-to-stitch monogram on a wedding present.

Or, use these letters to "sign" your intitials on your stitched pieces.

Try using this alphabet for initials with one of the floral borders from pages 39–40 above and below it.

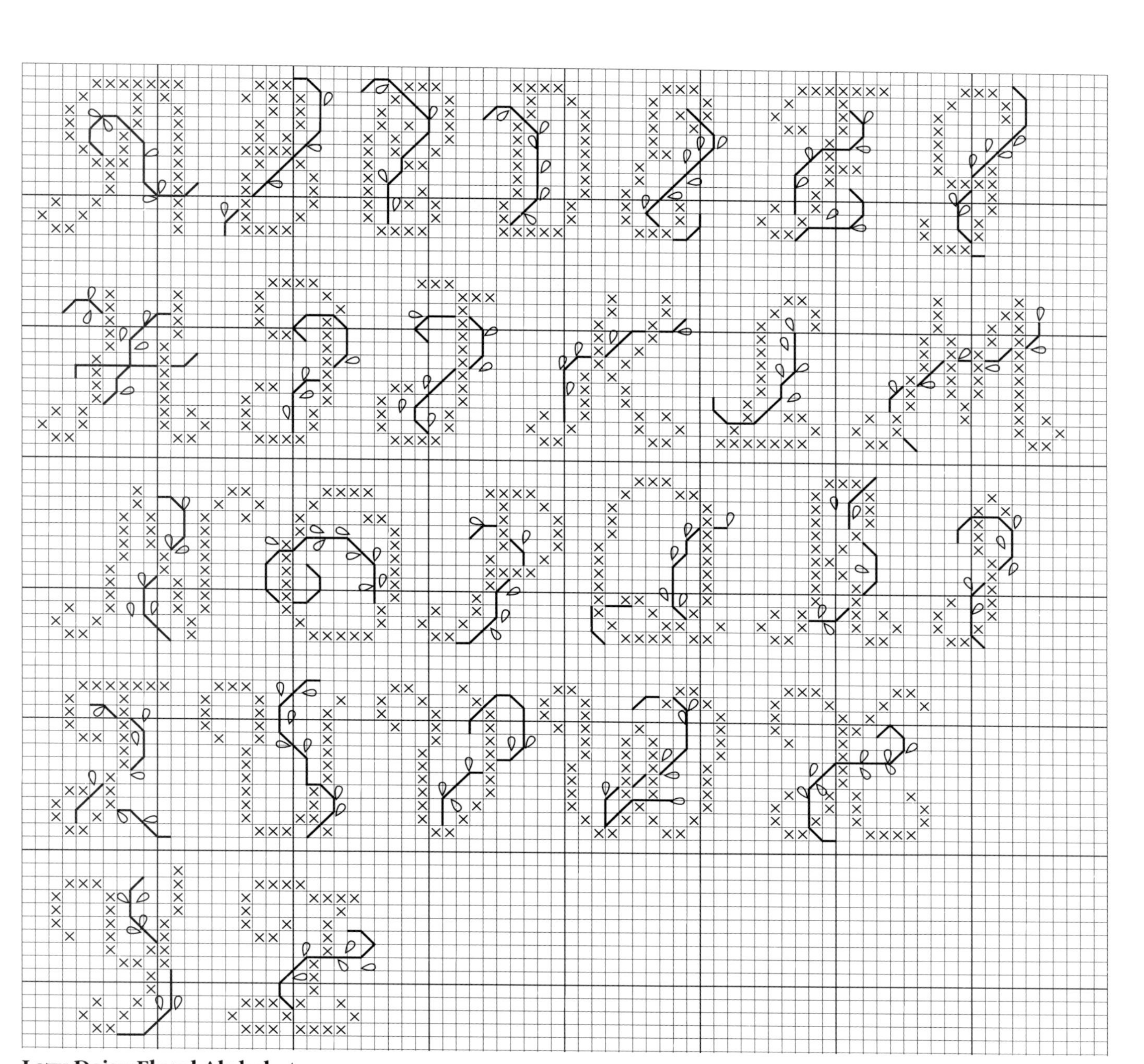

Lazy Daisy Floral Alphabet

Ideas for Use

Decorative letters such as these should be used only as initials.

Try cross-stitching these on a guest towel. You could spell out the word "Guest" using this uppercase G and the lowercase letters from the Floral Script Alphabet on page 36.

Floss

Symbol	Color name	DMC#	Anchor#
⬯	Light green**	966	214
	Dark green*	319	218

*Backstitch vines in dark green (two strands).
**Do lazy daisy stitches in light green (two strands).
Stitch letters in the colors of your choice.

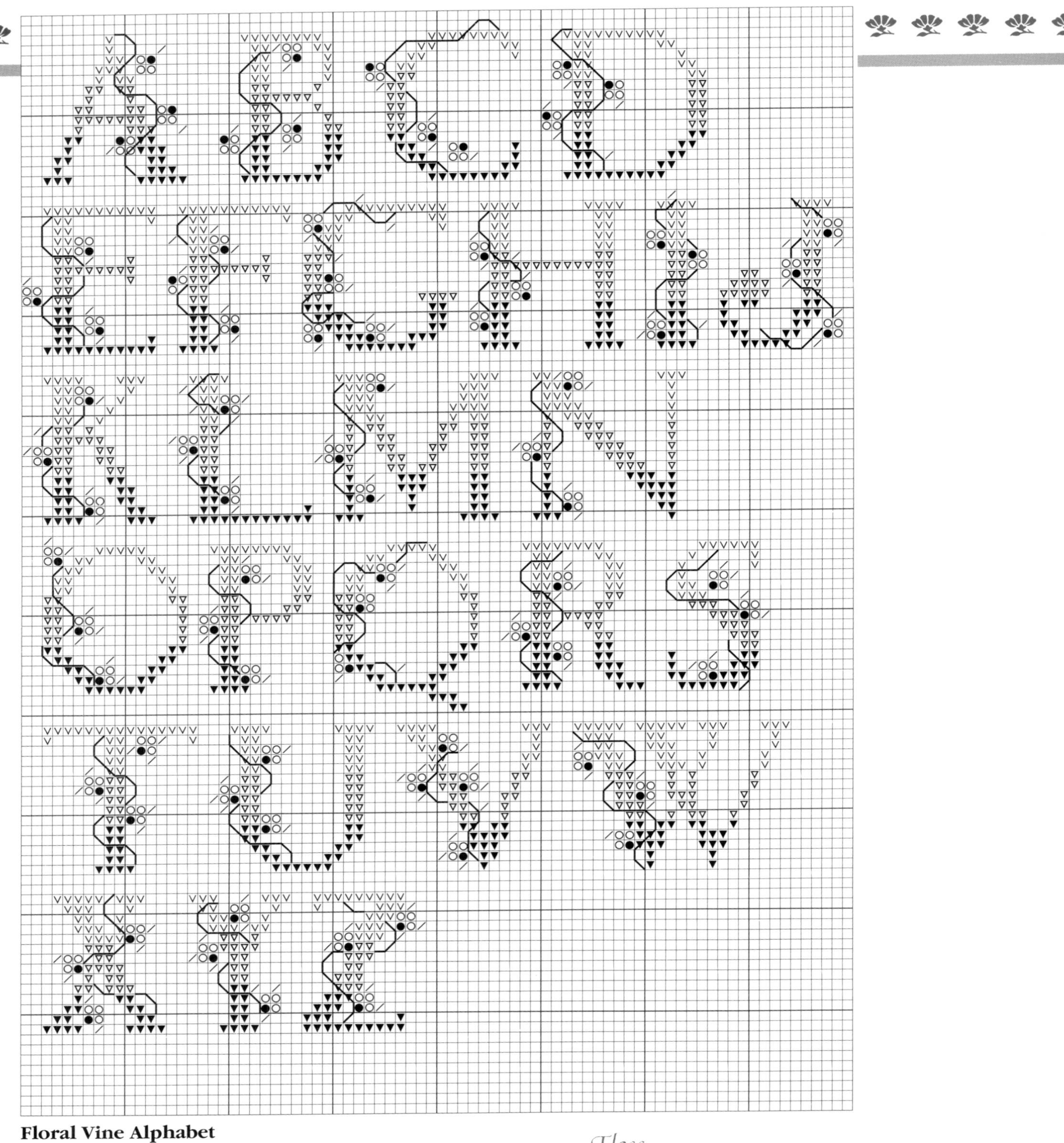

Floral Vine Alphabet

Ideas for Use

Use a letter from this alphabet and waste canvas to cross-stitch an initial on a sweater.

Also using waste canvas, try cross-stitching the bride and groom's initials on pillowcases using this alphabet.

Floss

Symbol	Color name	DMC#	Anchor#
○	Medium pink	3688	66
●	Dark pink	3687	68
V	Light blue	932	1035
▽	Medium blue	931	1034
▼	Dark blue	930	1033
/	Light green	966	214
	Dark green*	319	218

*Backstitch vines in dark green (two strands).

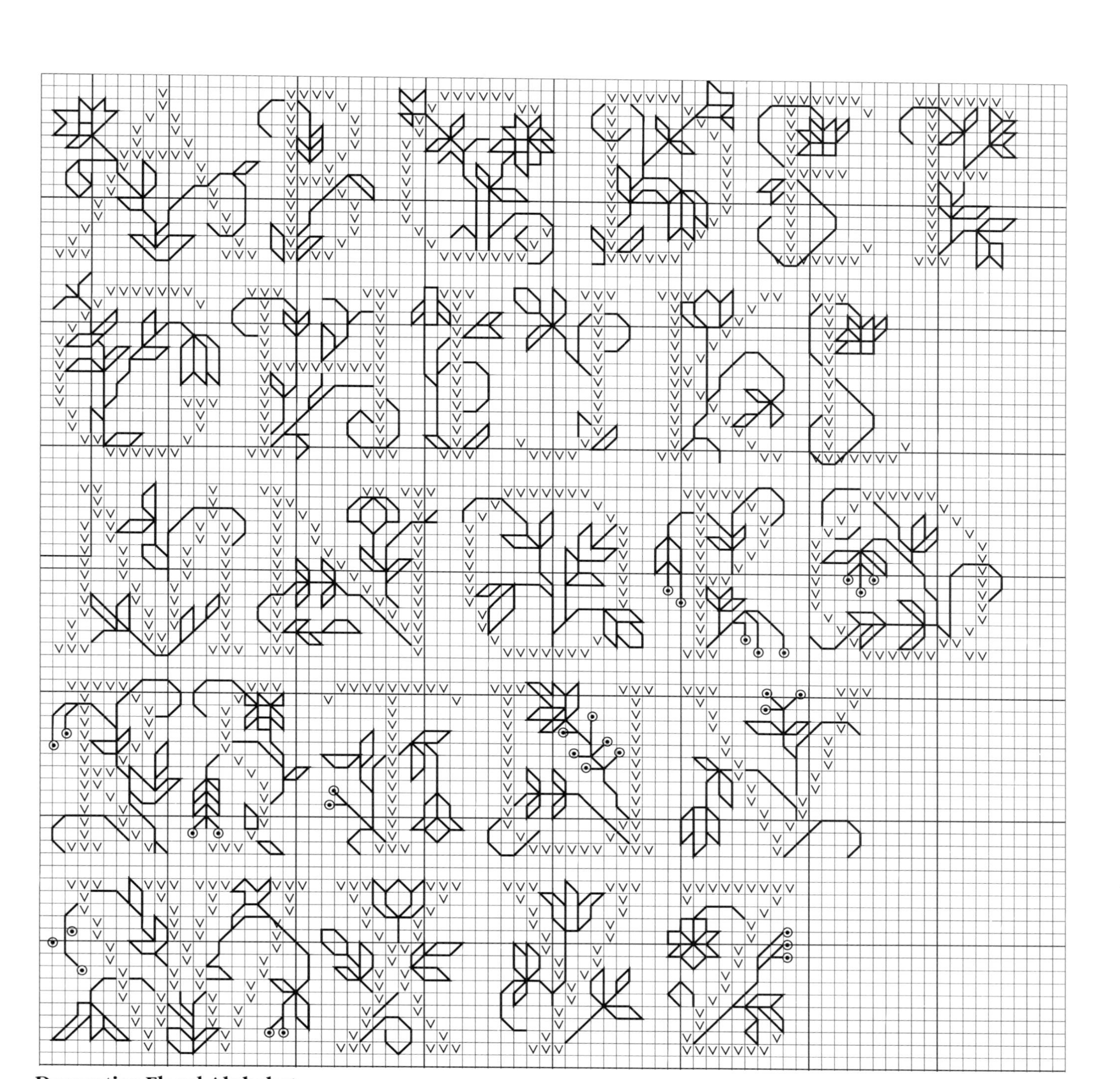

Decorative Floral Alphabet

Ideas for Use

These letters would be pretty cross-stitched on the pocket of a blouse. (Use waste canvas.)

Floss

Symbol	Color name	DMC#	Anchor#
V	Blue	931	1034
⊙	Pink French knot	3688	66
	Green*	320	215
	*Backstitch stems and leaves in green (two strands).		

Antique Alphabets

In years gone by, samplers were the only teaching tool for young girls. They learned their alphabet while perfecting the embroidery they would use to embellish items for their homes.

Most of these samplers were worked on linen; to carry on this tradition, our projects featuring the Antique Alphabet are stitched mainly on linen.

Antique Sampler

USE ANTIQUE SAMPLER CHART ON PAGES 52–57

USE ANTIQUE SAMPLER CHART ON PAGES 52–57

Materials

Fabric: Linen, 28 count, natural brown (undyed) (Wichelt), 17¼x9½ inches

Stitch

The stitches used include the following: cross-stitch, Smyrna cross-stitch, Algerian eye stitch, mosaic, herringbone, long-arm cross-stitch, and buttonhole.

Special Stitch Instructions

Algerian Eye Stitch

Bring the needle up at 1, down at 2, up at three, and down at four (this is the same hole as 2). Continue all the way around to complete the star shape.

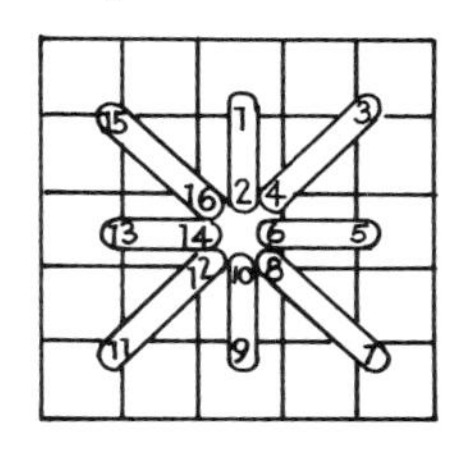

Smyrna Cross-Stitch

Work the same as a single cross-stitch. Bring the needle up at one, down at 2, up at 3, down at 4, up at 5, down at 6, up at 7, and down at 8. Make certain that the top stitch lies in the same direction on the entire sampler.

Herringbone Stitch

Come up at 1, down at 2, up at 3, and down at 4; continue.

Buttonhole Stitch

Come up at 1; go down at 2, leaving a small loop. Come up again at 3 directly above and close to 1. Pull thread through. Continue in the same manner.

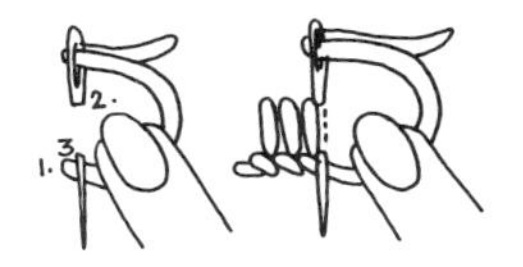

Long-Arm Cross-Stitch

Bring the needle up at 1, down at 2, up at 3, down at 4, up at 5 (the same place as 1), and down at 6; continue.

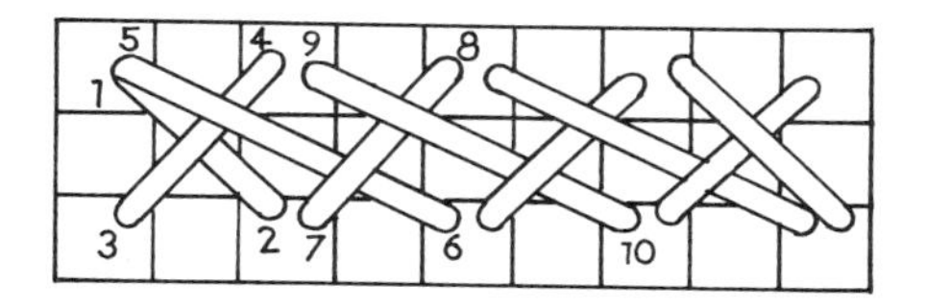

Mosaic Stitch

Bring the needle up at 1, down at 2, up at 3, and down at 4; continue. This stitch is very much like the satin stitch, except it is worked diagonally. The chart shows the direction of the slant.

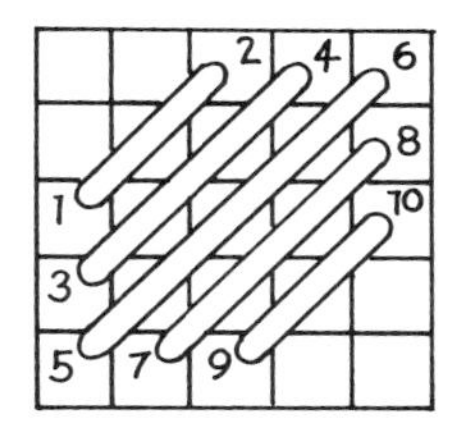

Table Runner

USE BOTTOM PART OF ANTIQUE SAMPLER CHART ON PAGES 56–57

Materials

Table runner: 27 count, cream fabric (Wichelt), 12x32 inches

Stitch

Fold the fabric in half lengthwise to find center. Measure up 3 inches. Start stitching here. You may stitch just one end or both ends of the runner. Follow the instructions for cross-stitching over two threads given in Cross-Stitch Basics.

Finish

Fringe ½ inch on all four sides.

Floss

Symbol	Color name	DMC#	Anchor
●	Fudge brown	632	936
◇	Light gold	3046	887
⬙	Medium gold	3045	888
—	Light gray	647	1040
=	Dark gray	645	273
×	Drab brown	610	889
/	Light green	3053	261
◢	Dark green	3051	681
V	Light blue	927	848
▽	Medium blue	926	850

Antique clock

USE BOTTOM THIRD OF ANTIQUE SAMPLER CHART ON PAGES 54–57

Materials

Fabric: Edinburgh, 36 count, cream (Zweigart®), 7x10 inches
Clock: Wheatland Crafts #CK4

Stitch

Follow the instructions for cross-stitching over two threads given in Cross-Stitch Basics.

Finish

Once cross-stitching is finished, trim fabric to fit mounting board in clock, leaving 1 inch all the way around for gluing to back of board. After mounting the fabric on the board, insert in clock.

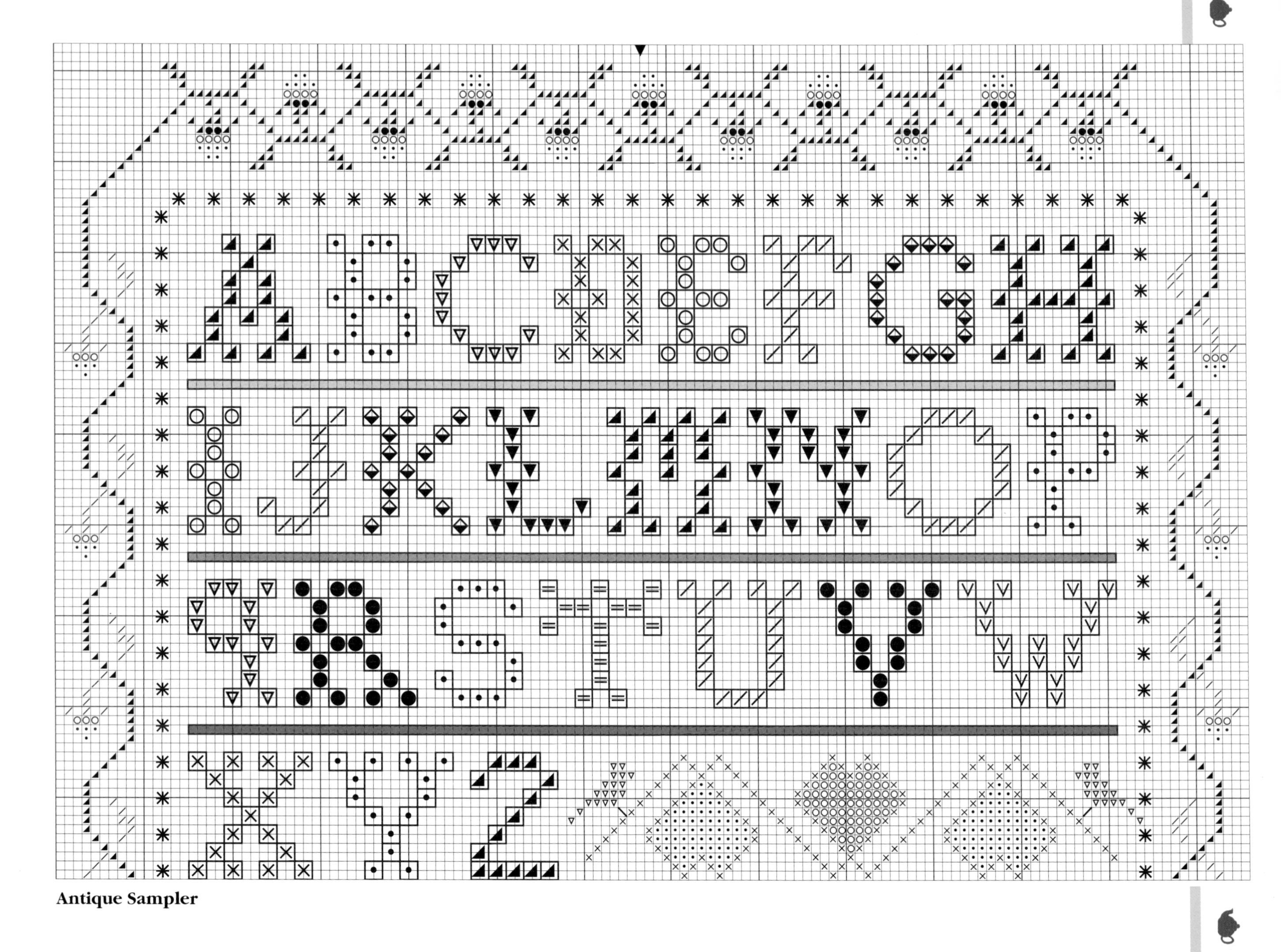

Antique Sampler

Floss

Symbol	Color name	DMC#	Anchor
•	Light flesh	950	4146
○	Fawn	3772	1007
●	Fudge brown	632	936
◇	Light gold	3046	887
⬘	Medium gold	3045	888
–	Light gray	647	1040
=	Dark gray	645	273
×	Drab brown	610	889
/	Light green	3053	261
◢	Dark green	3051	681
V	Light blue	927	848
▽	Medium blue	926	850
▼	Dark blue	3768	779
	Other stitches:		
	Mosaic Stitch (stitch in the direction indicated)		
	Yellow	3046	887
	Smyrna Cross-Stitch		
	Beige gray	(Pearl cotton) 822	(Pearl cotton) 830
	Algerian Eye Stitches		
	Flesh	950	4146
	Fawn	3772	1007
	Fudge brown	632	936
	Medium gold	3045	888
	Dark gray	645	273
	Drab brown	610	889
	Light green	3053	261
	Dark green	3051	681
	Light blue	927	848
	Medium blue	926	850
	Dark blue	3768	779

Stitch	Color name	DMC#	Anchor
Herringbone Stitch	Medium gold	3045	888
Long-Arm Cross-Stitch	Light green	3053	261
Buttonhole Stitch	Dark green	3051	681

When working on linen, cross-stitches are worked over two fabric threads using two strands of floss.

The large alphabet is completed in the Algerian eye stitch using two strands of floss in the color indicated.

Use one strand of DMC #822 size 8 pearl cotton for the Smyrna cross-stitch border.

Use two strands of DMC #3045 for the herringbone stitch row that is between the first two lines of the large alphabet.

Use two strands of DMC #3053 for the long-arm cross-stitch row that is between the second and third rows of the large alphabet.

Use two strands of DMC #3051 for the buttonhole stitch row that is between the third and fourth rows of the large alphabet.

The row immediately beneath the large alphabet uses a combination of the mosaic and Algerian eye stitches. Use two strands of DMC #3045 for the Algerian eye and two strands of DMC #3046 for the mosaic stitches.

See page 49 for special stitch instructions.

(continued)

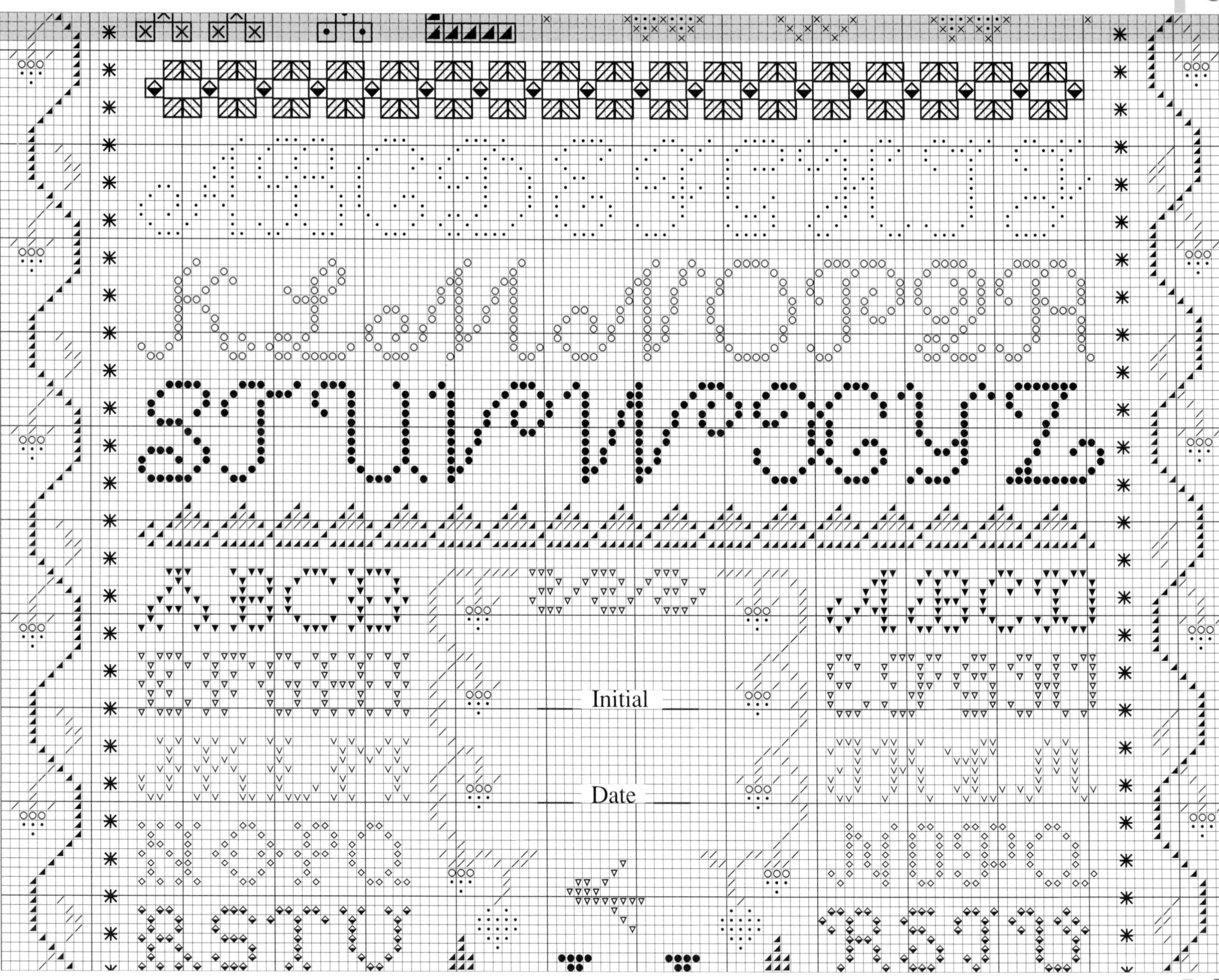
Initial
Date

Antique Sampler

Floss

Symbol	Color name	DMC#	Anchor
•	Light flesh	950	4146
○	Fawn	3772	1007
●	Fudge brown	632	936
◇	Light gold	3046	887
◆	Medium gold	3045	888
–	Light gray	647	1040
=	Dark gray	645	273
×	Drab brown	610	889
/	Light green	3053	261
◢	Dark green	3051	681
V	Light blue	927	848
▽	Medium blue	926	850
▼	Dark blue	3768	779
	Other stitches:		
	Mosaic Stitch (stitch in the direction indicated)		
	Yellow	3046	887
	Smyrna Cross-Stitch		
	Beige gray	(Pearl cotton) 822	(Pearl cotton) 830
	Algerian Eye Stitches		
	Flesh	950	4146
	Fawn	3772	1007
	Fudge brown	632	936
	Medium gold	3045	888
	Dark gray	645	273
	Drab brown	610	889
	Light green	3053	261
	Dark green	3051	681
	Light blue	927	848
	Medium blue	926	850
	Dark blue	3768	779

Stitch	Color name	DMC#	Anchor
Herringbone Stitch	Medium gold	3045	888
Long-Arm Cross-Stitch	Light green	3053	261
Buttonhole Stitch	Dark green	3051	681

When working on linen, cross-stitches are worked over two fabric threads using two strands of floss.

The large alphabet is completed in the Algerian eye stitch using two strands of floss in the color indicated.

Use one strand of DMC #822 size 8 pearl cotton for the Smyrna cross-stitch border.

Use two strands of DMC #3045 for the herringbone stitch row that is between the first two lines of the large alphabet.

Use two strands of DMC #3053 for the long-arm cross-stitch row that is between the second and third rows of the large alphabet.

Use two strands of DMC #3051 for the buttonhole stitch row that is between the third and fourth rows of the large alphabet.

The row immediately beneath the large alphabet uses a combination of the mosaic and Algerian eye stitches. Use two strands of DMC #3045 for the Algerian eye and two strands of DMC #3046 for the mosaic stitches.

See page 49 for special stitch instructions.

(continued)

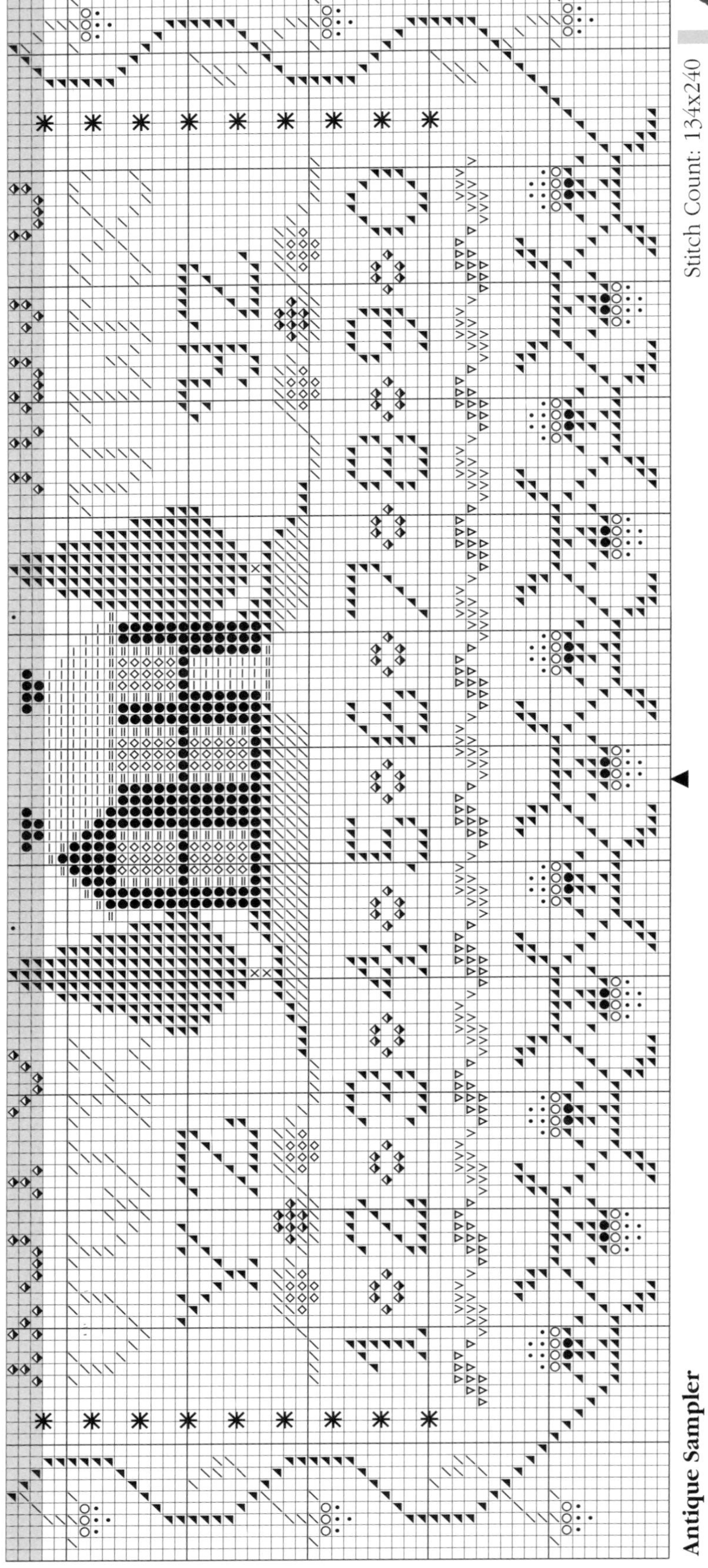

Stitch Count: 134x240

Antique Sampler

Ideas for Use

This sampler on pages 52–57 includes four alphabets that can be used in many different ways. Each one used separately, for example, would make a nice small sampler. Experiment with the different borders on page 60–61 to create a sampler that is all your own.

Floss

Symbol	Color name	DMC#	Anchor
•	Light flesh	950	4146
○	Fawn	3772	1007
●	Fudge brown	632	936
◇	Light gold	3046	887
◈	Medium gold	3045	888
–	Light gray	647	1040
=	Dark gray	645	273
×	Drab brown	610	889
/	Light green	3053	261
◢	Dark green	3051	681
V	Light blue	927	848
▽	Medium blue	926	850
▼	Dark blue	3768	779
	Other stitches:		
	Mosaic Stitch (stitch in the direction indicated)		
	Yellow	3046	887
	Smyrna Cross-Stitch		
	Beige gray	(Pearl cotton) 822	(Pearl cotton) 830
	Algerian Eye Stitches		
	Flesh	950	4146
	Fawn	3772	1007
	Fudge brown	632	936
	Medium gold	3045	888
	Dark gray	645	273
	Drab brown	610	889
	Light green	3053	261
	Dark green	3051	681
	Light blue	927	848
	Medium blue	926	850
	Dark blue	3768	779

Stitch	DMC#	Anchor
Herringbone Stitch		
Medium gold	3045	888
Long-Arm Cross-Stitch		
Light green	3053	261
Buttonhole Stitch		
Dark green	3051	681

When working on linen, cross-stitches are worked over two fabric threads using two strands of floss.

The large alphabet is completed in the Algerian eye stitch using two strands of floss in the color indicated.

Use one strand of DMC #822 size 8 pearl cotton for the Smyrna cross-stitch border.

Use two strands of DMC #3045 for the herringbone stitch row that is between the first two lines of the large alphabet.

Use two strands of DMC #3053 for the long-arm cross-stitch row that is between the second and third rows of the large alphabet.

Use two strands of DMC #3051 for the buttonhole stitch row that is between the third and fourth rows of the large alphabet.

The row immediately beneath the large alphabet uses a combination of the mosaic and Algerian eye stitches. Use two strands of DMC #3045 for the Algerian eye and two strands of DMC #3046 for the mosaic stitches.

See page 49 for special stitch instructions.

Towel

USE ANTIQUE STRAWBERRY BORDER ON PAGE 60

Materials

Towel: 14 count, ecru fingertip (Charles Craft #PT-6682)

Stitch

Follow the instructions for cross-stitching given in Cross-Stitch Basics.

Finish

Towel is prefinished; no finishing is necessary.

Tote Bag

USE ANTIQUE HEART BORDER ON PAGE 61

Materials

Tote bag: Linen, 28 count, cream (Janlynn)

Stitch

Follow the instructions for cross-stitching over two threads given in Cross-Stitch Basics.

Finish

Tote bag is prefinished; no finishing is necessary.

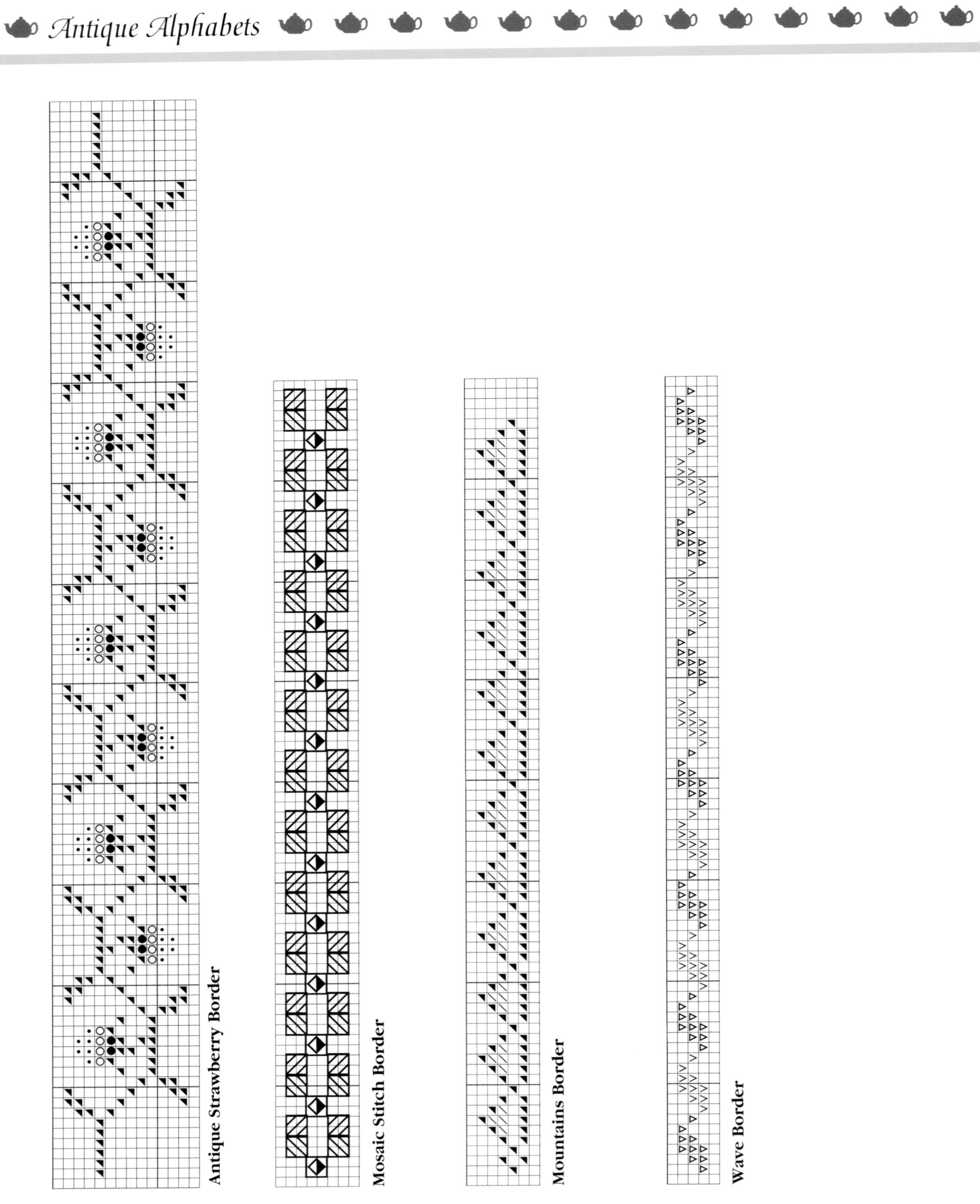
Antique Strawberry Border
Mosaic Stitch Border
Mountains Border
Wave Border

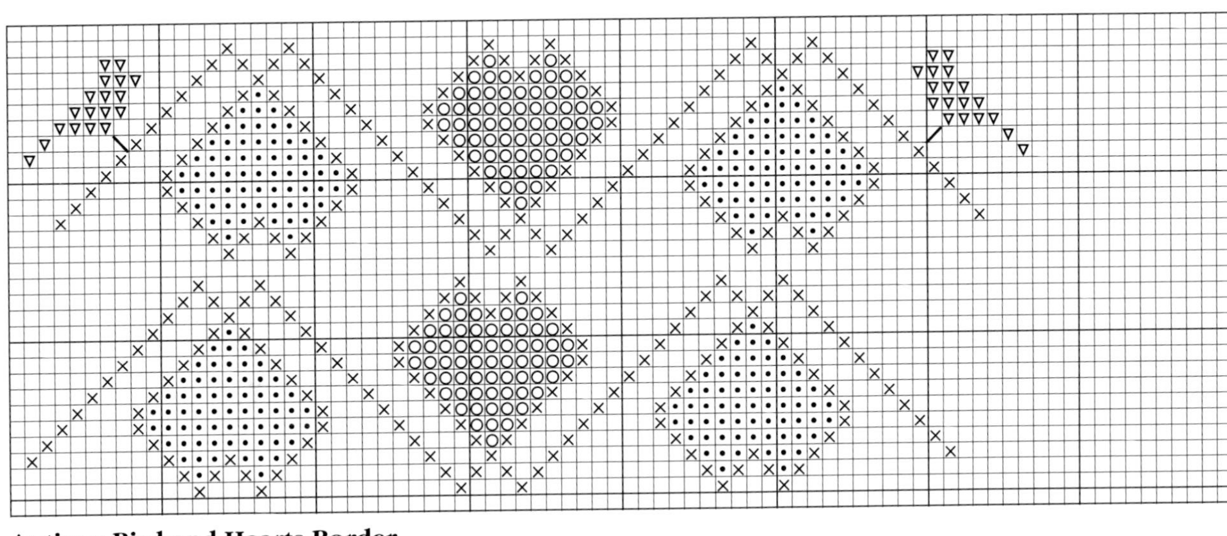

Antique Bird and Hearts Border
For an **Antique Heart Border**
repeat this border without the birds.

Floss

Symbol	*Color name*	*DMC#*	*Anchor*
•	Light flesh	950	4146
○	Fawn	3772	1007
●	Fudge brown	632	936
×	Drab brown	610	889
/	Light green	3053	261
◢	Dark green	3051	681
V	Light blue	927	848
▽	Medium blue	926	850
	Other stitches:		
	Mosaic Stitch (stitch in the direction indicated)		
	Yellow	3046	887
	Algerian Eye Stitches (use two strands)		
	Medium gold	3045	888
	When working on linen, cross-stitches are worked over two fabric threads using two strands of floss.		
	See page 49 for special stitch instructions.		

Home Sweet Home Sampler

Materials

Aida fabric: 14 count, ivory (Charles Craft)

Stitch

Follow the instructions for cross-stitching given in Cross-Stitch Basics.

Finish

Have your cross-stitched piece professionally framed and matted.

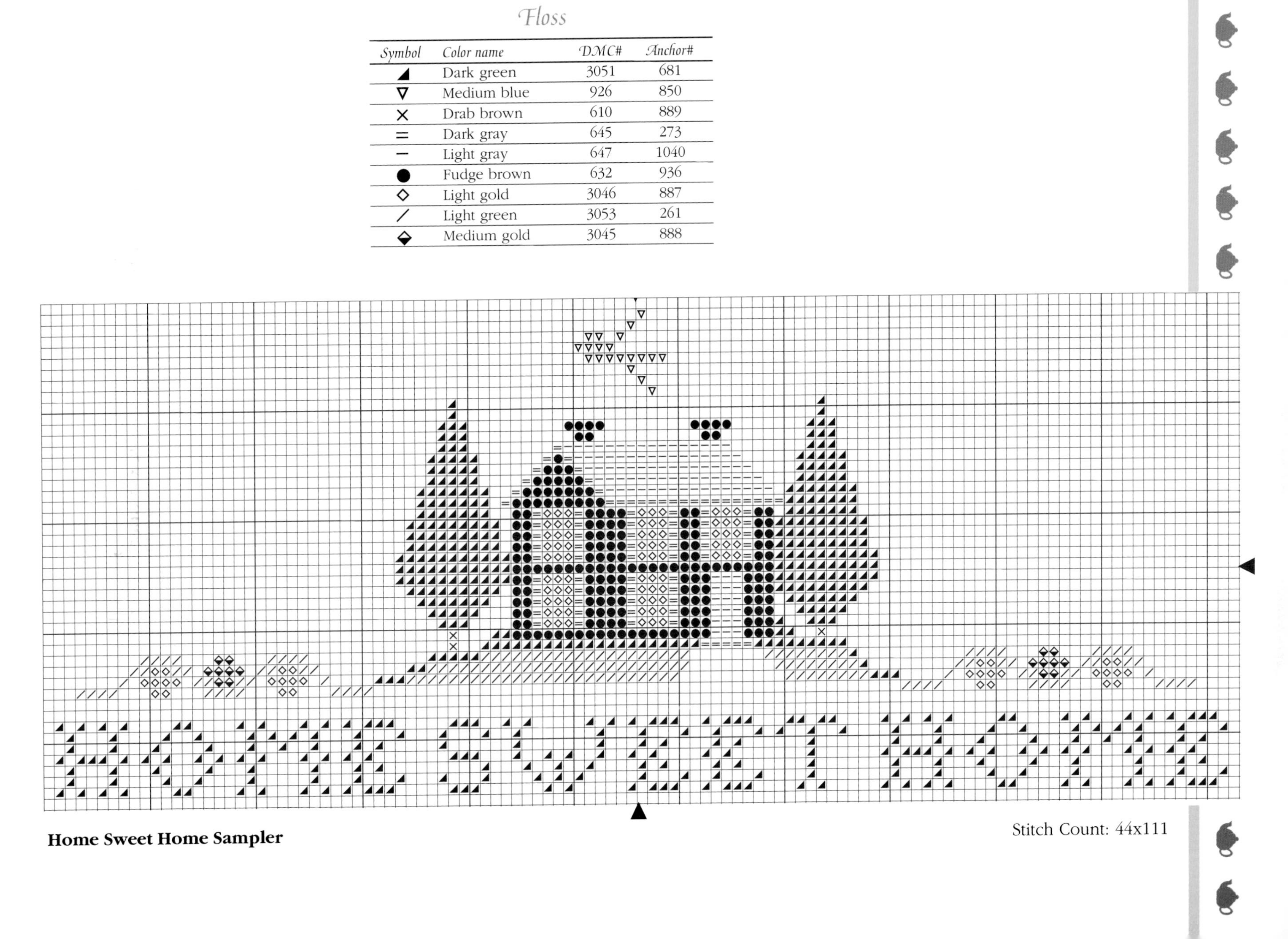

Floss

Symbol	Color name	DMC#	Anchor#
◢	Dark green	3051	681
▽	Medium blue	926	850
×	Drab brown	610	889
=	Dark gray	645	273
–	Light gray	647	1040
●	Fudge brown	632	936
◇	Light gold	3046	887
/	Light green	3053	261
⬙	Medium gold	3045	888

Home Sweet Home Sampler

Stitch Count: 44x111

Antique Initial Alphabet

Use the floss colors of your choice.

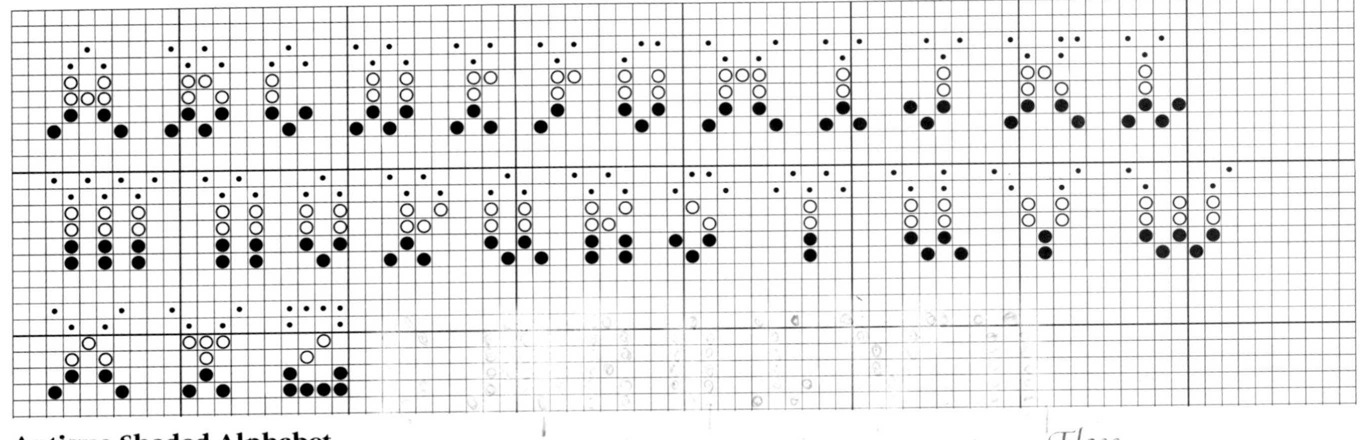

Antique Shaded Alphabet

Floss

Symbol	Color name	DMC#	Anchor#
•	Light flesh	950	4146
○	Fawn	3772	1007
●	Fudge brown	632	936

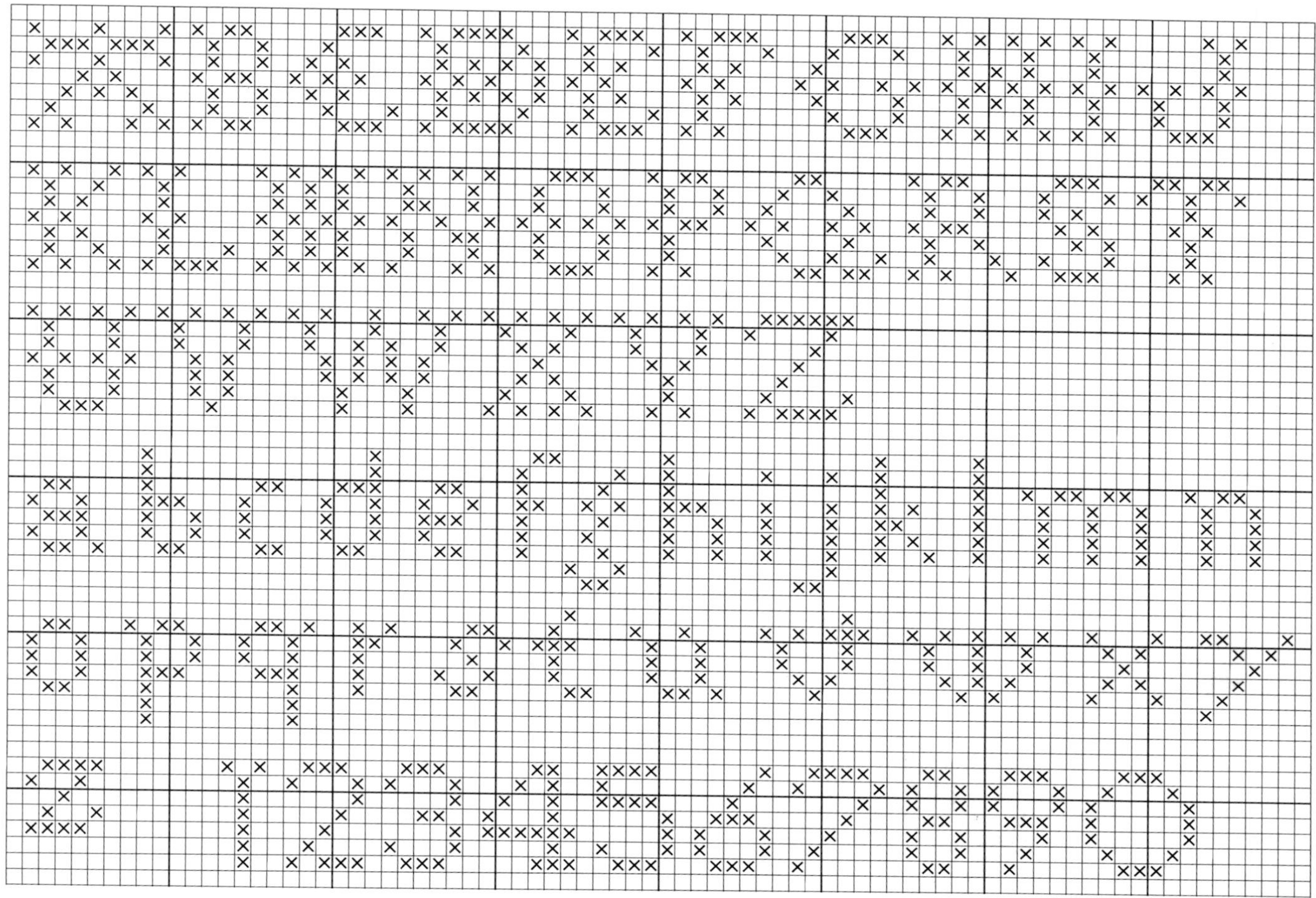

Antique Classic Alphabet

Use the floss colors of your choice.

Ideas for Use

The Antique Initial Alphabet would look lovely stitched with various antique shades of floss. To give it an even more antique appearance, try tea-dying it.

The Antique Shaded Alphabet would be adorable stitched on very fine fabric as a tiny doll house sampler.

Ideas for Use

These letters would work well combined with the Bird and Hearts Border on page 61 for a wedding or birth sampler.

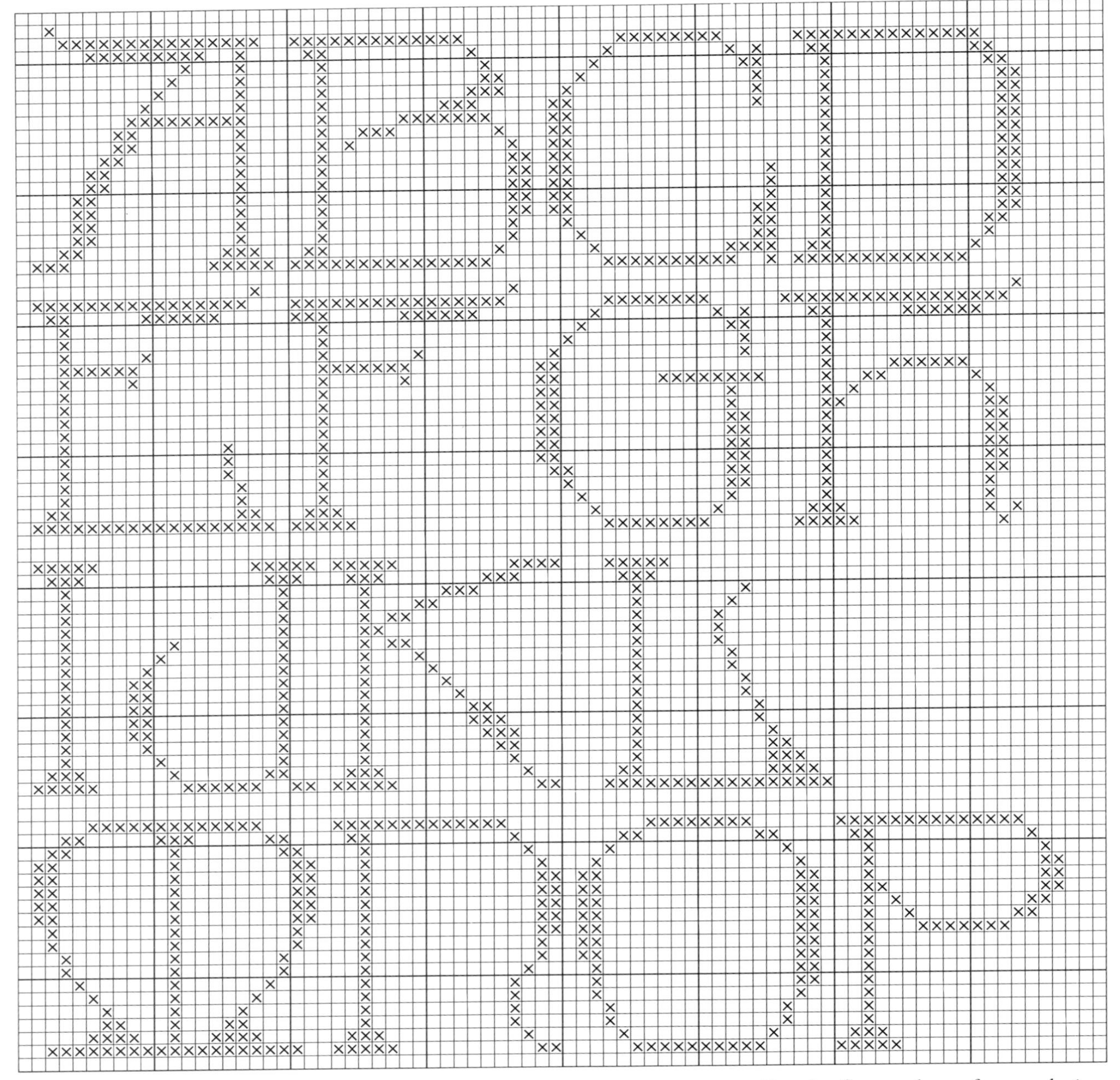

Antique Renaissance Alphabet

Use the floss colors of your choice.

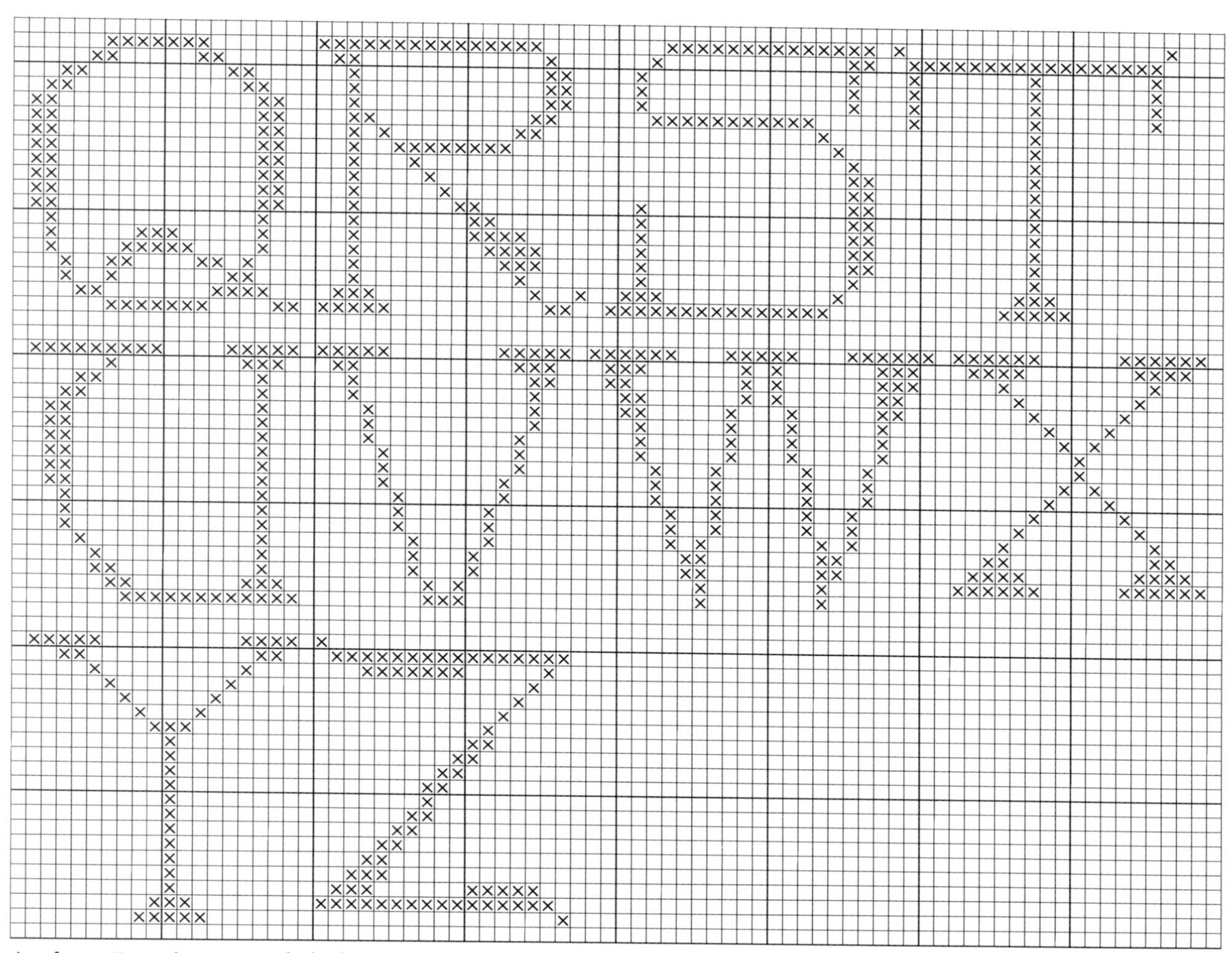

Antique Renaissance Alphabet

Use the floss colors of your choice.

Ideas for Use

Use this alphabet to cross-stitch a three-letter monogram and border it with a tapestry fabric for an elegant antique-looking pillow.

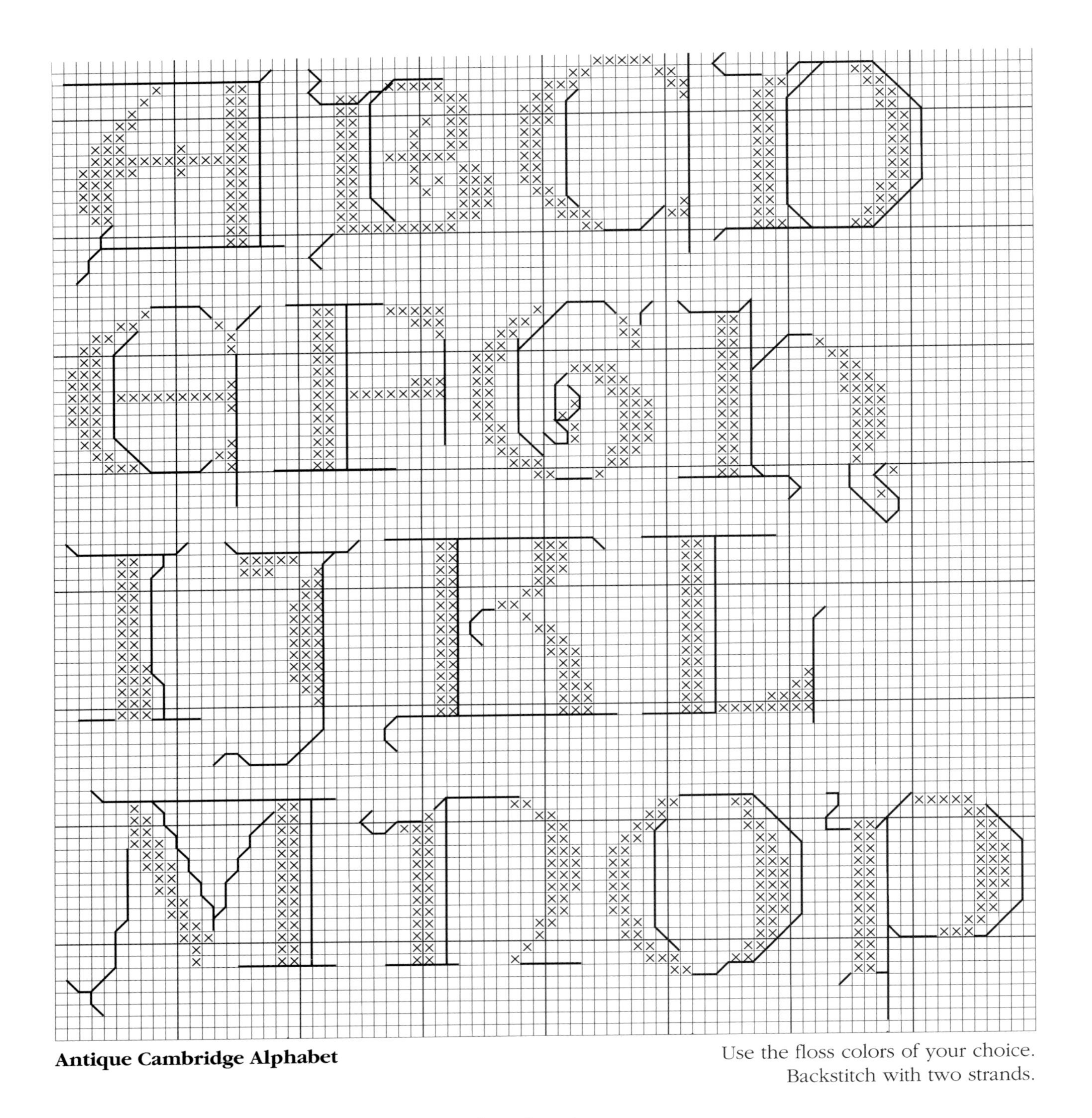

Antique Cambridge Alphabet

Use the floss colors of your choice.
Backstitch with two strands.

Ideas for Use

Choose a colored cross-stitch fabric and a contrasting color of floss to cross-stitch an initial for a personalized potpourri pouch. Add lace and a pretty ribbon.

Antique Cambridge Alphabet

Use the floss colors of your choice.
Backstitch with two strands.

Antique Serif Alphabet

Use the floss colors of your choice.
Backstitch with two strands.

Ideas for Use

Use this simple alphabet for adding your name and date to your sampler.

Country Alphabets

The universal appeal, warmth, and familiarity of country decor must be the reason it persists as one of the most popular home decorating themes. Our Country Alphabet projects have been designed to complement the variety of antiques, country collectibles, and Americana heirlooms found in so many households. All the versatile country motifs can be used with or without the letters for maximum flexibility.

A B C
D E F G H
I J K
N O
S T U
X Y
ENTER
A
HAPPY
HEART

Country Apron

USE LETTERS FROM COUNTRY ALPHABET ON PAGES 76–81 AND COUNTRY CHECKERBOARD BORDER ON PAGE 88

Note: A three-letter name or two initials can be used. If a longer name is desired, it could be stitched vertically.

Materials

Apron: Premade, natural
Waste canvas: 14 count, 6x9 inches
Chenille needle: Size 24

Stitch and Finish

Follow the cross-stitching and finishing instructions for waste canvas in Cross-Stitch Basics.

Welcome Wreath

USE COUNTRY ALPHABET ON PAGES 76–81

Materials

Fiddler's cloth: 18 count, seven pieces 3x3 inches each
Stik 'N Puffs: Seven 2x2-inch squares (BANAR DESIGNS, Inc.)
Rattail cord: Dark brown, 60 inches.
Fabric for backing: Brown felt, seven pieces 2x2 inches each
Wreath: 14 inches
Glue gun or thick craft glue
Wire-edged ribbon: Forest green, 1½ inches wide, 2 yards.

Stitch

Follow instructions for cross-stitching given in Cross-Stitch Basics.

Finish

Follow finishing instructions for covering padded shapes (Stik 'N Puffs) in General Project Instructions.

When forms are covered, add backing fabric. Then glue rattail cord around the edge of each square. Cut wire-edged ribbon in two 1-yard pieces. Wrap 1 yard of the ribbon around the wreath. With the other yard, tie a large bow and attach it to upper part of wreath. Crimp the tails of the bow.

Lay covered forms on wreath to get proper placement, then glue in place.

A B C
D E F G H
I J K L M
N O P Q R
S T U V W
X Y Z

Framed Country Alphabet

USE COUNTRY ALPHABET ON PAGES 76–81

Materials

Floba fabric: 14 count, oatmeal (Zweigart®), 24x28 inches

Stitch

Follow cross-stitching instructions given in Cross-Stitch Basics.

Finish

For best results, have this piece professionally matted and framed.

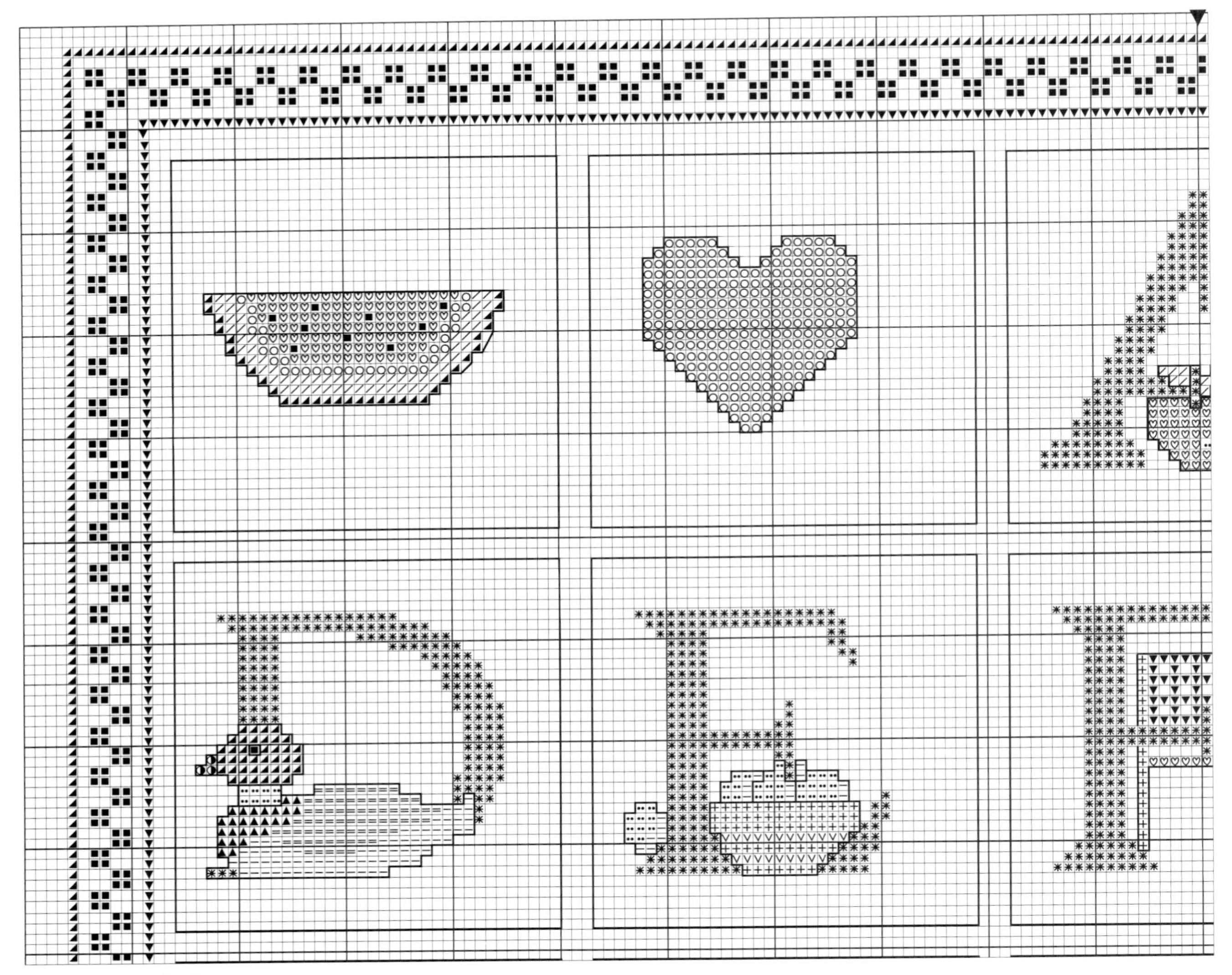

Country Alphabet

Floss

Symbol	Color name	DMC#	Anchor#
○	Medium pink*	3688	66
●	Dark pink	3687	68
♡	Red	321	9046
V	Light blue***	932	1033
▼	Dark blue**	930	1035
L	Lavender	211	342
/	Light green	502	877
◢	Dark green	500	879
I	Beige	437	362
+	Light brown	435	1046
×	Medium brown	433	358
✳	Dark brown****	801	359
◑	Orange	977	1002
–	Light gray	415	398
=	Dark gray	414	235
▲	Rust	919	340
••	White	Snow white	2
■	Black*****	310	403

Country Alphabet

*Backstitch pig's tail on P in medium pink (two strands).
**Backstitch thread on Y in dark blue (two strands).
***Backstitch stars on M and raindrops in U in light blue (two strands).
****Backstitch borders around letters in dark brown (two strands).
*****Backstitch everything else in black (one strand). Stitch bird's eye on N in black French knots. Use black to outline basket on O. Use black French knots in strawberries on S.

(continued)

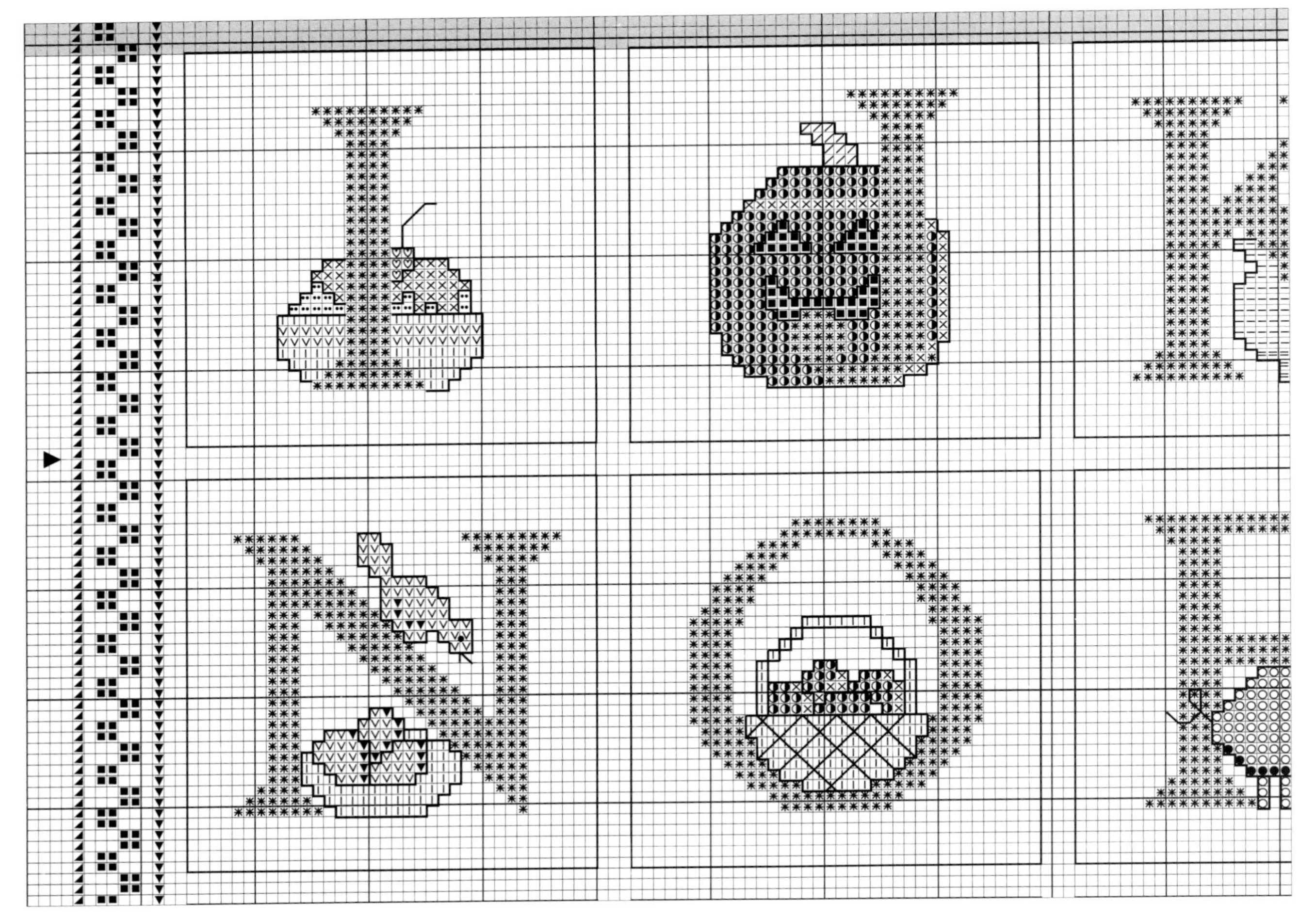

Country Alphabet

Floss

Symbol	Color name	DMC#	Anchor#
○	Medium pink*	3688	66
●	Dark pink	3687	68
♡	Red	321	9046
V	Light blue***	932	1033
▼	Dark blue**	930	1035
L	Lavender	211	342
/	Light green	502	877
◢	Dark green	500	879
I	Beige	437	362
+	Light brown	435	1046
×	Medium brown	433	358
✱	Dark brown****	801	359
◑	Orange	977	1002
–	Light gray	415	398
=	Dark gray	414	235
▲	Rust	919	340
••	White	Snow white	2
■	Black*****	310	403

Country Alphabet

*Backstitch pig's tail on P in medium pink (two strands).
**Backstitch thread on Y in dark blue (two strands).
***Backstitch stars on M and raindrops in U in light blue (two strands).
****Backstitch borders around letters in dark brown (two strands).
*****Backstitch everything else in black (one strand). Stitch bird's eye on N in black French knots. Use black to outline basket on O. Use black French knots in strawberries on S.

(continued)

Country Alphabet

Floss

Symbol	Color name	DMC#	Anchor#
○	Medium pink*	3688	66
●	Dark pink	3687	68
♡	Red	321	9046
V	Light blue***	932	1033
▼	Dark blue**	930	1035
L	Lavender	211	342
/	Light green	502	877
◢	Dark green	500	879
I	Beige	437	362
+	Light brown	435	1046
X	Medium brown	433	358
✱	Dark brown****	801	359
◑	Orange	977	1002
—	Light gray	415	398
=	Dark gray	414	235
▲	Rust	919	340
••	White	Snow white	2
■	Black*****	310	403

Country Alphabet

Stitch Count: 212x253

*Backstitch pig's tail on P in medium pink (two strands).
**Backstitch thread on Y in dark blue (two strands).
***Backstitch stars on M and raindrops in U in light blue (two strands).
****Backstitch borders around letters in dark brown (two strands).
*****Backstitch everything else in black (one strand). Stitch bird's eye on N in black French knots. Use black to outline basket on O. Use black French knots in strawberries on S.

Watermelon Pillow

Use Letter of Choice from Country Alphabet on Pages 76–81 and Country Watermelon Border Below

Materials

Premade pillow: 11 inch square with dark teal striped ruffle and Klostern fabric, 7 count (Adam Originals), sand
Pillow form: 11 inches square
Needle: Size #20

Stitch

Unzip the premade pillow and reach inside to cross-stitch the design. Follow the instructions for cross-stitching given in Cross-Stitch Basics. Use six strands of floss for all stitching.

Finish

When finished stitching, insert pillow form.

Floss

Symbol	Color name	DMC#	Anchor#
•	Pink	604	55
O	Red	321	9046
/	Light green	502	877
◢	Dark green	500	879

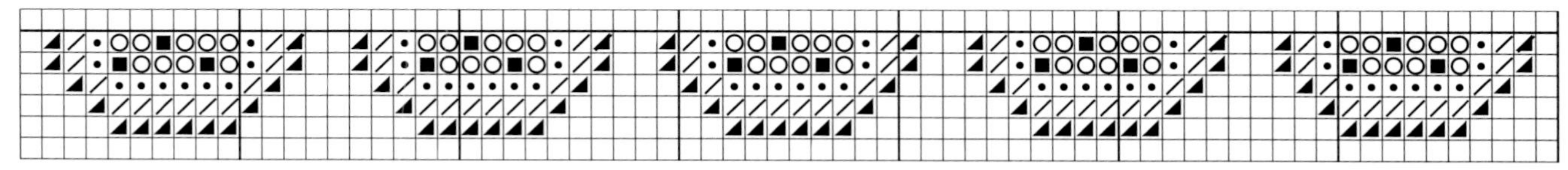

Country Watermelon Border Stitch Count: 68x5

Stacked Chipwood Boxes

USE COUNTRY HEARTS AND VINE, COUNTRY HOUSE, AND COUNTRY QUILT STAR BORDERS ON PAGES 87–88

Materials

Three chipwood boxes: 3x4 inches, 4x5 inches, and 5x6 inches
Fiddler's cloth: 14 count, three pieces: 2x11 inches, 2x16 inches, and 2x17 inches.
Acrylic paint: Peach, green, and blue
Small paintbrush
Thick craft glue

Stitch

Select the border of your choice. Stitch following cross-stitch instructions given in Cross-Stitch Basics.

Finish

Paint boxes the colors of your choice. Let dry. Hem bands, leaving three spaces at top and bottom. Trim fabric, leaving ½ of fabric top and bottom. Fold, press with iron, and glue. Spread cross-stitched bands with a thin layer of craft glue. Place bands on boxes, pressing fabric around box. Match fabric ends at the back of the box and trim. Let dry.

Mini Candle Screen

USE COUNTRY TRADITIONAL ALPHABET ON PAGE 89 AND COUNTRY HEARTS AND VINE BORDER BELOW

Materials

Candle screen: Wheatland Crafts #AC42
Floba fabric: 14 count (Zweigart®), 6x7 inches
Mounting board: With adhesive backing, 4x5 inches

Stitch

Follow the instructions for cross-stitching given in Cross-Stitch Basics.

Finish

Cut 1 inch off all sides of fabric leaving a 5x6-inch rectangle of fabric. Mount fabric on adhesive side of board. Place into frame of candle screen. The frame moves up and down on the dowel. Move to desired place and with pliers, squeeze the gold hooks until tight.

Floss

Symbol	Color name	DMC#	Anchor#
•	Light pink	3688	66
○	Medium pink	3688	66
●	Dark pink	3687	68
I	Beige	437	362
×	Brown	435	1046
L	Lavender	211	342
/	Light green	502	877
◢	Dark green	500	879
∧	Peach	353	8
V	Light blue	932	1033
◇	Gold	977	1002
▼	Dark blue	930	1035

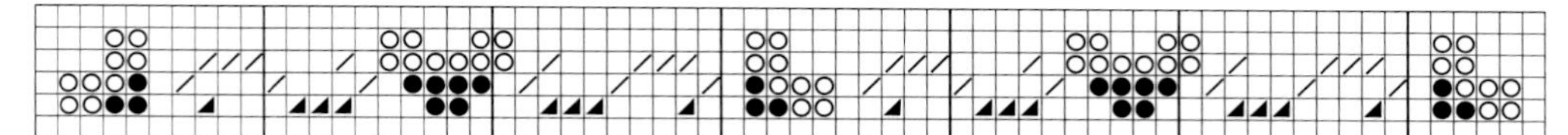
Country Hearts and Vine Border

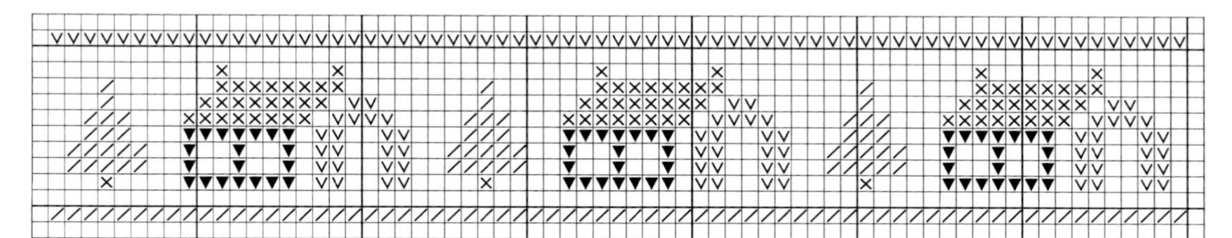
Country House Border

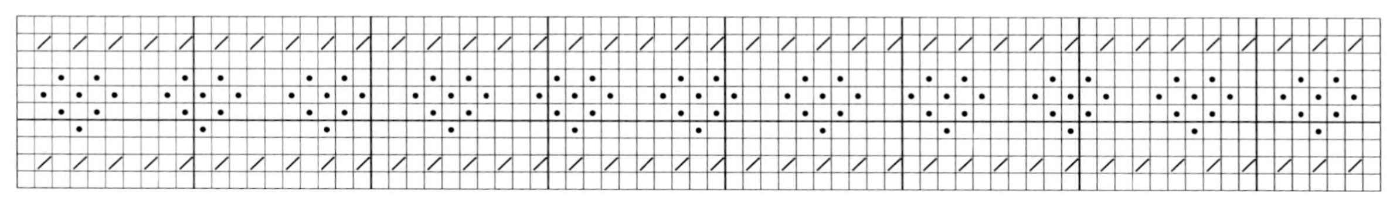
Little Country Heart Border

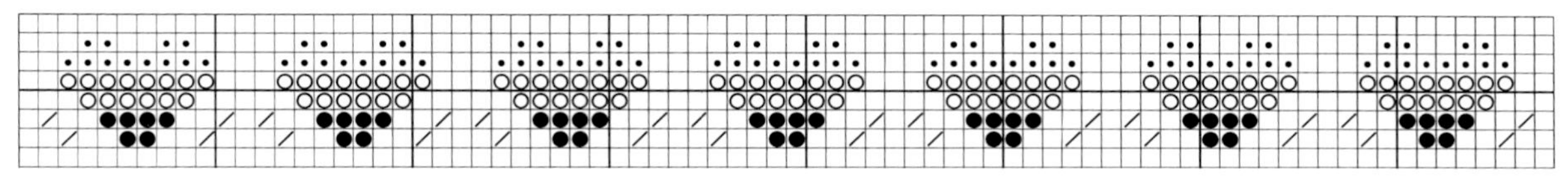
Shaded Heart Country Border

(continued)

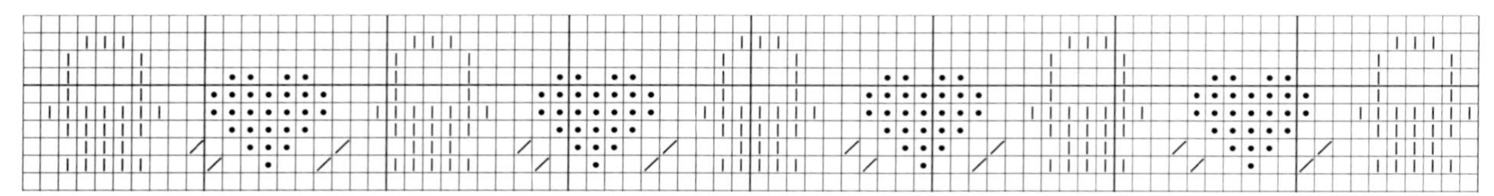

Country Baskets and Hearts Border

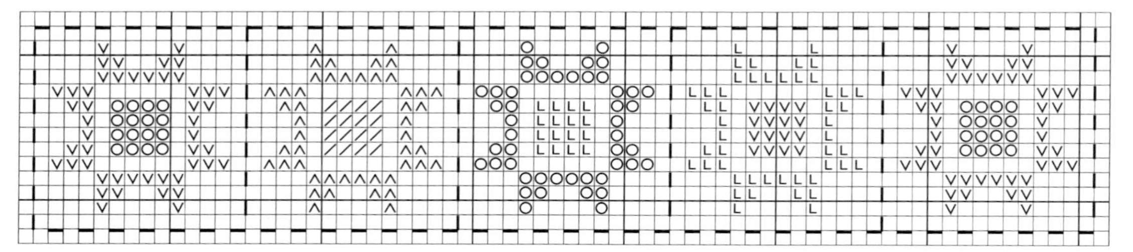

Country Quilt Star Border

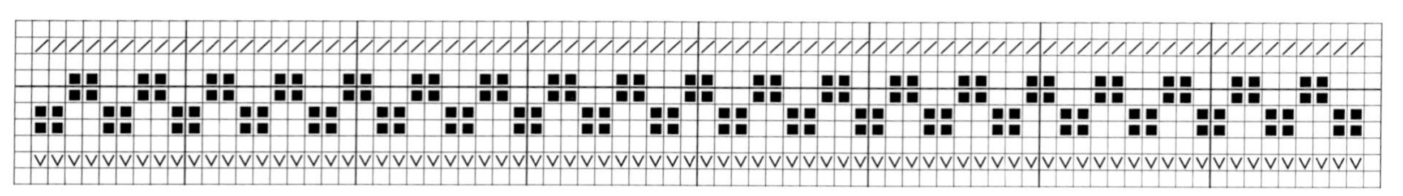

Country Checkerboard Border

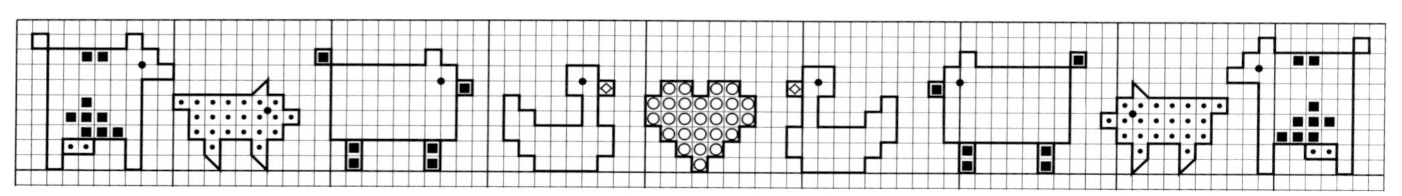

Country Barnyard Border

Floss

Symbol	Color name	DMC#	Anchor#
•	Light pink	3688	66
○	Medium pink	3688	66
●	Dark pink	3687	68
◇	Gold	977	1002
|	Beige	437	362
+	Brown	435	1046
L	Lavender	211	342
/	Light green	502	877
◢	Dark green	500	879
Λ	Peach	353	8
V	Light blue	932	1033
▼	Dark blue	930	1035
■	Black*	310	403

Use black running stitch around quilt star border (one strand).
*Backstitch in black (one strand).
*Stitch eyes in black French knots.

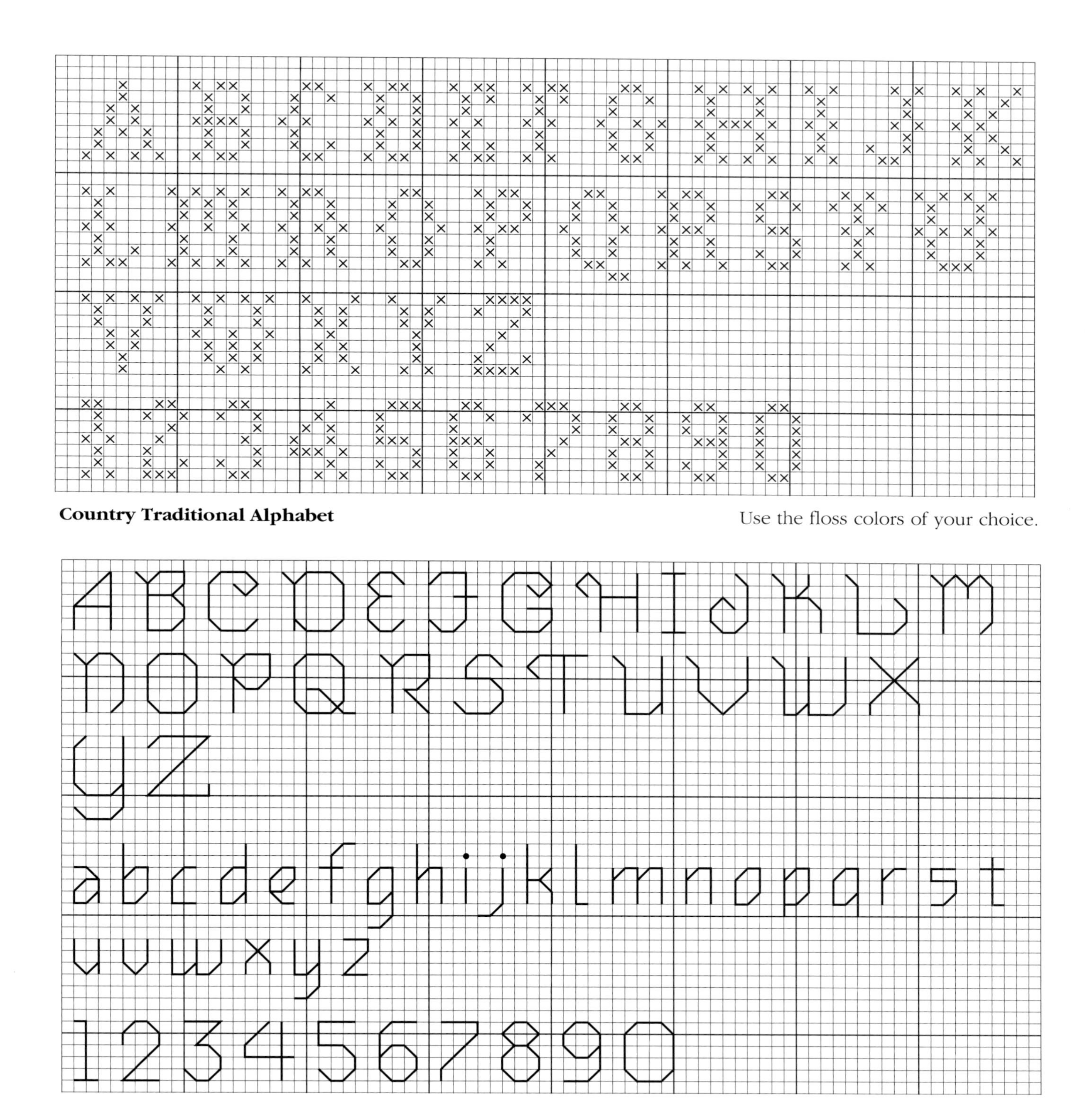

Country Traditional Alphabet

Use the floss colors of your choice.

Country Simplicity Alphabet

Use the floss colors of your choice.

Ideas for Use

This would be an excellent alphabet to use for "signing" your work. You could also use it accompanied by one of the borders on pages 87–88 and one of your favorite country sayings to create your own country sampler.

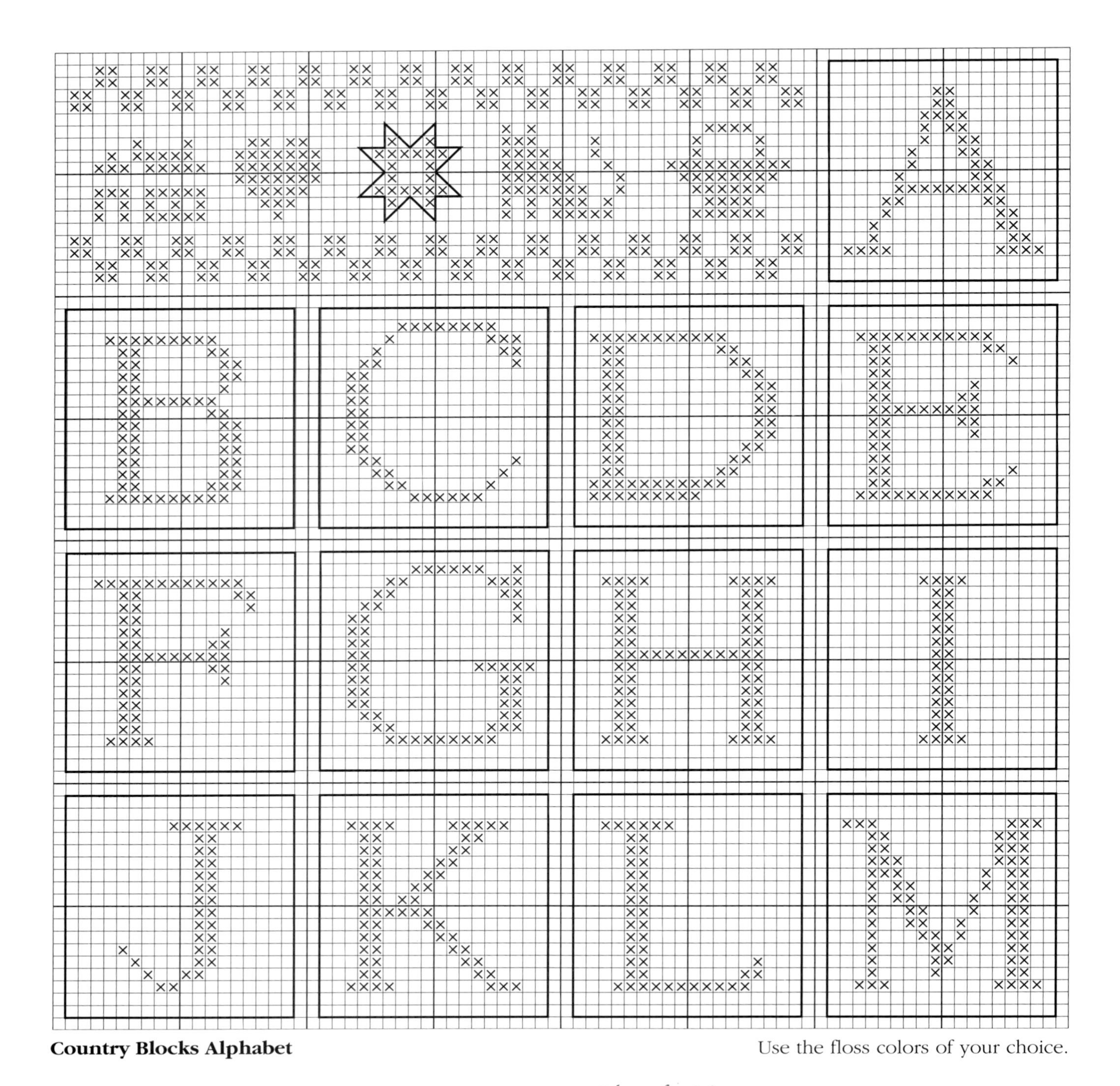

Country Blocks Alphabet

Use the floss colors of your choice.

Ideas for Use

This alphabet could be cross-stitched in its entirety as a sampler.

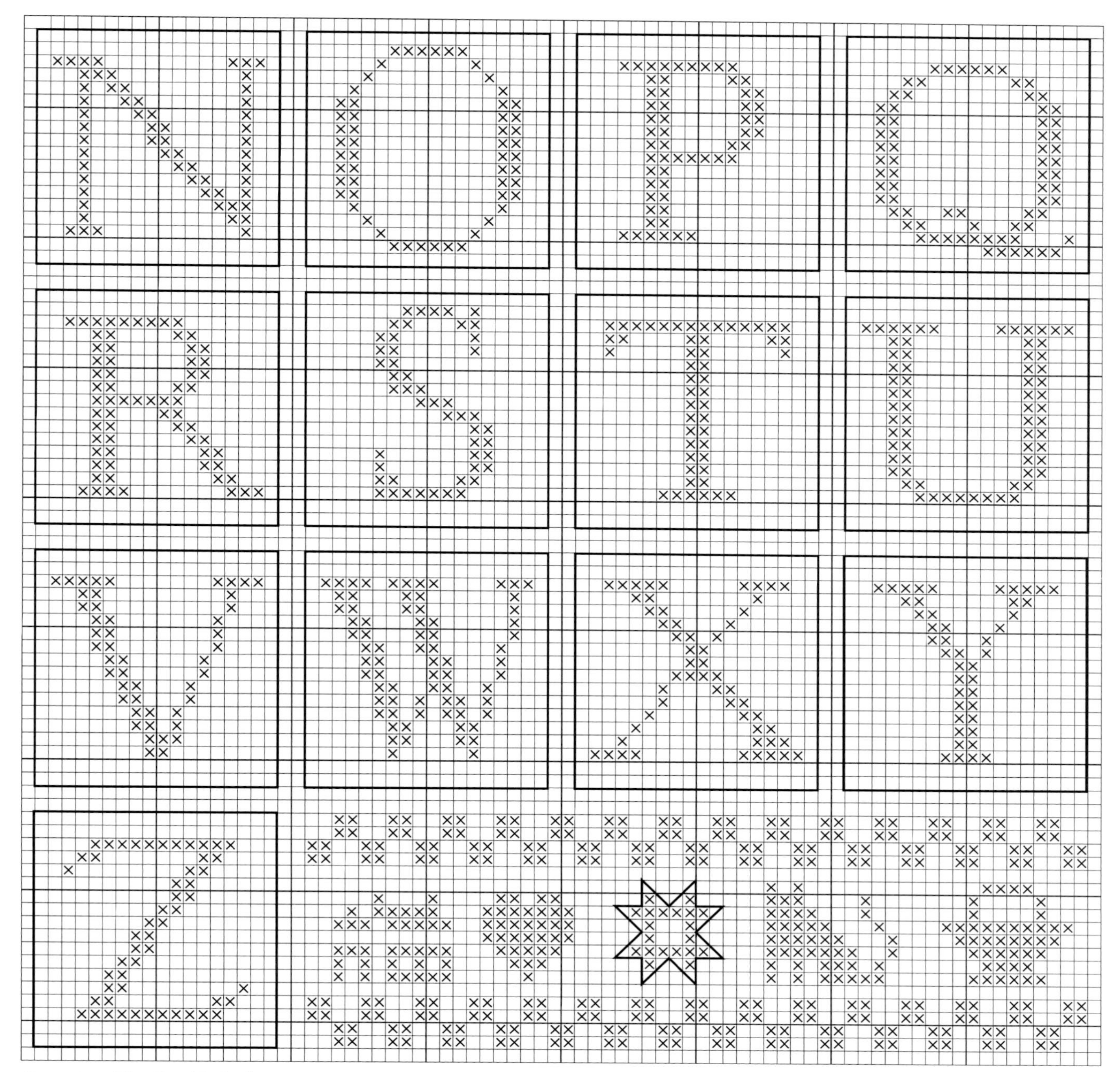

Country Blocks Alphabet

Stitch Count: 78x158

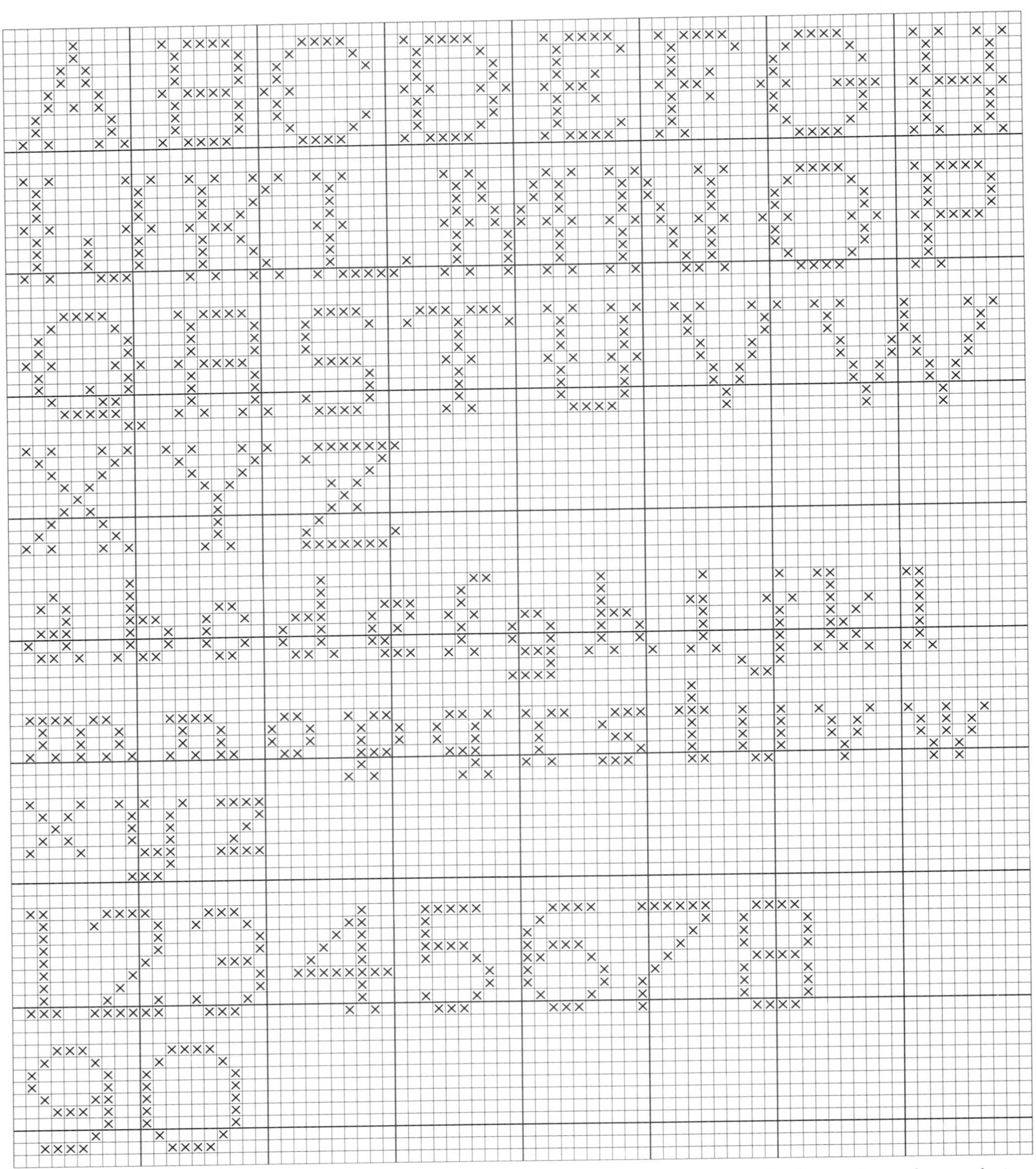

Country Sampler Alphabet

Use the floss colors of your choice.

Ideas for Use

This classic sampler alphabet would be perfect for teaching a child to cross-stitch. The beginner could spell out "stitched by me," his or her name, and the date. You'll probably need to help the beginner, using the instructions in the back of the book. When the sampler is done, tea-stain the piece, frame it in a simple frame, and you'll have a true family treasure.

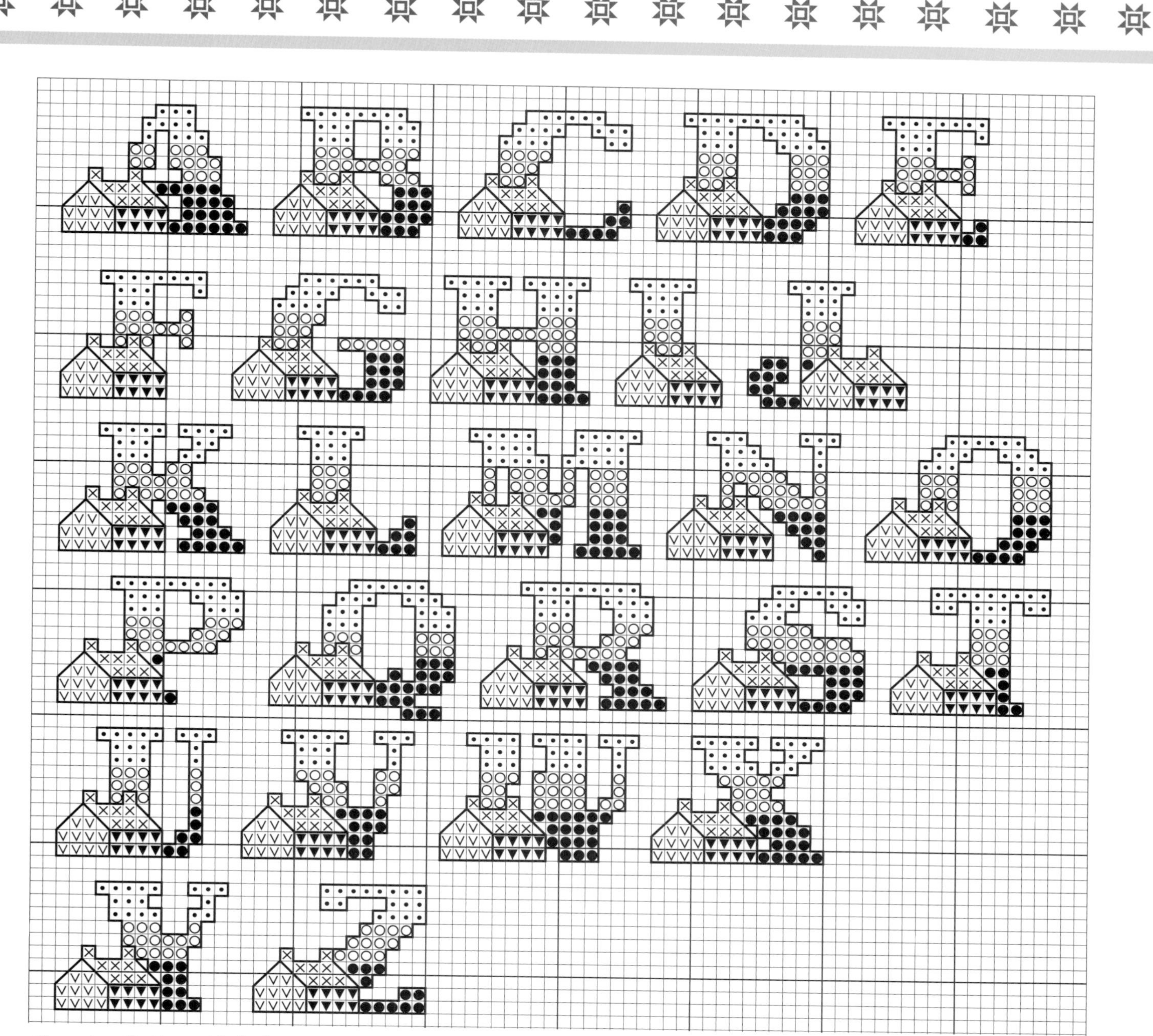

Country Cottage Alphabet

Ideas for Use

What a wonderful alphabet this would be for making a housewarming gift. Use it for the family name and stitch the number from the Cozy Country Alphabet on pages 96–97 for the date. Feel free to change the colors to match the home's decor.

Floss

Symbol	*Color name*	*DMC#*	*Anchor#*
•	Light pink	818	23
○	Medium pink	3688	66
●	Dark pink	3687	68
×	Brown	435	1046
V	Light blue	932	1033
▼	Dark blue	930	1035
	Black*	310	403

*Backstitch in black (one strand).

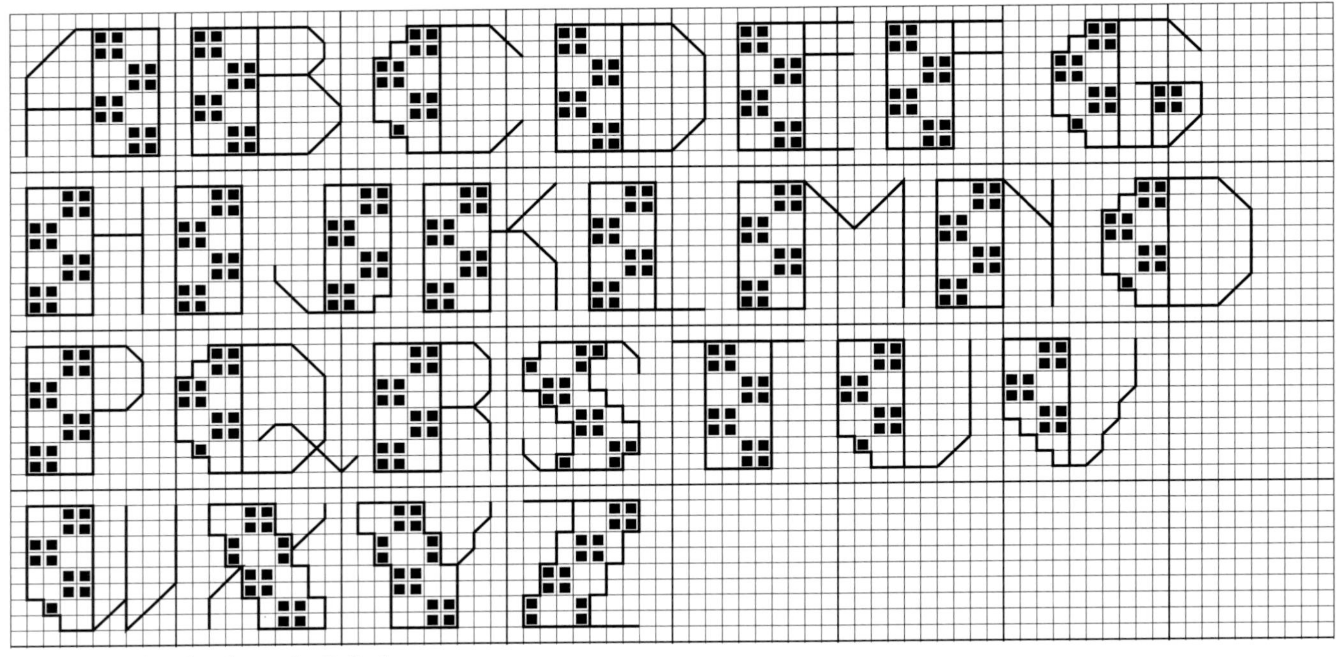

Country Checkerboard Alphabet

Ideas for Use

For a personal kitchen shower gift, cross-stitch the honoree's name and the word "Kitchen" in two lines, with either the Country Checkerboard or the Country Barnyard borders on page 88 above and below it.

Floss

Symbol	*Color name*	*DMC#*	*Anchor#*
■	Black*	310	403
	*Backstitch letters in black.		

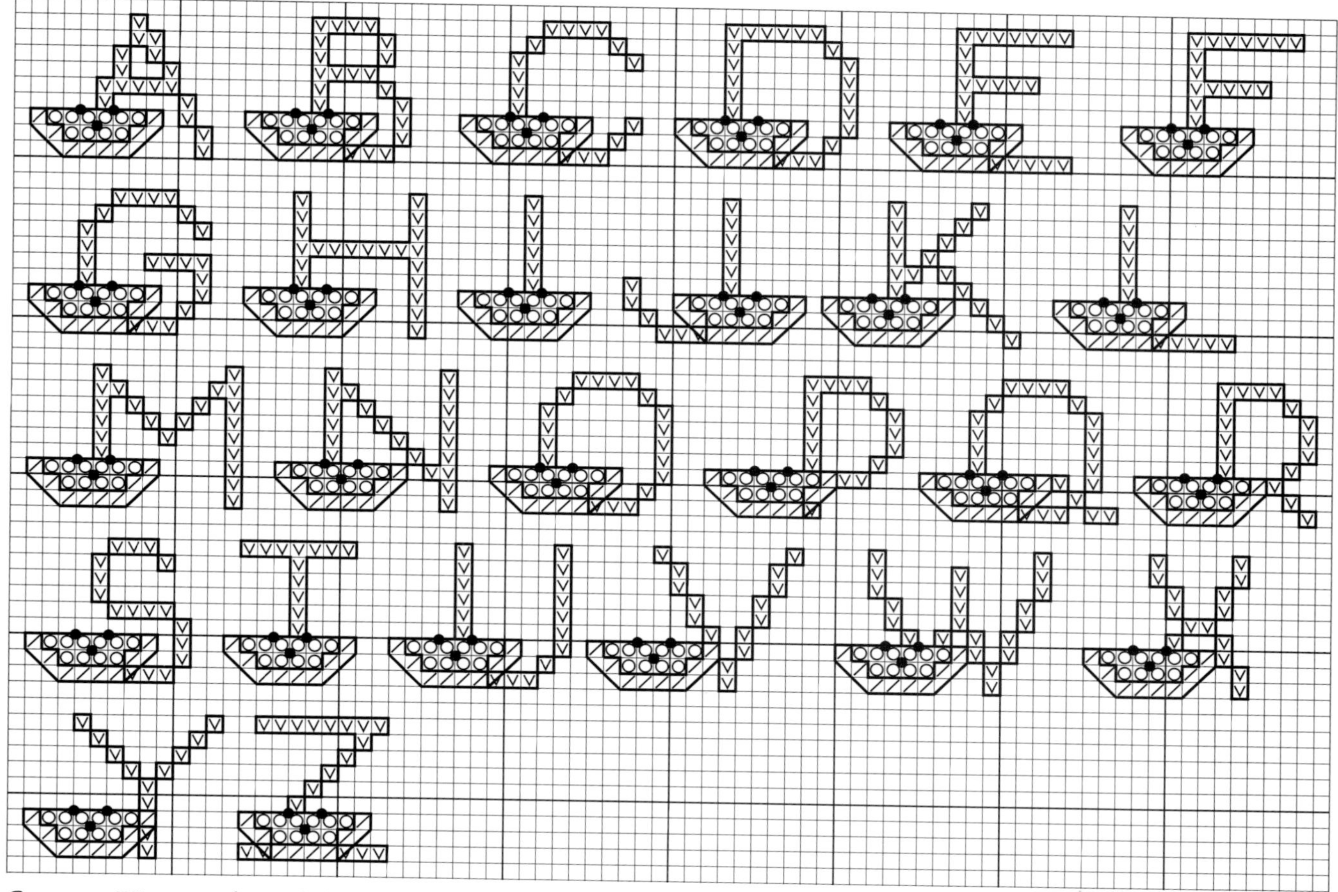

Country Watermelon Alphabet

Ideas for Use

This alphabet would be darling spelling out the word "Picnic" on a bread cloth, tablecloth, or napkins.

Floss

Symbol	Color name	DMC#	Anchor#
O	Pink	3688	66
/	Green	500	879
V	Blue	932	1033
	Black*	310	403
	*Backstitch in black (one strand). Stitch seeds in black French knots (one strand).		

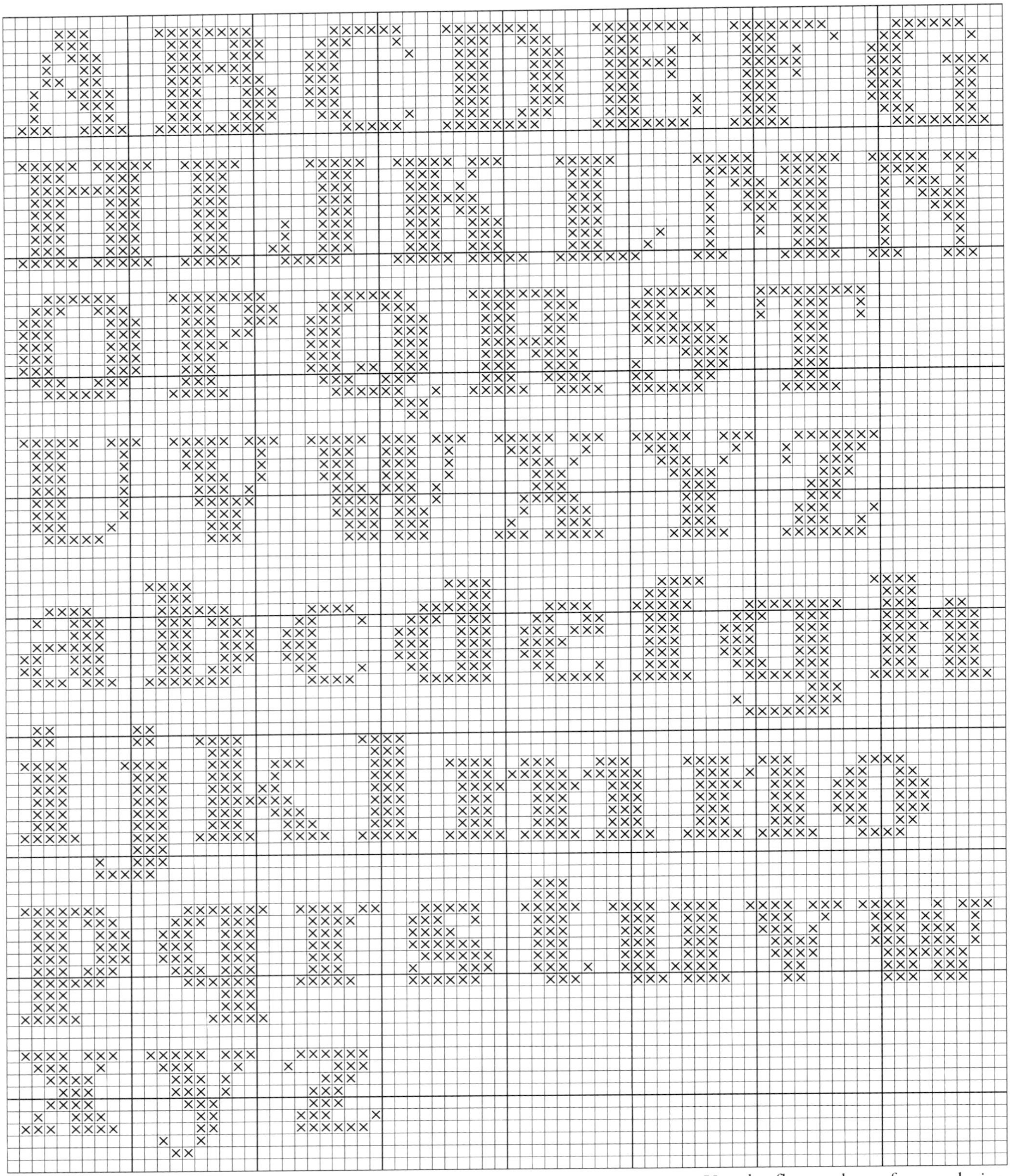

Cozy Country Alphabet

Use the floss colors of your choice.

Ideas for Use

This alphabet would give a homey feeling to the words "Home Sweet Home" or "Home is Where the Heart Is." Use it in combination with the Country House Border on page 87.

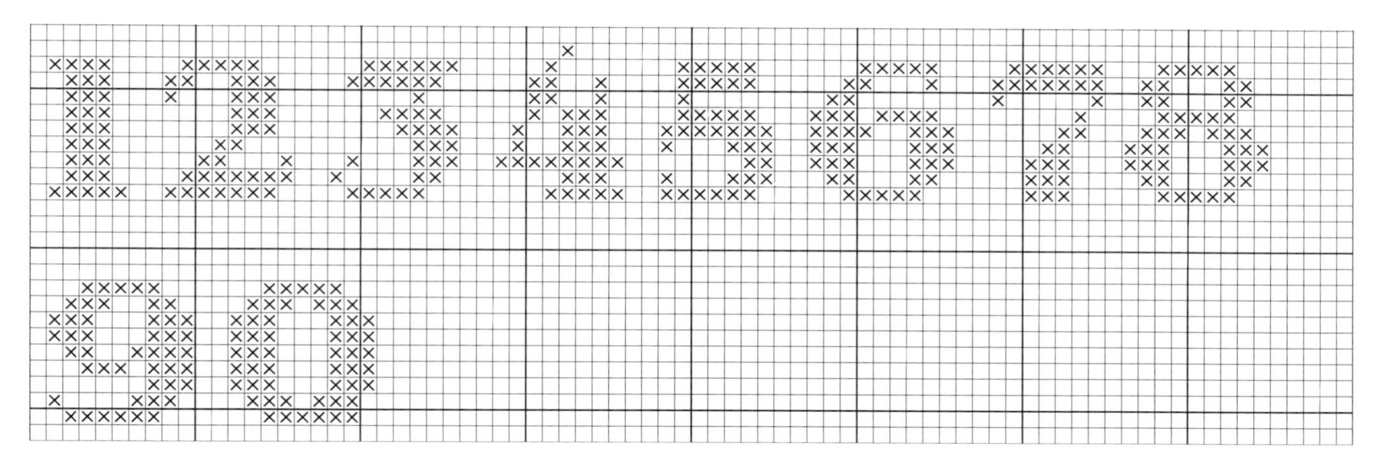

Cozy Country Alphabet *(continued)*

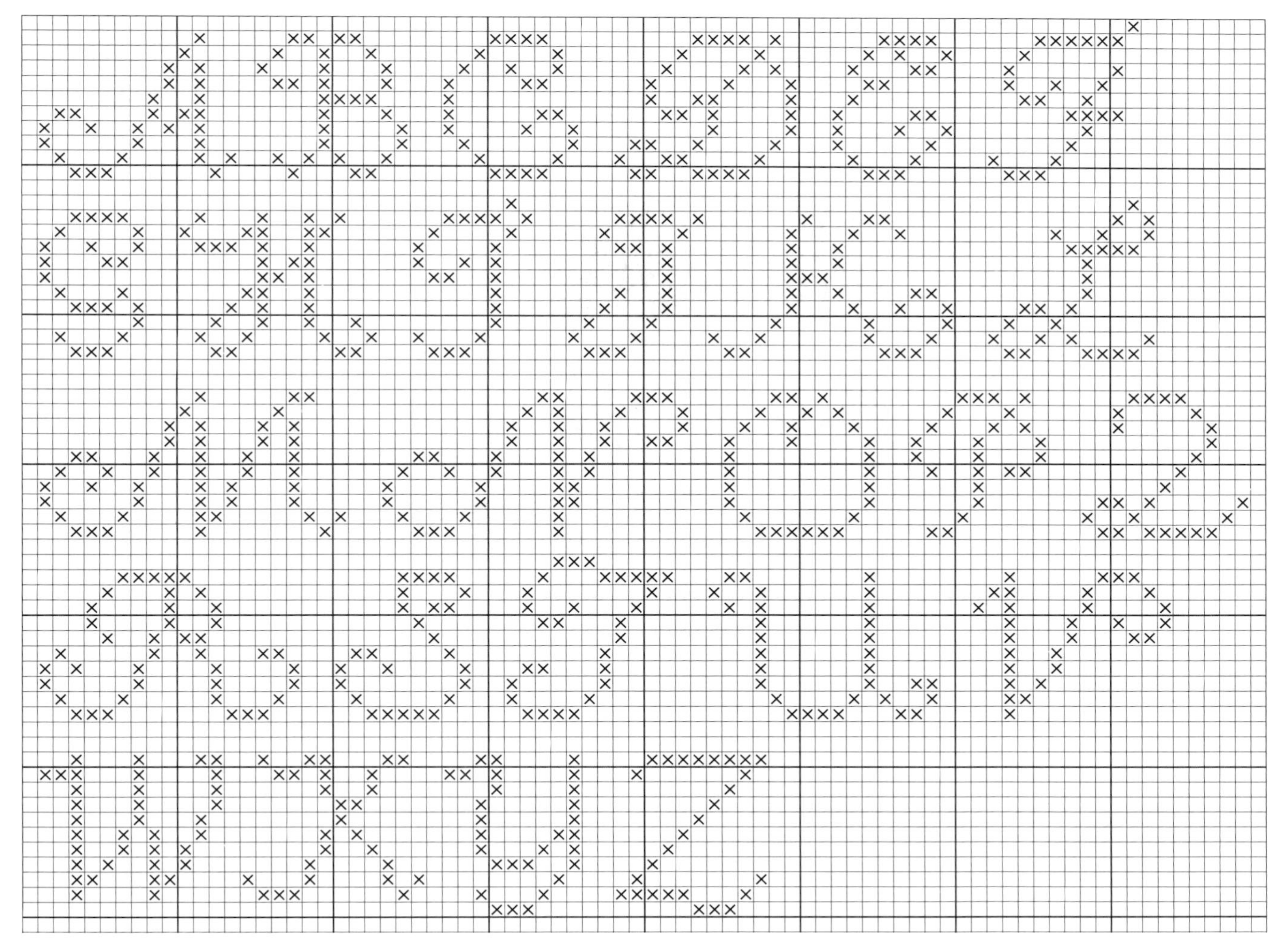

Country Sampler Script Alphabet

Use the floss colors of your choice.

Ideas for Use

This alphabet is best used as initials to personalize items such as guest towels or pillowcases. It can also be used with the lowercase letters from the Country Sampler Alphabet on page 92.

Victorian Alphabets

In tribute to the Victorian era, we present projects for the bride for every occasion from wedding shower to honeymoon. Queen Victoria reportedly was the first to choose white for a wedding, but the appeal lives on in classic white satin, ribbons, laces, roses, and beads—all utilized in this Victorian chapter.

One unique gift idea is an elegant bride's box, complete with monogram. It is the perfect repository for the bride's treasured mementos.

Framed Victorian Alphabet

USE LARGE VICTORIAN ALPHABET ON PAGES 106–111

Materials

Aida fabric: Black, 14 count (MCG Textiles), 21x29 inches
Lace: 2x84 inches, ivory
Ribbon: 1x100 inches, grosgrain, lavender
Buttons: Assorted, ivory
Charms: Hearts and cupid with wings (Creative Beginnings)
Ribbon roses: Five, periwinkle
Victorian picture: Cut from greeting cards or wrapping paper
Hot glue gun

Stitch

Follow the cross-stitch instructions given in Cross-Stitch Basics.

Finish

After cross-stitching, add lace to edge of fabric using hot glue gun. Miter corners. With hot glue gun, add all trims as pictured.

Wedding Album

Use Letter from Large Victorian Alphabet on Pages 106–111

Materials

Photo album: Ring-binder type
Aida fabric: Damask, 14 count, ivory (Zweigart® #3229), 8x10 inches
Satin fabric: ¼ yard (60 inches wide), ivory
Moire fabric: ¾ yard, ivory
8x10" oval photo frame (Better Homes and Gardens® Book Club), or 8½x11" poster board
Poster board: 2 pieces each 10x10 inches
Ribbon roses: 3, blue
Lace: 2 inches wide, 2 feet, ivory
Cord: Ivory, 46 inches
Batting: 1 inch thick, 11½x25 inches
Buttons: Assorted, ivory
Lace appliqués: 3
Hot glue gun

Stitch

Follow the cross-stitch instructions given in Cross-Stitch Basics.

Finish

Follow finishing instructions for covering photo albums in General Project Instructions. The following are additional instructions for this album.

After completing instructions #1 through #4, close album cover and smooth fabric again to cover inside corners. After instruction #7, cover the two pieces of poster board following the same instructions that were given for covering the album cover. Hot-glue covered boards inside album. In instructions #8 and #11, exclude adding lace.

Place inside cardboard oval piece onto wrong side of stitched piece, making sure that the initial is centered. Add 1 inch all the way around and cut fabric out. Use hot-glue gun to glue fabric onto back side of cardboard. Glue entire piece onto middle of album.

For outer oval, place oval cardboard frame onto batting and trace around it, inside and out. Cut out batting, and glue onto oval frame.

Measure around the outside of the oval. Cut satin fabric twice this length and twice as wide, plus 1 inch (set aside excess fabric for satin roses). Fold fabric lengthwise with right sides together, and sew a tube. Turn right side out. Cut one side of the oval so that fabric can slide onto it. Slip the tube over cardboard frame and batting. Space gathering out evenly, fold ends under, and glue. (Hide ends in gathers). Hot-glue finished satin oval frame onto cross-stitched piece.

Cover spine of album with two strips of lace glued side by side with lace ends tucked into the inside. Glue ivory cord around outside and inside of satin oval. Decorate corners as shown in photo with buttons, satin and ribbon roses, and other embellishments as desired.

To make a satin rose, cut a 4x12-inch piece of fabric. Fold it in half with rights sides together. Sew both ends closed (see diagram A–B), then turn

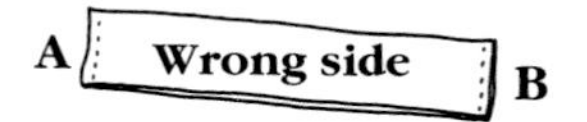

right side out. Sew a basting stitch along open edge of fabric (see diagram C),

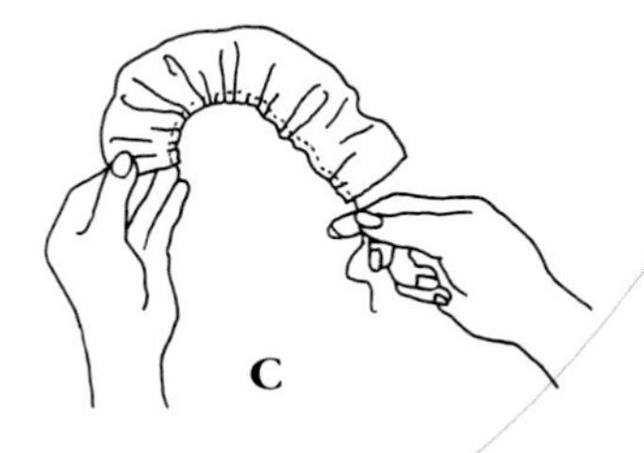

and tighten one of the threads to gather fabric. Coil the fabric around your finger, keeping the bottom, rough edge pinched (see diagram D). To secure rose shape, hand-stitch back and forth through the bottom of the rose.

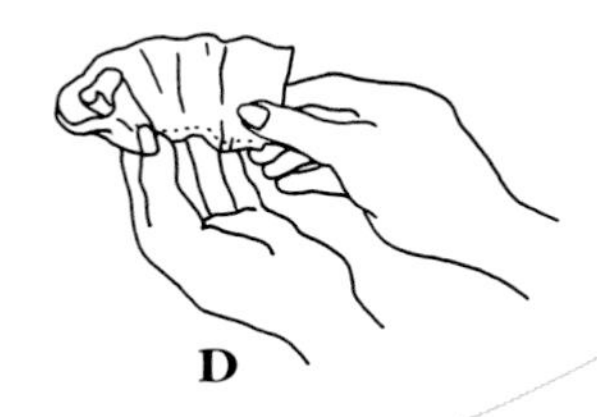

Oval Frame
Full-Size Pattern
(Cut out and retain both outer oval and inner oval. Both pieces will be used.)

Bride's Box

USE LETTERS FROM LARGE VICTORIAN ALPHABET ON PAGES 106–111 AND SMALL VICTORIAN ALPHABET ON PAGES 118–119

Note: These instructions are for a 12x4x38-inch hatbox. If using a different size hatbox, adjust measurements accordingly.

Materials

Aida: Damask, ivory (Zweigart #3229) 10x10 inches
Round hatbox: 4 inches deep, 12 inches in diameter
Moire fabric: Ivory, ¾ yard (60 inches wide)
Satin fabric: Ivory, ⅓ yard (60 inches wide)
Lace: 1½x40 inches, ivory
Satin ribbon: ¼x36 inches, periwinkle
Cord: 64 inches, ivory
Buttons: Assorted ivory buttons
Charm: Gold cupid (Creative Beginnings)
Ribbon roses: Cream and periwinkle

Stitch

Follow the cross-stitch instructions given in Cross-Stitch Basics.

Finish

Set hatbox onto cardboard; trace twice. Cut both circles about ⅛ inch smaller than tracings. Lay both cardboard circles on moire fabric, and cut fabric circles 1 inch away from edge. Wrap fabric around cardboard circles and glue onto back; set aside.

To cover hatbox base, cut a 10x60-inch piece of moire fabric. (Adjust this figure to fit height of your hatbox). Machine- or hand-sew two rows of basting stitches for gathering fabric. Stitch the first row 1 inch from bottom; stitch the second row at the height of your hatbox band. Tighten threads and gather to cover the full circumference of hatbox. Fold and glue section A of fabric (see diagram below) to inside of hatbox. Fold and glue section B to outside bottom of hatbox.

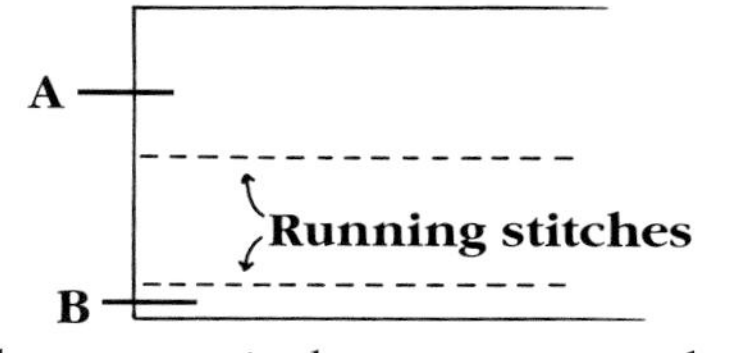

(Gathers remain loose on outside of hatbox.) Glue one fabric-covered cardboard circle to outside bottom and the other to the inside bottom of hatbox (see diagram C).

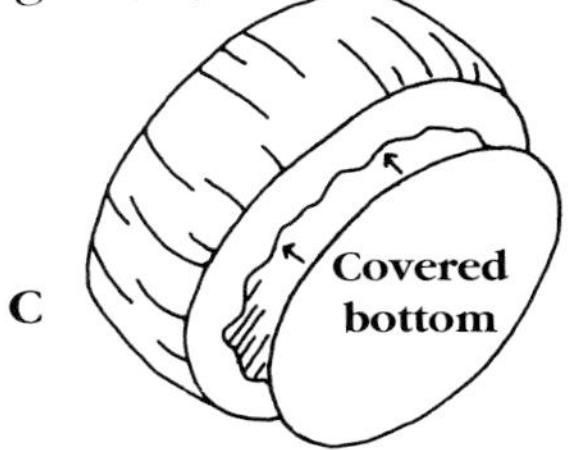

C

To mount the cross-stitched piece, cut a 7-inch-diameter circle out of cardboard (approximately two-thirds the size of hatbox). Place cardboard circle on batting, trace, and cut out (see diagram D). Also, place cardboard circle on prestitched cross-stitch fabric and cut out, leaving 1 inch all around (see diagram E). Stretch cross-stitched fabric over batting and cardboard circle and glue onto back (see diagram F); set aside.

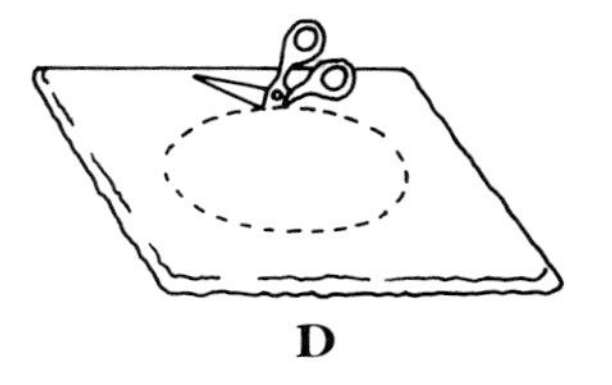

D

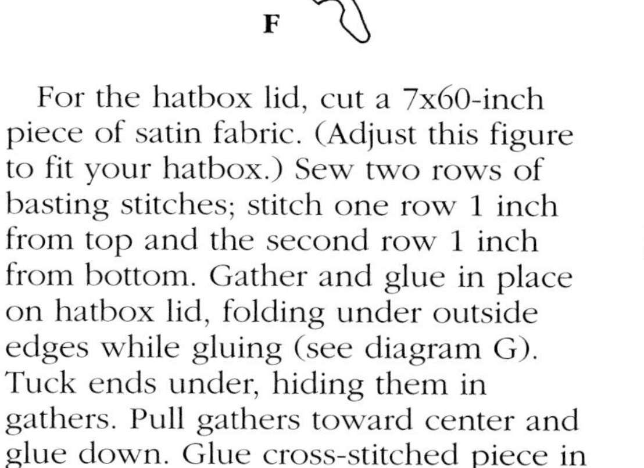

E

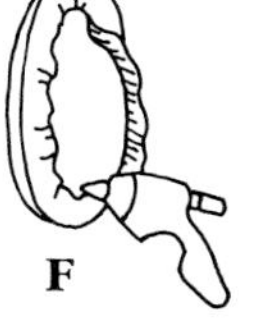

F

For the hatbox lid, cut a 7x60-inch piece of satin fabric. (Adjust this figure to fit your hatbox.) Sew two rows of basting stitches; stitch one row 1 inch from top and the second row 1 inch from bottom. Gather and glue in place on hatbox lid, folding under outside edges while gluing (see diagram G). Tuck ends under, hiding them in gathers. Pull gathers toward center and glue down. Glue cross-stitched piece in the center, covering up rough gathered edges (see diagram H).

G

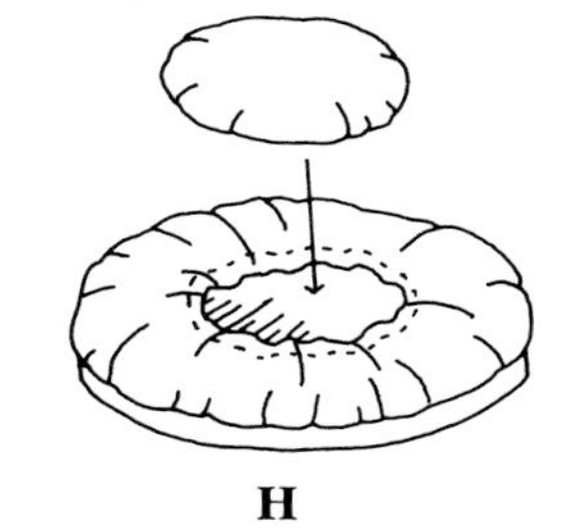

H

Embellish lid top with satin and ribbon roses, charms, ribbon, and buttons as shown in photo. Glue lace and ivory cord around lid edge. Also glue cord around cross-stitched circle.

To make satin roses, cut a 4x12-inch piece of fabric . Fold it in half with right sides together. Sew both ends (see diagram I-J) closed, then turn right side out. Sew a basting stitch along open edge of fabric (see diagram K), and tighten one of the threads to gather fabric. Coil the fabric around your finger, keeping the bottom, rough edge (see diagram L) pinched. To secure rose shape, hand-stitch back and forth through the bottom of the rose as pictured.

I Wrong side J

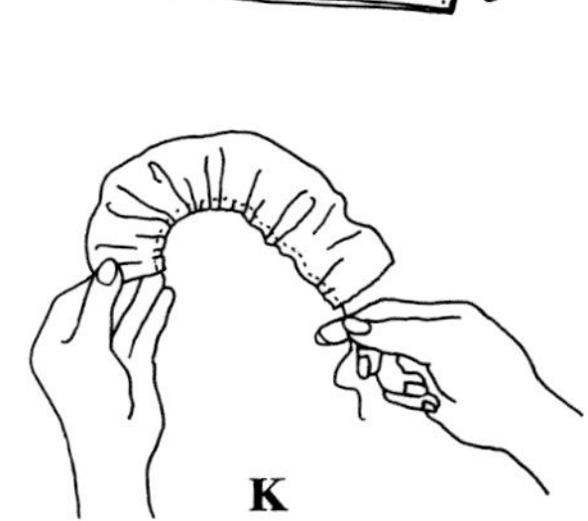

K

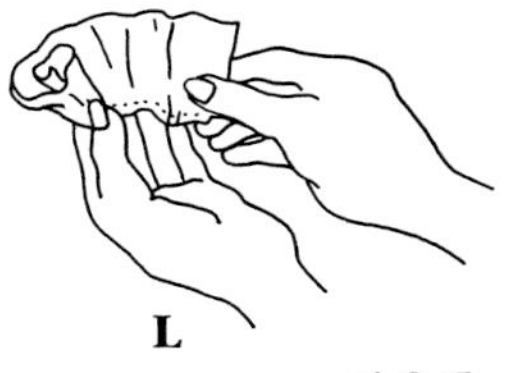

L

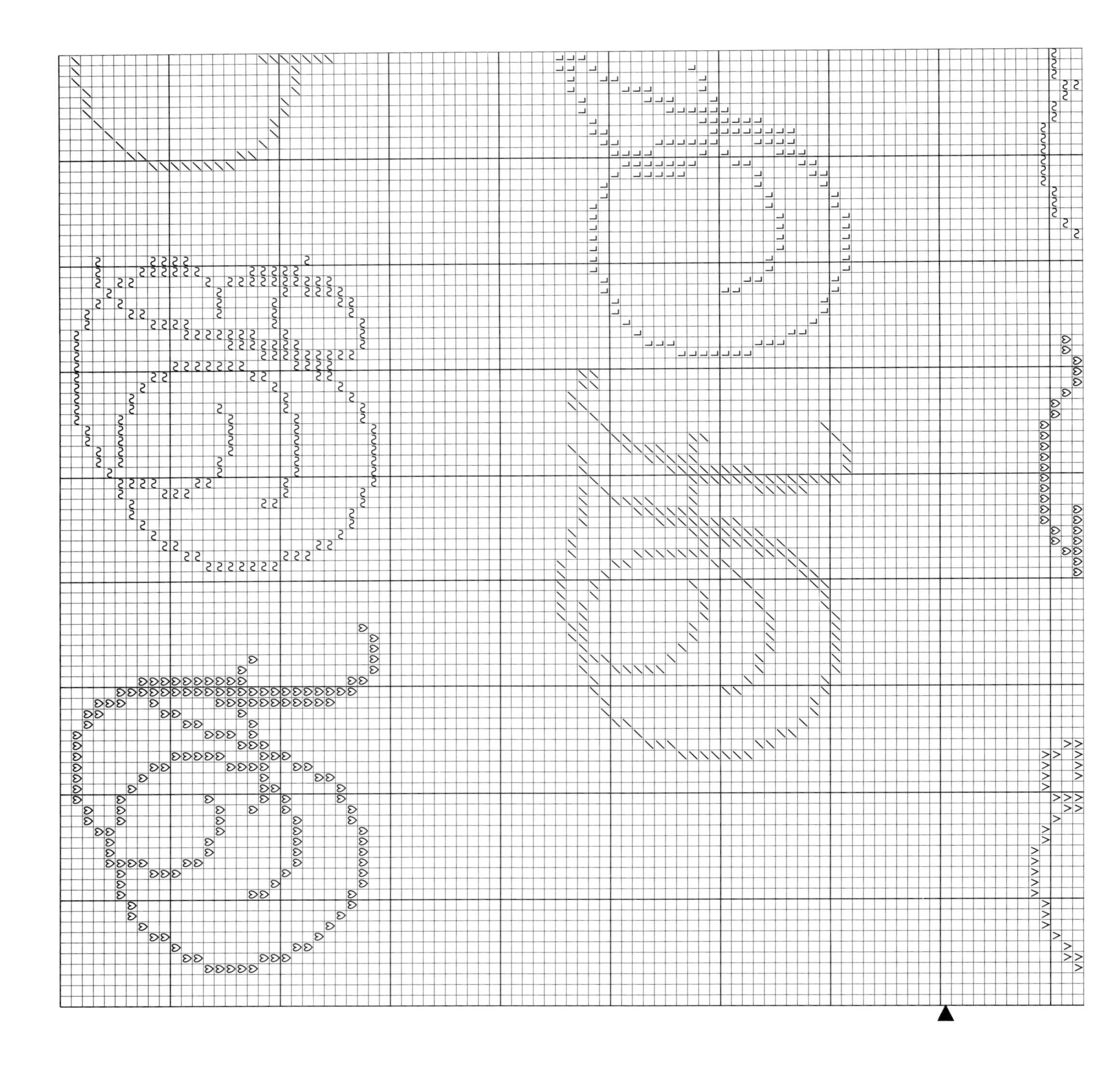

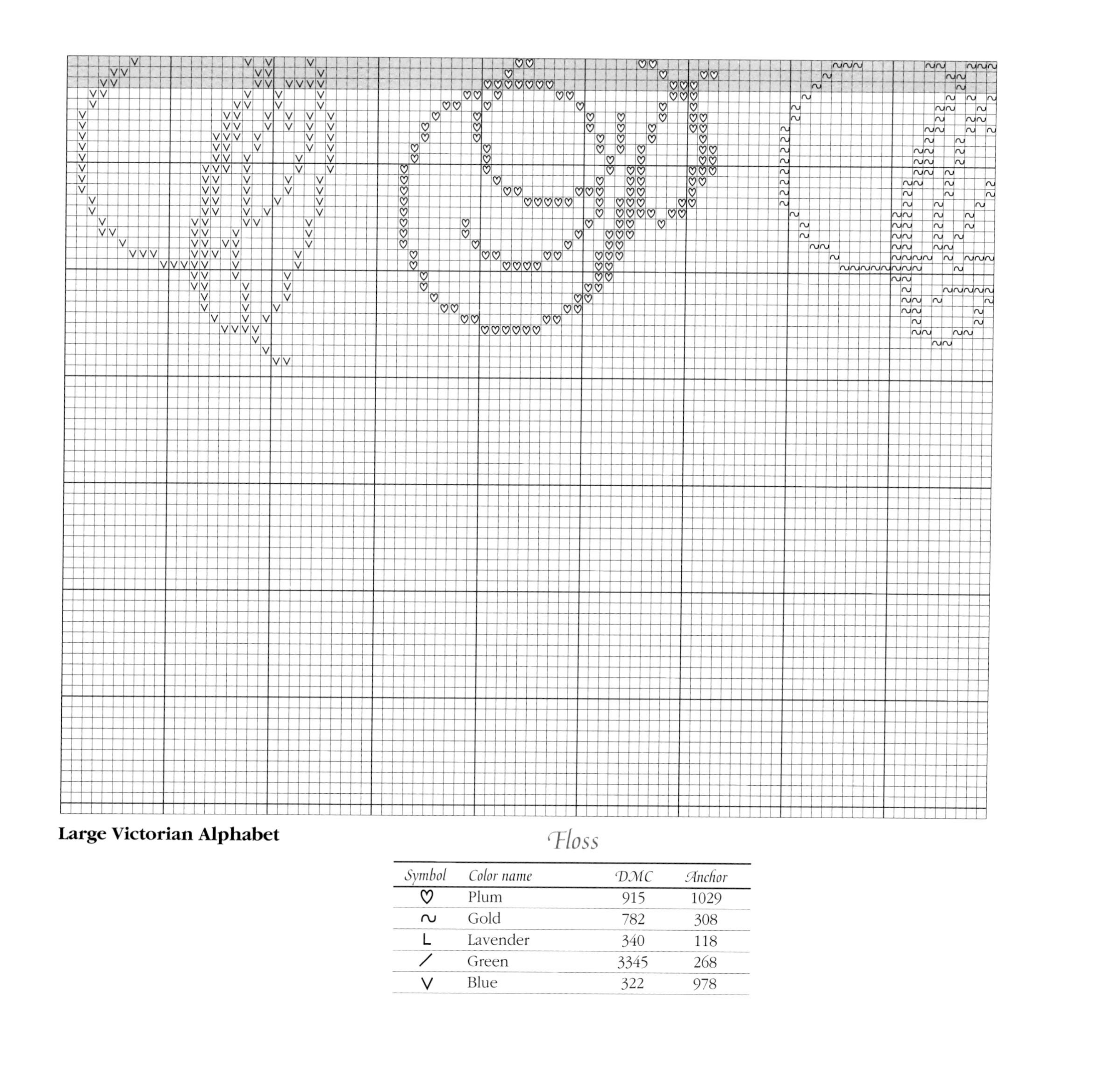

Large Victorian Alphabet

Floss

Symbol	Color name	DMC	Anchor
♡	Plum	915	1029
~	Gold	782	308
L	Lavender	340	118
/	Green	3345	268
V	Blue	322	978

(continued)

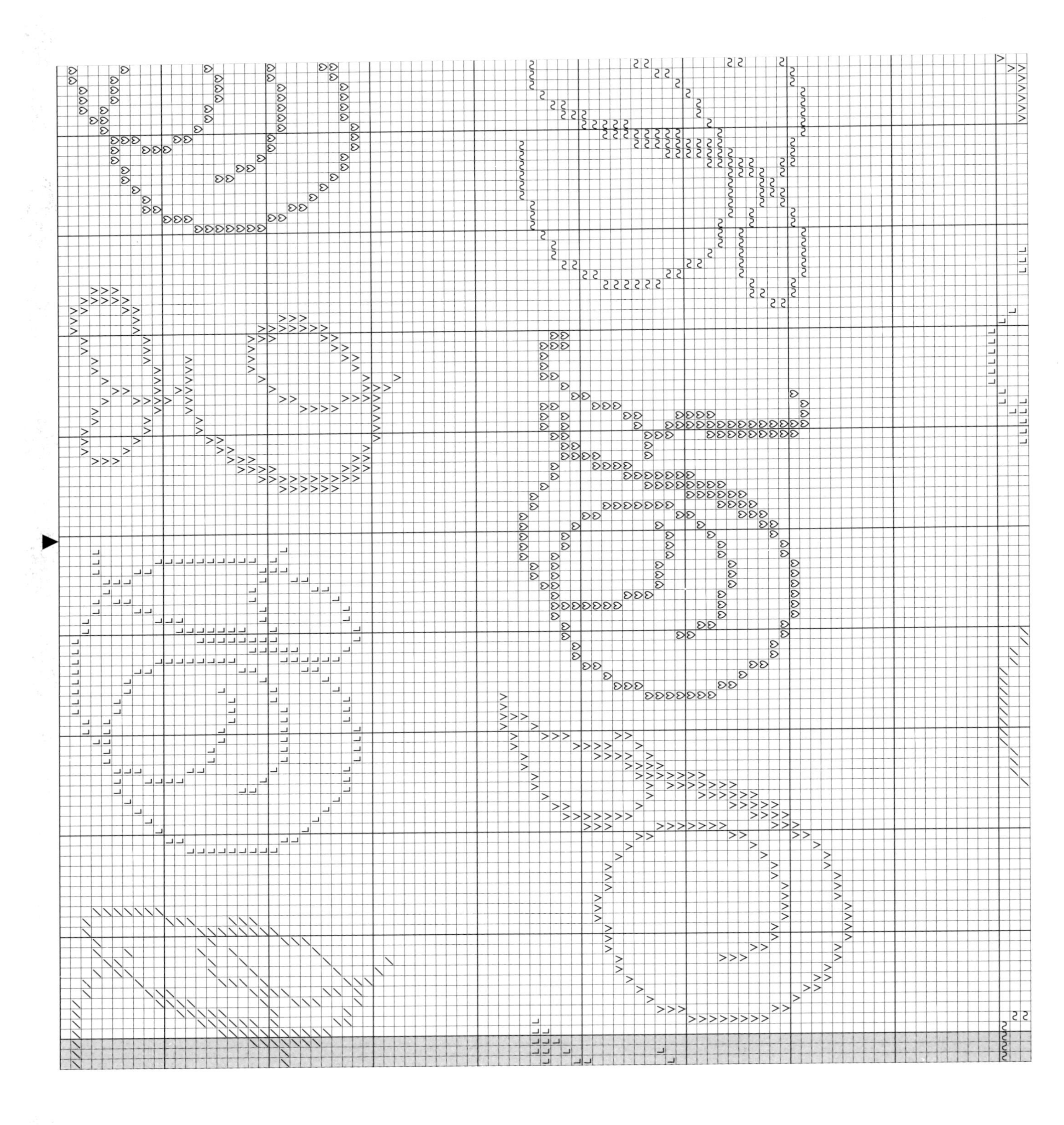

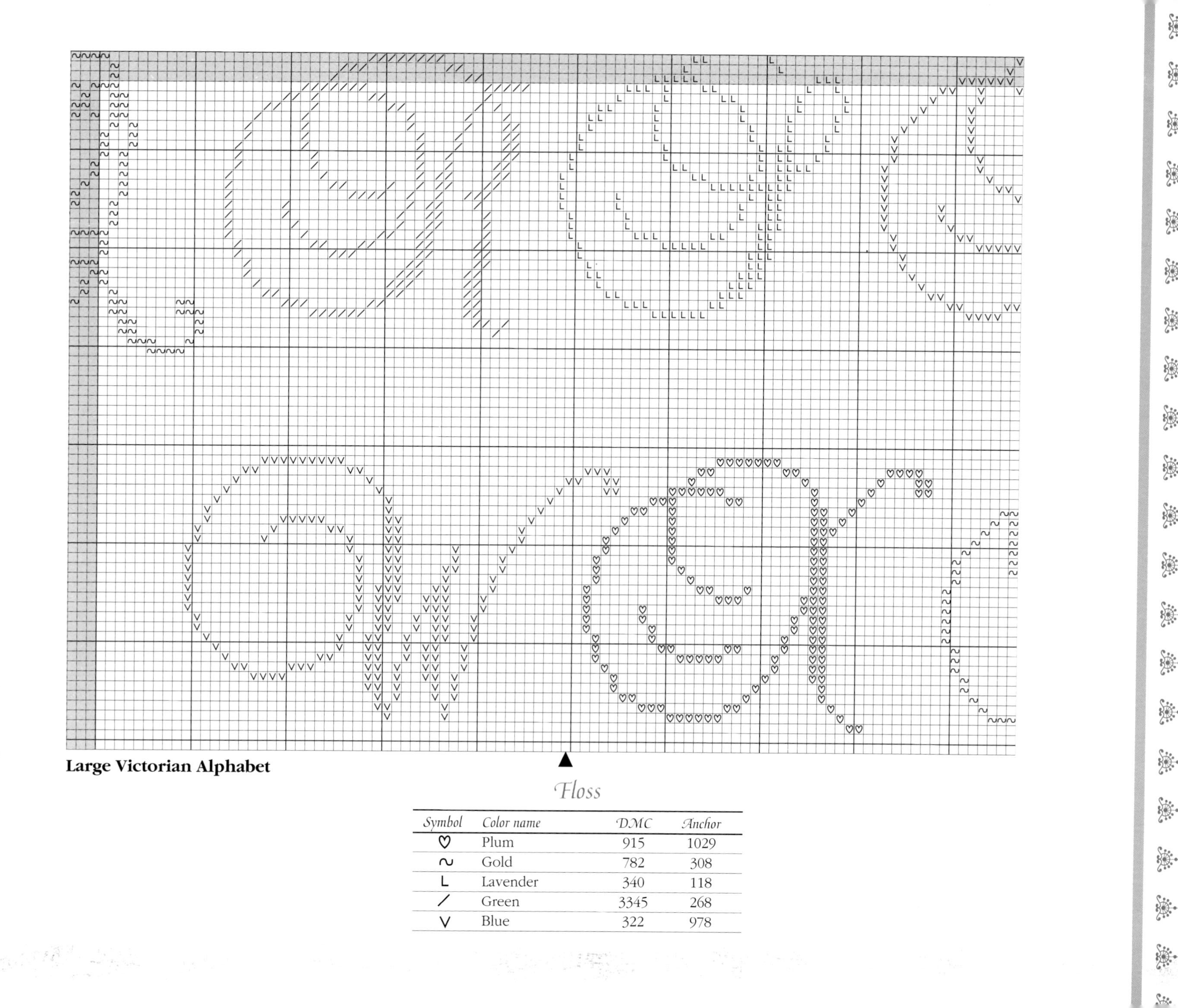

Large Victorian Alphabet

Floss

Symbol	Color name	DMC	Anchor
♡	Plum	915	1029
∾	Gold	782	308
L	Lavender	340	118
/	Green	3345	268
V	Blue	322	978

(continued)

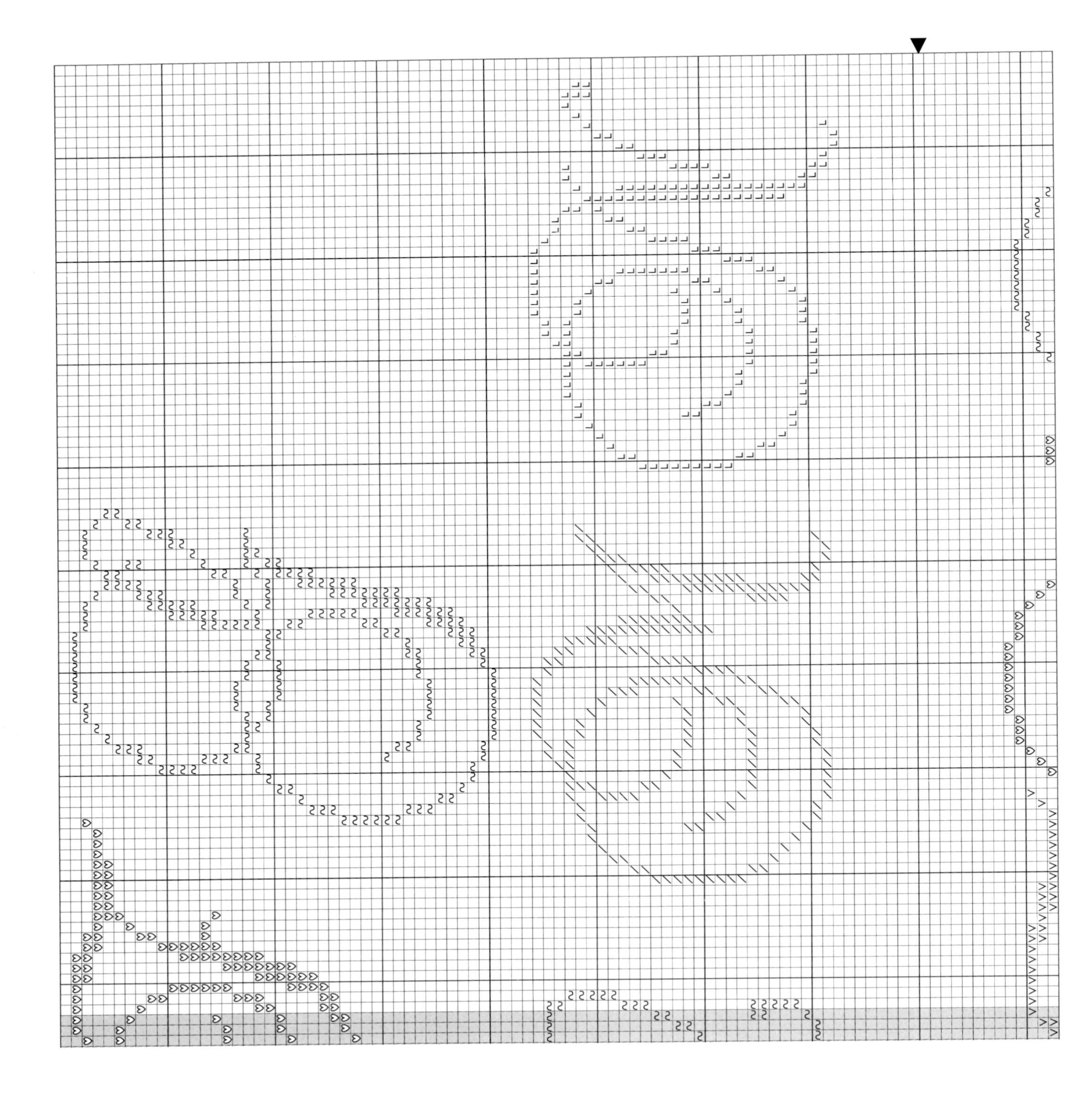

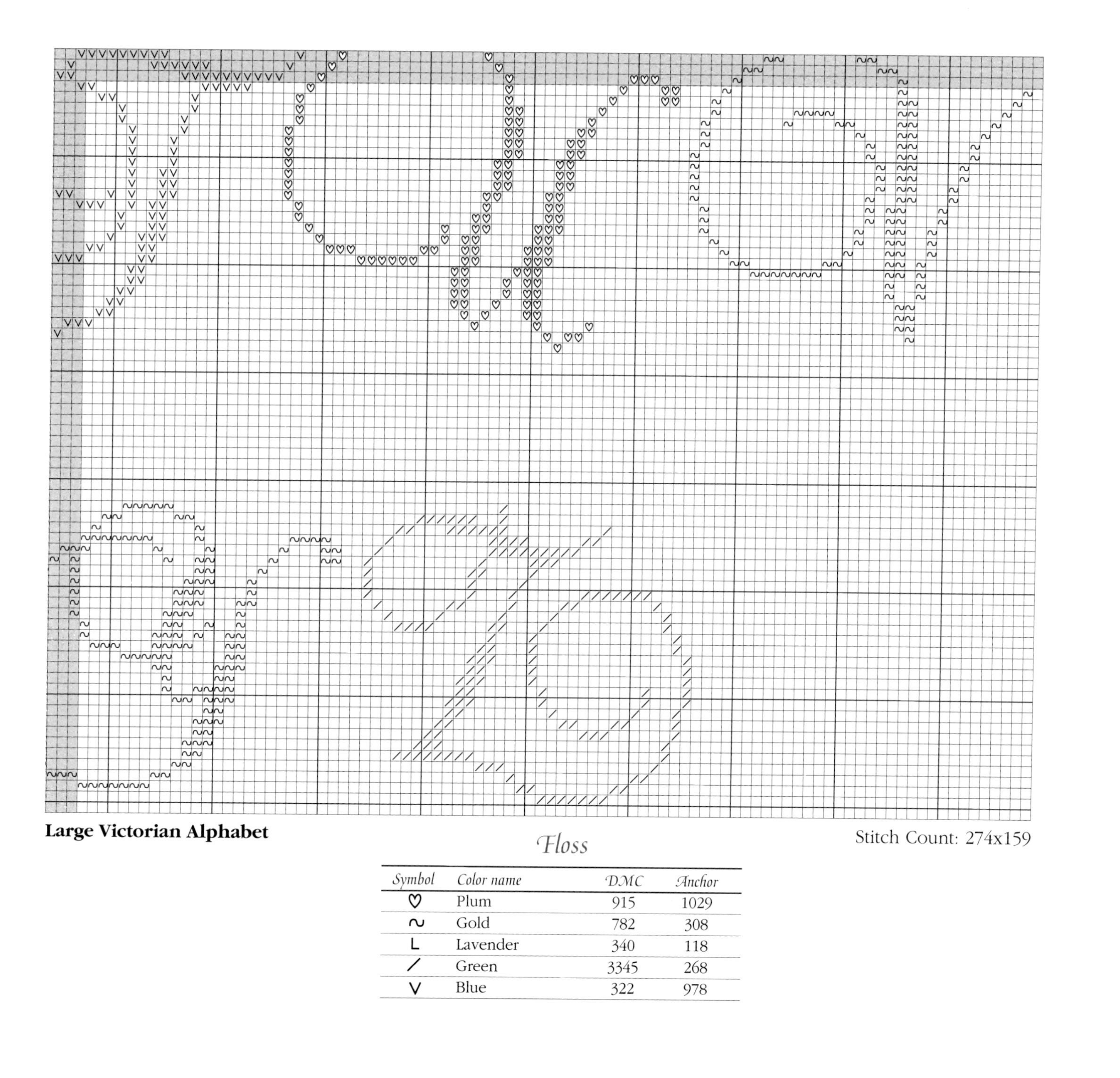

Large Victorian Alphabet

Stitch Count: 274x159

Floss

Symbol	Color name	DMC	Anchor
♡	Plum	915	1029
∾	Gold	782	308
L	Lavender	340	118
/	Green	3345	268
V	Blue	322	978

Lingerie Bag

USE VICTORIAN SIGNET BORDER ON PAGE 115 AND LARGE VICTORIAN ALPHABET ON PAGES 106–111

Materials

Aida fabric: Ivory, 14 count, 8x10 inches
Chintz fabric: Floral, ⅓ yard
Moire fabric: Solid, ⅓ yard
Lace: 1½x16 inches
Braid: 27 inches
Tassel: 3 inches
Batting: 11x25 inches

Stitch

Follow the cross-stitch instructions given in Cross-Stitch Basics.

Finish

Use the triangular pattern on page 114 to cut cross-stitched piece for front flap. Also cut an 11x17-inch rectangle of floral fabric. Place right sides of floral fabric and cross-stitched fabric together, and sew a ¼-inch seam. Turn right side out and press. Use this finished shape as a pattern to cut liner and batting.

Lay batting down and top with piece A (see diagram below), right side

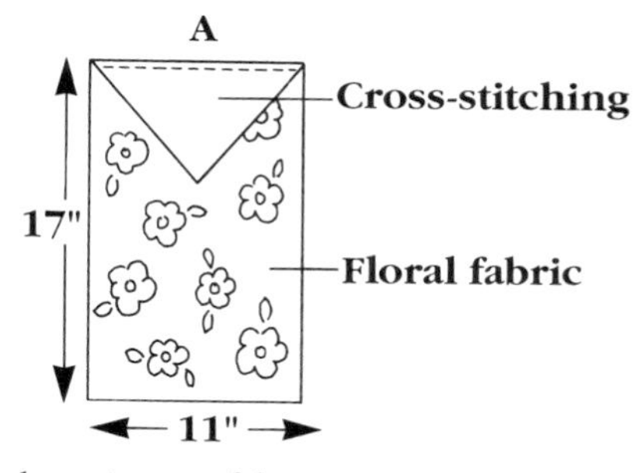

up. Lay the piece of lace onto cross-stitched fabric edge so that scalloped edge of lace is facing inward. Place moire liner on top, wrong side up (see diagram B). Pin and sew all pieces

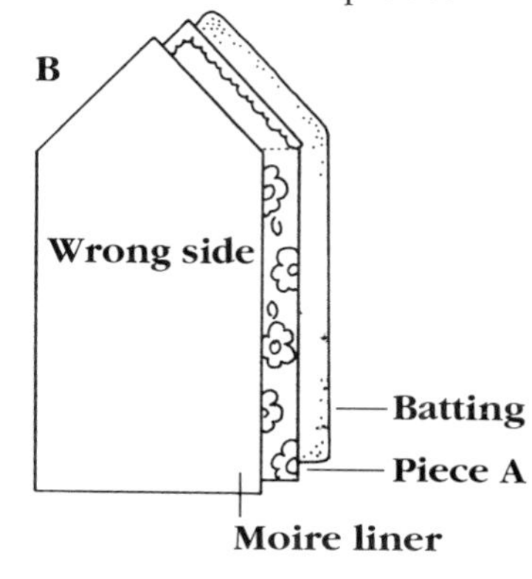

together on three sides, leaving the bottom edge open ½ inch (see diagram C). Clip corners; trim batting to ⅛ inch

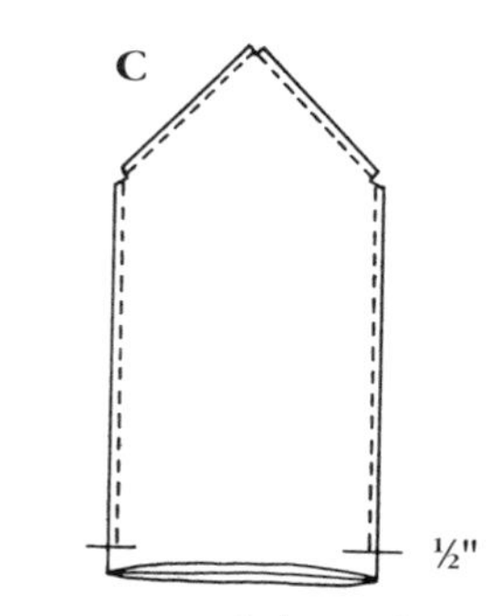

from seams, turn right side out, and press.

Fold in raw bottom edges and hand-sew closed. Fold bottom edge up to meet bottom edge of cross-stitched piece, floral sides together (see diagram D). Sew both sides of lingerie bag

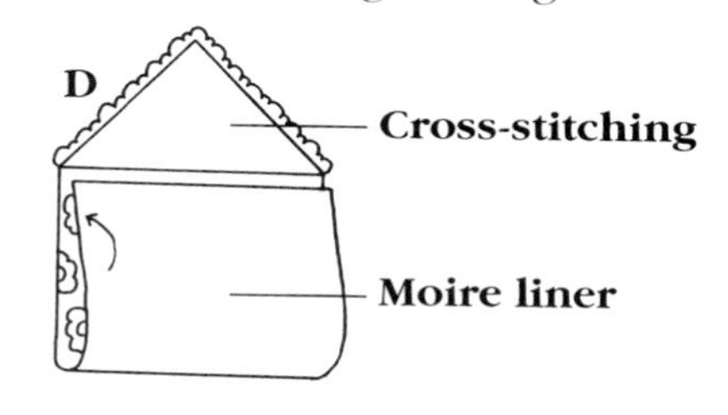

closed (see diagram E). Turn right side out and press again.

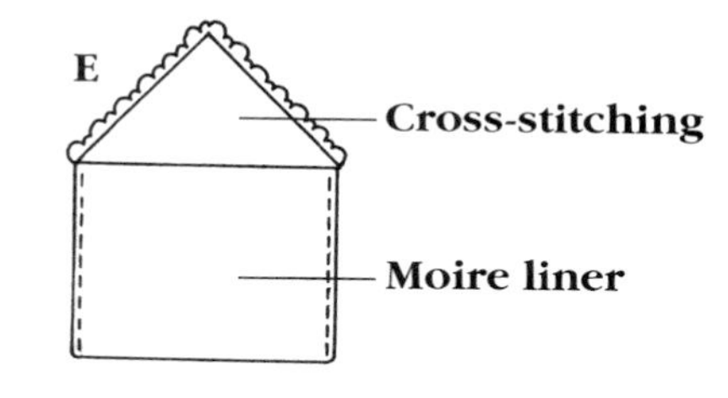

To embellish, glue cord around entire cross-stitched flap along lace. Hand-sew tassel to end of flap.

(continued)

Lingerie Bag
(continued)

Lingerie Bag
Full-Size Pattern

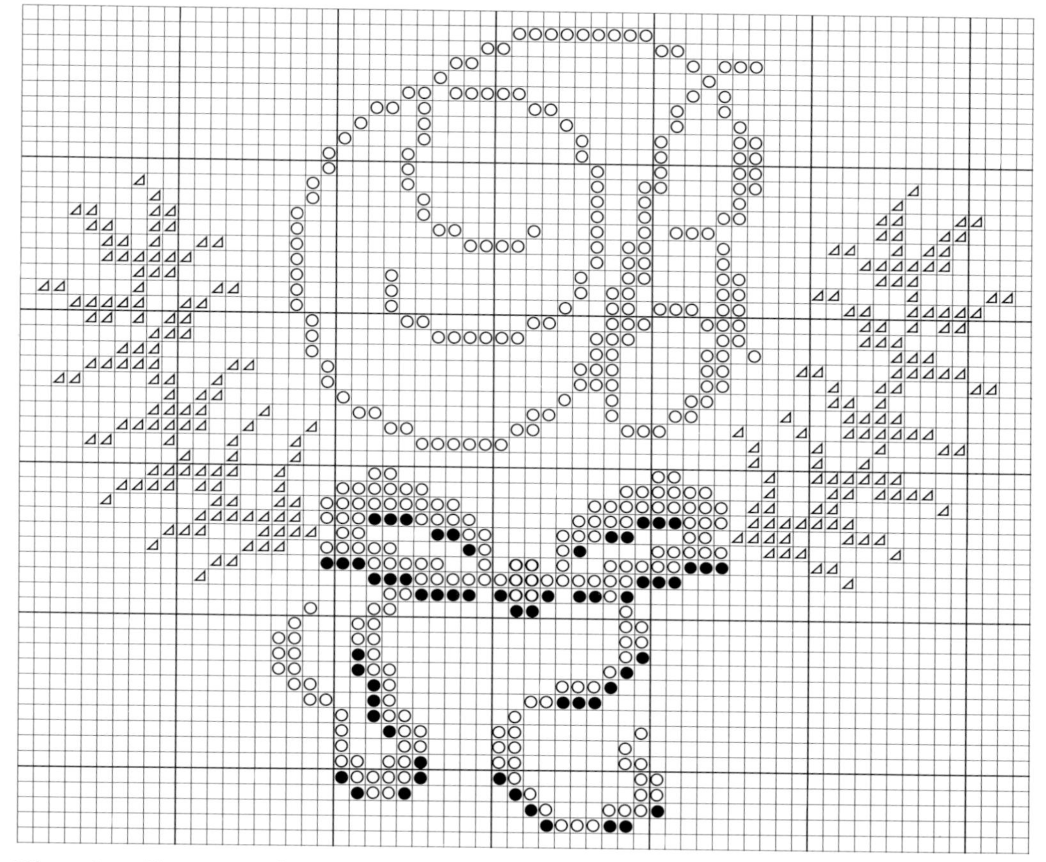

Victorian Signet Border

Stitch Count: 62x43
(without initial)

Floss

Symbol	Color name	DMC	Anchor
○	Medium pink	223	895
●	Dark pink*	815	43
◿	Green	502	877
	*Stitch the monogram in dark pink.		

Silk Chemise

USE VICTORIAN GARDEN PATH BORDER ON PAGE 117 AND SMALL VICTORIAN ALPHABET ON PAGES 118–119

Materials

Chemise: Taupe, silk
Waste canvas: 14 count, 5x10 inches
Crewel needle: Size #9

Stitch and Finish

Follow cross-stitching and finishing instructions for waste canvas in Cross-Stitch Basics.

Floss

Symbol	Color name	DMC	Anchor
•	Light pink	3689	49
○	Medium pink*	3687	68
●	Dark pink	915	1029
|	Yellow	676	891
L	Light lavender	340	118
◣	Dark lavender	333	119
◿	Green	3345	268
▽	Blue	793	176
	*Stitch the monogram in medium pink.		

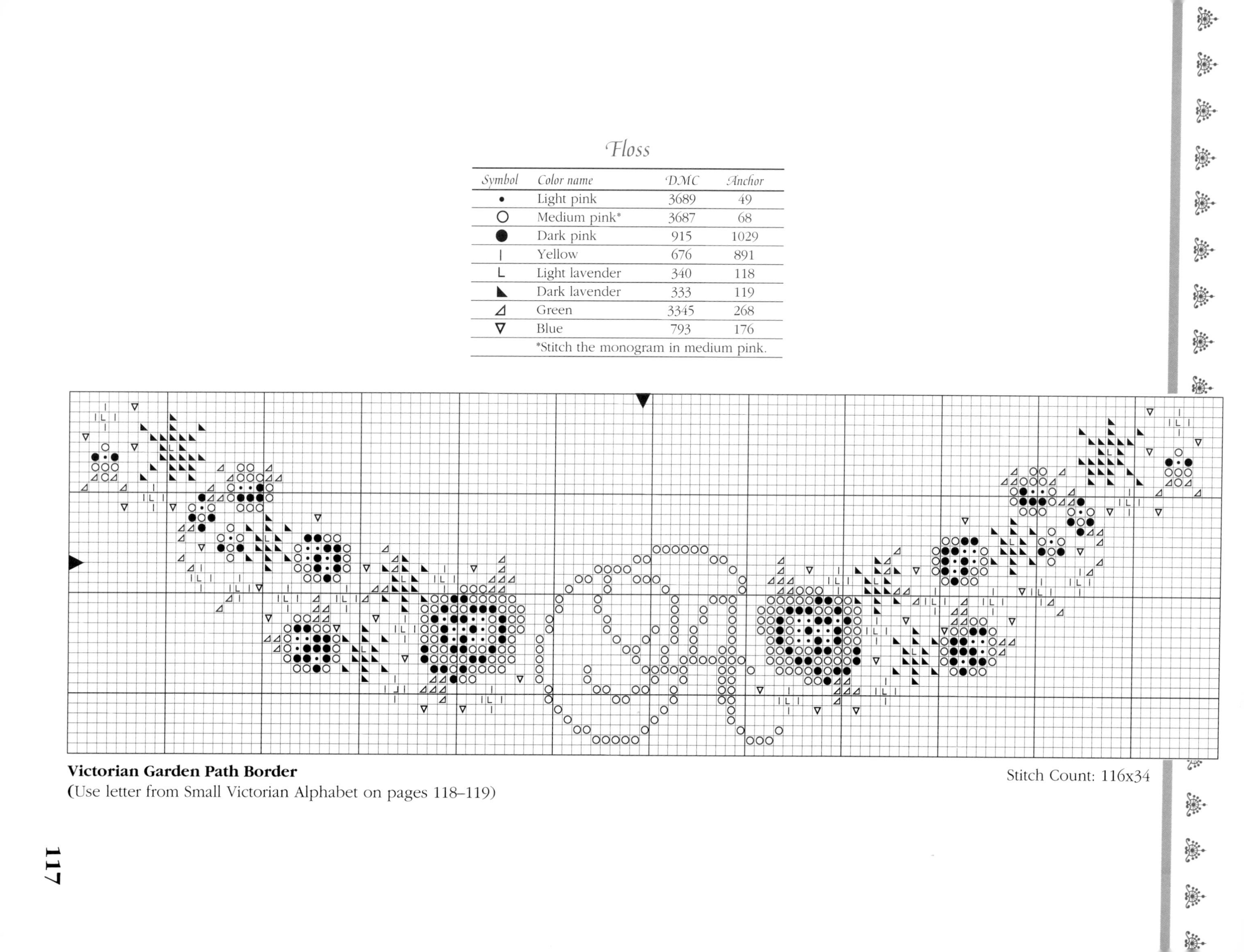

Victorian Garden Path Border
(Use letter from Small Victorian Alphabet on pages 118–119)

Stitch Count: 116x34

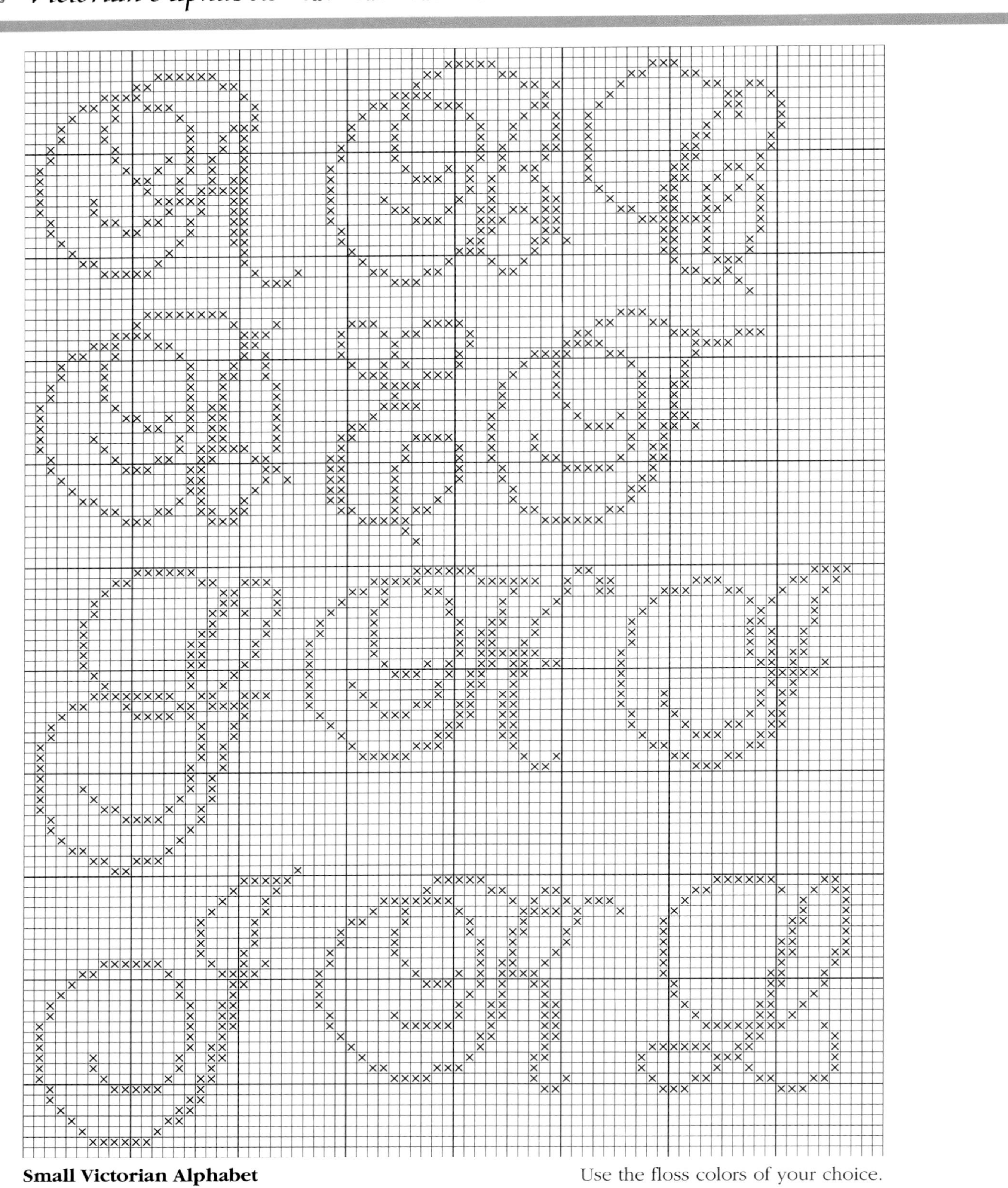

Small Victorian Alphabet

Use the floss colors of your choice.

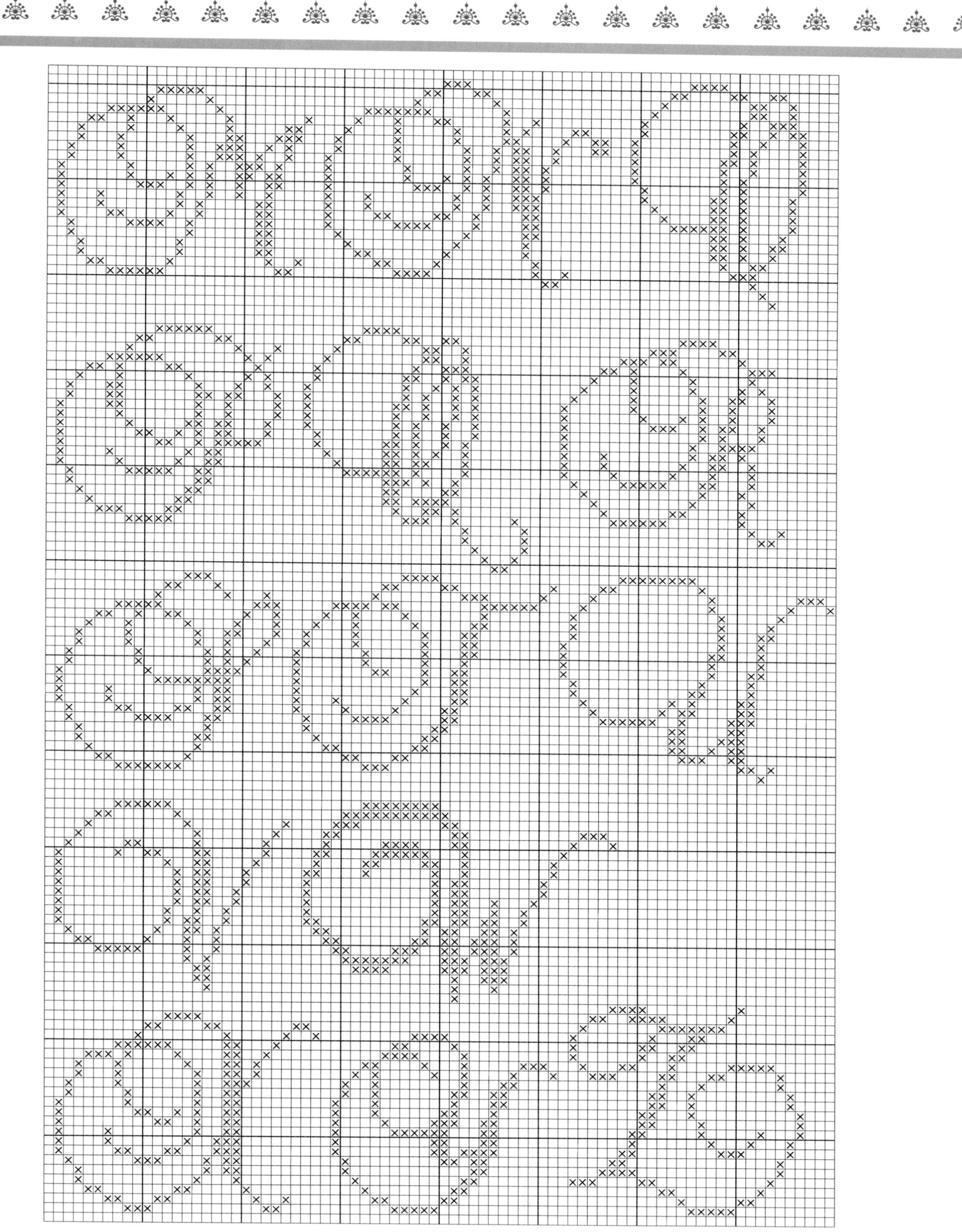

Small Victorian Alphabet

Use the floss colors of your choice.

Potpourri Bag

USE VICTORIAN VINE BORDER BELOW

Materials

Potpourri bag: Premade, ivory (Hirschberg/Schutz, Inc.)
Aida fabric: Damask, ivory (Zweigart® #3229), 14 count, 3x15 inches
Lace: Ivory, 1¼x28 inches
Satin ribbon: Periwinkle, ⅛x28 inches
White pearls: Approximately 26, medium size
Satin cord: Ivory, 16 inches
Fabric glue

Stitch

Follow cross-stitch instructions given in Cross-Stitch Basics.

Finish

To hem the stitched piece, fold back the top and bottom edges ¼ inch. Sew or glue in place. Spread a thin layer of fabric glue on the back of the stitched piece. Glue to potpourri bag about 1½ inches from bottom. Trim stitched piece at the back of the bag. Glue lace to top and bottom edges of cross-stitched fabric, and glue ribbon on top of lace. Glue pearls to lace. Thread cord through the openings in the top of the bag.

Floss

Symbol	Color name	DMC	Anchor
L	Light lavender	340	118
	Green*	3346	267
	*Backstitch leaves and stems in green (one strand).		

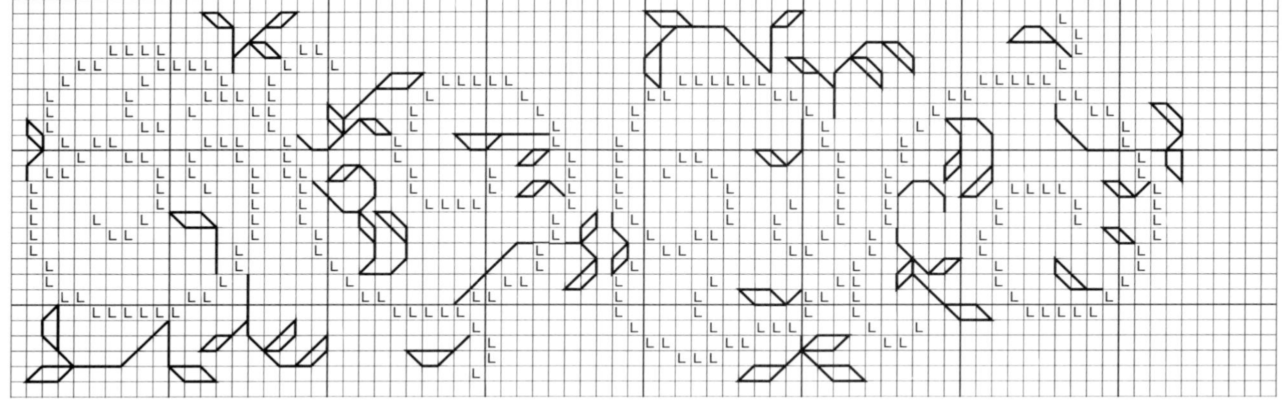

Victorian Vine Border

Repeat design as needed.

Beaded Hatband

USE VICTORIAN SCROLL BORDER AT RIGHT

Materials

Aida fabric: Black, 14 count, 3x24 inches (MCG Textiles)
Beads: Glass seed beads (Mill Hill Glass Seed Beads, Gay Bowles Sales)
Straw hat

Stitch

Follow the instructions for stitching with beads given in Cross-Stitch Basics. Use a single strand of floss in the same color as the bead. If desired, the design can be cross-stitched without beads using two strands of floss and making full cross-stitches.

Finish

To hem the stitched piece, fold back the top and bottom edges ¼ inch. Sew or glue in place. Spread a thin layer of glue on the back of the stitched piece, and glue around hat. Join fabric in the back of the hat and trim.

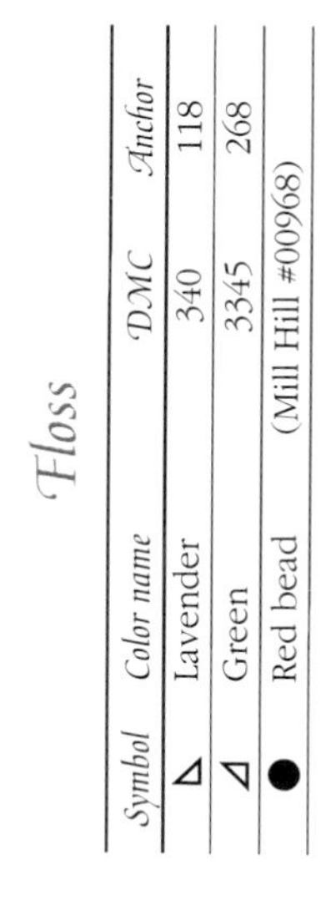

Floss

Symbol	*Color name*	*DMC*	*Anchor*
△	Lavender	340	118
◺	Green	3345	268
●	Red bead	(Mill Hill #00968)	

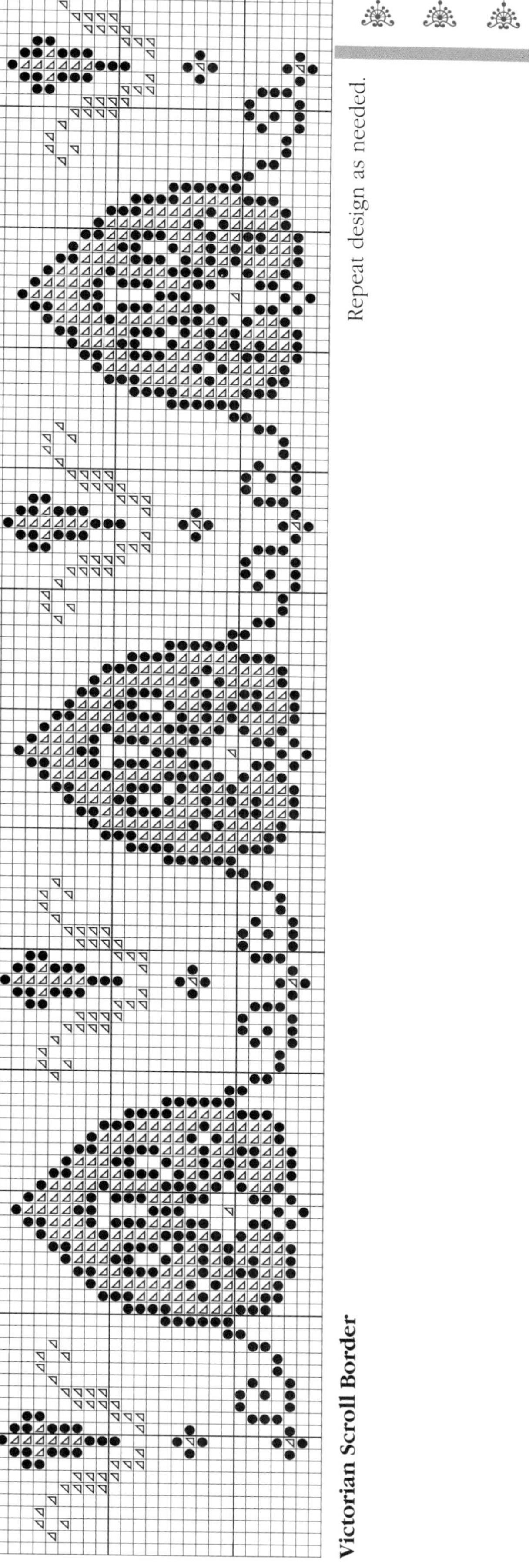

Victorian Scroll Border

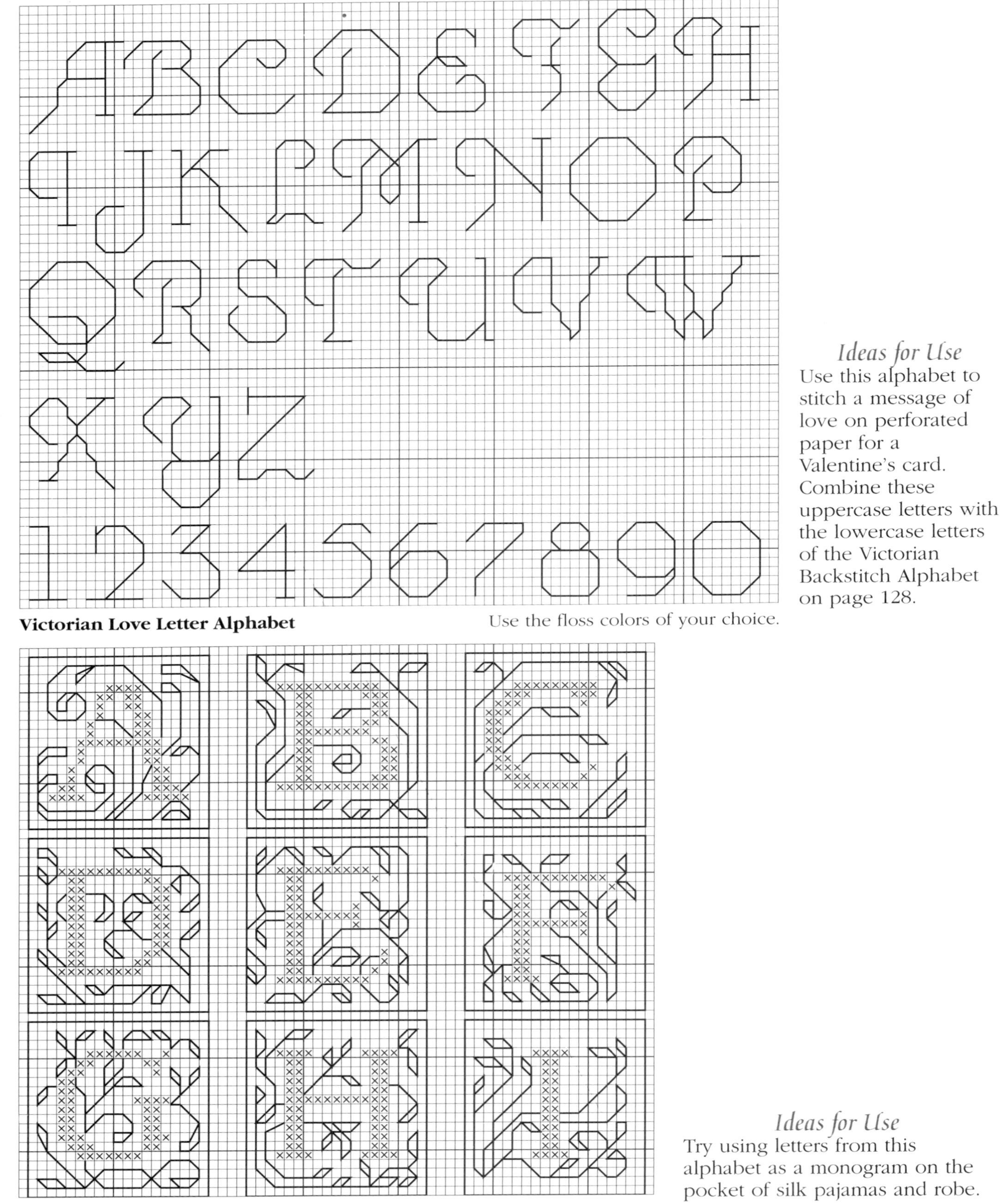

Victorian Love Letter Alphabet

Use the floss colors of your choice.

Ideas for Use

Use this alphabet to stitch a message of love on perforated paper for a Valentine's card. Combine these uppercase letters with the lowercase letters of the Victorian Backstitch Alphabet on page 128.

Victorian Ivy Alphabet

Use the floss colors of your choice. Backstitch leaves and stems in green (one strand).

Ideas for Use

Try using letters from this alphabet as a monogram on the pocket of silk pajamas and robe.

Victorian Ivy Alphabet

Use the floss colors of your choice.
Backstitch leaves and stems in green (one strand).

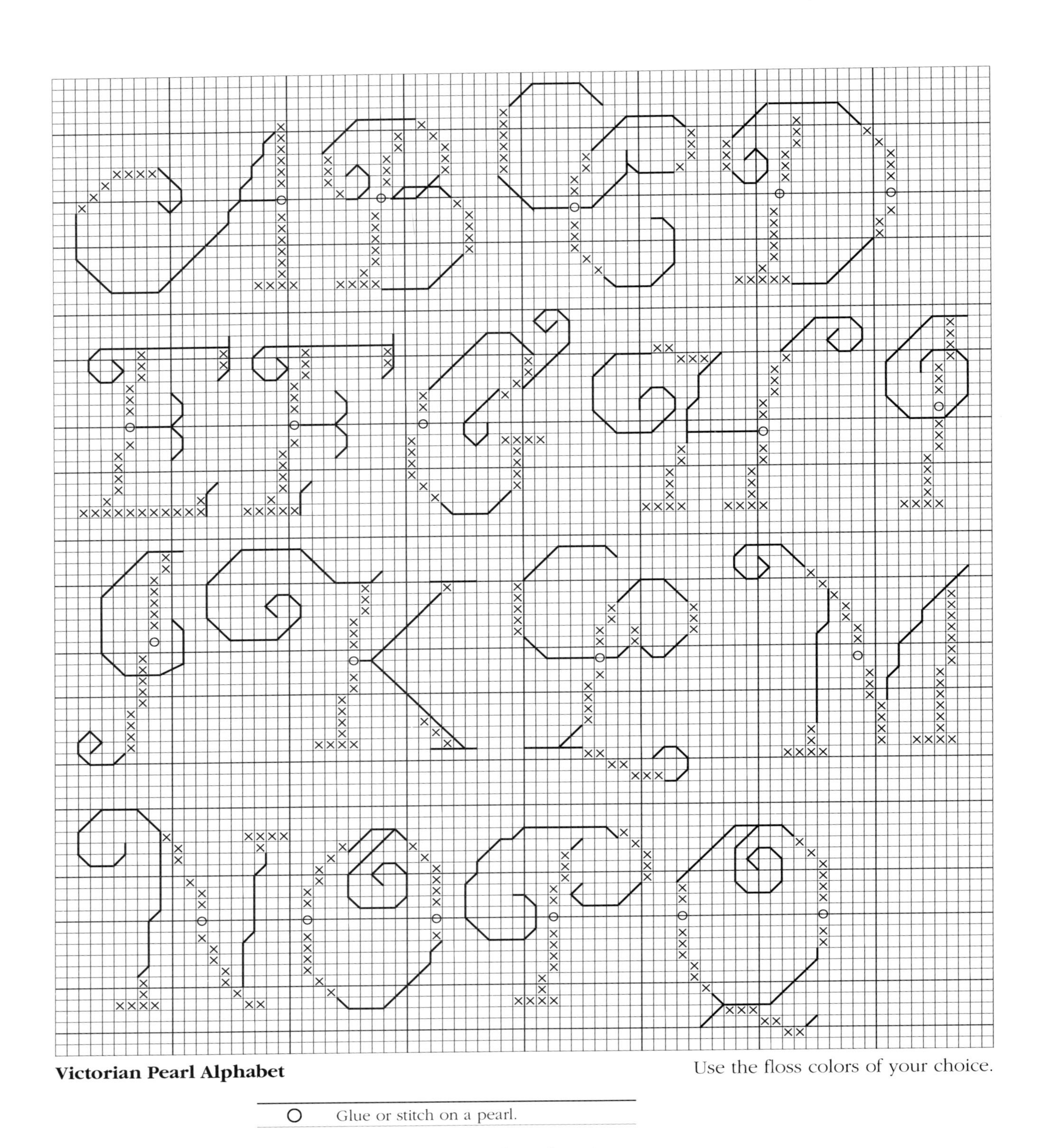

Victorian Pearl Alphabet

Use the floss colors of your choice.

O	Glue or stitch on a pearl.

Ideas for Use

This alphabet would be elegant used as the initial letters on a Victorian sample that says, for example, "All Love Is Sweet Given or Returned."

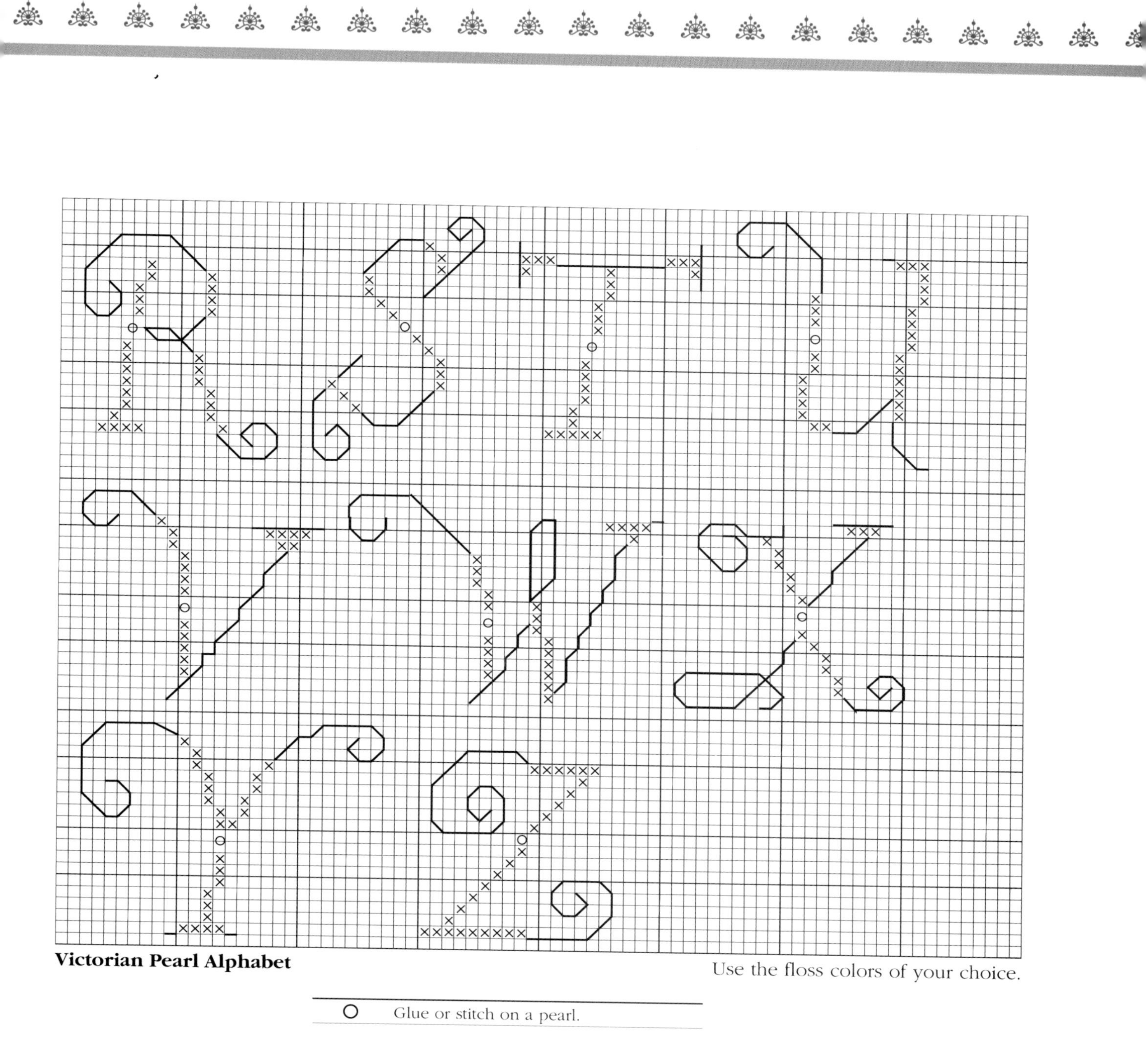

Victorian Pearl Alphabet

Use the floss colors of your choice.

O	Glue or stitch on a pearl.

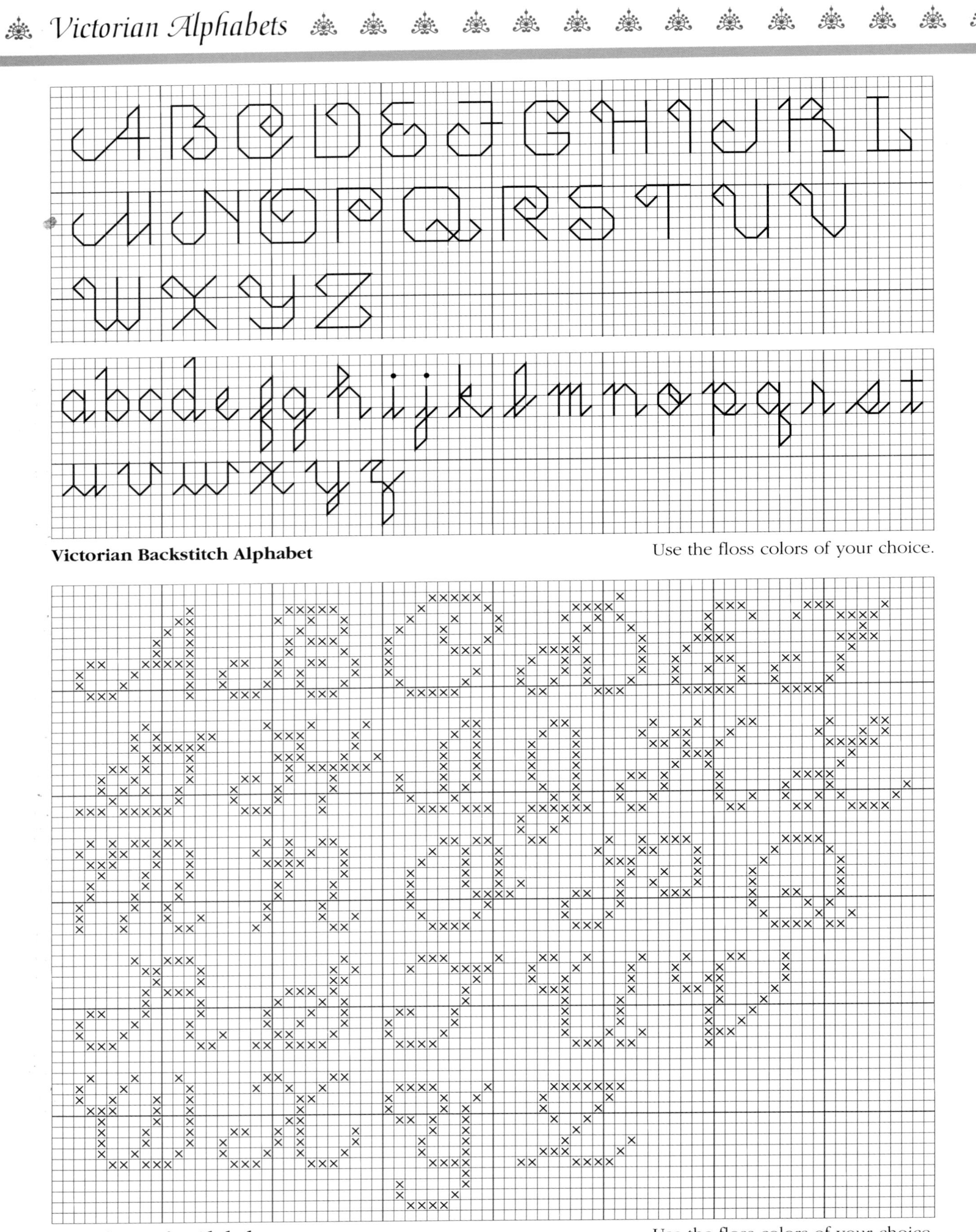

Victorian Backstitch Alphabet

Use the floss colors of your choice.

Victorian Script Alphabet

Use the floss colors of your choice.

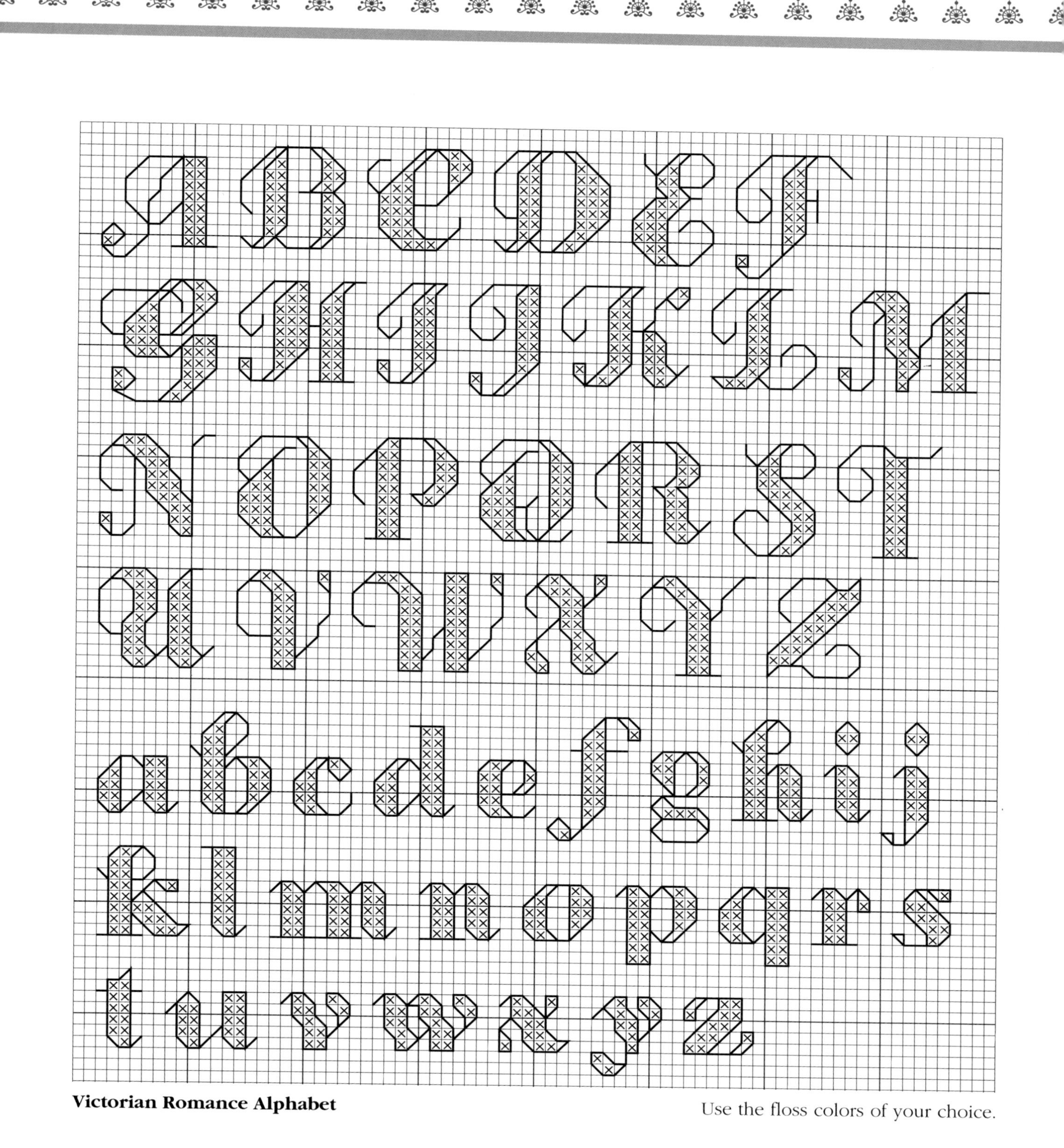

Victorian Romance Alphabet

Use the floss colors of your choice.

Ideas for Use

The two alphabets on page 128 would combine nicely. Use the uppercase letters from the Victorian Script Alphabet and the lowercase letters from the Victorian Backstitch Alphabet.

Ideas for Use

Wouldn't the alphabet above be pretty spelling out a teenage girl's name with the Victorian Bow Border on page 133 above and below it? It could be framed or made into a pillow for her room.

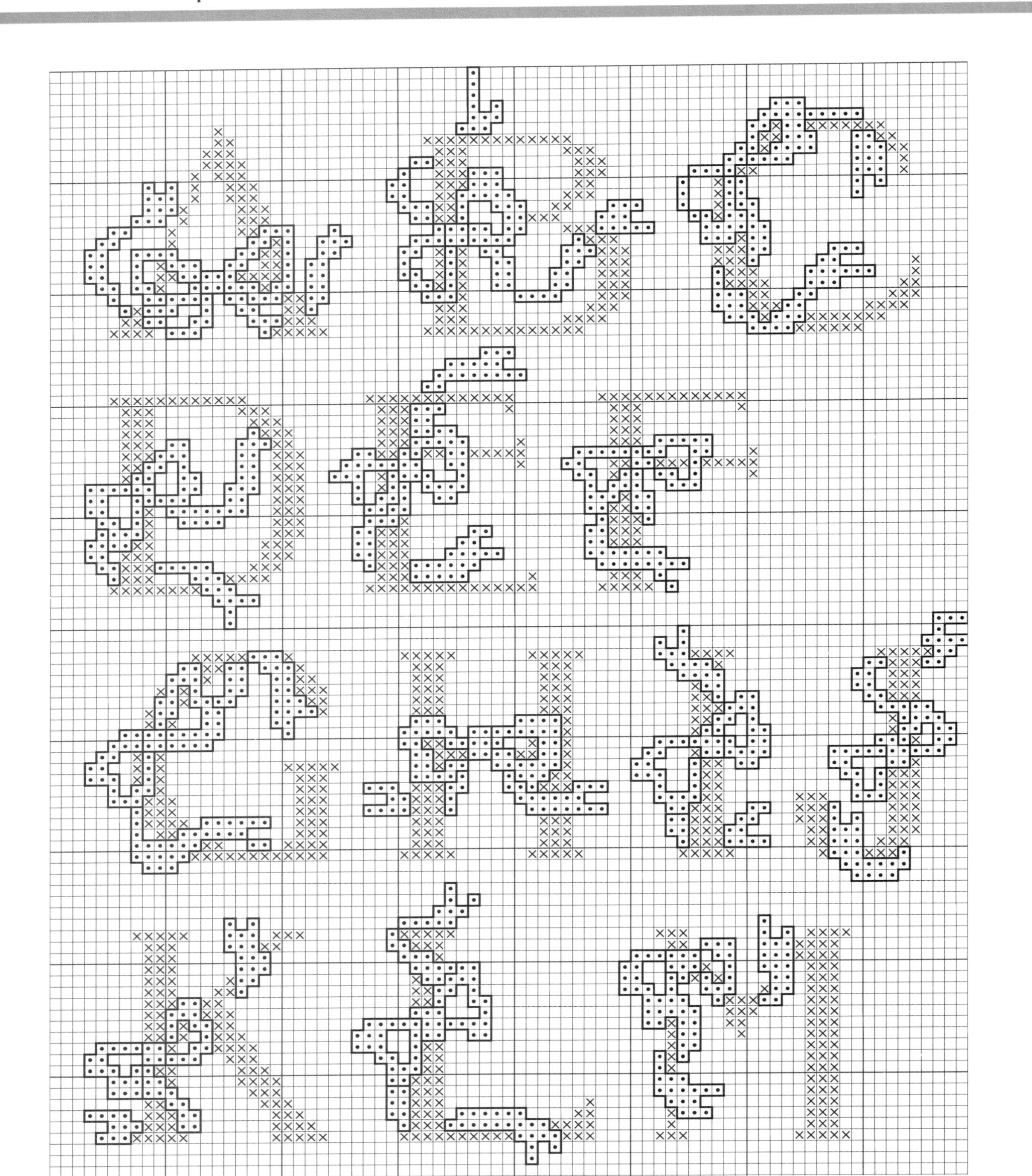

Victorian Ribbon Alphabet

Use the floss colors of your choice.

Ideas for Use

Use one of these letters as the centerpiece initial on a velvet pillow. Add ribbons, ribbon roses, and buttons. Such a pillow would make a beautiful addition to a Victorian bedroom.

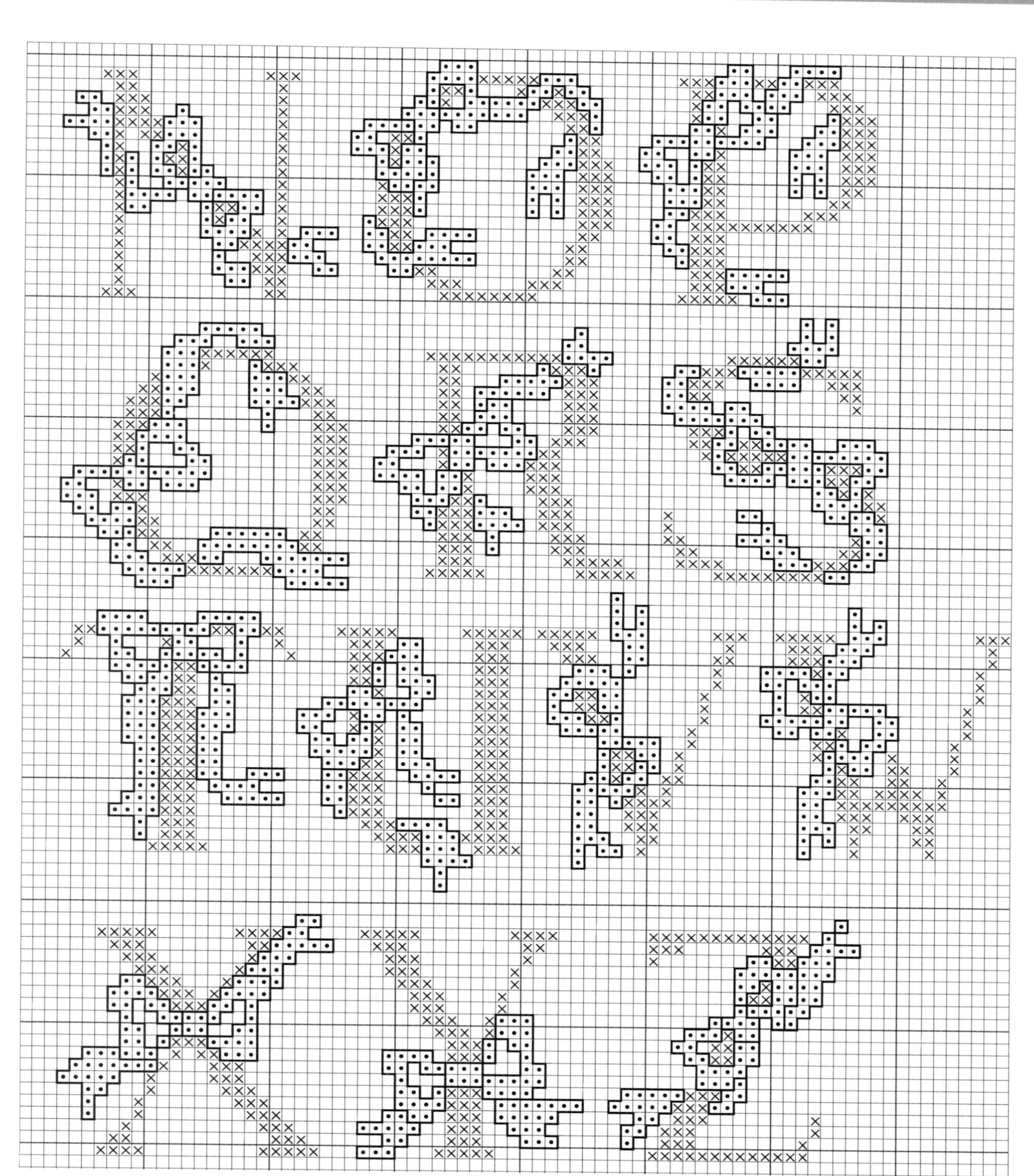

Victorian Ribbon Alphabet

Use the floss colors of your choice.

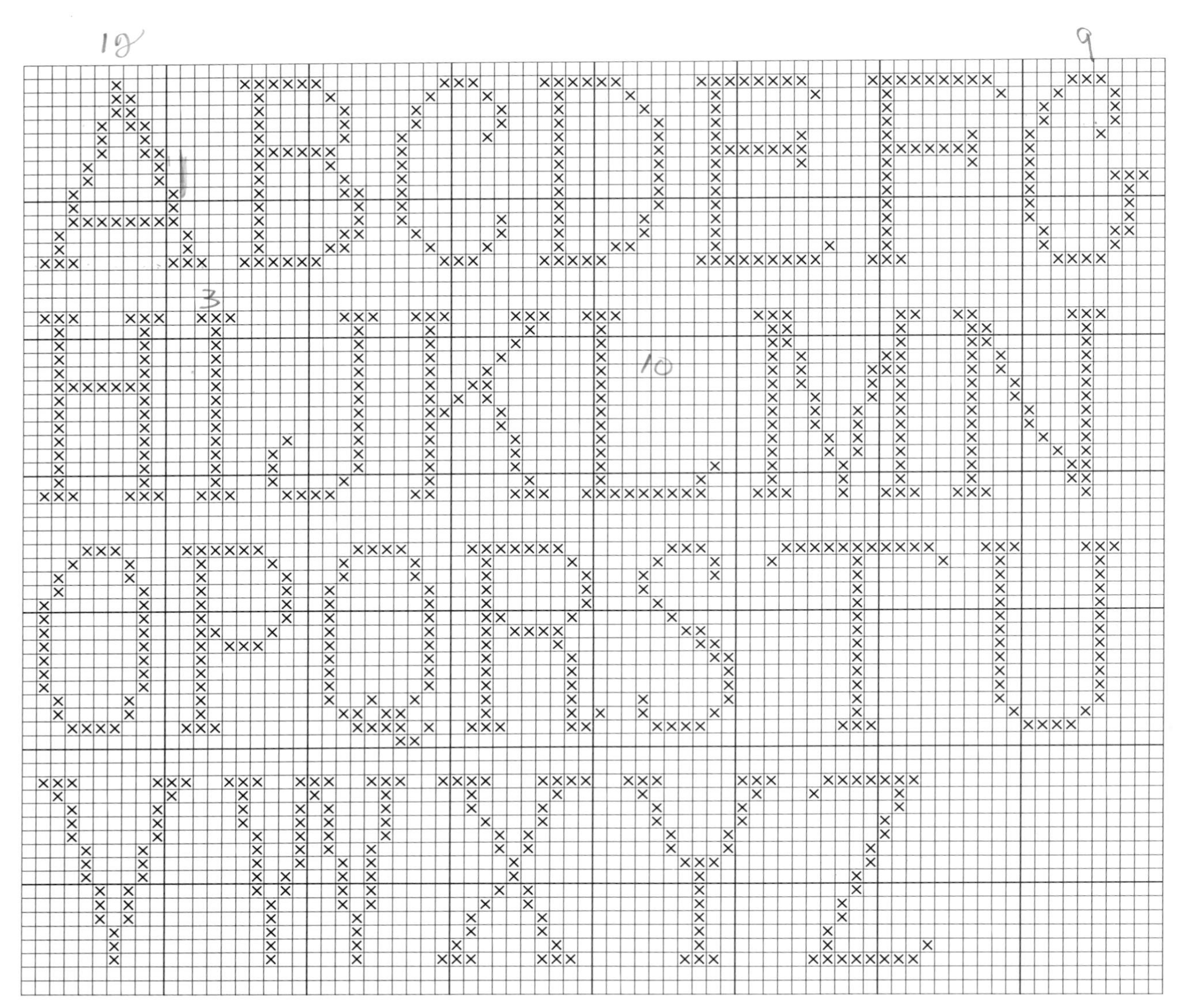

Victorian Stately Alphabet

Use the floss colors of your choice.

34
9
43

Ideas for Use

This simple, formal alphabet looks nice in combination with the Victorian Ribbon Alphabet on pages 130–131. Add the Victorian Bow Border on page 133 all around for a beautiful sampler.

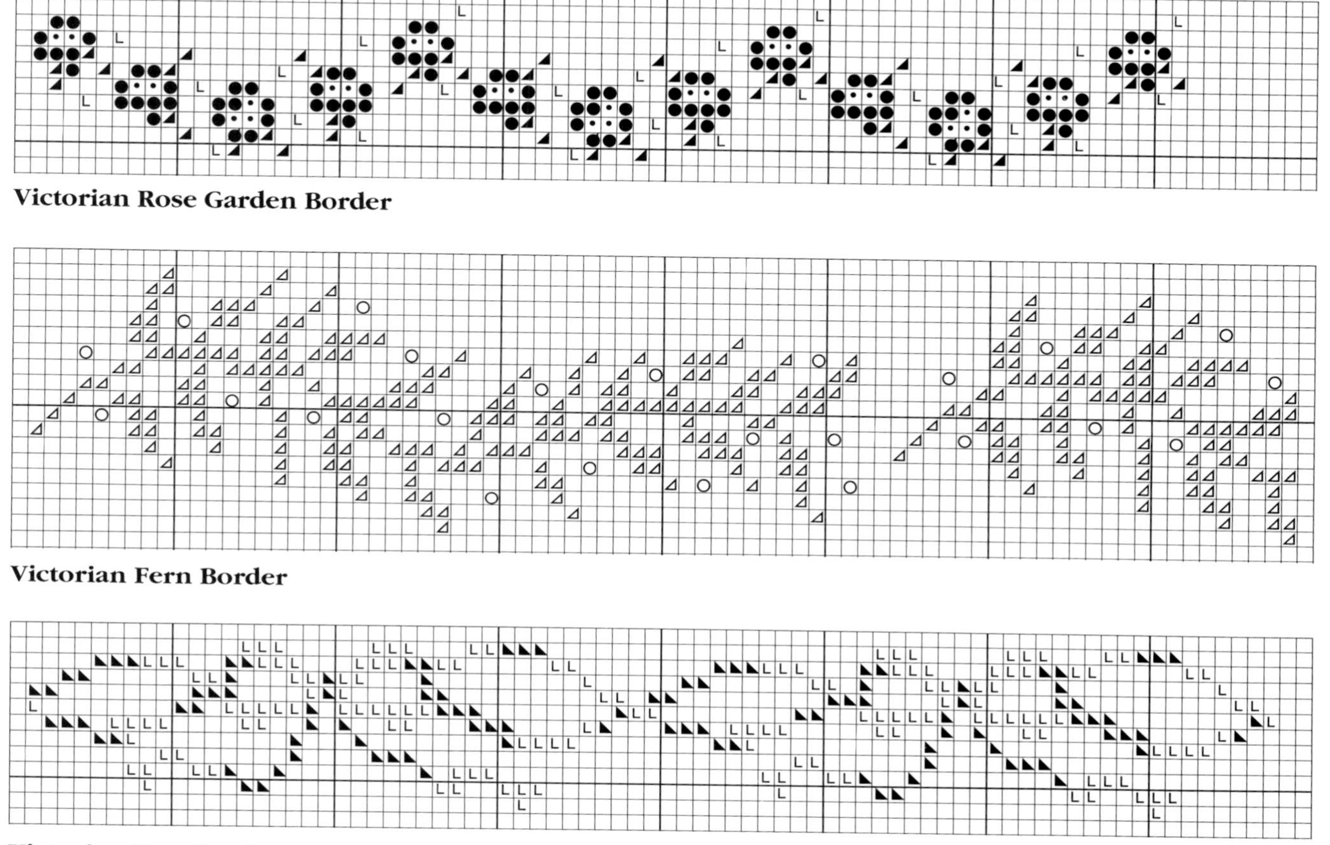

Victorian Rose Garden Border

Victorian Fern Border

Victorian Bow Border

Floss

Symbol	*Color name*	*DMC*	*Anchor*
•	Light pink	3689	49
○	Medium pink	3687	68
●	Dark pink	915	1029
L	Light lavender	340	118
◣	Dark lavender	333	119
◿	Medium green	3347	266
◢	Dark green	3345	268

Ideas for Use

These borders would make delightful enhancements to guest towels, curtain hems, or a blouse's pocket or collar. Or, cross-stitch a border on a strip of colored Aida fabric, and use it to trim a pillow.

Elegant Alphabets

Transform simple decor into elegant decor with rich fabrics, deep vibrant colors, golden accents, braids, and tassels. All of these have been incorporated in the Elegant Alphabet—letters uniquely intertwined with tassels in deep jewel tones and metallic fibers. Now any home can have a touch of elegance with these exquisite projects.

Tassel Alphabet Sampler

USE TASSEL ALPHABET SAMPLER ON PAGES 138–145

Materials

Fabric: Linen, 28 count (Zweigart®), champagne, 20x26 inches

Stitch

Follow instructions for cross-stitching over two threads given in Cross-Stitch Basics. Note that special metallic threads by Madeira have been mixed with floss to give these pieces an extra elegance.

Finish

Have this piece professionally framed.

Floss for Tassel Alphabet Sampler

Symbol	Color name	Madeira	DMC	Anchor
♡	Red + Rainbow**	0811 + R610	221	897
/	Light teal	1114	958	187
◢	Dark teal	1204	991	189
V	Medium blue	1711	931	1034
▼	Dark blue***	1007	336	150
■	Black/gold metallic flash*FL03		310	403

*Backstitch border line in black/gold metallic flash (three strands).
**Rainbow is a metallic thread. Combine three strands of red and one strand of rainbow.
***Backstitch letters in dark blue (one strand).
Note: For all projects in this chapter, if using Madeira, stitch with two strands; if using regular floss, stitch with three strands.

Floss for Waffle Stitch

Symbol	Color name	Madeira	DMC	Anchor
XXXX	Dark blue	1007	336	150

Use all four strands of Madeira silk. Use three strands if stitching with regular floss.

Floss for Bargello Border

Symbol	Color name	Madeira	DMC	Anchor
I (light)	Dark teal	1204	991	189
I	Red + Rainbow*	0811 + R610	221	897
▌	Dark blue	1007	336	150

*Combine three strands of red and one strand of rainbow.

Tassel Alphabet Sampler

(continued)

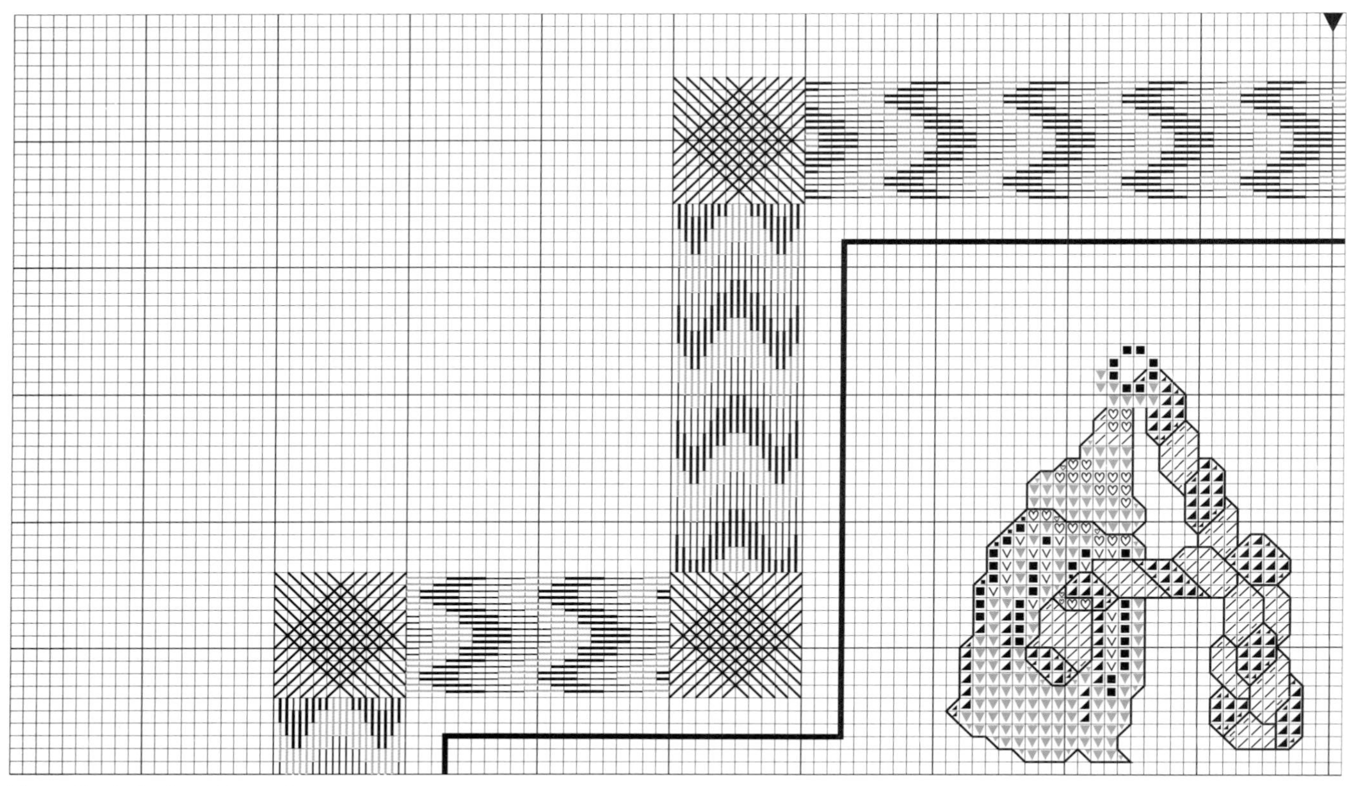

Tassel Alphabet Sampler

Floss for Tassel Alphabet Sampler

Symbol	Color name	Madeira	DMC	Anchor
♡	Red + Rainbow**	0811 + R610	221	897
/	Light teal	1114	958	187
◢	Dark teal	1204	991	189
V	Medium blue	1711	931	1034
▼	Dark blue***	1007	336	150
■	Black/gold metallic flash*FL03		310	403

*Backstitch border line in black/gold metallic flash (three strands).
**Rainbow is a metallic thread. Combine three strands of red and one strand of rainbow.
***Backstitch letters in dark blue (one strand).
Note: For all projects in this chapter, if using Madeira, stitch with two strands; if using regular floss, stitch with three strands.

Tassel Alphabet Sampler

Floss for Waffle Stitch

Symbol	Color name	Madeira	DMC	Anchor
XXX	Dark blue	1007	336	150
	Use all four strands of Madeira silk. Use three strands if stitching with regular floss.			

Floss for Bargello Border

Symbol	Color name	Madeira	DMC	Anchor
ǀ	Dark teal	1204	991	189
ǀ	Red + Rainbow*	0811 + R610	221	897
ǀ	Dark blue	1007	336	150
	*Combine three strands of red and one strand of rainbow.			

(continued)

Tassel Alphabet Sampler

(continued)

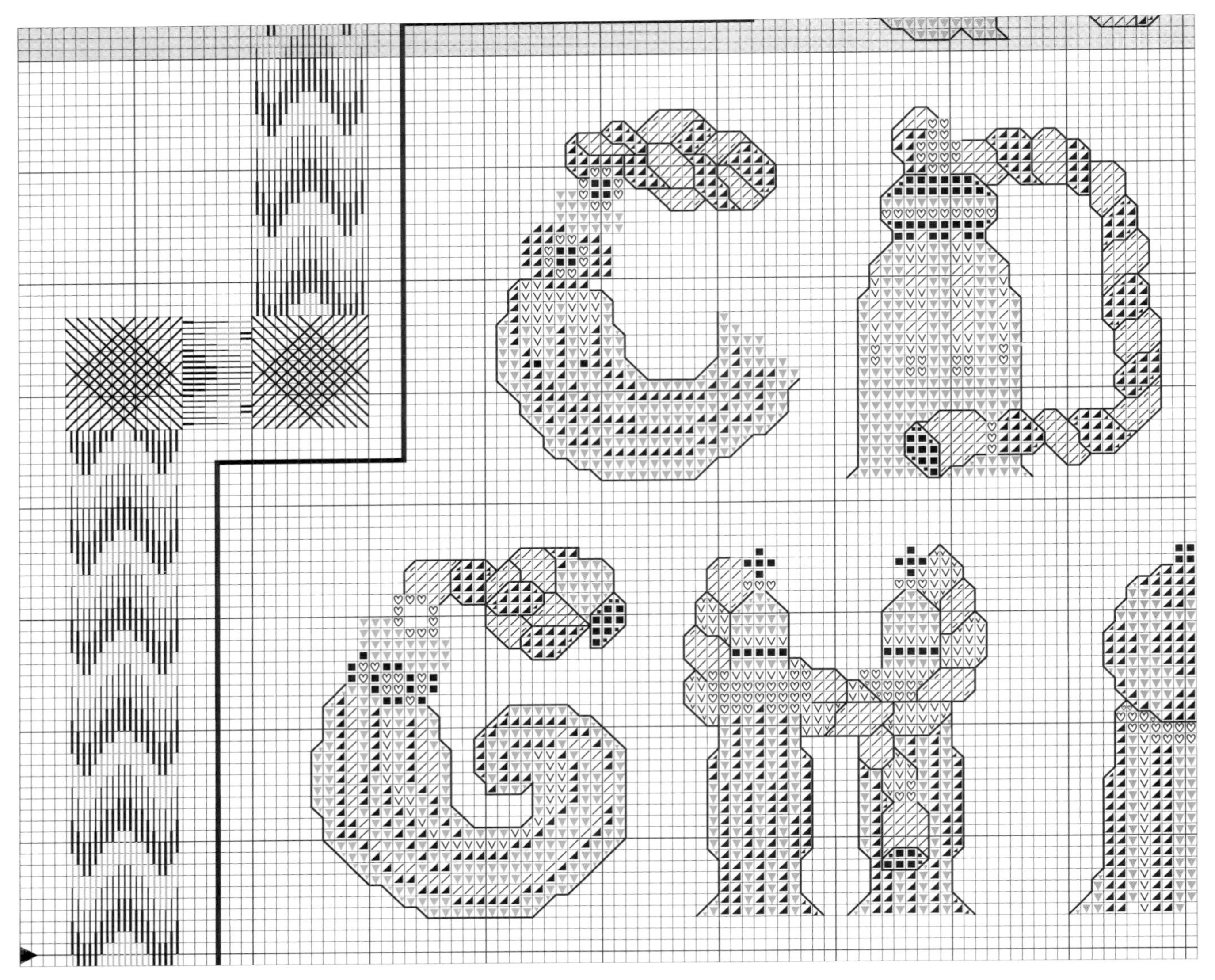

Tassel Alphabet Sampler

Floss for Tassel Alphabet Sampler

Symbol	Color name	Madeira	DMC	Anchor
♡	Red + Rainbow**	0811 + R610	221	897
/	Light teal	1114	958	187
◢	Dark teal	1204	991	189
V	Medium blue	1711	931	1034
▼	Dark blue***	1007	336	150
■	Black/gold metallic flash*	FL03	310	403

*Backstitch border line in black/gold metallic flash (three strands).
**Rainbow is a metallic thread. Combine three strands of red and one strand of rainbow.
***Backstitch letters in dark blue (one strand).
Note: For all projects in this chapter, if using Madeira, stitch with two strands; if using regular floss, stitch with three strands.

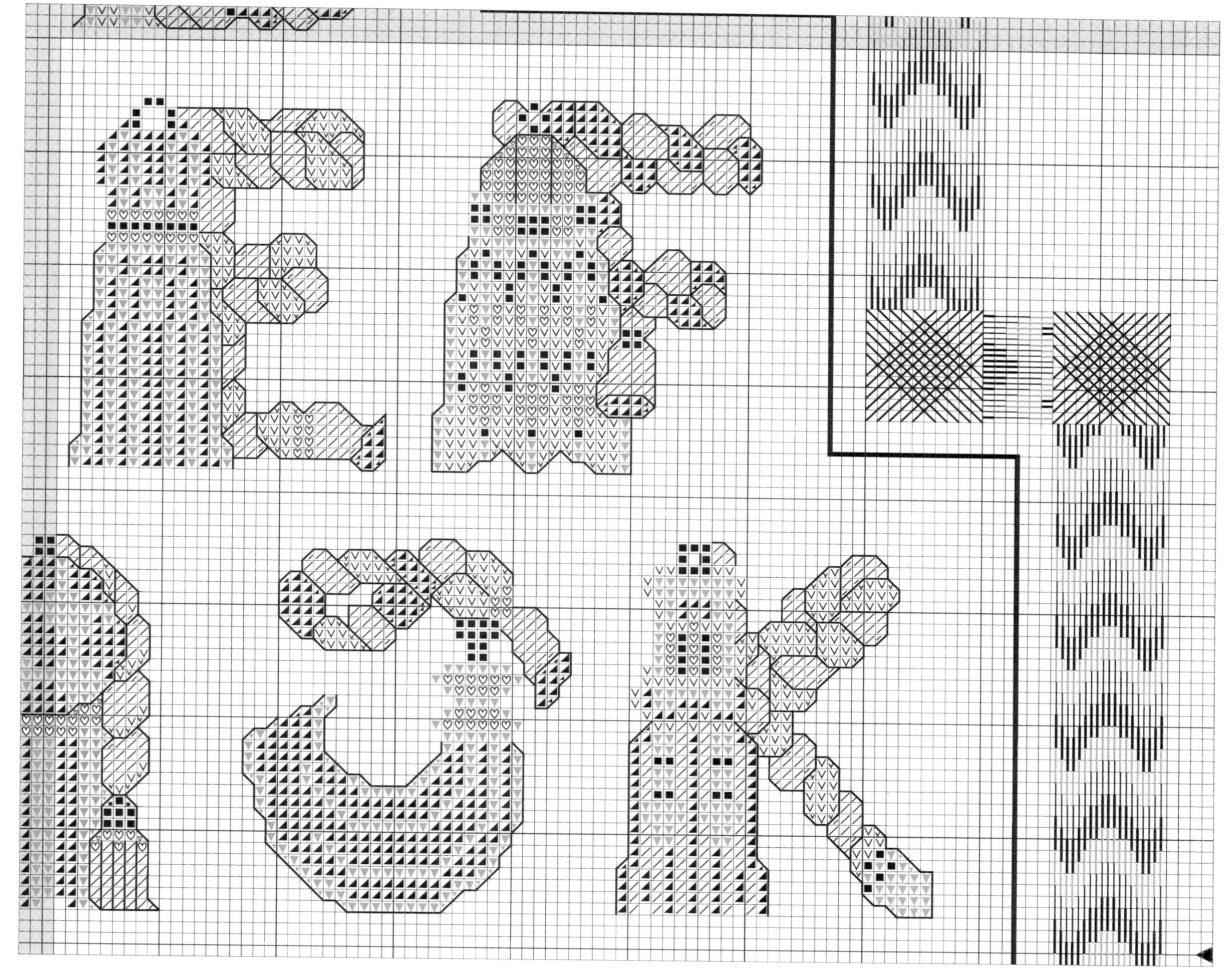

Tassel Alphabet Sampler

Floss for Waffle Stitch

Symbol	Color name	Madeira	DMC	Anchor
XXX	Dark blue	1007	336	150
	Use all four strands of Madeira silk. Use three strands if stitching with regular floss.			

Floss for Bargello Border

Symbol	Color name	Madeira	DMC	Anchor
I	Dark teal	1204	991	189
I	Red + Rainbow*	0811 + R610	221	897
I	Dark blue	1007	336	150

*Combine three strands of red and one strand of rainbow.

(continued)

Tassel Alphabet Sampler

(continued)

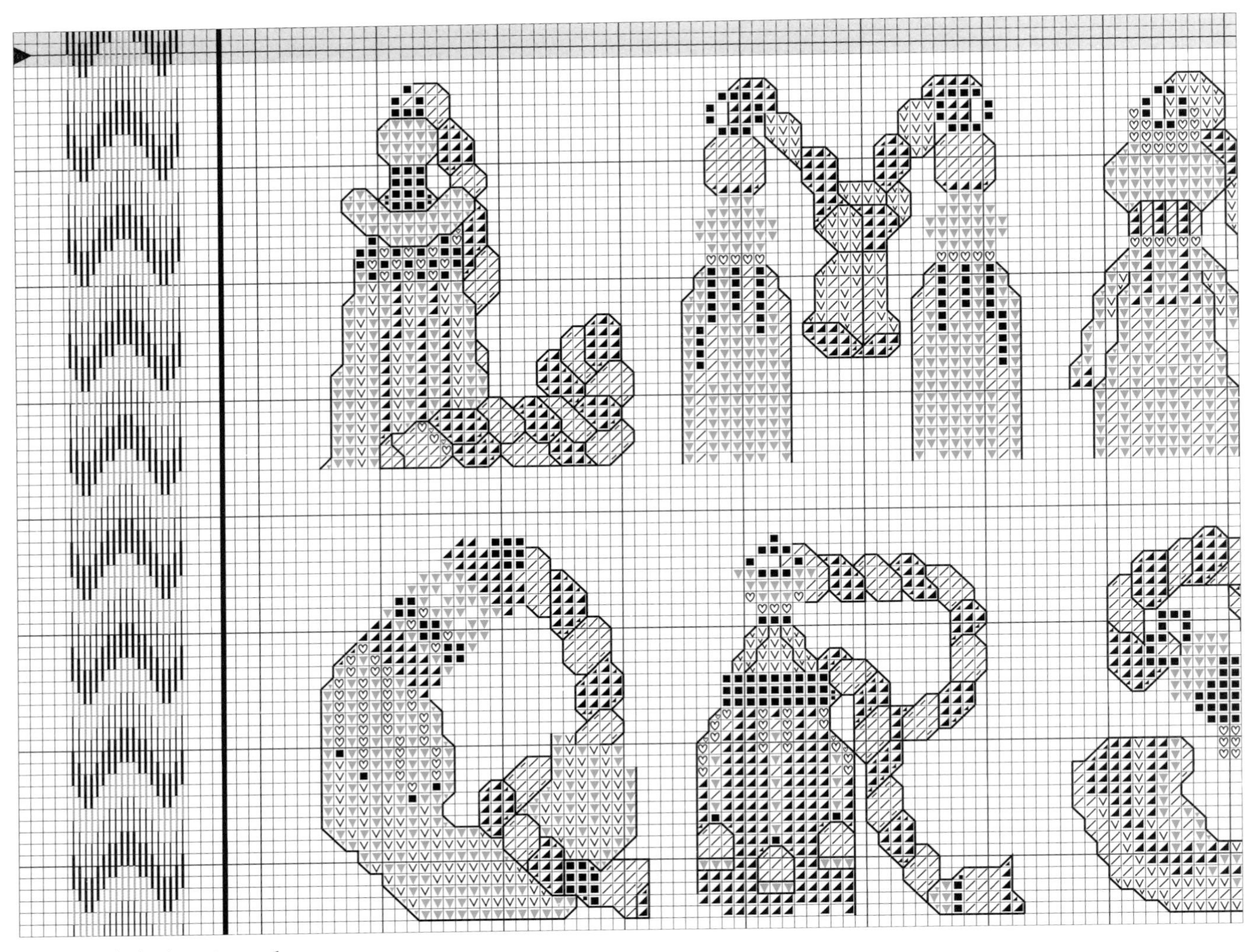

Tassel Alphabet Sampler

Floss for Tassel Alphabet Sampler

Symbol	Color name	Madeira	DMC	Anchor
♡	Red + Rainbow**	0811 + R610	221	897
/	Light teal	1114	958	187
◢	Dark teal	1204	991	189
V	Medium blue	1711	931	1034
▼	Dark blue***	1007	336	150
■	Black/gold metallic flash*	FL03	310	403

*Backstitch border line in black/gold metallic flash (three strands).
**Rainbow is a metallic thread. Combine three strands of red and one strand of rainbow.
***Backstitch letters in dark blue (one strand).
Note: For all projects in this chapter, if using Madeira, stitch with two strands; if using regular floss, stitch with three strands.

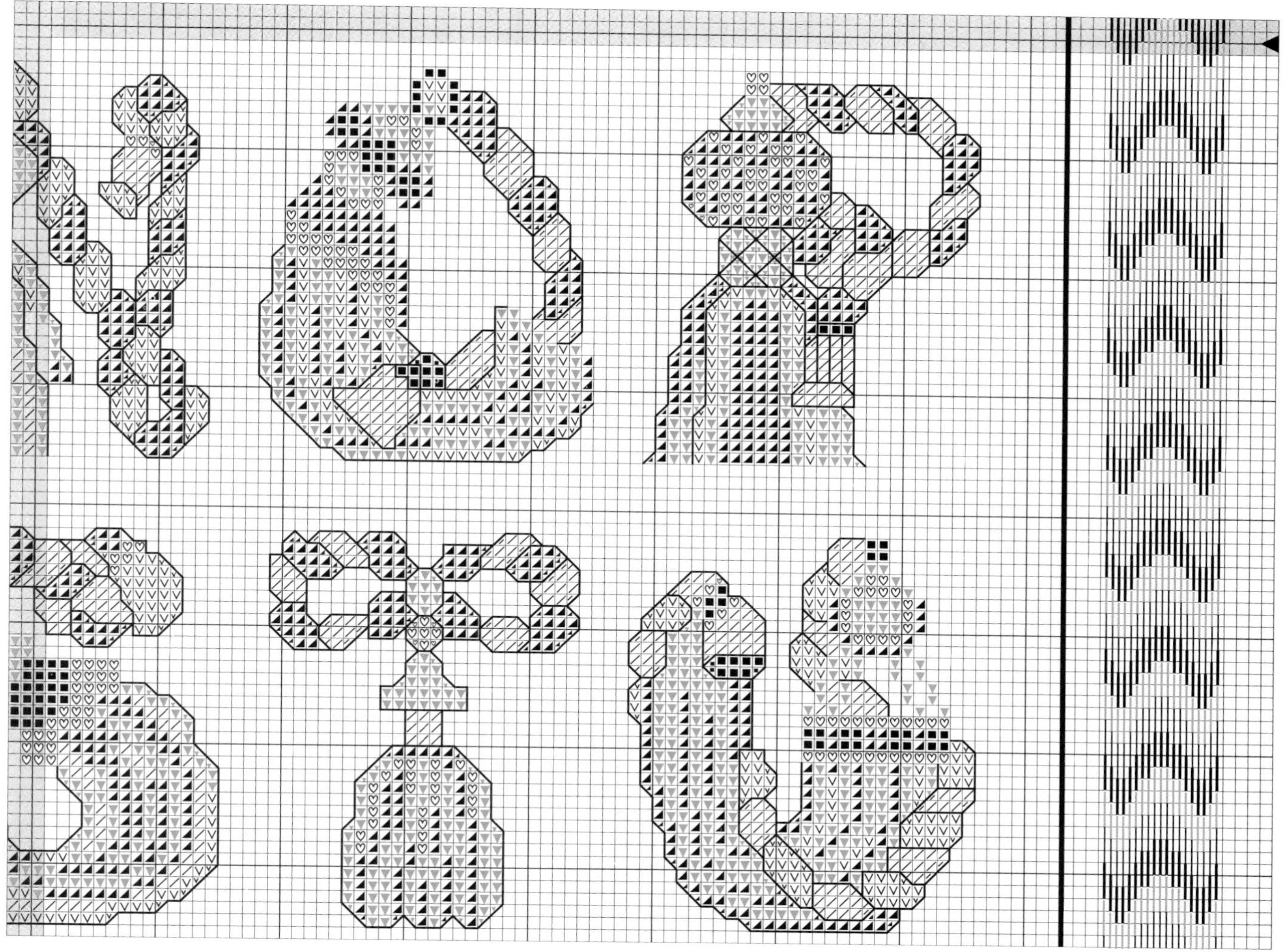

Tassel Alphabet Sampler

Floss for Waffle Stitch

Symbol	Color name	Madeira	DMC	Anchor
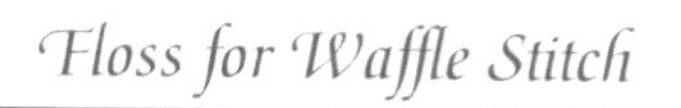	Dark blue	1007	336	150
	Use all four strands of Madeira silk. Use three strands if stitching with regular floss.			

Floss for Bargello Border

Symbol	Color name	Madeira	DMC	Anchor
I	Dark teal	1204	991	189
I	Red + Rainbow*	0811 + R610	221	897
I	Dark blue	1007	336	150
	*Combine three strands of red and one strand of rainbow.			

(continued)

Tassel Alphabet Sampler

(continued)

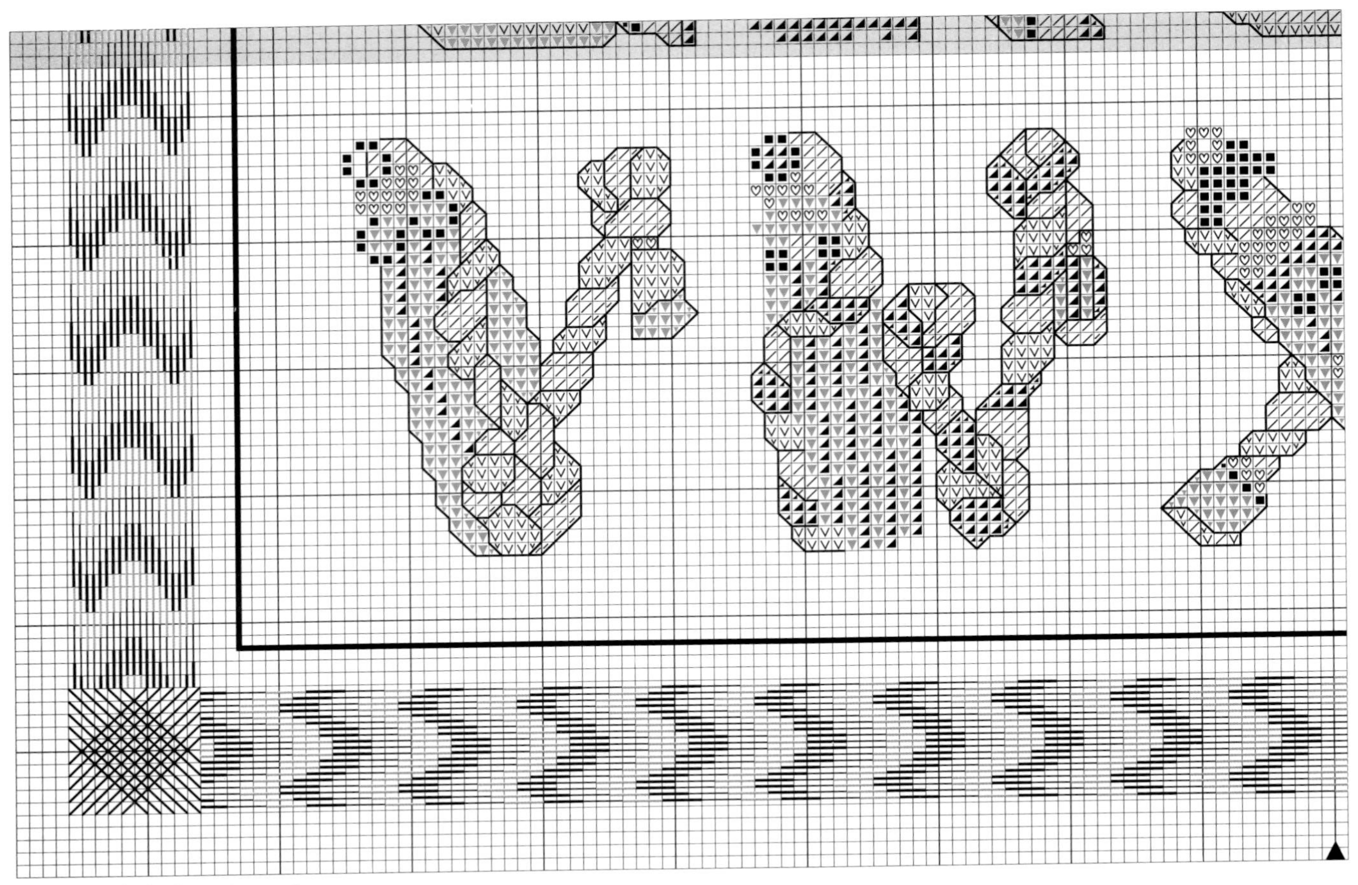

Tassel Alphabet Sampler

Floss for Tassel Alphabet Sampler

Symbol	Color name	Madeira	DMC	Anchor
♡	Red + Rainbow**	0811 + R610	221	897
/	Light teal	1114	958	187
◢	Dark teal	1204	991	189
V	Medium blue	1711	931	1034
▼	Dark blue***	1007	336	150
■	Black/gold metallic flash*FL03		310	403

*Backstitch border line in black/gold metallic flash (three strands).
**Rainbow is a metallic thread.
***Backstitch letters in dark blue (one strand).
Note: For all projects in this chapter, if using Madeira, stitch with two strands; if using regular floss, stitch with three strands.

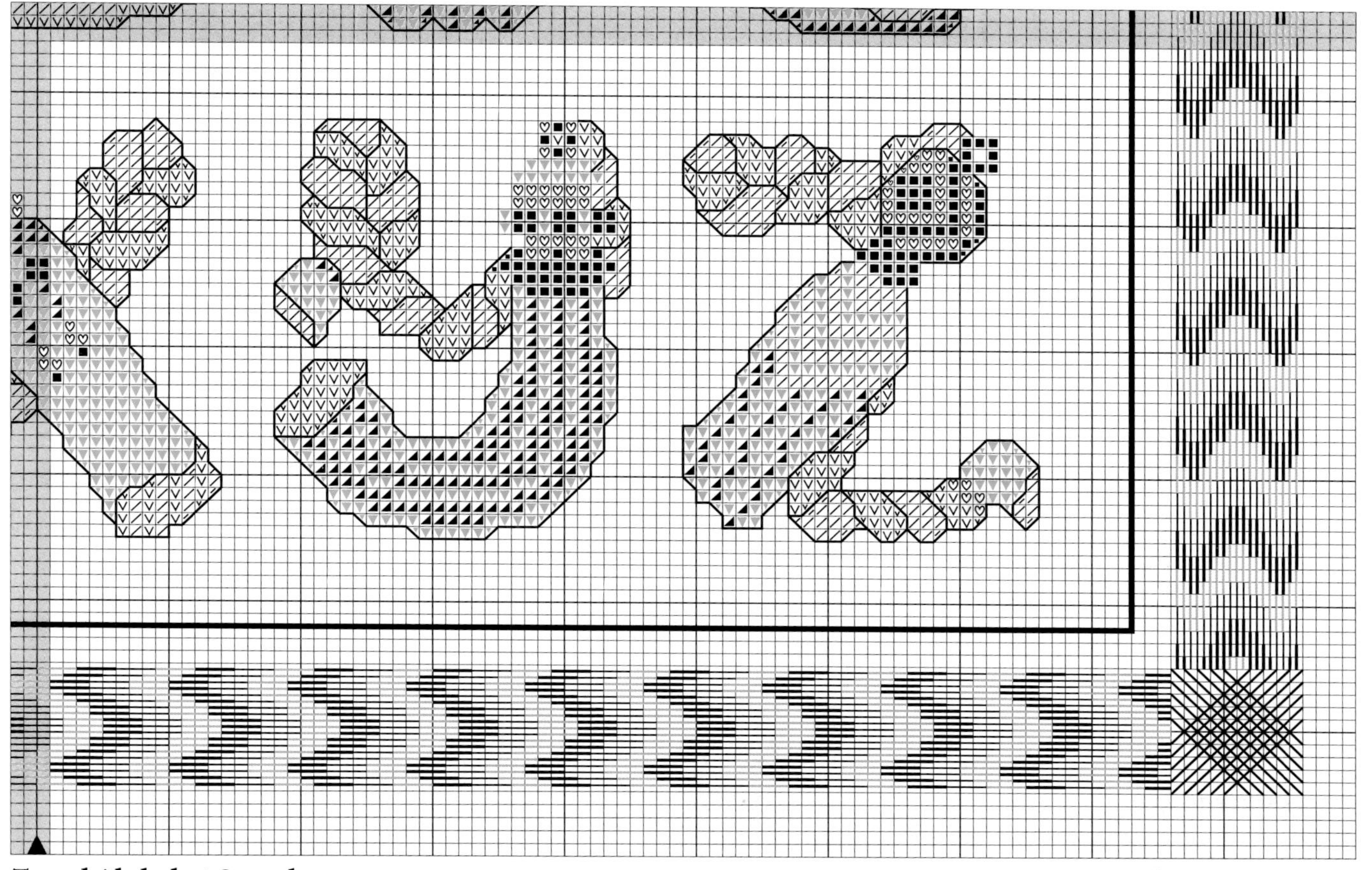

Tassel Alphabet Sampler Stitch Count: 192x270

Floss for Waffle Stitch

Symbol	Color name	Madeira	DMC	Anchor
⨯⨯⨯	Dark blue	1007	336	150
	Use all four strands of Madeira silk. Use three strands if stitching with regular floss.			

Floss for Bargello Border

Symbol	Color name	Madeira	DMC	Anchor
I	Dark teal	1204	991	189
I	Red + Rainbow*	0811 + R610	221	897
I	Dark blue	1007	336	150
	*Combine three strands of red and one strand of rainbow.			

Monogram Bell Pull

USE LETTER FROM ONE OF THE ELEGANT ALPHABETS ON PAGES 151–158

Materials

Fabric: Linen, Jobelan, 28 count (Zweigart®), shell, 6x16 inches
Backing fabric: Dusty green corduroy
Cord: Monk's cord and tassel (all silk colors combined), 28 yards
Tapestry needle: Size #26

Stitch

Follow instructions for cross-stitching over two threads given in Cross-Stitch Basics.

Finish

We had this bell pull finished professionally.

Floss for Monogram Bell Pull

Symbol	Color name	Madeira	DMC	Anchor
▼	Dark blue silk*	1712	930	922
V	Light blue silk	1710	932	343
◢	Gray/blue silk + Rainbow multi-white	1707 + R001	926	850
/	Green silk	1703	502	877
♡	Mauve silk	0812	223	895
■	Luster gold	LS02		
	*Backstitch letters in dark blue (one strand).			

Floss for Monogram Drapery Tieback

Symbol	Color name	Madeira	DMC	Anchor
▼	Dark blue*	1007	336	150
V	Medium blue silk	1711	931	1034
◢	Dark teal silk	1204	991	189
/	Light teal silk	1114	958	187
♡	Red + Rainbow	0811 + R610	221	897
■	Black/gold metallic flash	FL03	310	403
	*Backstitch letter in dark blue (one strand).			

Monogram Drapery Tieback

USE LETTERS FROM ONE OF THE ELEGANT ALPHABETS ON PAGES 151–158

Materials

Fabric: Linen, Jobelan, 28 count (Zweigart®), champagne, 10x10 inches
Tieback: Big Bold Button (Liz Turner Diehl Designs)
Cord: Monk's cord, Glamour by Madeira, light teal, 42 inches
Tassels: Persian yarn to match light teal floss color, 75 yards
Tapestry needle: Size #26 (or smaller)

Stitch

Follow instructions for cross-stitching over two threads given in Cross-Stitch Basics.

Finish

Follow instructions for making tassels in General Project Instructions. Use Persian yarn to match floss color. Follow manufacturer's instructions for covering Big Bold Button. Glue monk's cord made of Glamour by Madeira, light teal (see General Project Instructions) around edge of button. Use remaining monk's cord to tie onto tassels. Glue the ends of the monk's cord onto the back of the button at different heights so that the two tassels are not the same length.

Monogram Pillow with Border

Use Letter and Border from One of the Elegant Alphabets and Borders on Pages 151–159

Materials

Fabric: Linen, Jobelan, 16 count (Zweigart®), charcoal, 14x14 inches.

Backing fabric: Use a coordinating stripe upholstery fabric

Stitch

Follow instructions for cross-stitching over two threads given in Cross-Stitch Basics.

Finish

Have your pillow finished professionally.

Floss for Monogram Pillow with Border

Symbol	Color name	Madeira	DMC	Anchor
▼	Dark blue silk*	1007	336	150
V	Medium blue silk	1711	931	1034
◢	Dark teal green	1205	561	212
/	Light teal green silk	1114	958	187
♡	Burgundy	0602	3685	70
■	Black/gold metallic flash**	FL03	310	403

*Backstitch letter in dark blue (two strands).
**Backstitch border line in black/gold metallic flash (two strands).

Floss for Waffle Stitch

Symbol	Color name	Madeira	DMC	Anchor
XXX	Dark blue	1007	336	150

Floss for Bargello Border

Symbol	Color name	Madeira	DMC	Anchor
I	Dark teal green	1205	561	212
I	Burgundy	0602	3685	70
I	Dark blue silk	1007	336	150

Monogram Tray

USE LETTER FROM ONE OF THE ELEGANT ALPHABETS ON PAGES 151–158

Materials

Fabric: Constance damask, 10 count (Zweigart® #2208), cream, 12x14 inches

Stitch

Follow instructions for cross-stitching given in Cross-Stitch Basics.

Finish

Our tray was made by a framer. Molding was used for the handles.

Floss for Monogram Tray

Symbol	Color name	Madeira	DMC	Anchor
▼	Dark blue silk*	1712	930	922
V	Light blue silk	1710	932	343
/	Light green	3	504	1042
◢	Dark green silk	1703	502	877
♡	Mauve silk	0812	223	895
■	Luster gold	LS02	282	4640

Use three strands for all cross-stitching.
Use two strands for all backstitching.
*Backstitch letter in dark blue (two strands).

Elegant Boston Alphabet

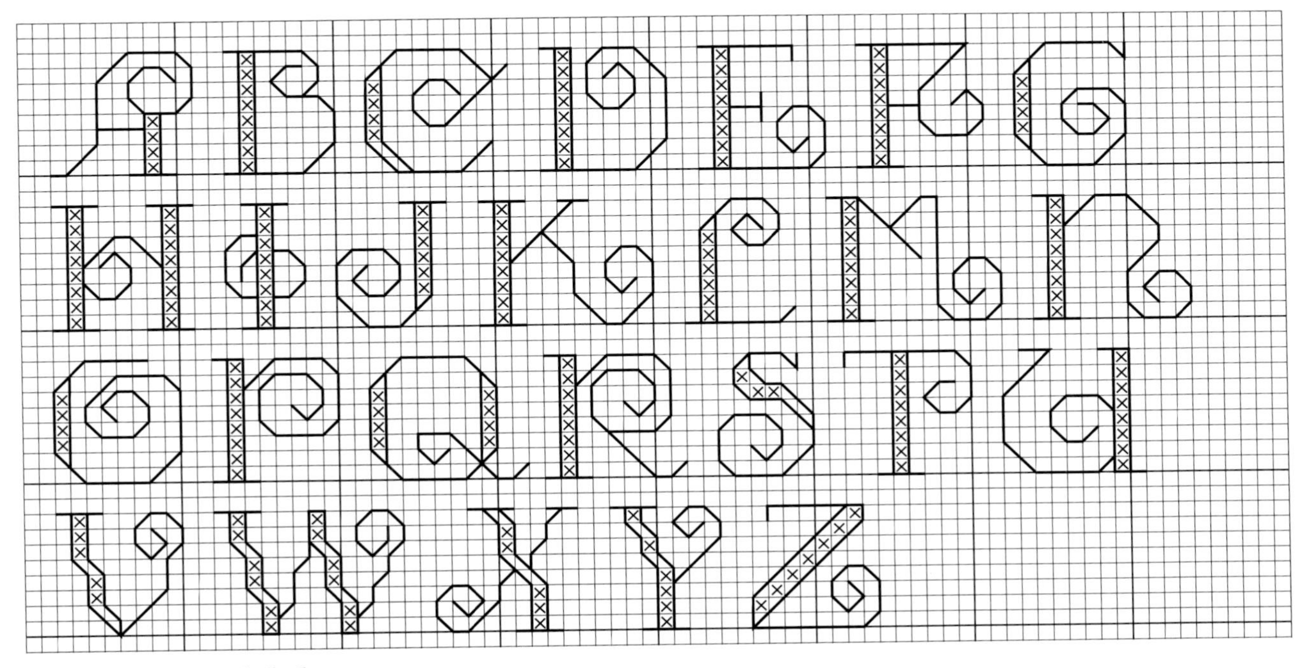

Elegant Swerve Alphabet

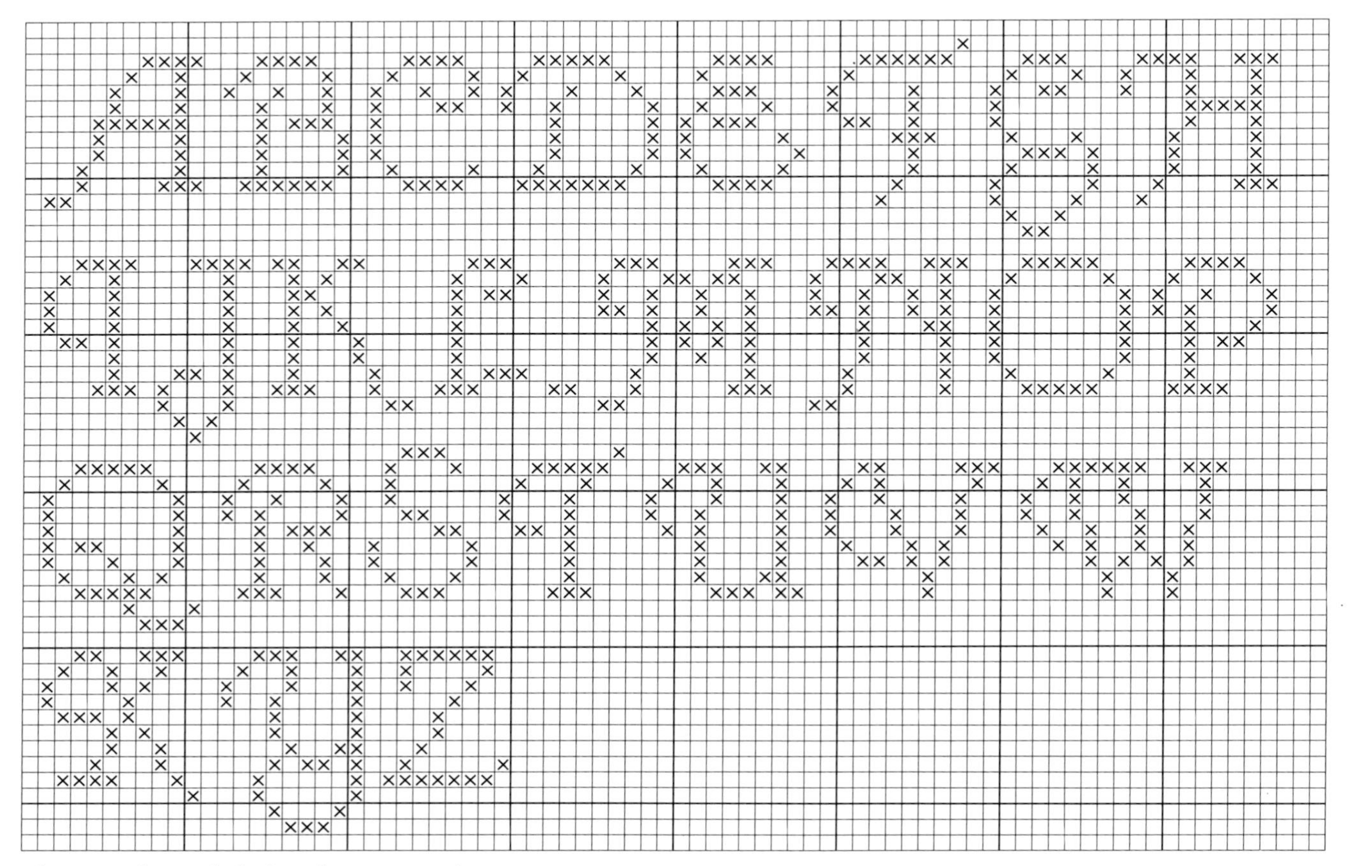

Elegant Plaza Alphabet (uppercase)

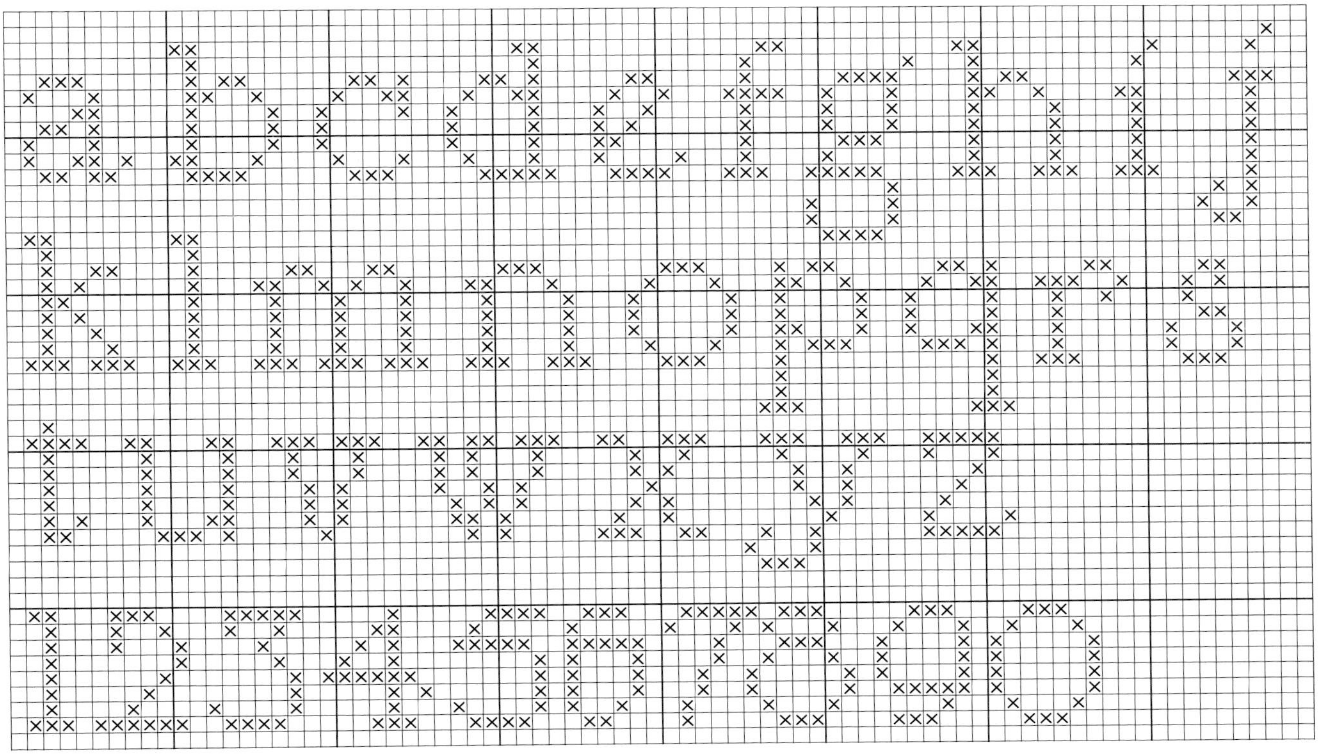

Elegant Plaza Alphabet (lowercase)

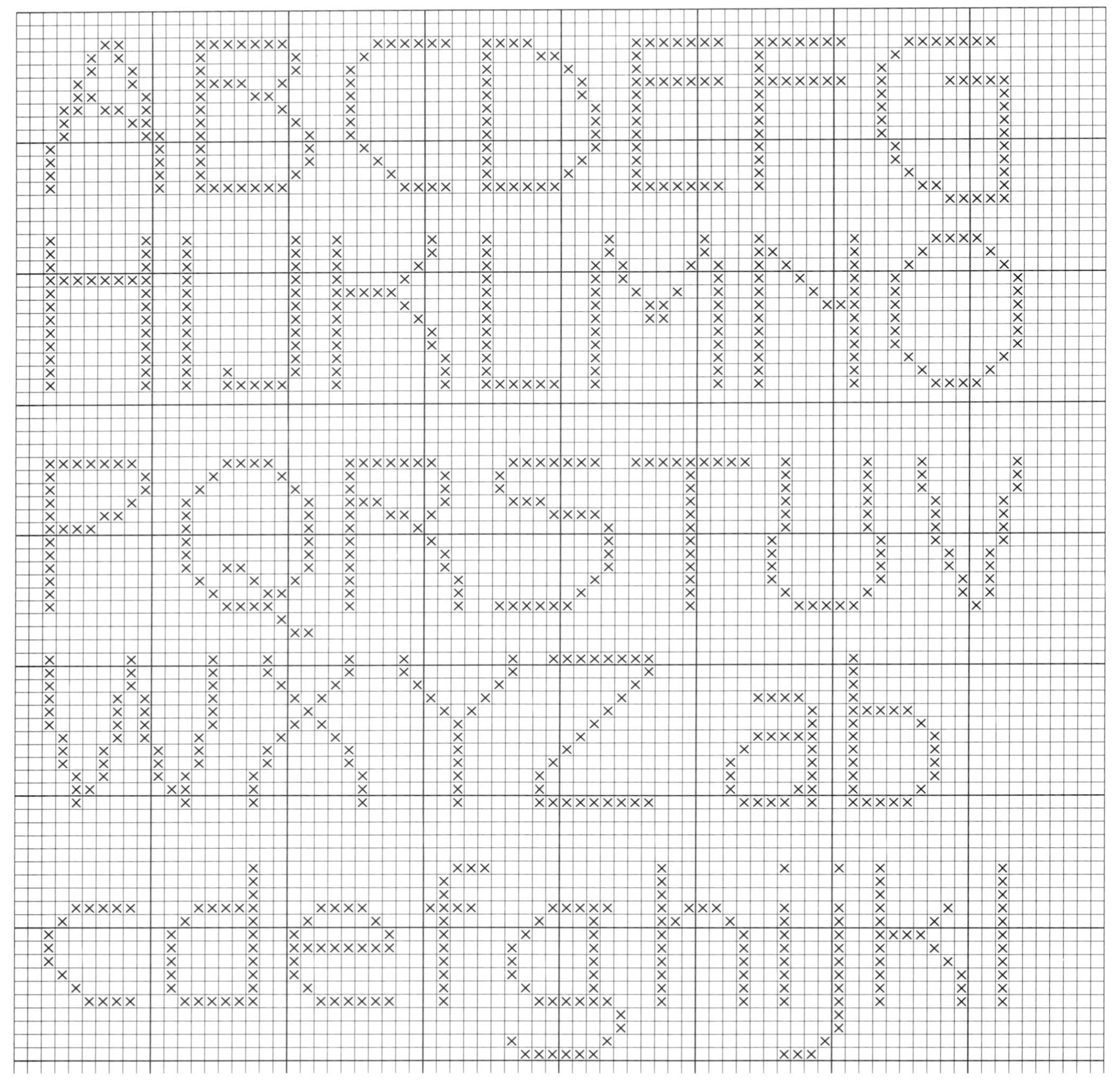

Elegant Westminster Alphabet

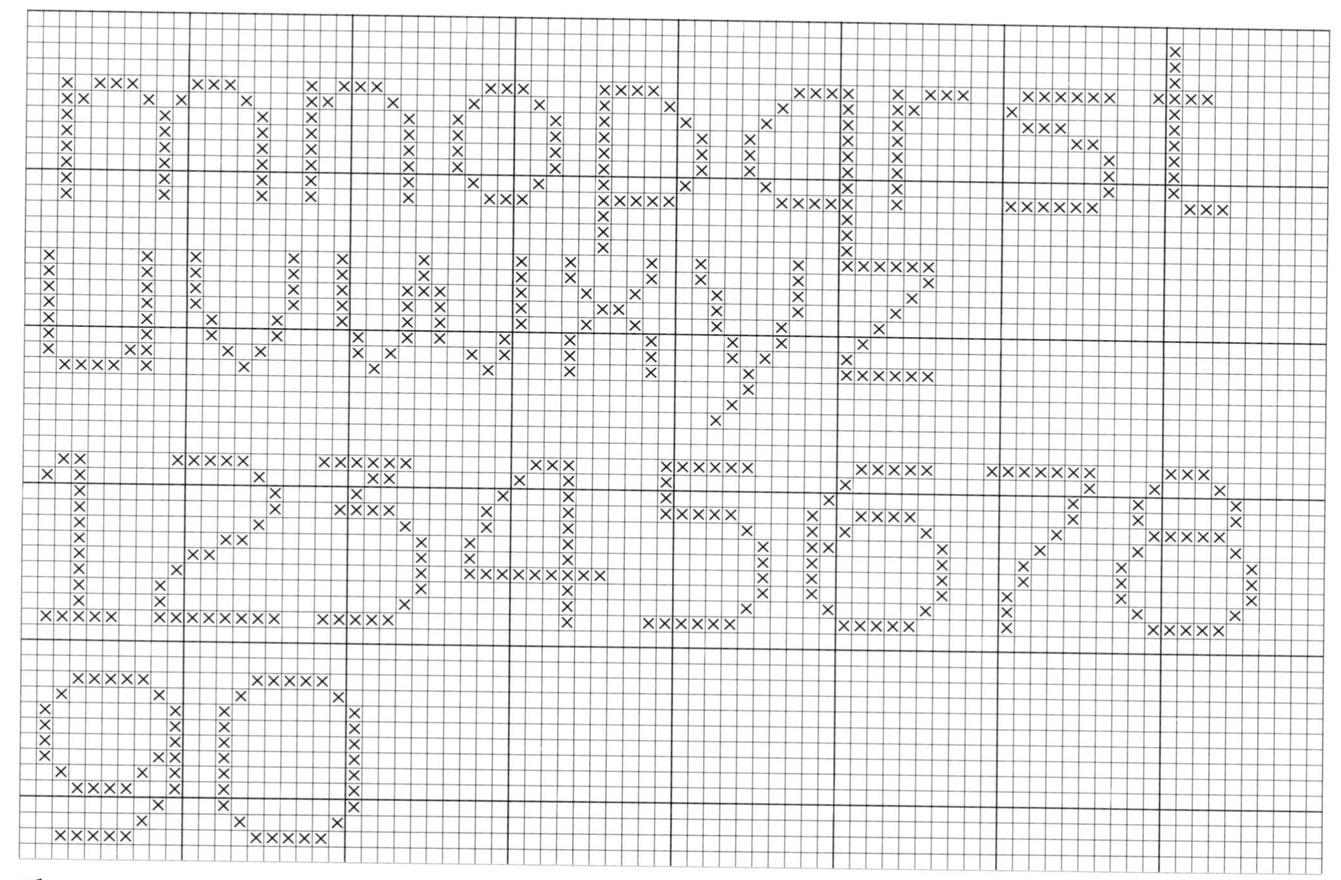

Elegant Westminster Alphabet

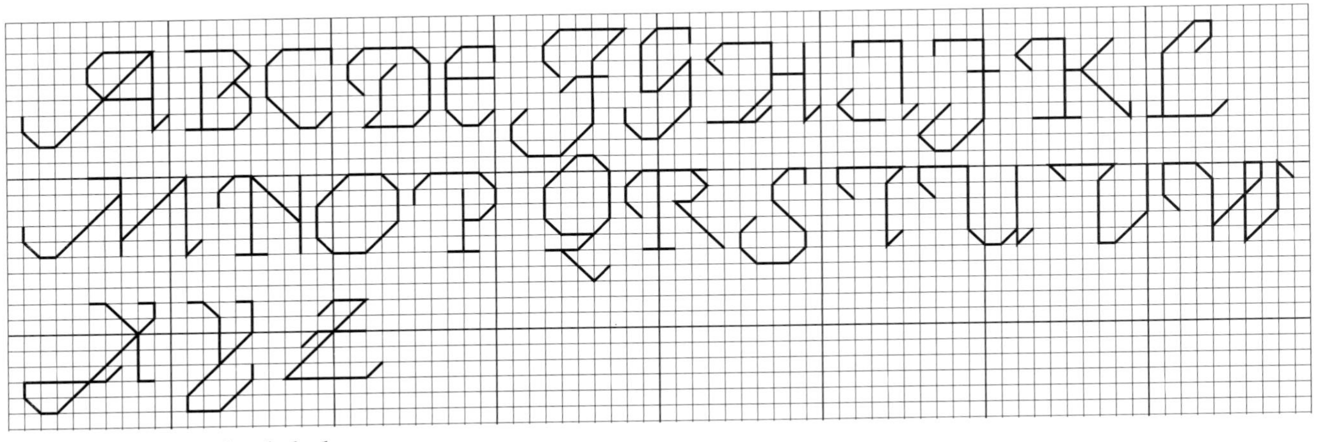

Elegant Backstitch Alphabet

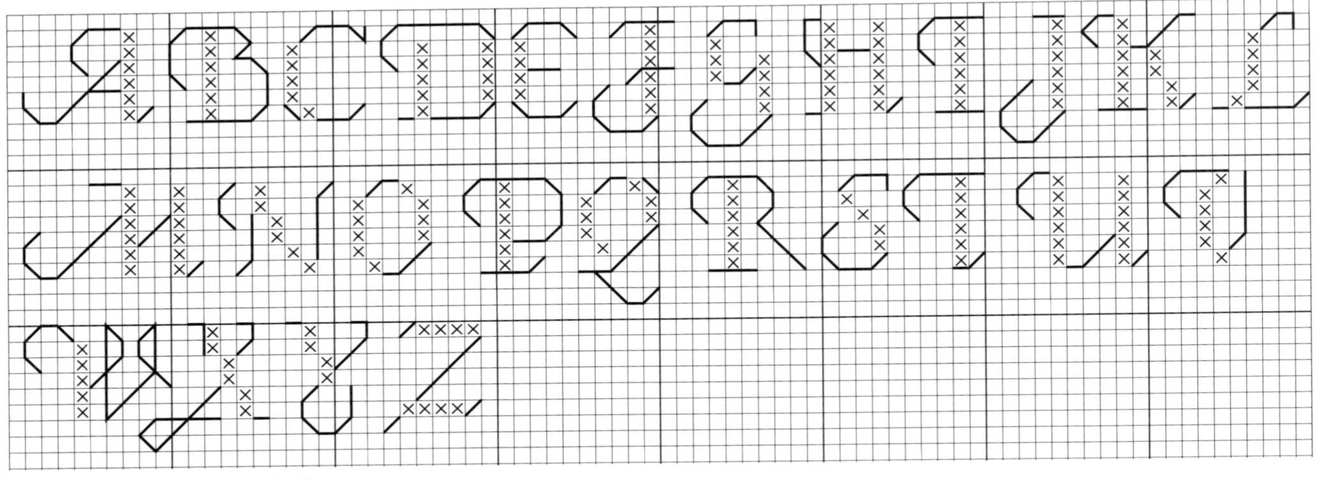

Elegant Berkeley Alphabet

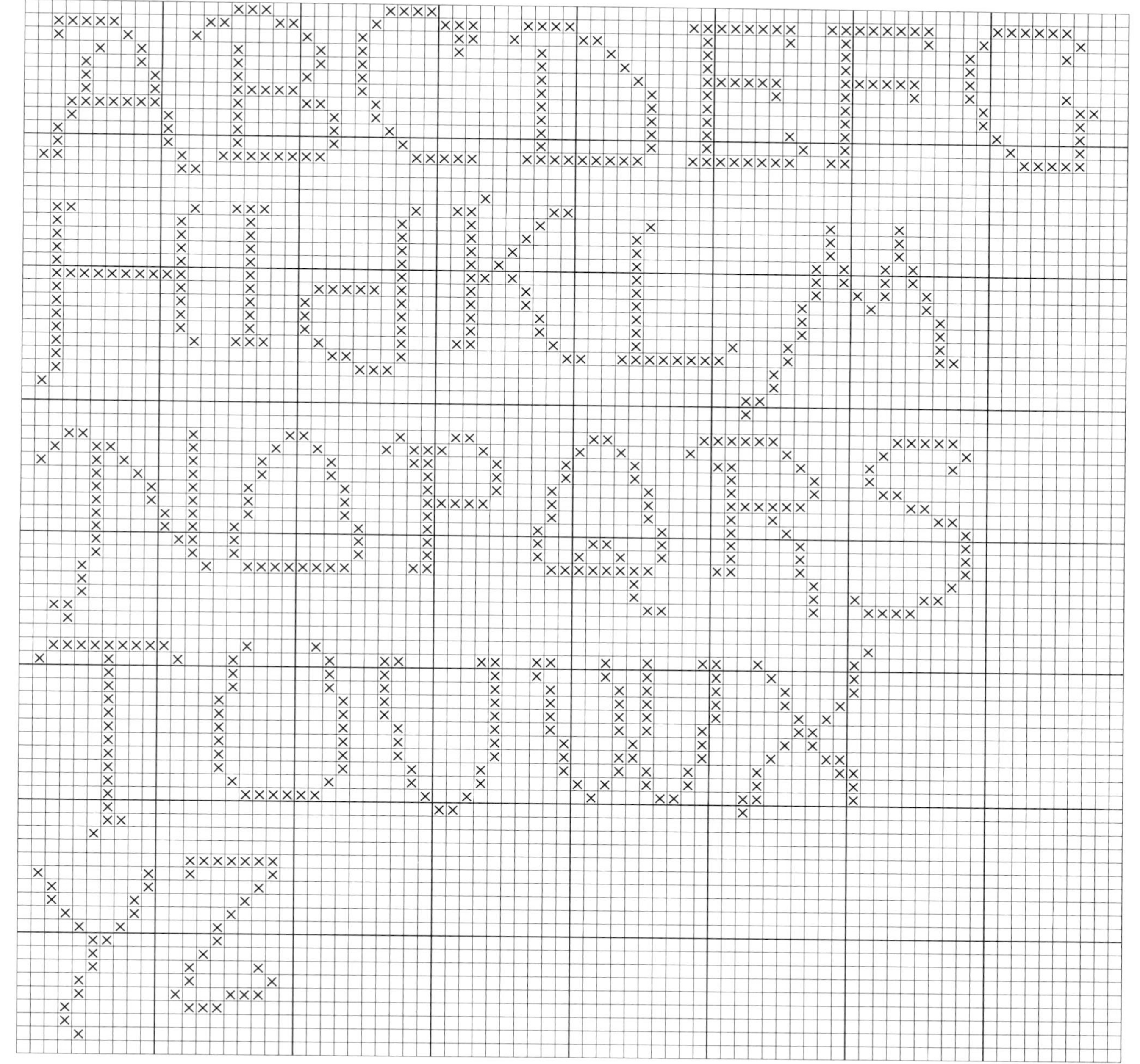

Elegant Emerson Alphabet

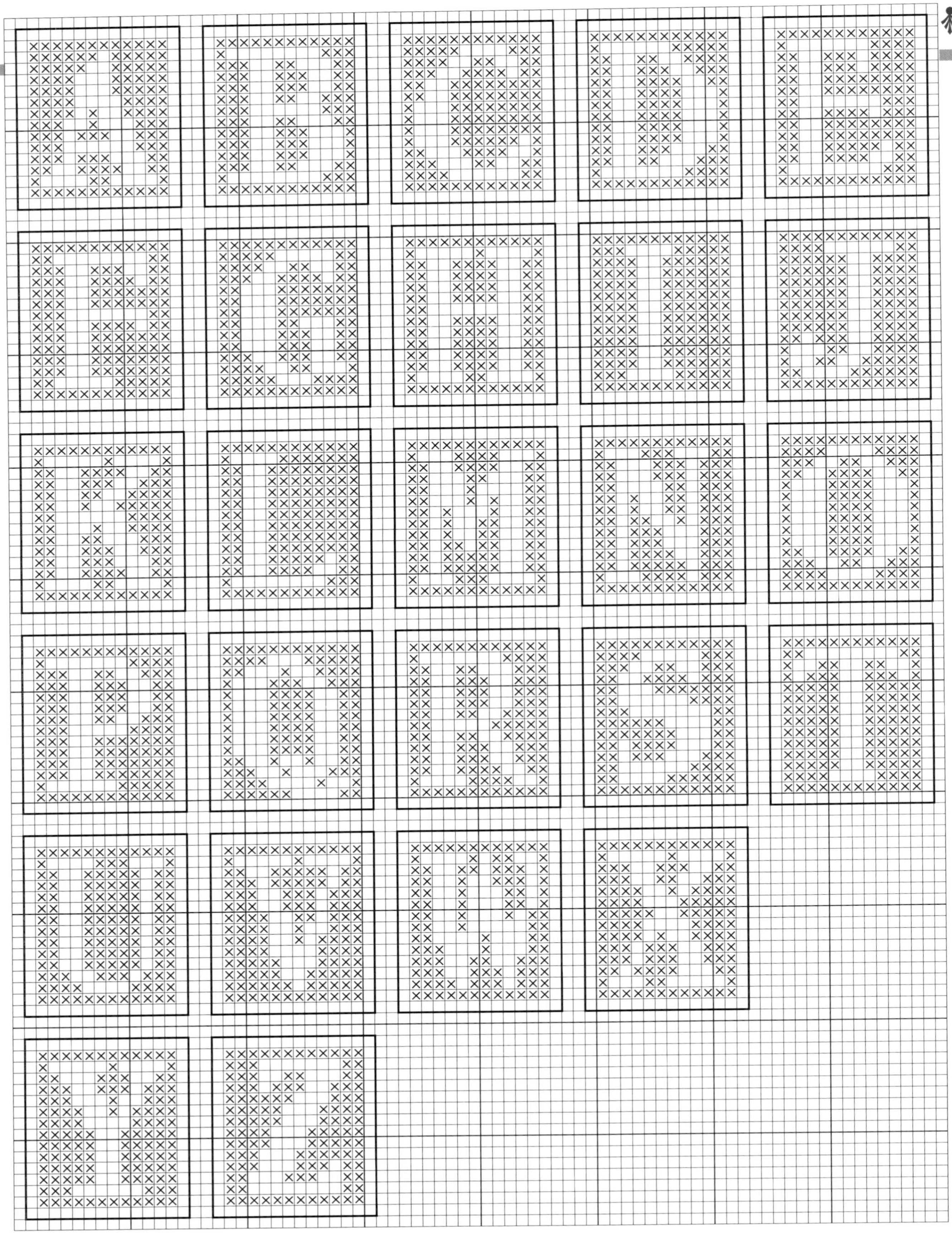

Elegant Princeton Alphabet

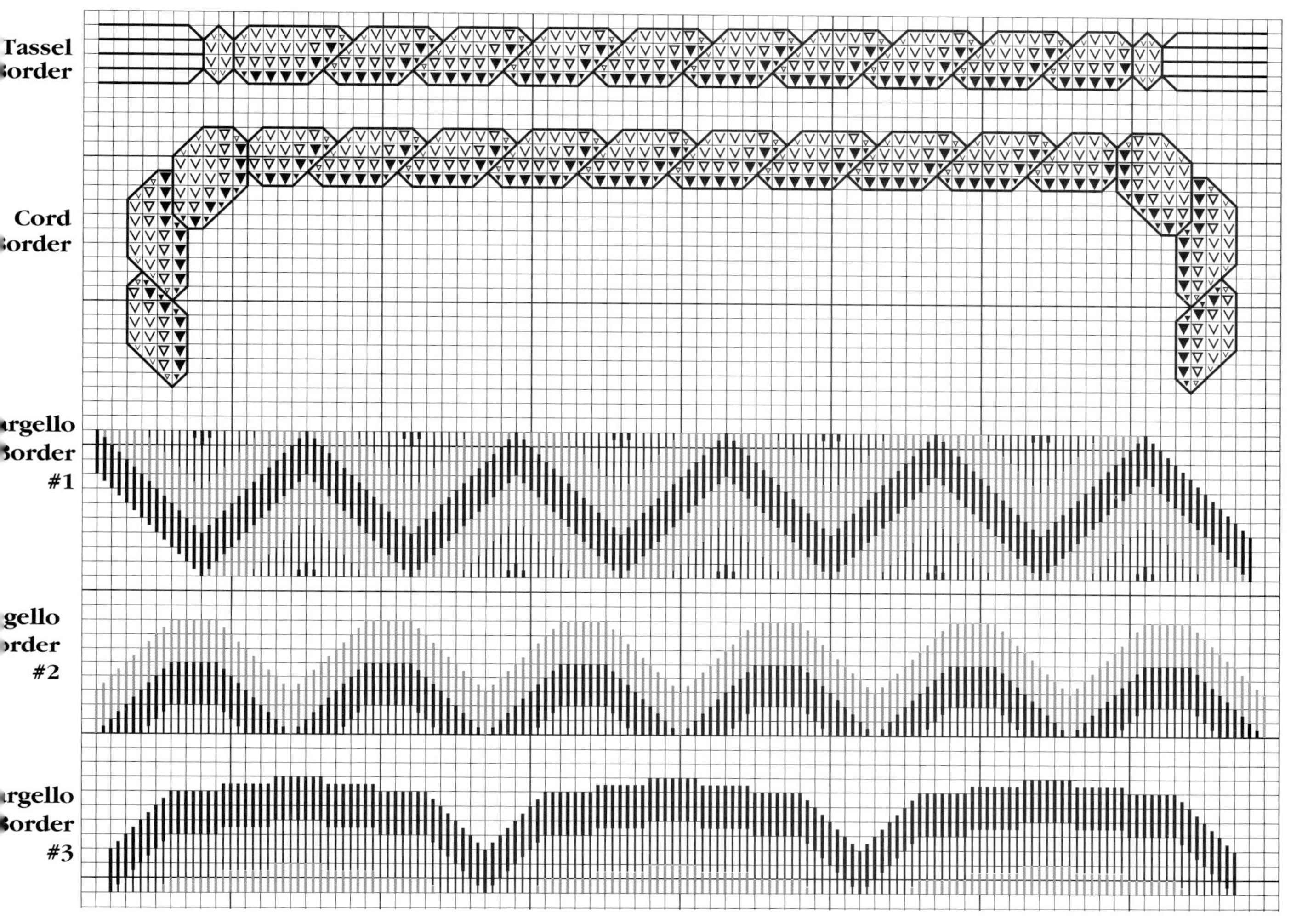

Elegant Borders

Floss for Tassel and Cord Borders

Symbol	Color name	DMC	Anchor
V	Light blue	3752	1032
▽	Medium blue	931	1034
▼	Dark blue*	336	150
	*Backstitch in dark blue (one strand).		

Floss for Bargello Borders

Symbol	Color name	Madeira	DMC	Anchor
I	Dark teal	1204	991	189
I	Red + Rainbow*	0811 + R610	221	897
I	Dark blue	1007	336	150
	*Combine three strands of red and one strand of rainbow.			

Baby Alphabets

Irresistible! That's the word for our adorable Baby Alphabet. Grandmothers will delight in stitching the alphabet on a charming afghan for a wall hanging or decorative coverlet for baby's first bed. Whether you use all the letters or just a few, you'll create eye-catching and wonderful accessories and wearables for the special babies in your life.

SUE
MEGAN

Baby Afghan

USE BABY ALPHABET ON PAGES 163–172

Materials

Anne cloth: Baby blue windowpane (Leisure Arts #11637-10), 28x45 inches
Tapestry needle: Size #24

Stitch

Follow the instructions for cross-stitching over two threads and for cross-stitching on an afghan given in Cross-Stitch Basics.

Finish

After cross-stitching the design, stay-stitch on the outside of the horizontal and vertical colored lines near the edges of the afghan. Cut evenly around afghan before fringing. Fringe all four sides to the stitching line (in about 2 inches) by pulling out the horizontal threads.

Floss

Symbol	Color name	DMC#	Anchor#	Skeins
•	Light pink	818	23	1
○	Medium pink	776	24	1
●	Dark pink	3688	66	1
∾	Yellow	3078	292	1
◇	Light gold	744	301	1
◑	Dark gold	977	1002	1
−	Light gray	415	398	2
=	Dark gray	414	235	1
I	Beige	738	361	1
+	Light brown	436	1045	4
✳	Dark brown	434	310	1
L	Lavender	211	342	1
/	Light green	368	214	1
◢	Dark green	320	216	1
Λ	Peach	353	8	1
V	Light blue	747	158	2
▽	Medium blue	598	167	1
▼	Dark blue	3766	168	25
♡	Red	309	42	1
■	Black***	310	403	1
	Dark dark blue**	806	169	2
⊙	French knot*			

*Use black French knots except where otherwise indicated.
**Backstitch letters in dark dark blue (two strands).
***Backstitch everything in black, except where otherwise indicated (two strands).
I: Stitch French knots on ice cream in red.
L: Stitch French knots on flowers in lavender, medium blue, and medium pink.
P: Backstitch pig's tail in medium pink (two strands).
R: Backstitch raindrops in dark blue (two strands).
X: Stitch French knots on Christmas tree in red.

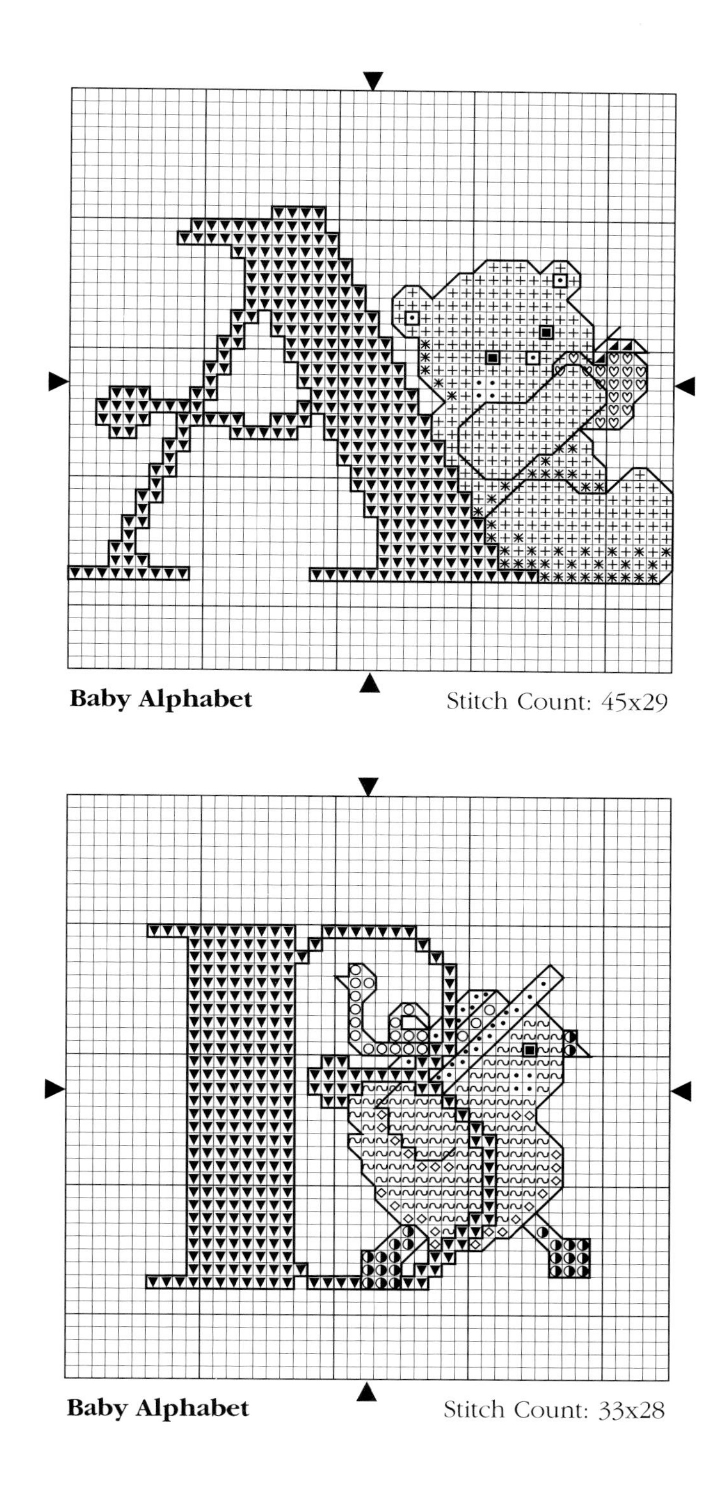

Baby Alphabet Stitch Count: 45x29

Baby Alphabet Stitch Count: 33x28

(continued)

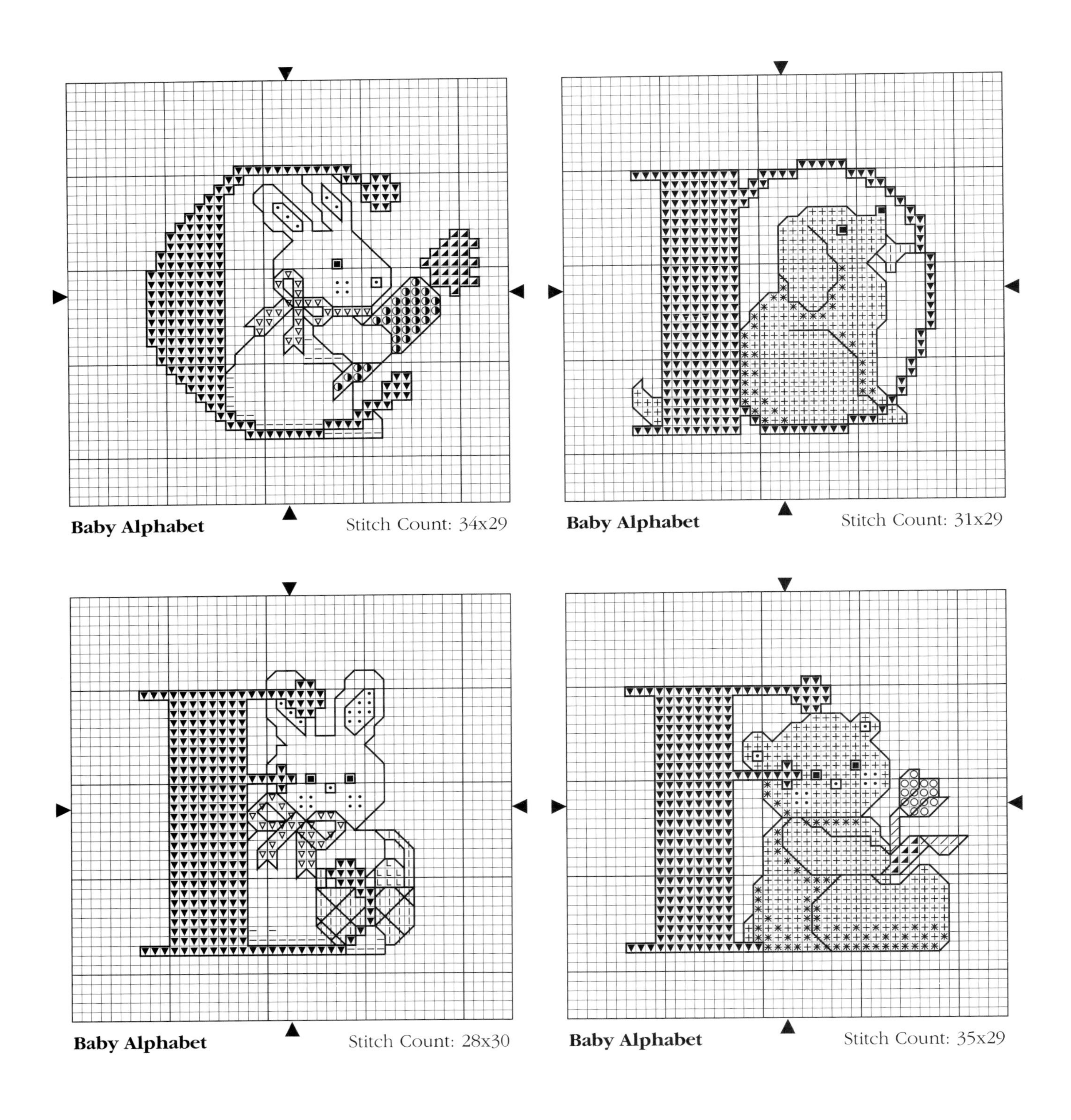

Baby Alphabet Stitch Count: 34x29

Baby Alphabet Stitch Count: 31x29

Baby Alphabet Stitch Count: 28x30

Baby Alphabet Stitch Count: 35x29

Floss

Symbol	*Color name*	*DMC#*	*Anchor#*	*Skeins*
•	Light pink	818	23	1
○	Medium pink	776	24	1
●	Dark pink	3688	66	1
∾	Yellow	3078	292	1
◇	Light gold	744	301	1
◑	Dark gold	977	1002	1
—	Light gray	415	398	2
=	Dark gray	414	235	1
|	Beige	738	361	1
+	Light brown	436	1045	4
✳	Dark brown	434	310	1
L	Lavender	211	342	1
/	Light green	368	214	1
◢	Dark green	320	216	1
Λ	Peach	353	8	1
V	Light blue	747	158	2
▽	Medium blue	598	167	1
▼	Dark blue	3766	168	25
♡	Red	309	42	1
■	Black***	310	403	1
	Dark dark blue**	806	169	2
⊙	French knot*			

*Use black French knots except where otherwise indicated.
**Backstitch letters in dark dark blue (two strands).
***Backstitch everything in black, except where otherwise indicated (two strands).
I: Stitch French knots on ice cream in red.
L: Stitch French knots on flowers in lavender, medium blue, and medium pink.
P: Backstitch pig's tail in medium pink (two strands).
R: Backstitch raindrops in dark blue (two strands).
X: Stitch French knots on Christmas tree in red.

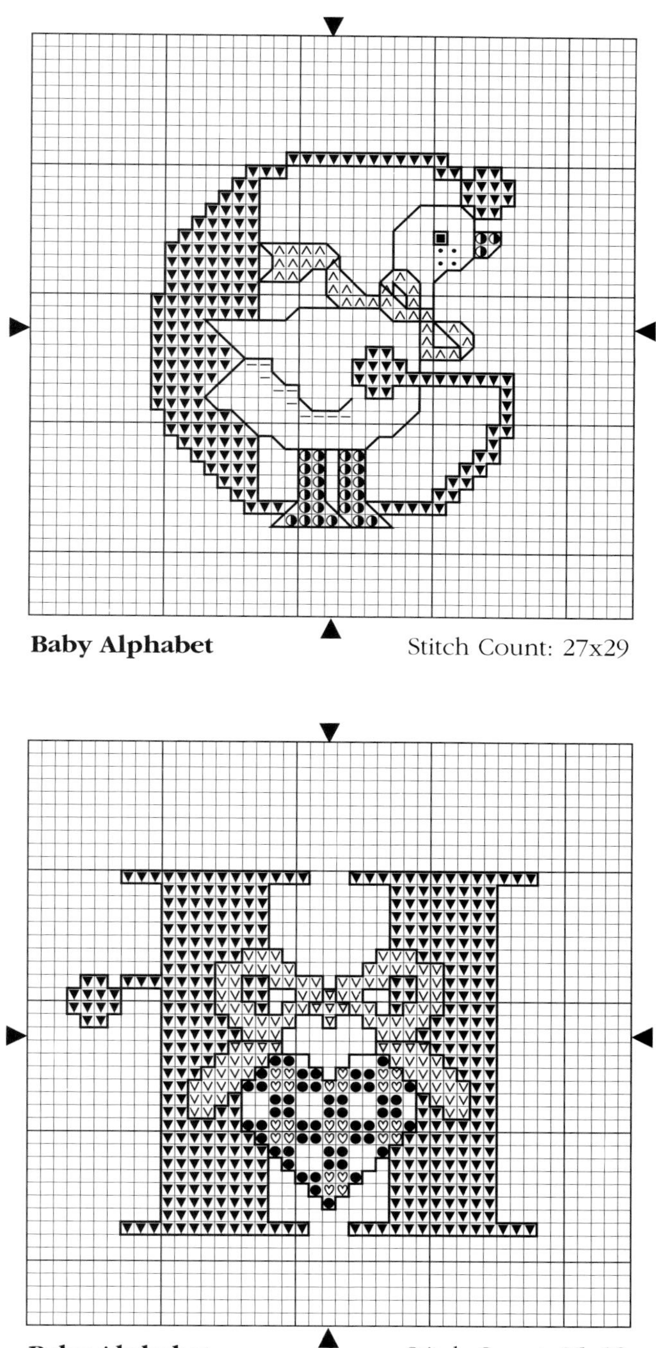

Baby Alphabet Stitch Count: 27x29

Baby Alphabet Stitch Count: 35x28

(continued)

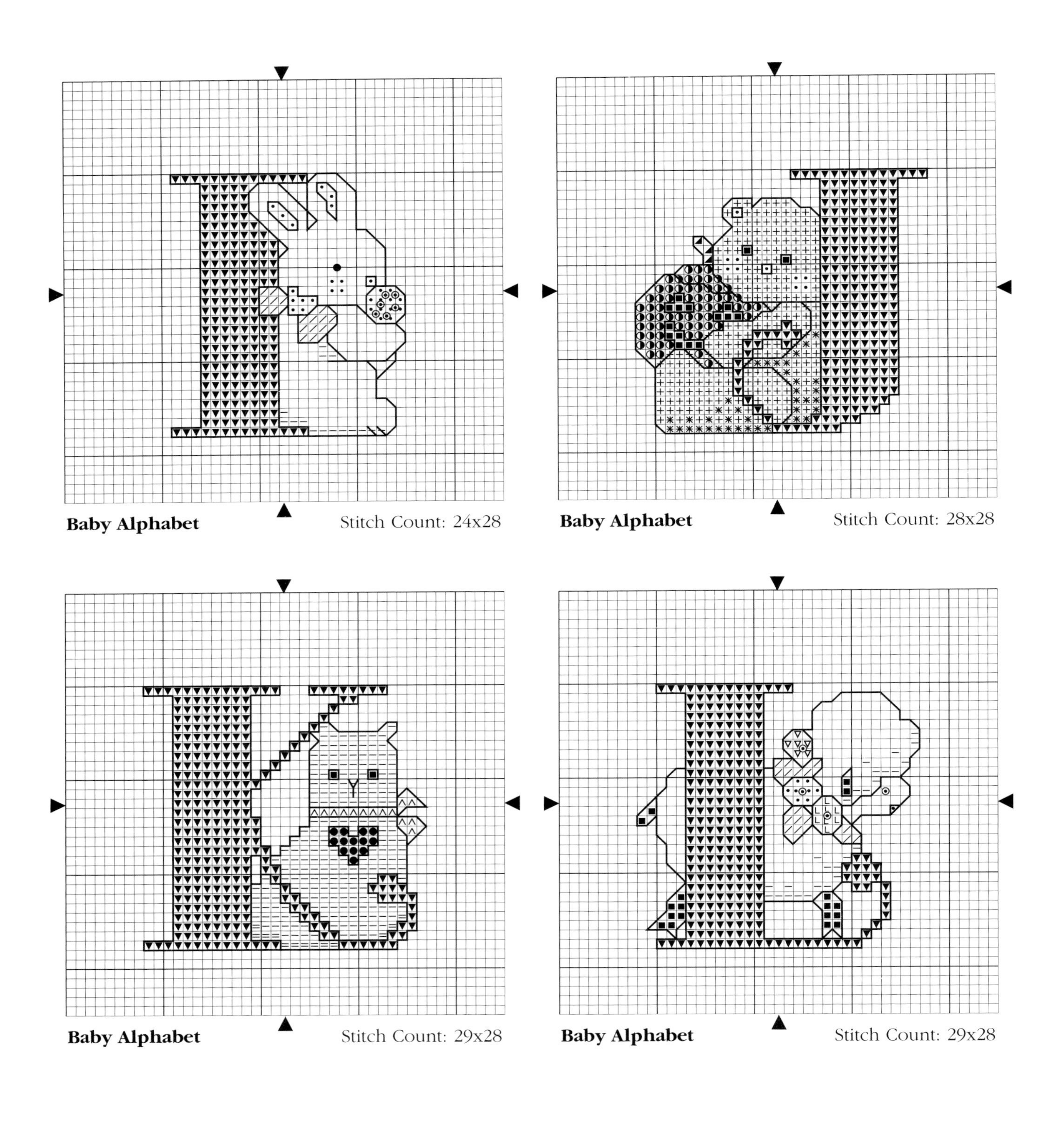

Baby Alphabet Stitch Count: 24x28

Baby Alphabet Stitch Count: 28x28

Baby Alphabet Stitch Count: 29x28

Baby Alphabet Stitch Count: 29x28

Floss

Symbol	Color name	DMC#	Anchor#	Skeins
•	Light pink	818	23	1
○	Medium pink	776	24	1
●	Dark pink	3688	66	1
∿	Yellow	3078	292	1
◇	Light gold	744	301	1
◑	Dark gold	977	1002	1
–	Light gray	415	398	2
=	Dark gray	414	235	1
I	Beige	738	361	1
+	Light brown	436	1045	4
✱	Dark brown	434	310	1
L	Lavender	211	342	1
/	Light green	368	214	1
◢	Dark green	320	216	1
Λ	Peach	353	8	1
V	Light blue	747	158	2
▽	Medium blue	598	167	1
▼	Dark blue	3766	168	25
♡	Red	309	42	1
■	Black***	310	403	1
	Dark dark blue**	806	169	2
⊙	French knot*			

*Stitch black French knots except where otherwise indicated.
**Backstitch letters in dark dark blue (two strands).
***Backstitch everything in black, except where otherwise indicated (two strands).
I: Stitch French knots on ice cream in red.
L: Stitch French knots on flowers in lavender, medium blue, and medium pink.
P: Backstitch pig's tail in medium pink (two strands).
R: Backstitch raindrops in dark blue (two strands).
X: Stitch French knots on Christmas tree in red.

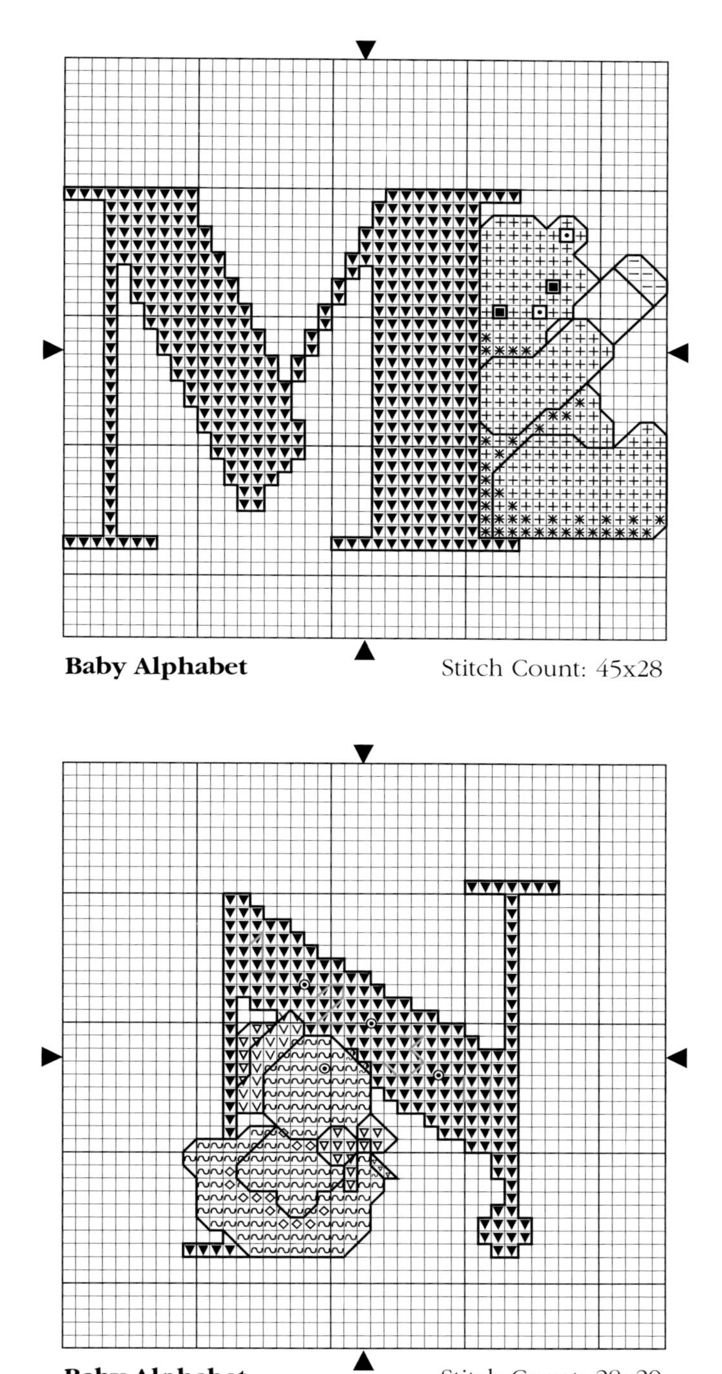

Baby Alphabet Stitch Count: 45x28

Baby Alphabet Stitch Count: 28x29

(continued)

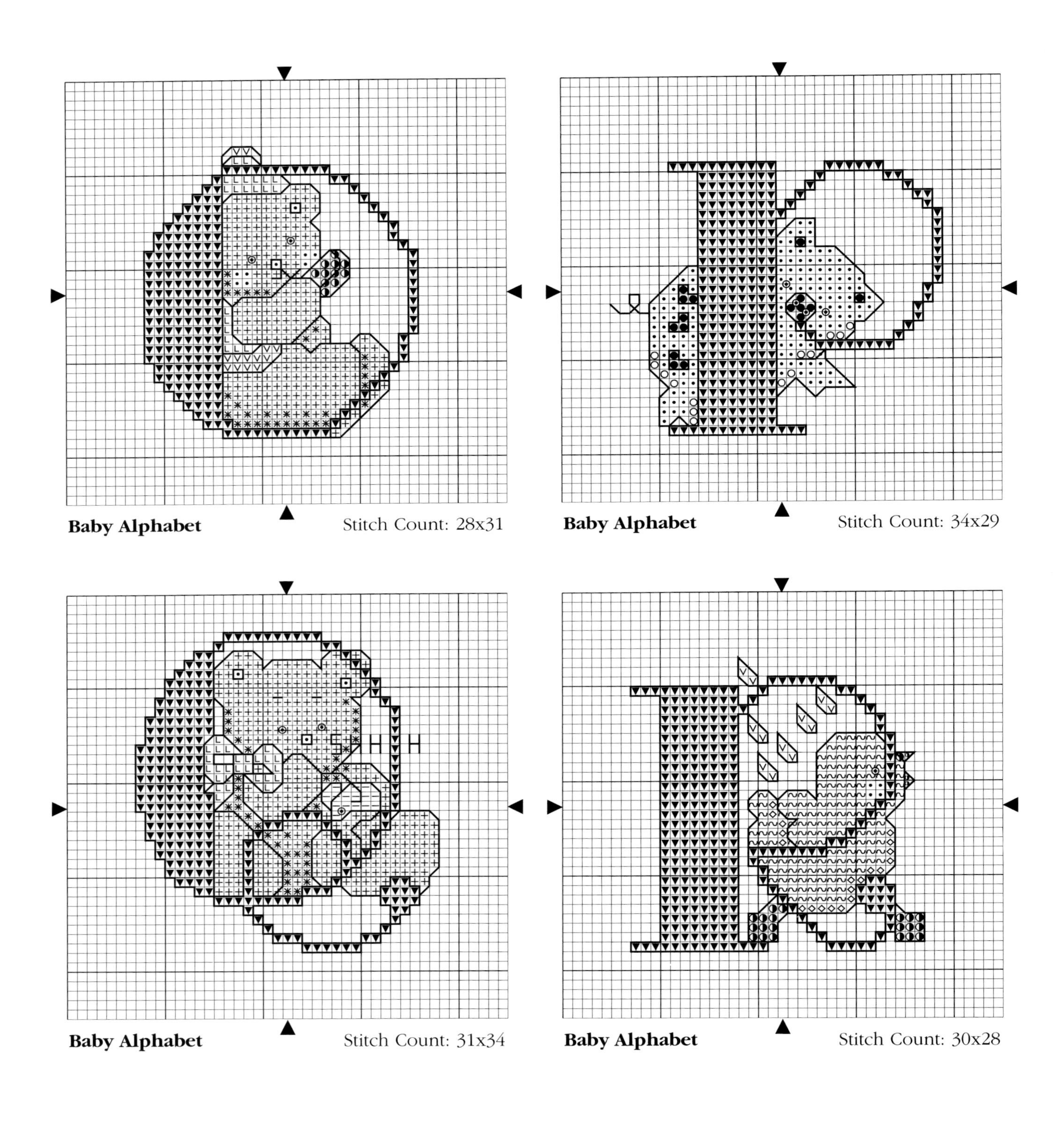

Baby Alphabet Stitch Count: 28x31

Baby Alphabet Stitch Count: 34x29

Baby Alphabet Stitch Count: 31x34

Baby Alphabet Stitch Count: 30x28

Floss

Symbol	Color name	DMC#	Anchor#	Skeins
•	Light pink	818	23	1
○	Medium pink	776	24	1
●	Dark pink	3688	66	1
∾	Yellow	3078	292	1
◇	Light gold	744	301	1
◑	Dark gold	977	1002	1
–	Light gray	415	398	2
=	Dark gray	414	235	1
I	Beige	738	361	1
+	Light brown	436	1045	4
✱	Dark brown	434	310	1
L	Lavender	211	342	1
/	Light green	368	214	1
◢	Dark green	320	216	1
Λ	Peach	353	8	1
V	Light blue	747	158	2
▽	Medium blue	598	167	1
▼	Dark blue	3766	168	25
♡	Red	309	42	1
■	Black***	310	403	1
	Dark dark blue**	806	169	2
⊙	French knot*			

*Stitch black French knots except where otherwise indicated.
**Backstitch letters in dark dark blue (two strands).
***Backstitch everything in black, except where otherwise indicated (two strands).
I: Stitch French knots on ice cream in red.
L: Stitch French knots on flowers in lavender, medium blue, and medium pink.
P: Backstitch pig's tail in medium pink (two strands).
R: Backstitch raindrops in dark blue (two strands).
X: Stitch French knots on Christmas tree in red.

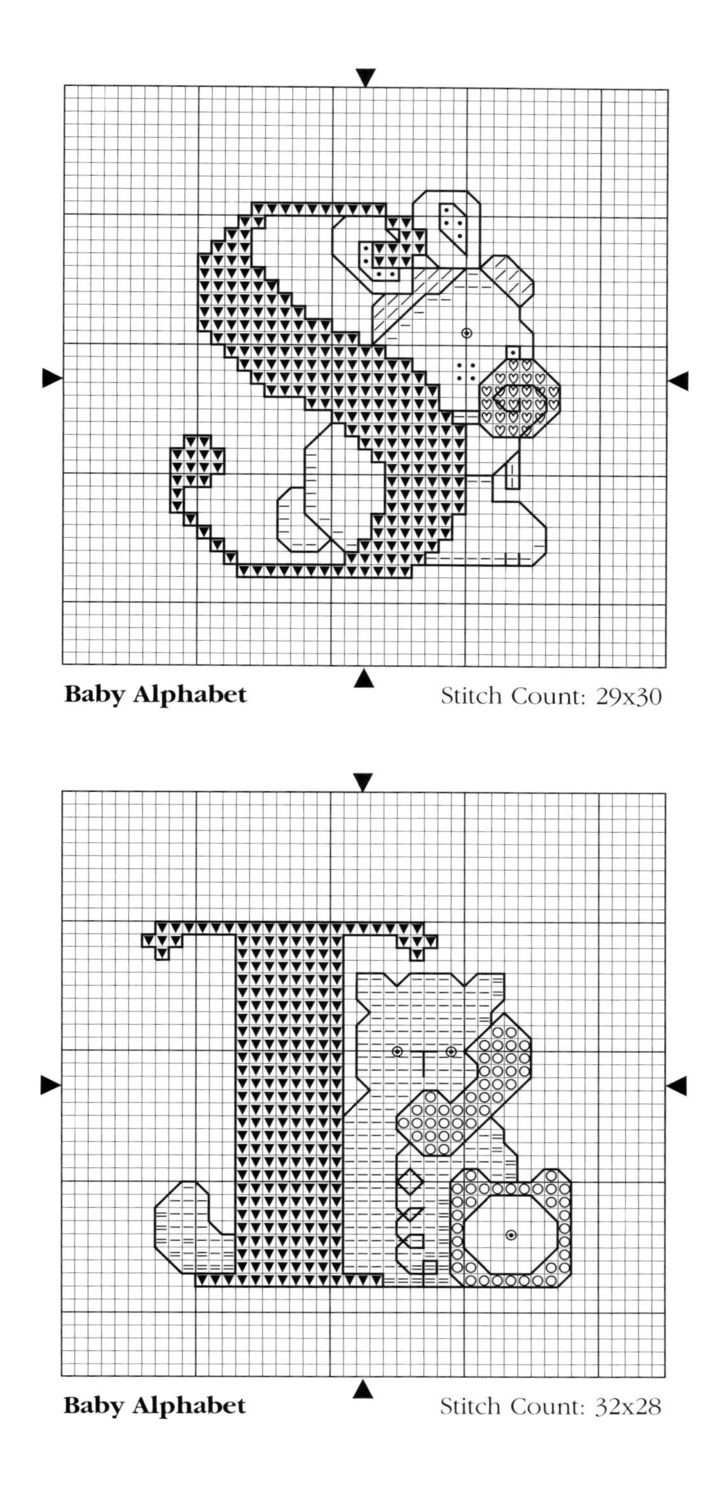

Baby Alphabet Stitch Count: 29x30

Baby Alphabet Stitch Count: 32x28

(continued)

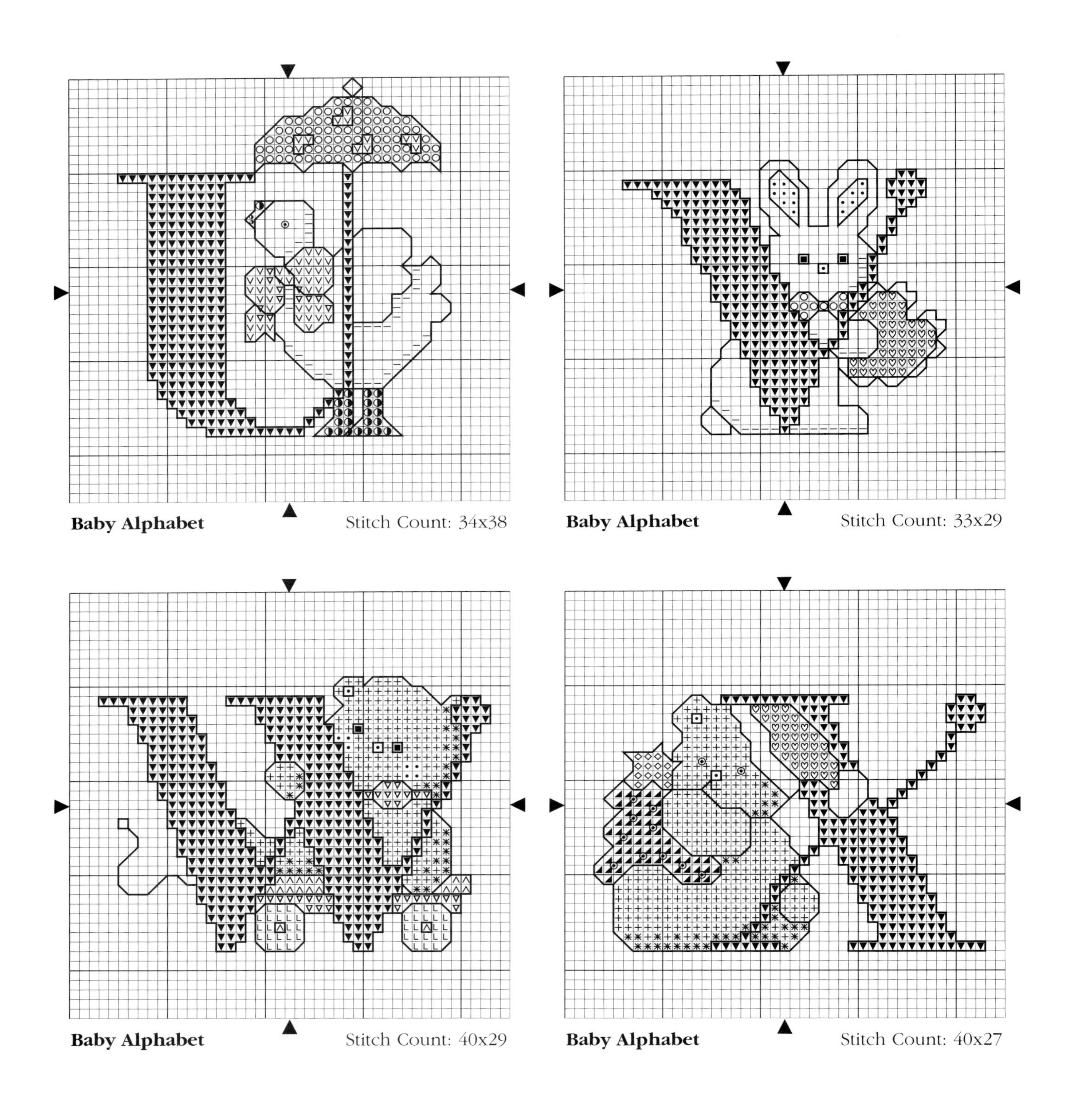

Baby Alphabet Stitch Count: 34x38

Baby Alphabet Stitch Count: 33x29

Baby Alphabet Stitch Count: 40x29

Baby Alphabet Stitch Count: 40x27

Floss

Symbol	Color name	DMC#	Anchor#	Skeins
•	Light pink	818	23	1
○	Medium pink	776	24	1
●	Dark pink	3688	66	1
∾	Yellow	3078	292	1
◇	Light gold	744	301	1
◑	Dark gold	977	1002	1
−	Light gray	415	398	2
=	Dark gray	414	235	1
I	Beige	738	361	1
+	Light brown	436	1045	4
✳	Dark brown	434	310	1
L	Lavender	211	342	1
/	Light green	368	214	1
◢	Dark green	320	216	1
Λ	Peach	353	8	1
V	Light blue	747	158	2
▽	Medium blue	598	167	1
▼	Dark blue	3766	168	25
♡	Red	309	42	1
■	Black***	310	403	1
	Dark dark blue**	806	169	2
⊙	French knot*			

*Stitch black French knots except where otherwise indicated.
**Backstitch letters in dark dark blue (two strands).
***Backstitch everything in black, except where otherwise indicated (two strands).
I: Stitch French knots on ice cream in red.
L: Stitch French knots on flowers in lavender, medium blue, and medium pink.
P: Backstitch pig's tail in medium pink (two strands).
R: Backstitch raindrops in dark blue (two strands).
X: Stitch French knots on Christmas tree in red.

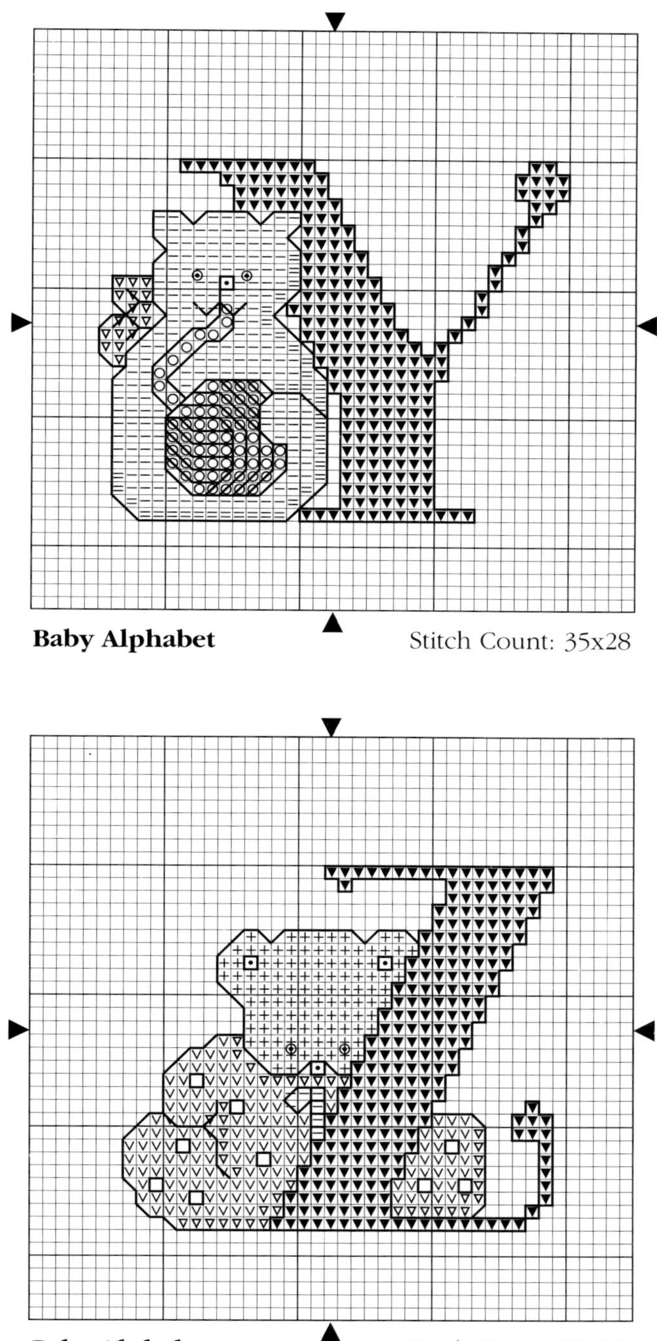

Baby Alphabet Stitch Count: 35x28

Baby Alphabet Stitch Count: 32x28

(continued)

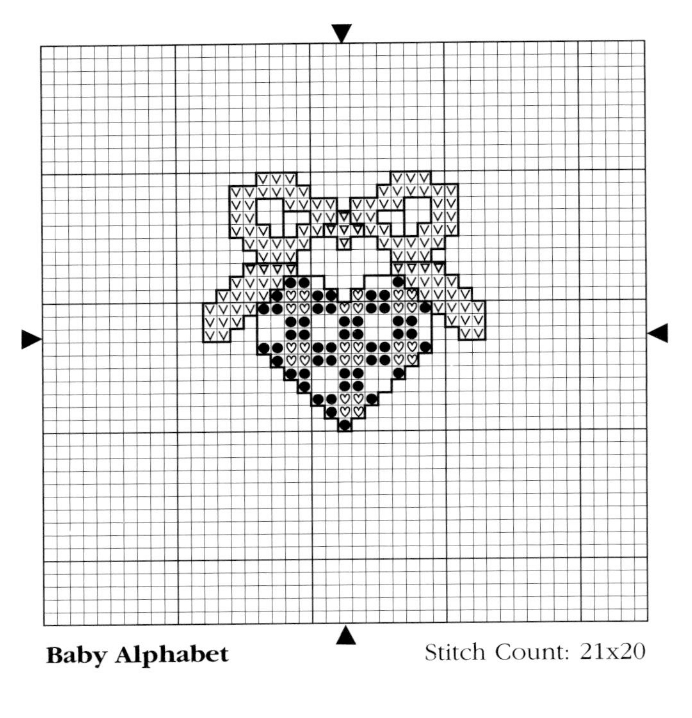

Baby Alphabet Stitch Count: 21x20

Floss

Symbol	Color name	DMC#	Anchor#	Skeins
•	Light pink	818	23	1
○	Medium pink	776	24	1
●	Dark pink	3688	66	1
∾	Yellow	3078	292	1
◇	Light gold	744	301	1
◑	Dark gold	977	1002	1
—	Light gray	415	398	2
=	Dark gray	414	235	1
|	Beige	738	361	1
+	Light brown	436	1045	4
✳	Dark brown	434	310	1
L	Lavender	211	342	1
/	Light green	368	214	1
◢	Dark green	320	216	1
Λ	Peach	353	8	1
V	Light blue	747	158	2
▽	Medium blue	598	167	1
▼	Dark blue	3766	168	25
♡	Red	309	42	1
■	Black***	310	403	1
	Dark dark blue**	806	169	2
⊙	French knot*			

*Stitch black French knots except where otherwise indicated.
**Backstitch letters in dark dark blue (two strands).
***Backstitch everything in black, except where otherwise indicated (two strands).
I: Stitch French knots on ice cream in red.
L: Stitch French knots on flowers in lavender, medium blue, and medium pink.
P: Backstitch pig's tail in medium pink (two strands).
R: Backstitch raindrops in dark blue (two strands).
X: Stitch French knots on Christmas tree in red.

Baby Bib

Use Letter from Baby Alphabet on Pages 163–172

Materials

Bib: Premade, white (Charles Craft), with 14-count white Aida
Lace: White gathered eyelet, ½ inch wide, 22 inches
Satin ribbon: Color to match floss, ⅛ inch wide, 24 inches
Fabric glue

Stitch

Follow the instructions for cross-stitching given in Cross-Stitch Basics.

Finishing

The premade bib requires no finishing. To embellish, sew or glue on the eyelet lace. Glue on the ribbon for trim. Add two bows (see photo for placement).

Baby Cup

Use Letter from Baby Alphabet on Pages 163–172

Materials

Baby cup: Pink top (Crafter's Pride), with 14-count vinyl Aida insert
Satin ribbon: Pink, ⅛ inch wide, 12 inches
Craft glue

Stitch

Follow the instructions for cross-stitching given in Cross-Stitch Basics.

Finish

If desired, after stitching add ribbon using craft glue (see photo for placement). Insert vinyl Aida into cup, and snap lid on top according to manufacturer's instructions.

Framed Name Sign

SPELL THE NAME OF YOUR CHOICE USING LETTERS FROM BABY ALPHABET ON PAGES 163–172

Materials

Aida fabric: White, 14 count, 10x16 inches

Stitch

Follow cross-stitching instructions given in Cross-Stitch Basics.

Finishing

We had this piece professionally framed using two mats.

Baby Pillow

SPELL THE NAME OF YOUR CHOICE USING LETTERS FROM BABY ALPHABET ON PAGES 163–172

Materials

Pillow cover: Soft-Touch, premade, with 14-count Aida front, EZ stitch back, 10x10 inches plus 3-inch ruffle (Charles Craft #PS 5560-6750)

Satin Ribbon: Pink, ⅜ inch wide, 18 inches; blue, ⅛ inch wide, 18 inches

Stitch

Follow the instructions for cross-stitching given in Cross-Stitch basics.

Finish

The premade pillow requires no finishing. After stitching, insert pillow form and glue or sew on bow.

The Little Car

Baby Romper

USE DUCK FROM BABY ALPHABET LETTER N AND BABY HEARTS AND BABY WAVES BORDERS BELOW

Materials

T-shirt: White, infant
Waste canvas: 8.5 count, 4x9 inches
Chenille needle: Size #24

Stitch and Finish

Follow instructions for cross-stitching using waste canvas given in Cross-Stitch Basics. Cross-stitch with the top of the design about 2½ inches below the neckline of the shirt.

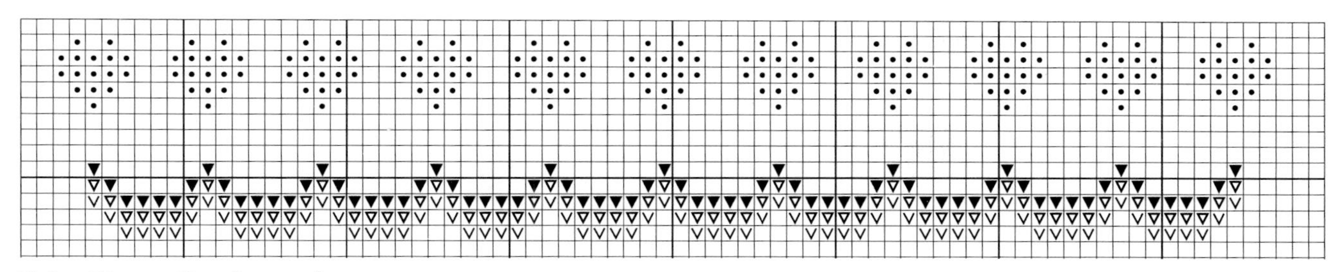

Baby Hearts Border and Baby Waves Border

Floss

Symbol	Color name	DMC#	Anchor#
•	Pink	3688	66
V	Light blue	747	158
▽	Medium blue	598	167
▼	Dark blue	3766	168

Baby Socks

USE BABY BOW BORDER BELOW

Materials

Socks: 1 pair, infant, with cuff
Waste canvas: 14 count, 2x6 inches
Chenille needle: Size 7
Lace: 2 pieces, each 6½x1 inch

Stitch

Turn the socks inside out. Attach the waste canvas to the top edges of the socks, following the instructions for using waste canvas given in Cross-Stitch Basics. Turn the socks upside down, and cross-stitch the design right side up about ¼ inch from the top of the socks. (Be sure the socks are inside out while cross-stitching). When finished stitching, turn socks right side out and turn down cuffs.

Finish

Sew lace along edges of cuffs.

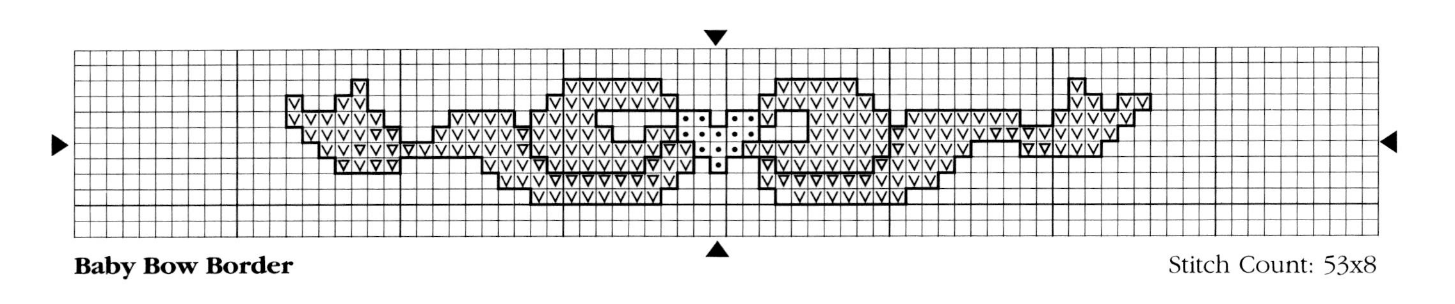

Baby Bow Border Stitch Count: 53x8

Floss

Symbol	Color name	DMC#	Anchor#
•	Pink*	3688	66
V	Light blue	747	158
▽	Medium blue	598	167
	Dark blue**	3766	168
	*Backstitch hearts in pink (one strand). **Backstitch bow in dark blue (two strands).		

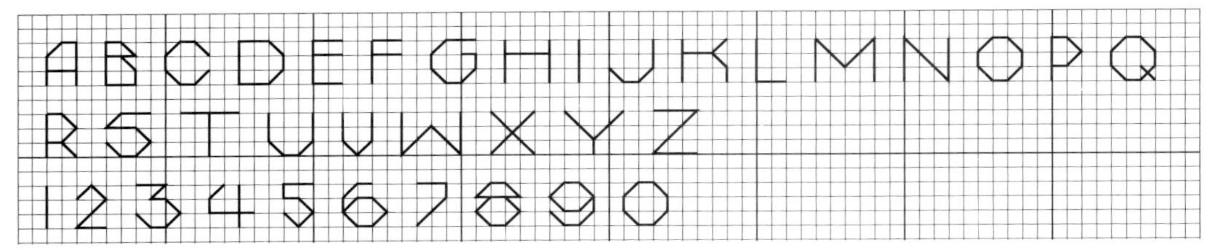

Baby Basic Alphabet

Ideas for Use

This little alphabet would be perfect to use for "signing" your work.

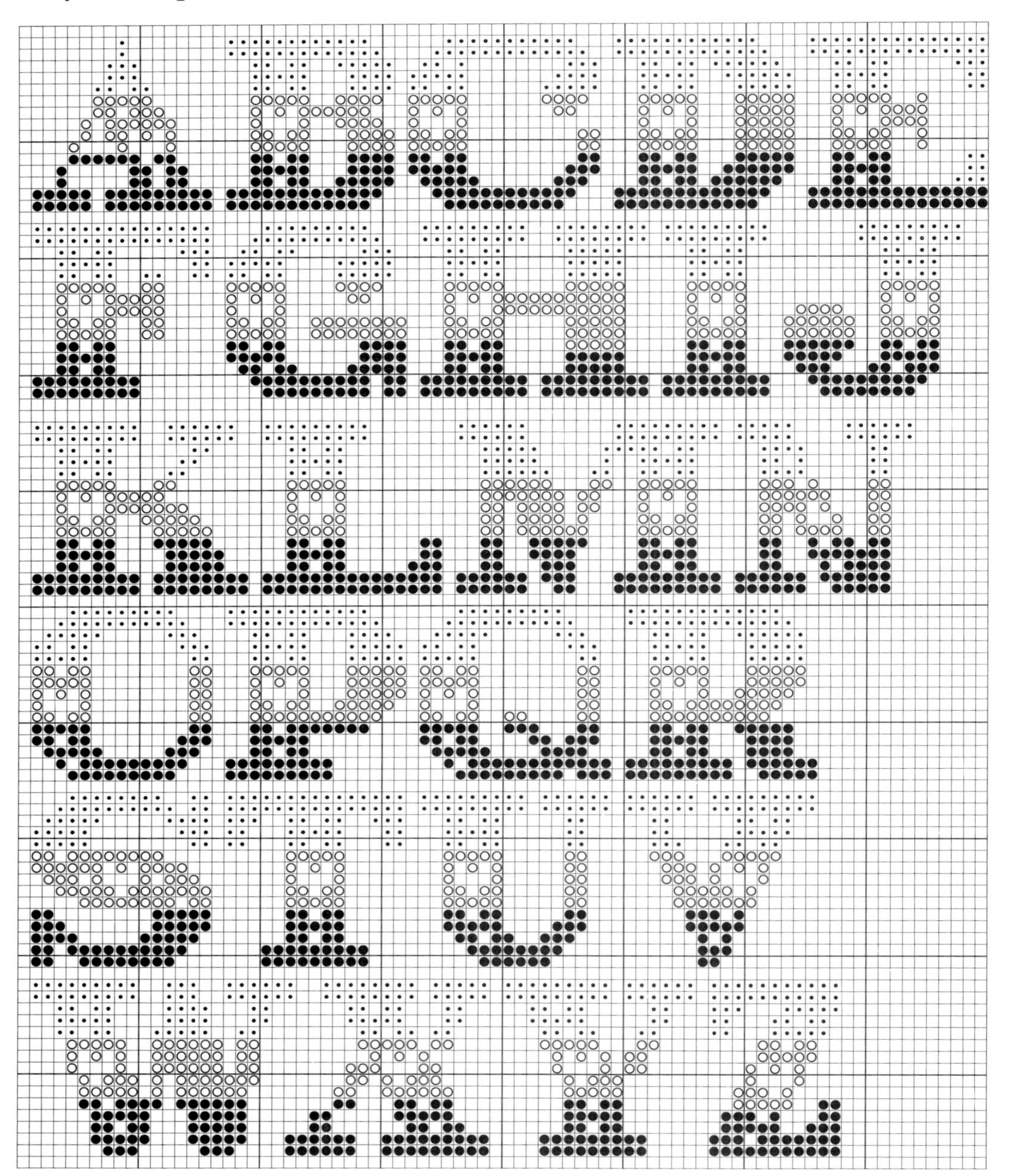

Baby Pink Shaded Alphabet

Ideas for Use

This alphabet could be used in so many different ways. Cross-stitch the entire alphabet on a baby afghan, an initial on a bib or T-shirt, or spell out the baby's name for a framed piece. You can use floss in shades of any color of your choice.

Floss

Symbol	Color name	DMC#	Anchor#
•	Light pink	818	23
○	Medium pink	776	24
●	Dark pink	3688	66

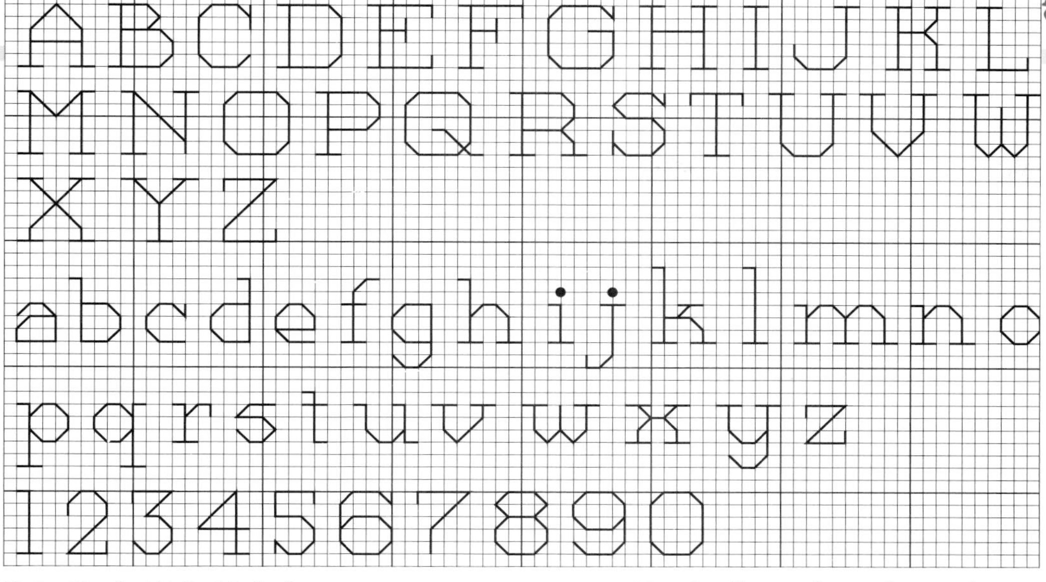

Baby Backstitch Alphabet Use the floss colors of your choice.

Ideas for Use

This is a handy alphabet to use for "signing" your cross-stitched pieces.

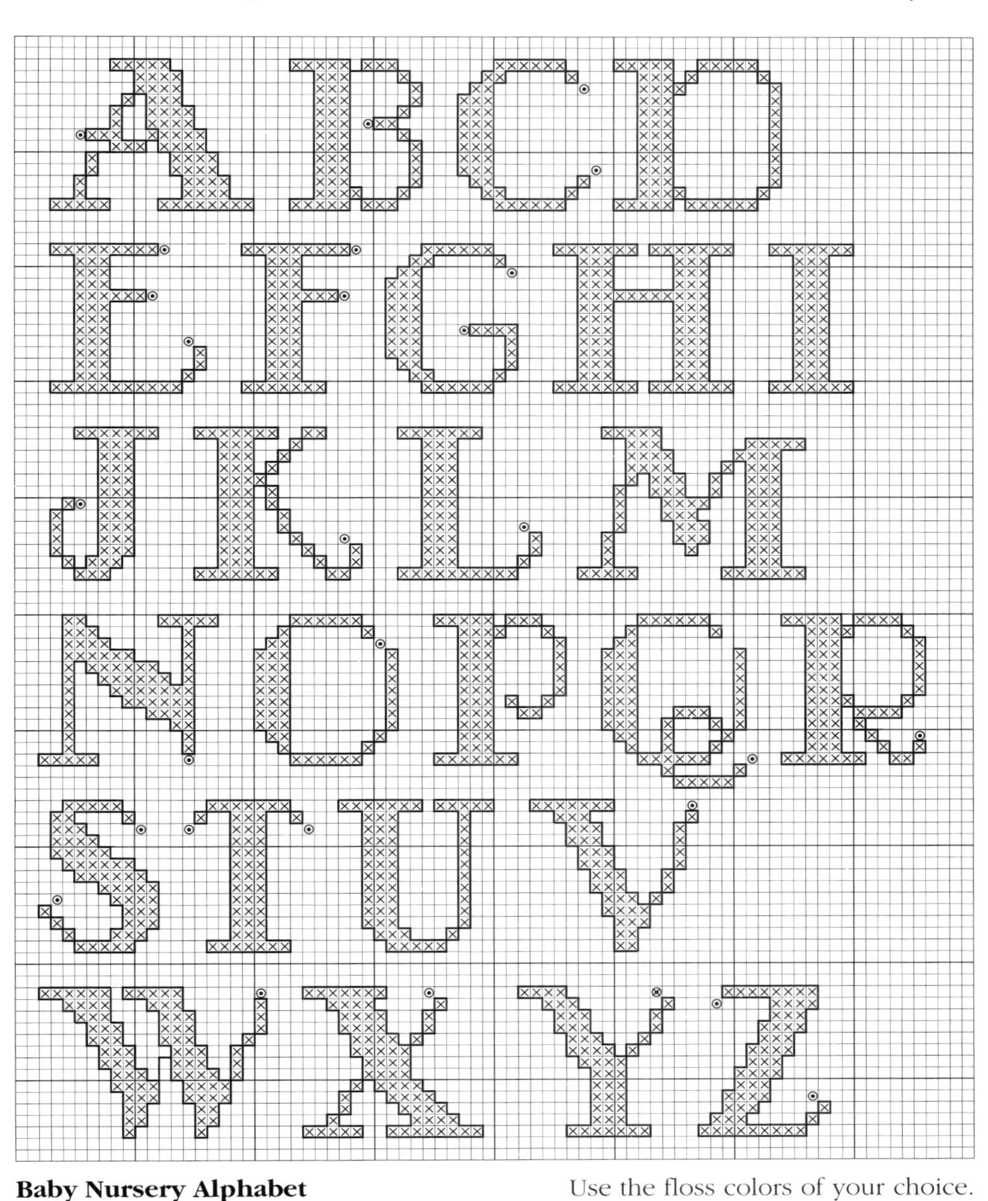

Baby Nursery Alphabet Use the floss colors of your choice.

⊙ French knots in color of your choice.

Ideas for Use

This is a small version of the large Baby Alphabet on page 163–172 used in the afghan. When spelling out a name, use the initial letter from the large alphabet and these smaller letters for the rest of the name.

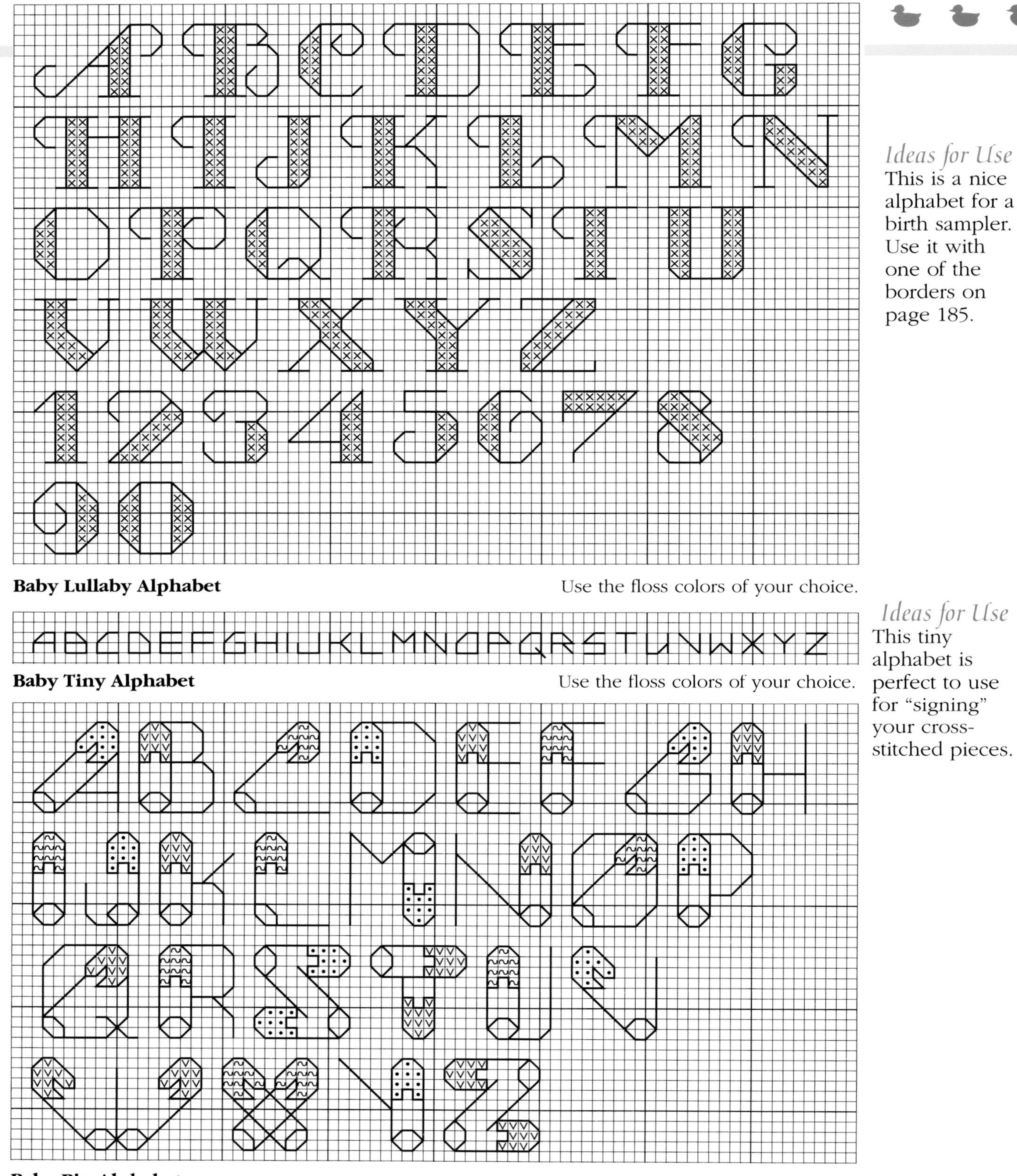

Baby Lullaby Alphabet

Use the floss colors of your choice.

Ideas for Use
This is a nice alphabet for a birth sampler. Use it with one of the borders on page 185.

Baby Tiny Alphabet

Use the floss colors of your choice.

Ideas for Use
This tiny alphabet is perfect to use for "signing" your cross-stitched pieces.

Baby Pin Alphabet

Note: When using this alphabet, decide what letters you will be using, then alternate floss colors accordingly.

Ideas for Use
This would be cute on a diaper bag.

Floss

Symbol	*Color name*	*DMC#*	*Anchor#*
•	Pink	818	23
∾	Yellow	3078	292
V	Blue	747	158
	Black*	310	403

*Backstitch in black (two strands).

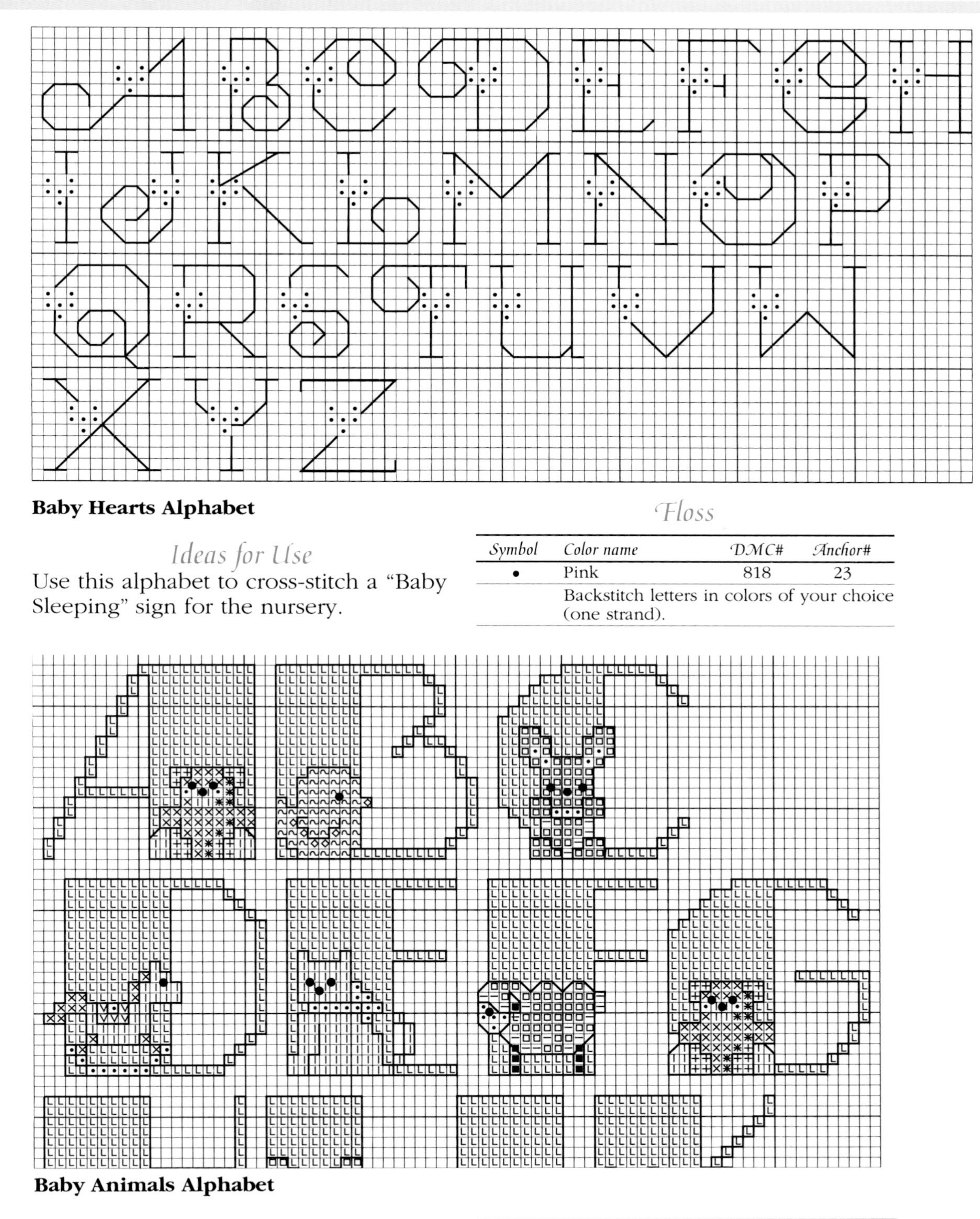

Baby Hearts Alphabet

Ideas for Use

Use this alphabet to cross-stitch a "Baby Sleeping" sign for the nursery.

Floss

Symbol	Color name	DMC#	Anchor#
•	Pink	818	23
	Backstitch letters in colors of your choice (one strand).		

Baby Animals Alphabet

Floss

Symbol	Color name	DMC#	Anchor#
□	White	Snow white	1
•	Pink	818	23
∾	Yellow	3078	292
◇	Gold	744	301
I	Beige	738	361
—	Gray	415	398
+	Light brown	436	1045
×	Medium brown	434	310
✳	Dark brown	433	371
L	Lavender	211	342
■	Black*	310	403
V	Blue	747	158

*Backstitch in black (one strand)
*Stitch black French knots for eyes and noses.

(continued)

Baby Animals Alphabet

Floss

Symbol	Color name	DMC#	Anchor#
□	White	Snow white	1
•	Pink	818	23
∾	Yellow	3078	292
◇	Gold	744	301
I	Beige	738	361
—	Gray	415	398
+	Light brown	436	1045
X	Medium brown	434	310
✱	Dark brown	433	371
L	Lavender	211	342
■	Black*	310	403
V	Blue	747	158

*Backstitch in black (one strand).
*Stitch black French knots for eyes and noses.

Ideas for Use

This alphabet would be perfect for cross-stitching on an afghan.

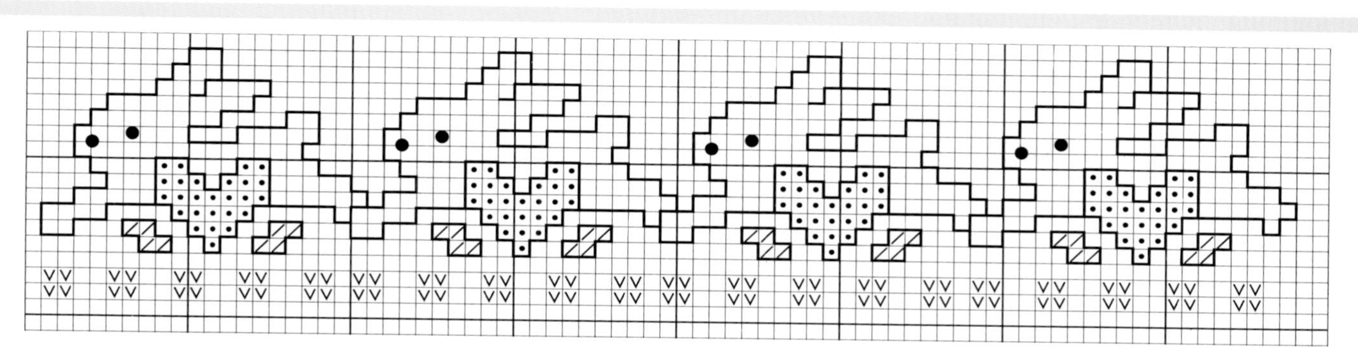

Baby Bunny Border

Baby Tiny Heart Border

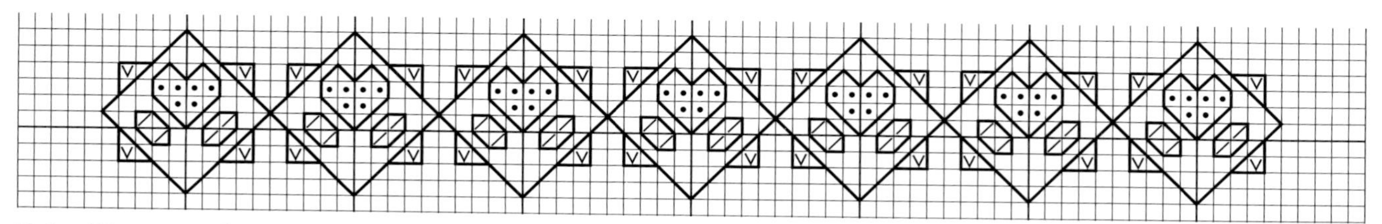

Baby Hearts and Diamonds Border

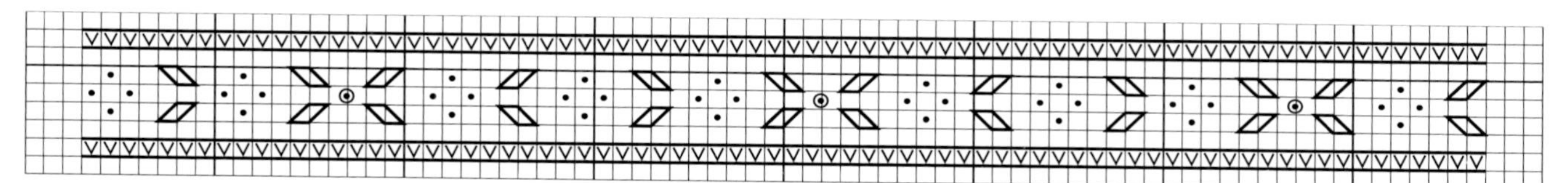

Baby Floral Border

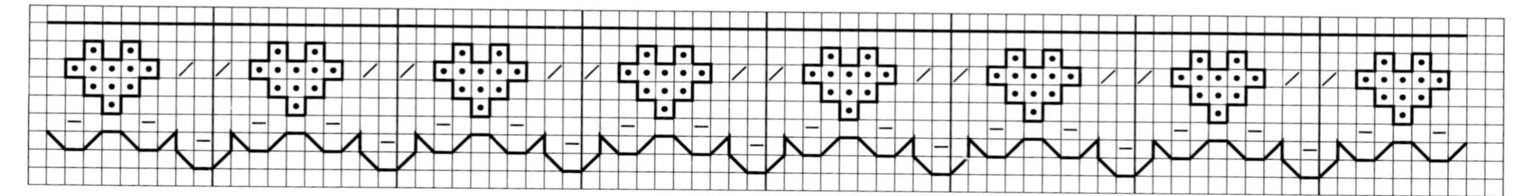

Baby Lace Border

Ideas for Using Baby Borders

These delightful borders can be used with waste canvas to stitch around the edge of a receiving blanket. Use them with any of the alphabets in this chapter for a birth sampler. Or, trim baby clothes for a layette.

Floss

Symbol	*Color name*	*DMC#*	*Anchor#*
•	Pink*	3688	66
—	Gray	415	398
/	Green	368	214
V	Light blue	747	158
	Medium blue****	598	167
	Dark gray**	413	401
	Dark green***	320	216
⊙	Pink French knots*		

*Stitch pink French knots for rabbit's nose and eyes. Backstitch hearts in pink (one strand).
**Backstitch rabbits in dark gray (one strand). Backstitch lace in Lace Border in dark gray (one strand).
***Backstitch leaves in dark green (one strand).
****Backstitch lines around hearts in Hearts and Diamonds Border in medium blue (one strand).

Kids Alphabets

All aboard! Brightly colored letters on tiny flatbed cars roll right along on this moving afghan. The husky engine pulls all the letters, and the classic caboose brings up the rear. Use this train motif to "haul" a child's name across decorative items for his or her room or a closet full of wearables.

All-Aboard Afghan

USE KIDS' TRAIN ALPHABET ON PAGES 191–195

Materials

Anne cloth: White, 28x45 inches (Leisure Arts)

Stitch

Follow the instructions for cross-stitching over two threads and for cross-stitching on an afghan given in Cross-Stitch Basics.

Finish

After cross-stitching is complete, cut off selvage edge. Machine-stitch right next to decorative bars. (If desired, zigzag-stitch over two threads). Carefully pull out threads right up to machine stitching.

Pillowcase

USE KIDS' TRAIN ALPHABET ON PAGES 191–195

Materials

Pillowcase: Premade, white, 14 count (Designs for the Needle)

Stitch

Choose letters to spell child's name. Colors may be substituted accordingly. Follow instructions for cross-stitching given in Cross-Stitch Basics.

Finish

The premade pillowcase requires no finishing.

Floss

Symbol	Color name	DMC#	Anchor#	Skeins
○	Pink	603	57	2
◇	Yellow	742	303	2
I	Flesh	754	6	1
◺	Light lavender	211	342	1
L	Dark lavender	208	110	3
/	Green**	911	205	2
V	Blue	799	145	2
♡	Red	321	9046	2
■	Black*	310	403	1

*Backstitch in black where indicated (one strand).
**Backstitch stem of flower on hat in green (two strands).

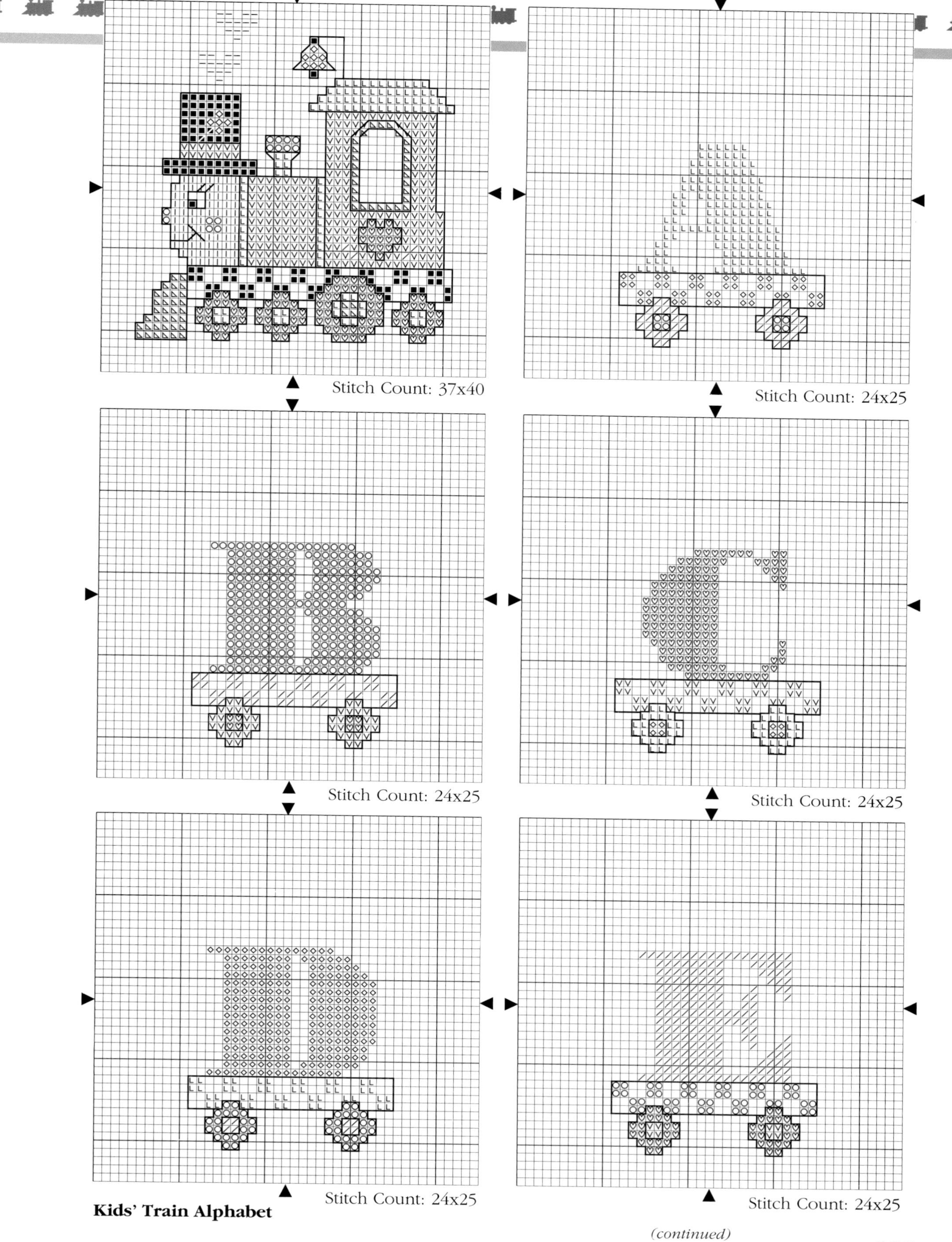

Stitch Count: 37x40

Stitch Count: 24x25

Stitch Count: 24x25

Stitch Count: 24x25

Stitch Count: 24x25

Stitch Count: 24x25

Kids' Train Alphabet

(continued)

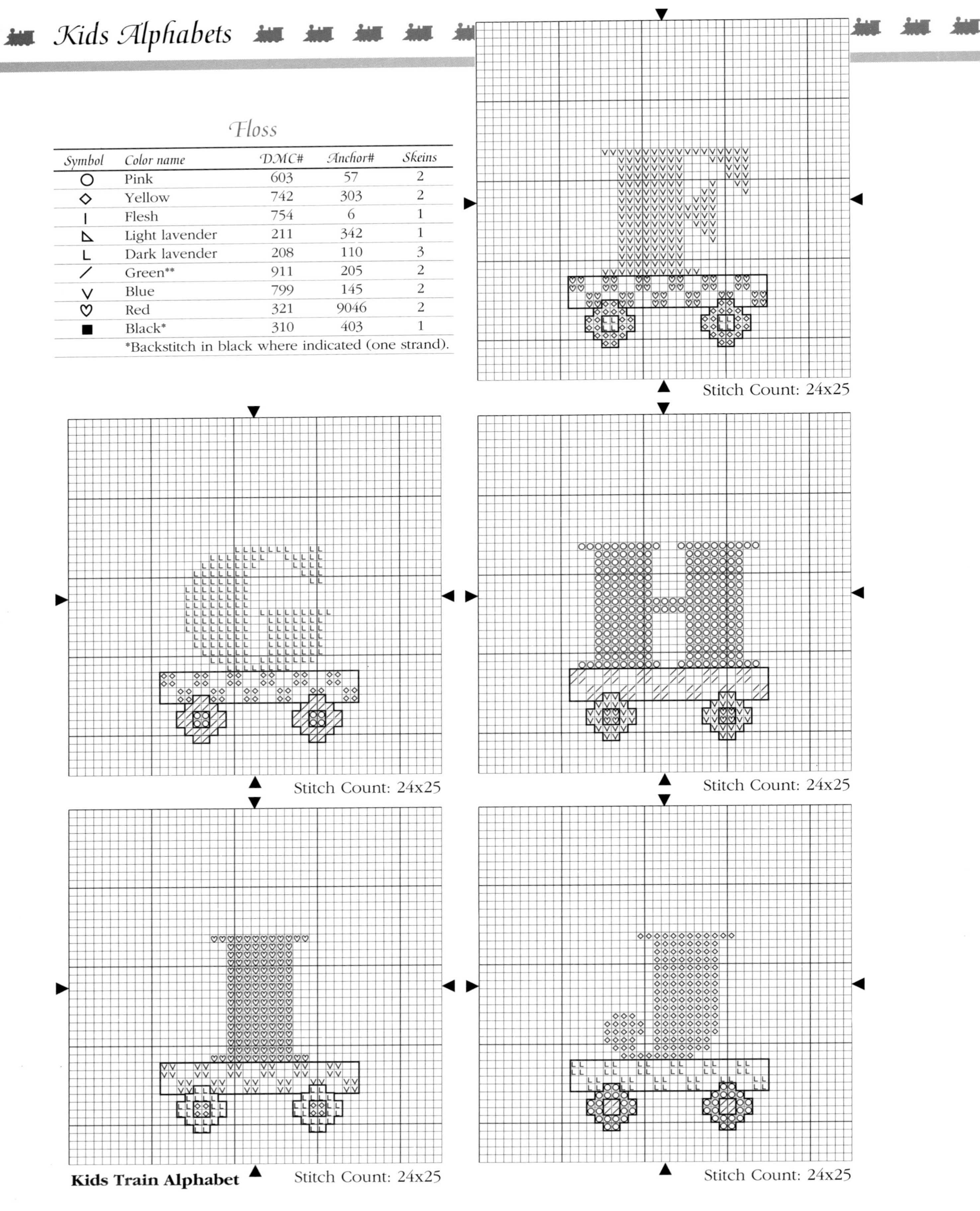

Floss

Symbol	Color name	DMC#	Anchor#	Skeins
○	Pink	603	57	2
◇	Yellow	742	303	2
I	Flesh	754	6	1
◺	Light lavender	211	342	1
L	Dark lavender	208	110	3
/	Green**	911	205	2
V	Blue	799	145	2
♡	Red	321	9046	2
■	Black*	310	403	1

*Backstitch in black where indicated (one strand).

Stitch Count: 24x25

Stitch Count: 24x25

Stitch Count: 24x25

Kids Train Alphabet

Stitch Count: 24x25

Stitch Count: 24x25

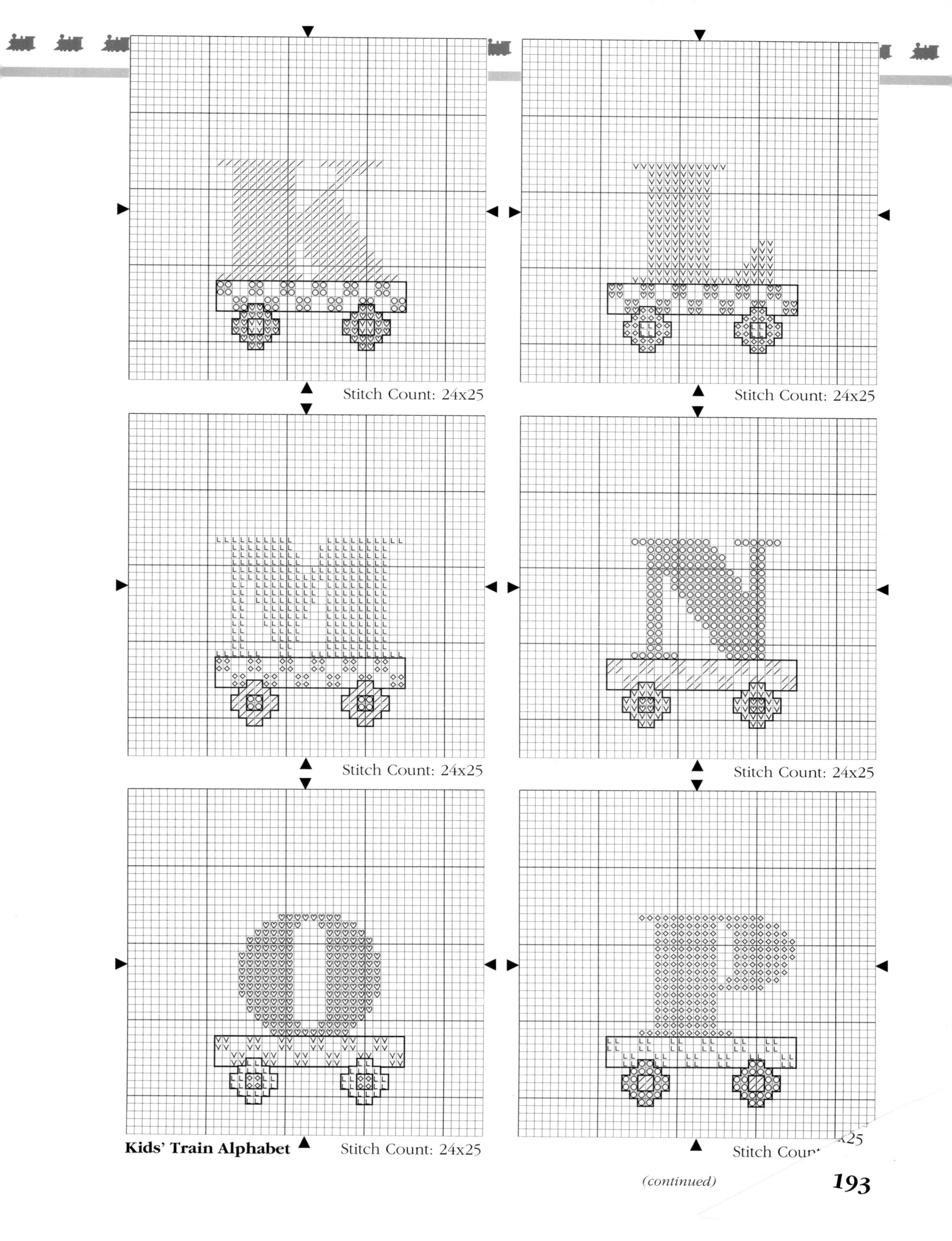
Stitch Count: 24x25
Stitch Count: 24x25
Stitch Count: 24x25
Stitch Count: 24x25
Stitch Count: 24x25

(continued)

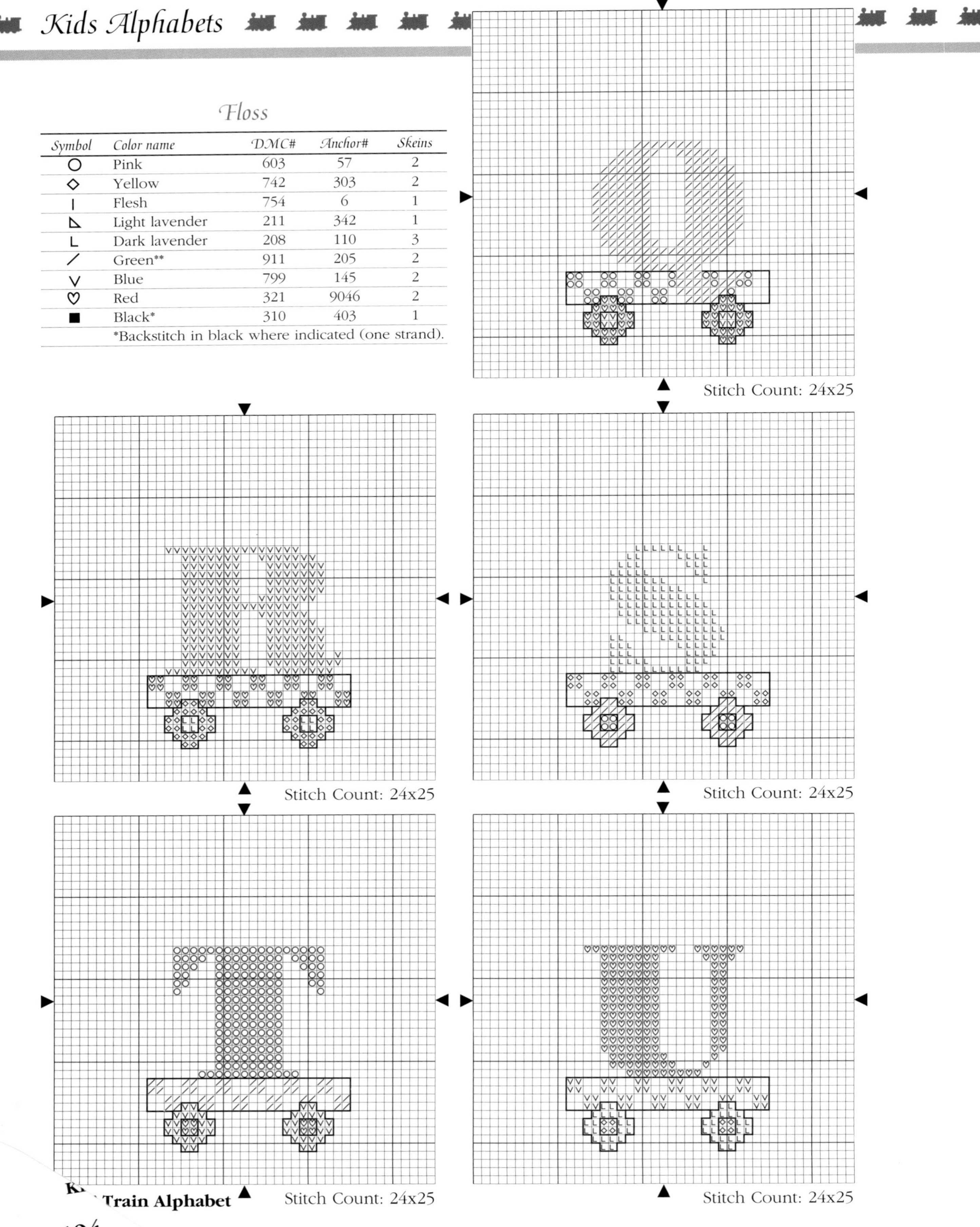

Floss

Symbol	Color name	DMC#	Anchor#	Skeins
○	Pink	603	57	2
◇	Yellow	742	303	2
|	Flesh	754	6	1
◺	Light lavender	211	342	1
L	Dark lavender	208	110	3
/	Green**	911	205	2
V	Blue	799	145	2
♡	Red	321	9046	2
■	Black*	310	403	1
	*Backstitch in black where indicated (one strand).			

Stitch Count: 24x25

Stitch Count: 24x25

Stitch Count: 24x25

Stitch Count: 24x25

Stitch Count: 24x25

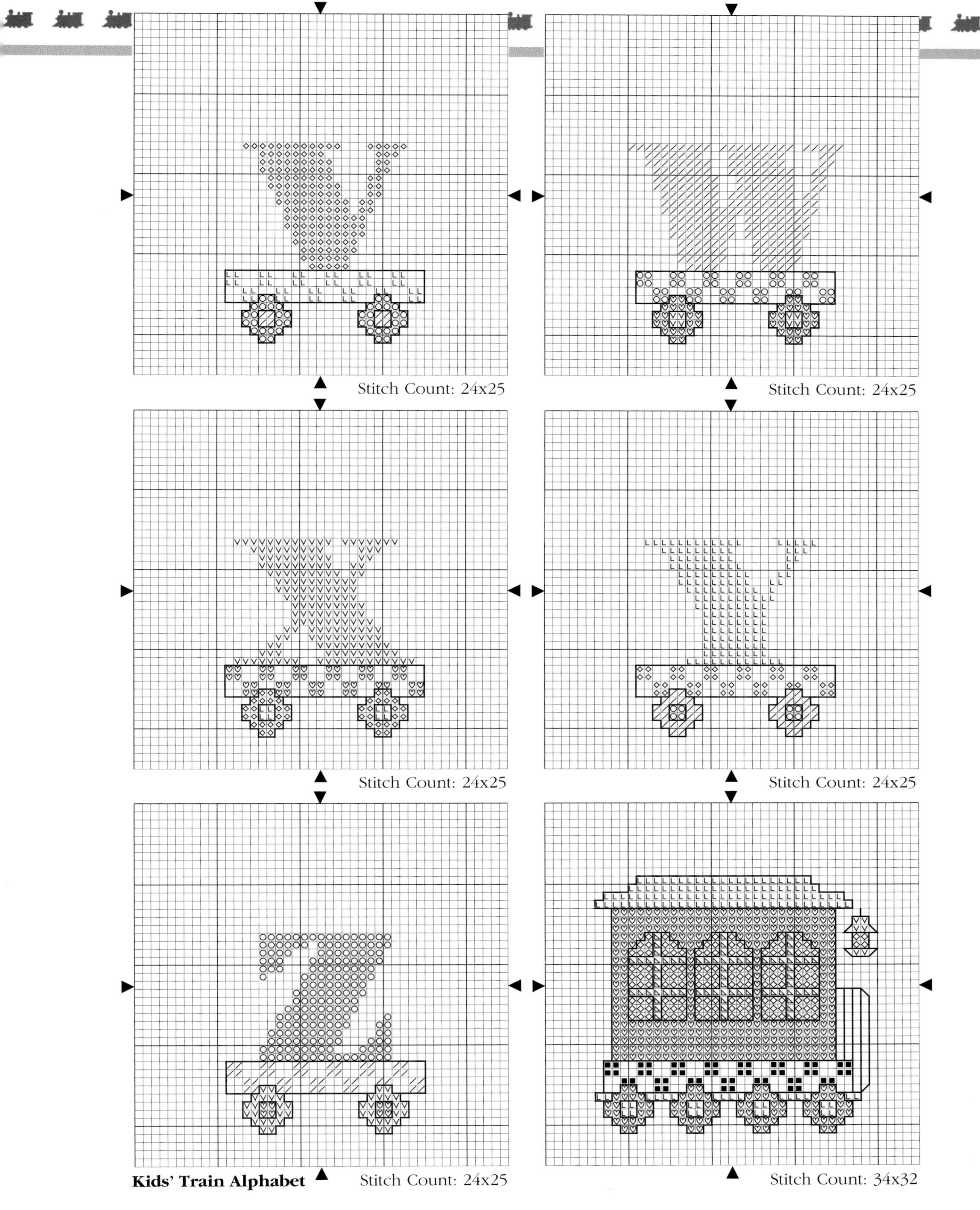

Kids' Train Alphabet

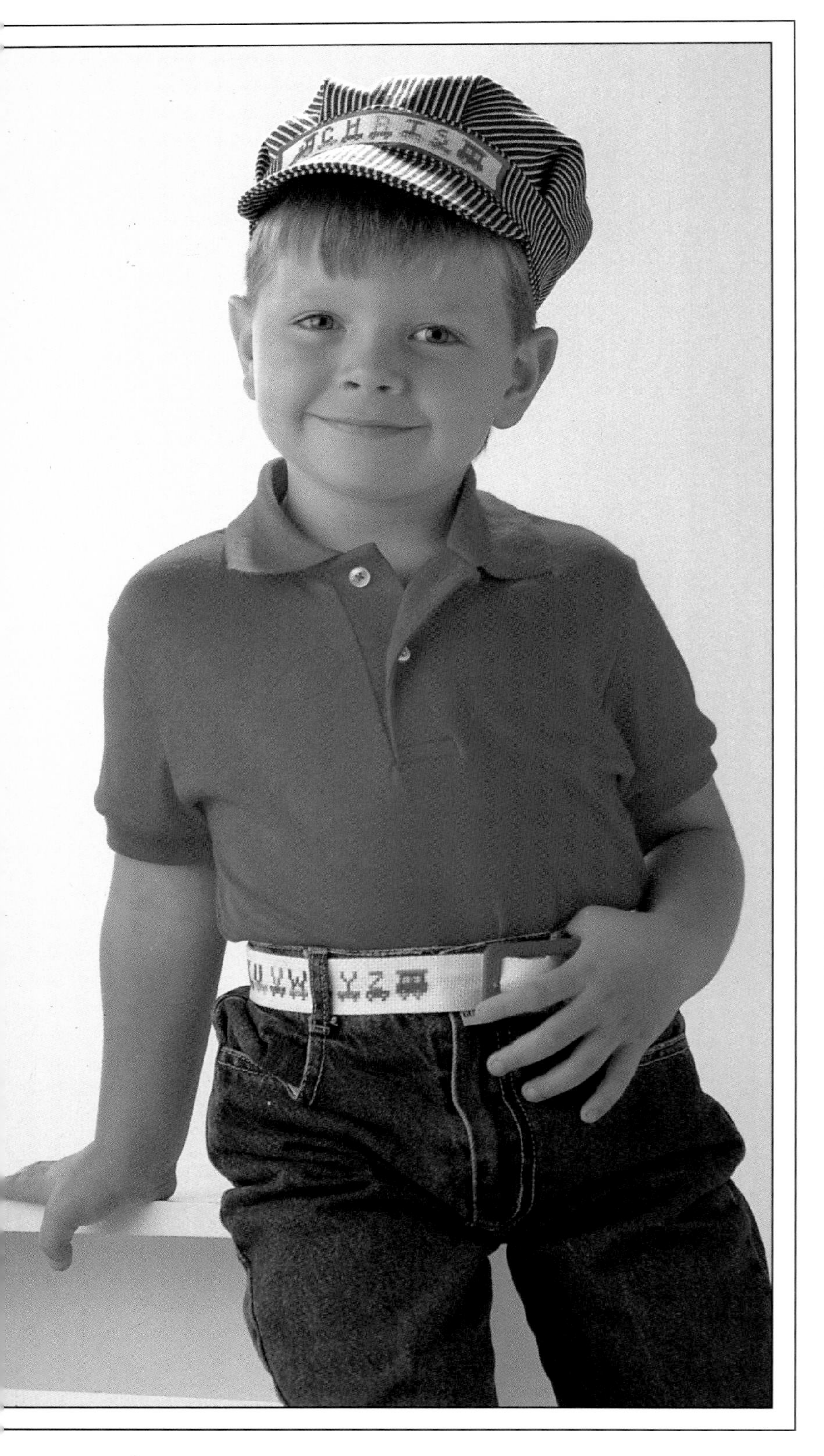

Conductor's Hat

USE TINY TRAIN ALPHABET ON PAGE 197

Materials

Hat: Child's conductor's hat (Lillian Vernon catalog) or denim cap
Aida fabric: White, 14 count, 2x7 inches
Satin ribbon: Red, 1/8 inch wide, 26 inches
Fabric glue

Stitch

Follow the instructions for cross-stitching given in Cross-Stitch Basics.

Finish

Trim cross-stitched fabric to fit hat; hem. Spread thin layer of fabric glue on back of fabric. Glue to hat. Glue ribbon around edge of cross-stitched fabric.

Conductor's Belt

USE TINY TRAIN ALPHABET BELOW

Materials

Aida fabric: White, 14 count, 2¼x26 inches (or fit waist measurement)
Belt buckle kit: Dritz
Cotton fabric: Red, 4x4 inches
Ribbon: Red, 1x24 inches (or to fit waist measurement)

Stitch

Belt was made to fit a Size 2. The alphabet, engine, and caboose cover 19 inches of the fabric.

Cross-stitch the train alphabet border centered on the strip of fabric. If you're making a belt larger than specified, begin cross-stitching the engine about 2½ inches from the end of the fabric. Stop stitching at the middle of the alphabet (M). Start stitching the caboose at the other end of the fabric and cross-stitch the last 13 letters. This will give you an empty space in the middle to stitch in a name, using the letters from this alphabet.

Finish

After cross-stitching, hem long edges about ½ inch and each short end about ¼ inch. Glue or sew 1-inch-wide red ribbon on back.

Follow the manufacturer's instructions for completing the belt and the buckle.

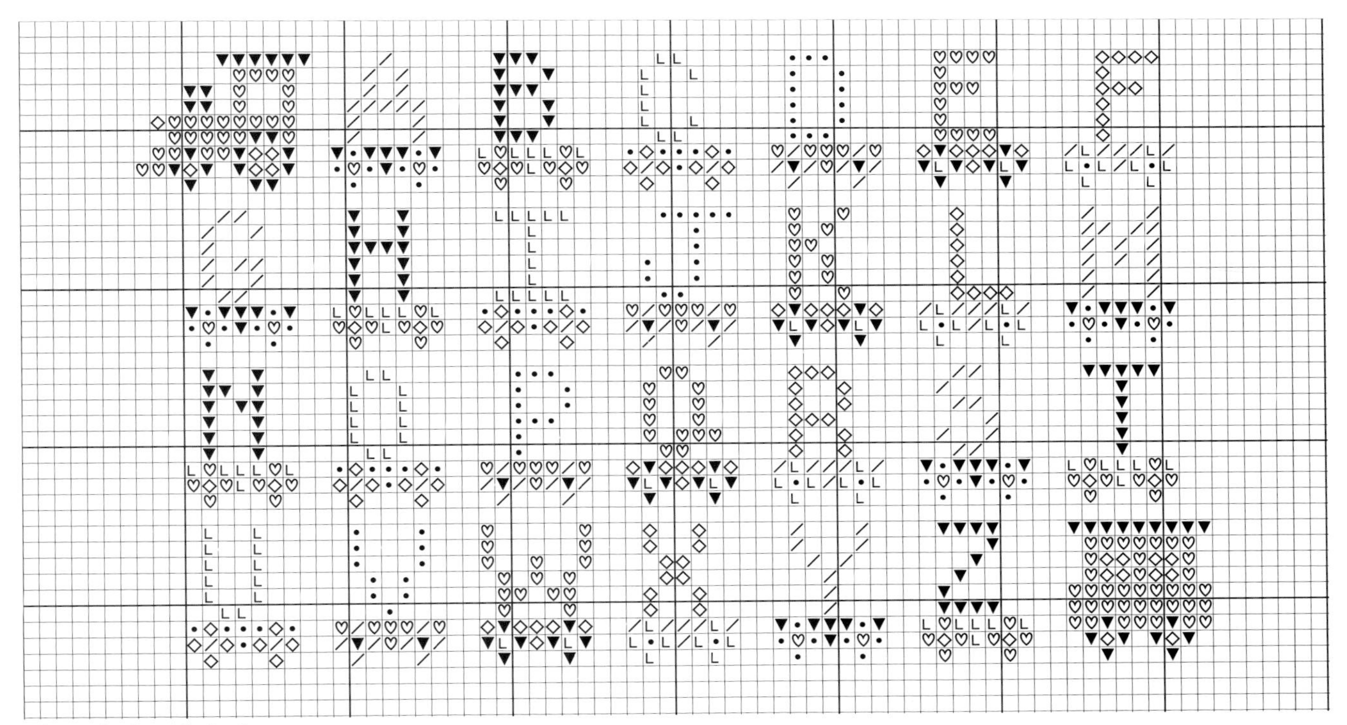

Tiny Train Alphabet

Floss

Symbol	Color name	DMC#	Anchor#
•	Pink	603	57
◇	Yellow	742	303
L	Lavender	211	342
/	Green	911	205
▼	Blue	799	145
♡	Red	321	9046

Mug

USE RUBBER DUCKY ALPHABET ON PAGE 199

Materials

Mug: Stitch-A-Mug (Crafter's Pride #30100W), with 14-count vinyl Aida insert

Satin ribbon: Blue, ⅓ inch wide, 20 inches

Stitch

Follow the instructions for cross-stitching given in Cross-Stitch Basics.

Finish

After cross-stitching, glue ribbon four stitches above and below design. Insert vinyl Aida into mug according to manufacturer's instructions.

Floss

Symbol	Color name	DMC#	Anchor#
◇	Yellow	742	303
◆	Orange	971	316
▼	Blue	799	145
♡	Red	321	9046
■	Black	310	403
	Backstitch wheels and around ducks' eyes in black (one strand).		

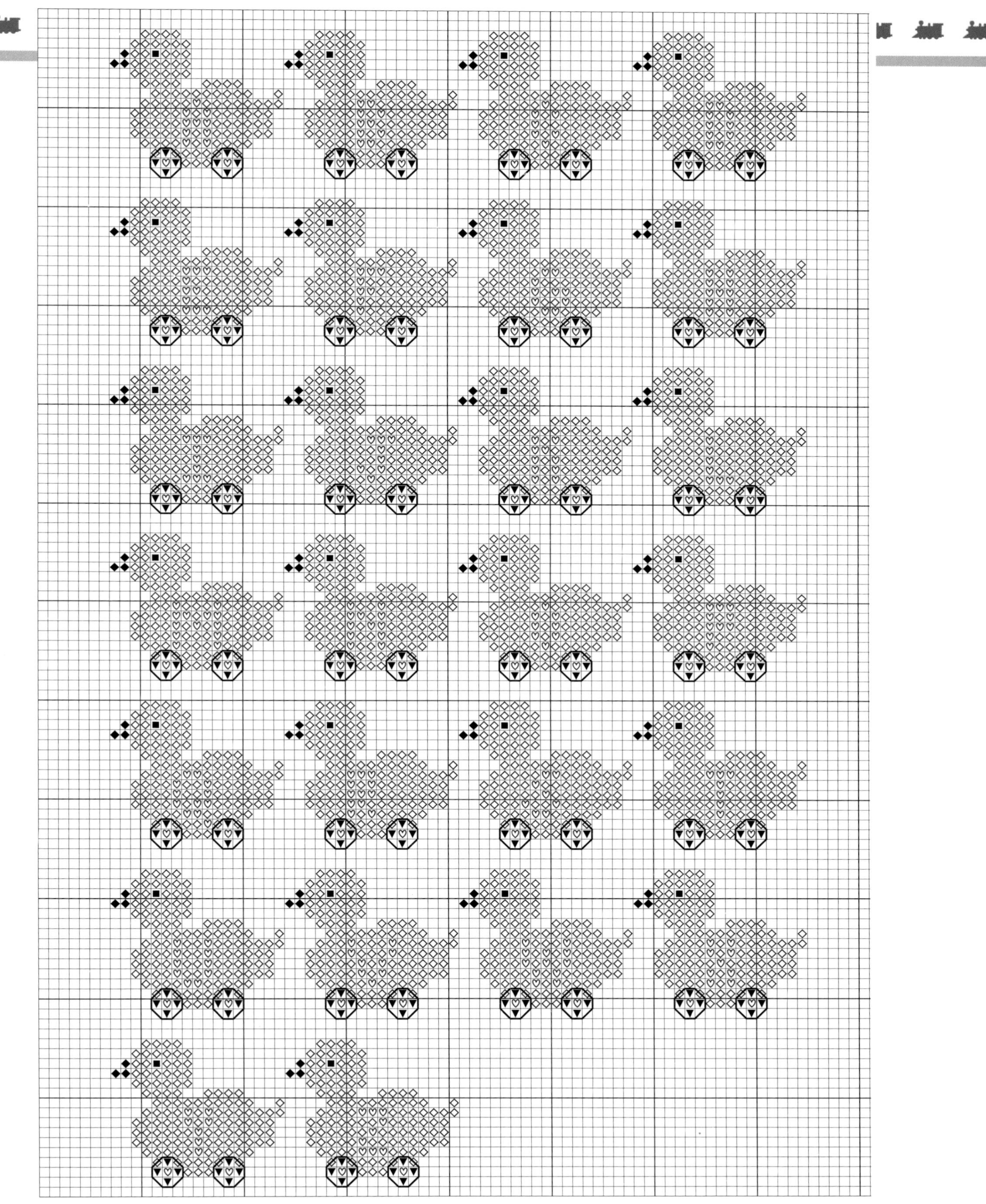

Rubber Ducky Alphabet

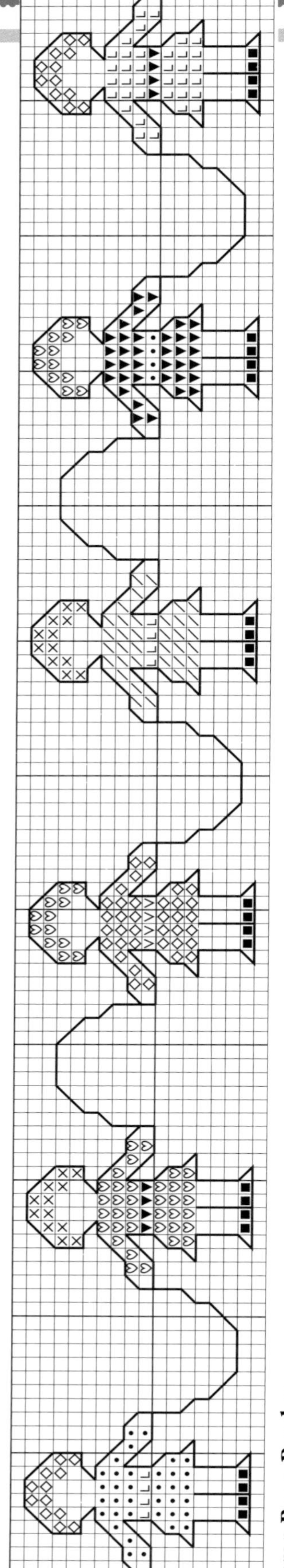

Jump Rope Border

Tote Bag

USE JUMP ROPE BORDER AT LEFT

Materials

Tote bag: Red, 13x14 inches
Ribband®: White, 2x27 inches, 18 count (The Finish Line)
Rickrack: Blue, 56 inches
Fabric glue

Stitch

Follow the instructions for cross-stitching given in Cross-Stitch Basics.

Finish

After cross-stitching, glue or sew band to tote bag about 1 inch from top. Glue or sew rickrack above and below the cross-stitched band for a border.

Floss

Symbol	Color name	DMC#	Anchor#
•	Light pink	605	60
◇	Yellow	742	303
L	Lavender	211	342
/	Green	911	205
V	Light blue	794	175
▶	Medium blue	799	145
♡	Red	321	904
×	Brown	435	1046
■	Black*	310	403

*Backstitch in black (one strand).
*Backstitch rope in black (two strands).

Flamingo T-shirt

USE LETTERS FROM FLAMINGO ALPHABET ON PAGES 203–204 TO SPELL THE NAME OF YOUR CHOICE

Note: If stitching a longer name, use smaller-size waste canvas, such as 14 count.

Materials

Child's T-shirt
Waste canvas: 8.5 count, 4x9 inches
Chenille needle: Size 24

Stitch and Finish

Follow the instructions for cross-stitching using waste canvas given in Cross-Stitch Basics.

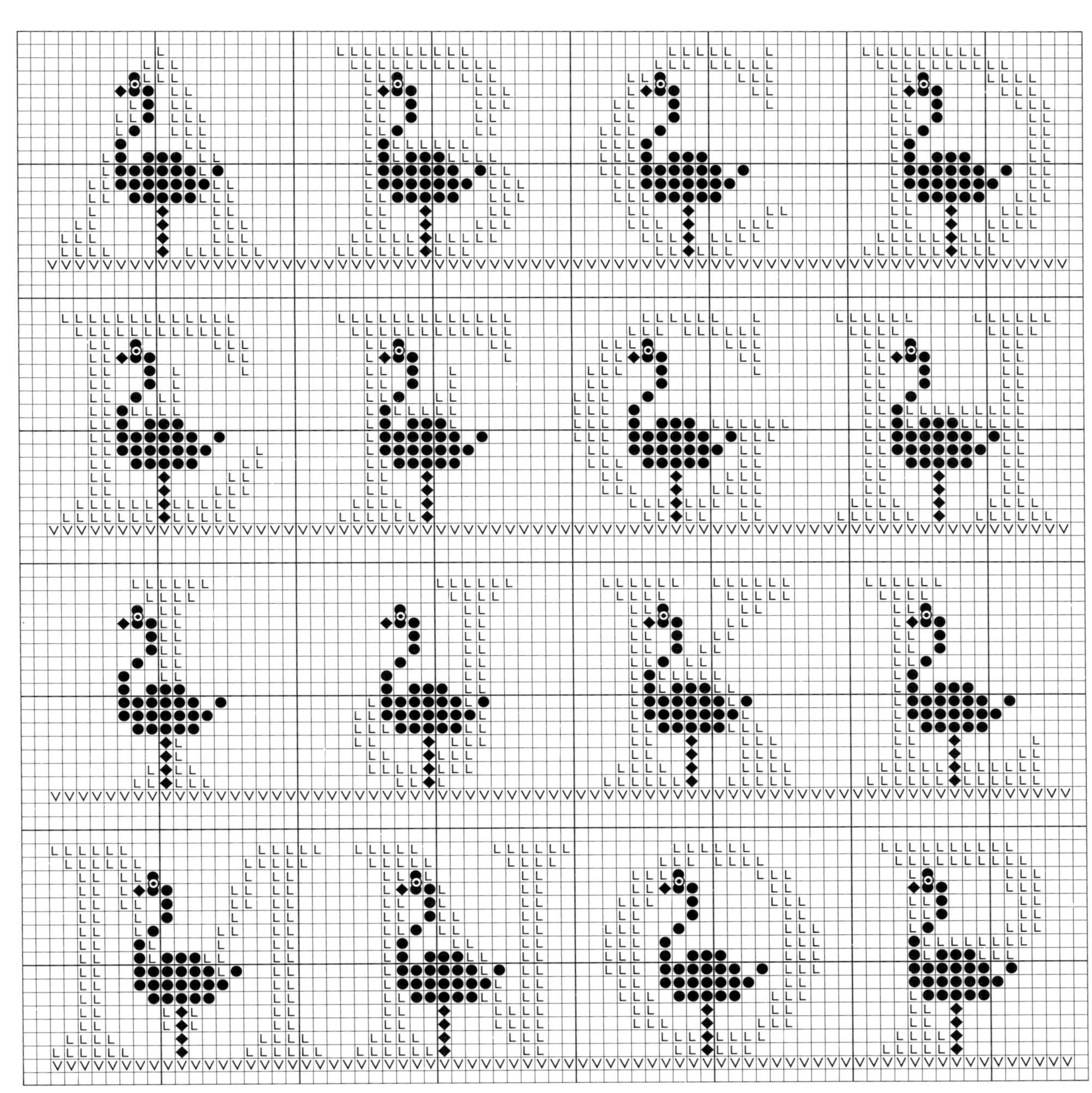

Flamingo Alphabet

Ideas for Other Uses

Try this alphabet on an Anne cloth afghan. Use flamingoes without letters for the empty squares.

Floss

Symbol	Color name	DMC#	Anchor#
●	Pink	603	57
L	Lavender	208	110
V	Blue	799	145
◆	Yellow	742	303
	Black*	310	403
	*Use black French knots for eyes.		

(continued)

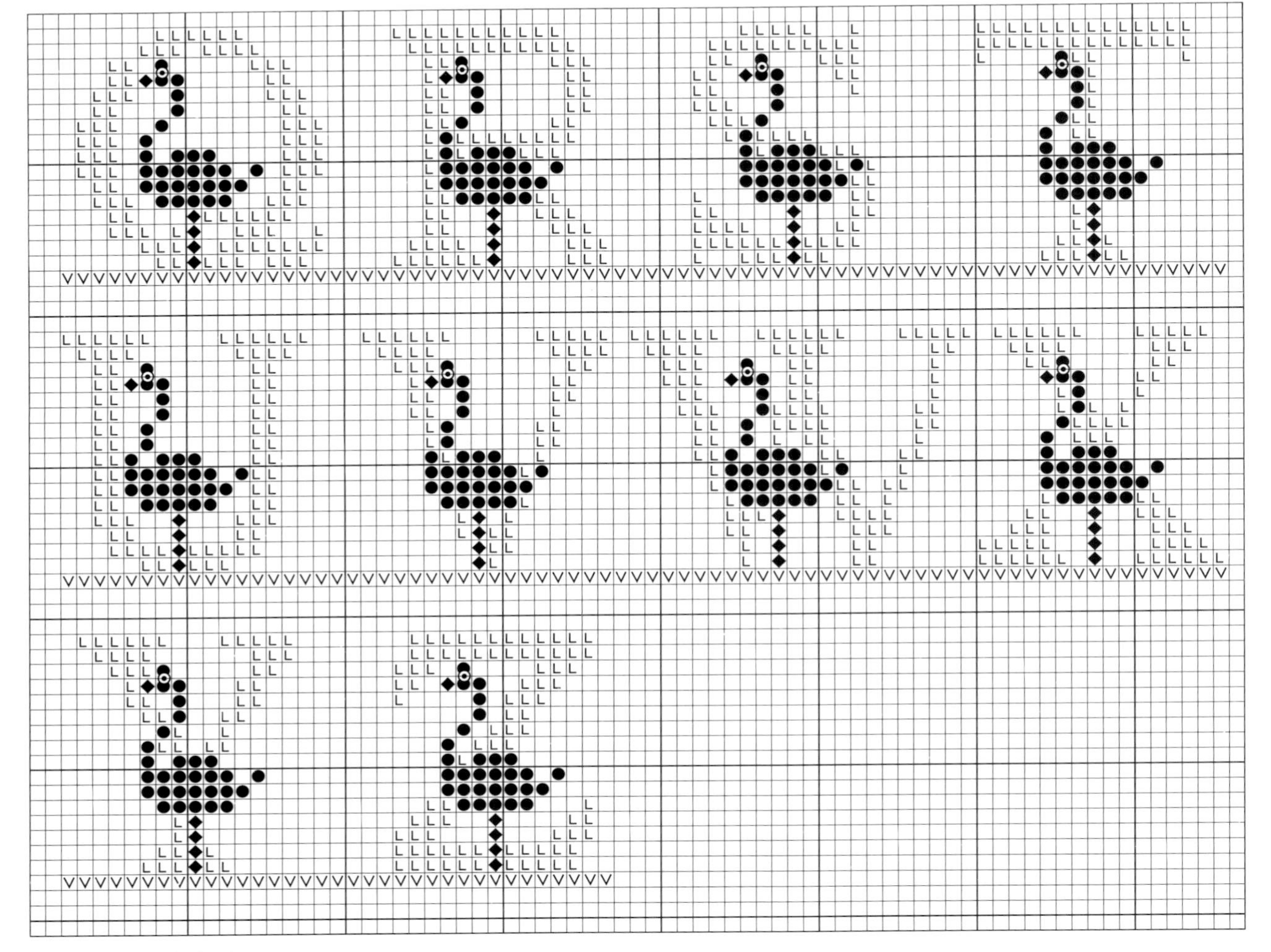

Flamingo Alphabet

Floss

Symbol	Color name	DMC#	Anchor#
●	Pink	603	57
L	Lavender	208	110
V	Blue	799	145
◆	Yellow	742	303
	Black*	310	403
	*Use black French knots for eyes.		

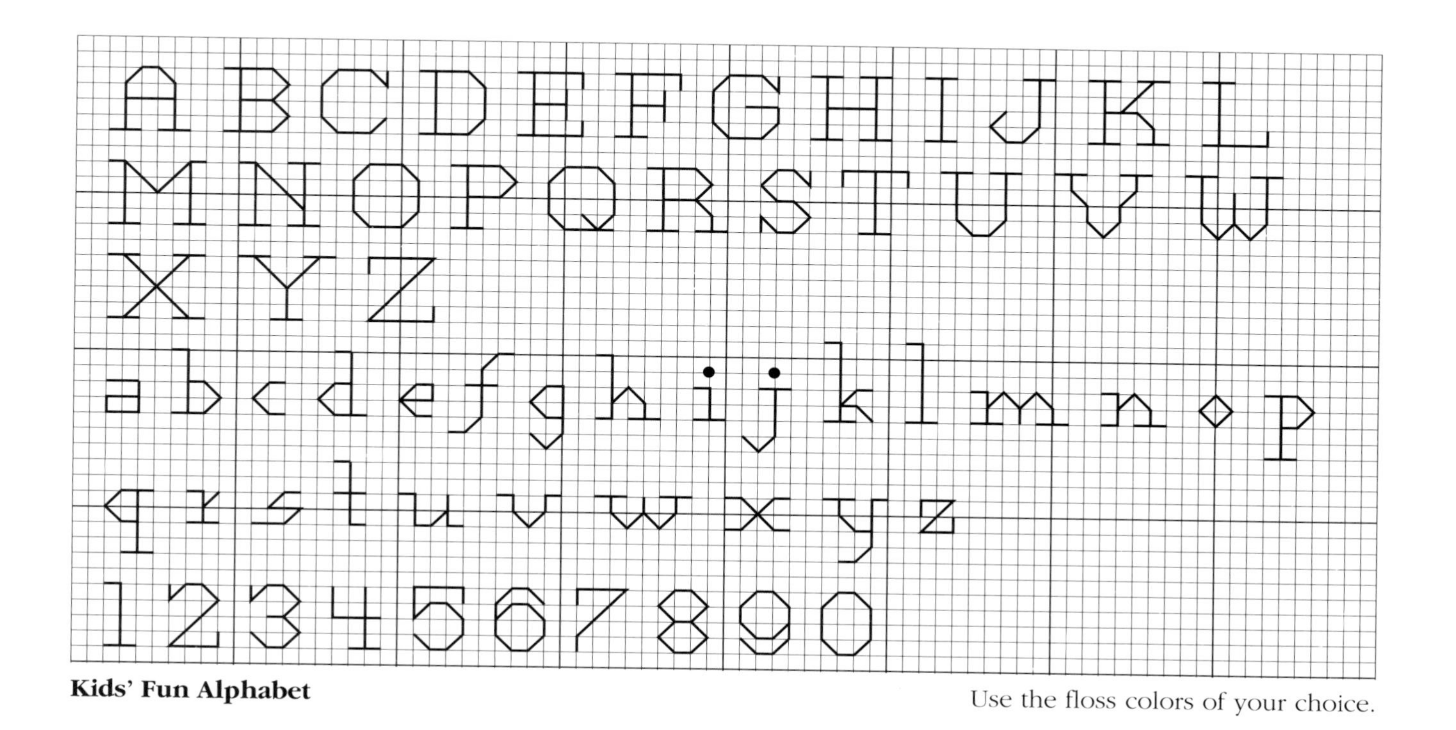

Kids' Fun Alphabet

Use the floss colors of your choice.

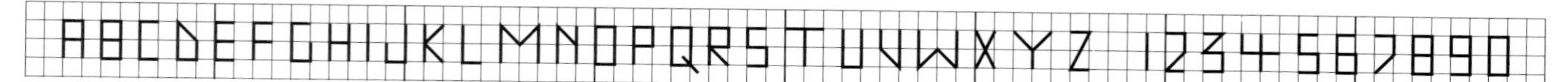

Kids' Mini Alphabet

Use the floss colors of your choice.

Ideas for Use

Use both of these alphabets for personalizing items such as towels, hats, photo frames, album covers, and framed items.

Balloon Alphabet

Floss

Symbol	Color name	DMC#	Anchor#
○	Pink	603	57
∾	Yellow	742	303
L	Lavender	211	342
/	Green	911	205
V	Blue	799	145
♡	Red	321	9046
	Black*	310	403

*Backstitch balloon strings in black (one strand).

Balloon Alphabet

(continued)

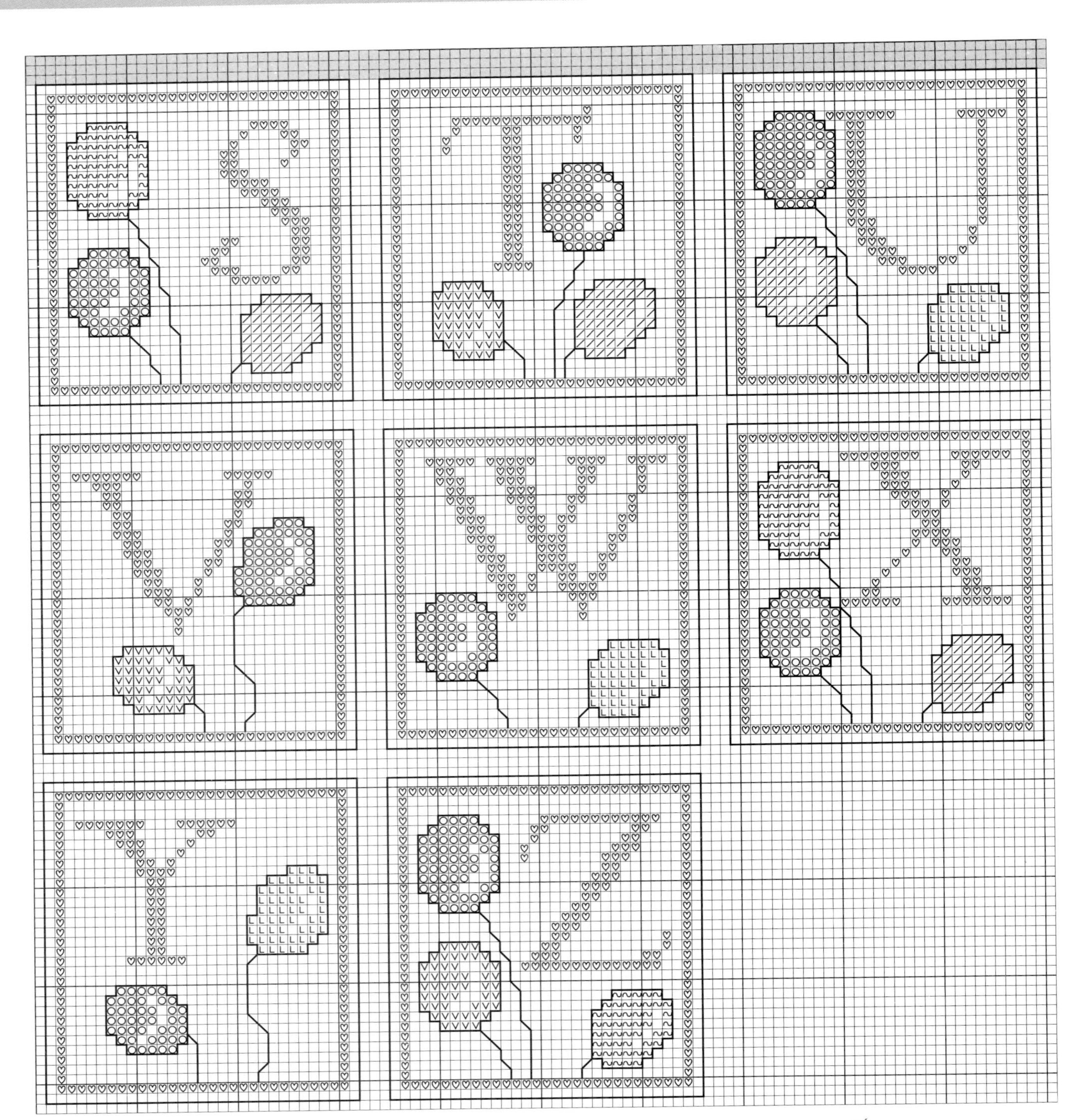

Balloon Alphabet

Ideas for Use

Use these letters to spell out a child's name for a door sign or a framed room sign.

Use the complete alphabet for afghan using Anne cloth. Fill empty squares with balloons only.

Floss

Symbol	Color name	DMC#	Anchor#
O	Pink	603	57
∾	Yellow	742	303
L	Lavender	211	342
/	Green	911	205
V	Blue	799	145
♡	Red	321	9046
	Black*	310	403

*Backstitch balloon strings in black (one strand).

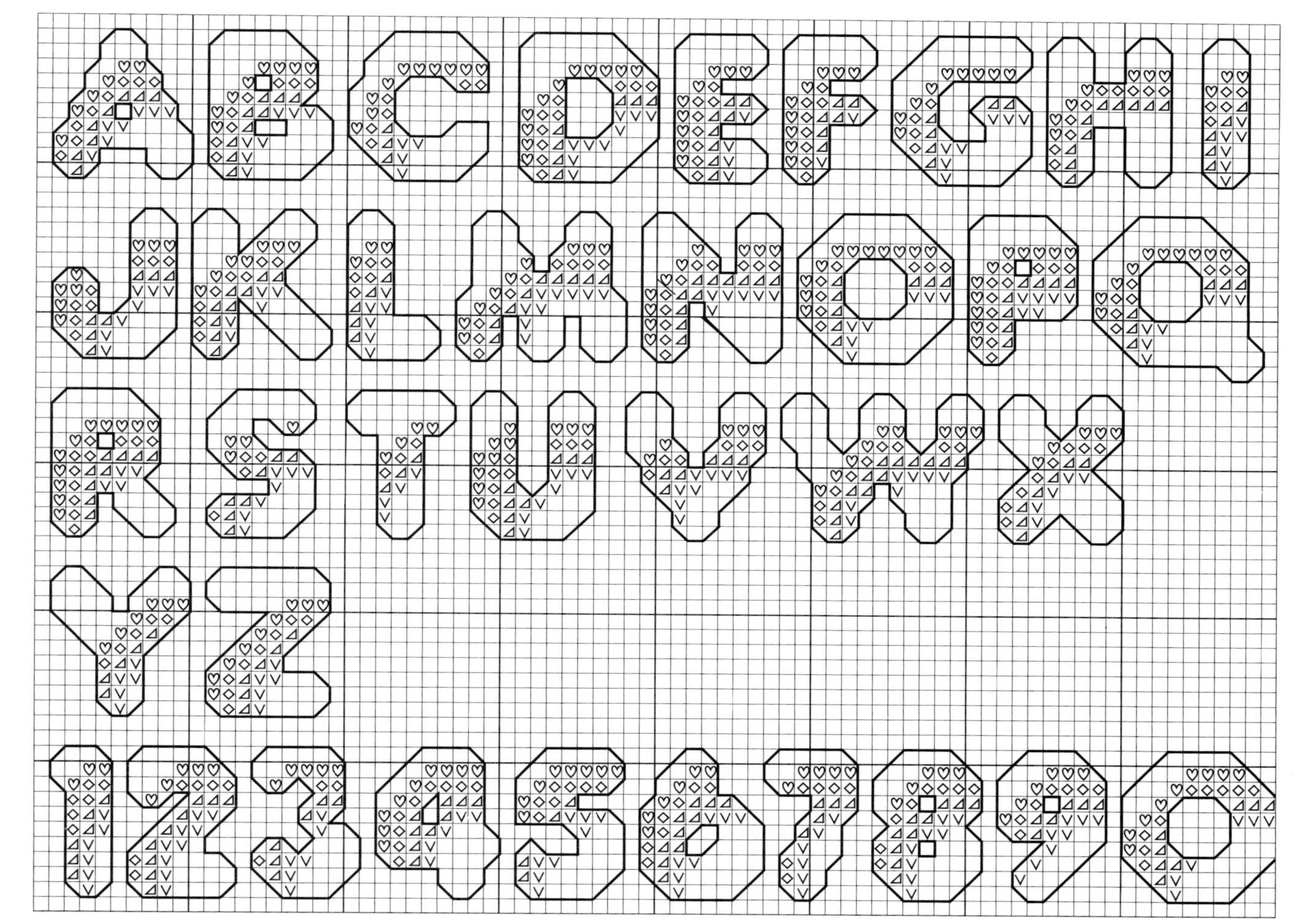

Rainbow Alphabet

Ideas for Use

Spell out a child's name with this alphabet on a T-shirt using waste canvas.

Or, make a birth sampler with name and date of birth. Have it framed with a colorful frame and mat that brings out one of the floss colors used.

Floss

Symbol	Color name	DMC#	Anchor#
◇	Yellow	742	303
⊿	Green	911	205
V	Blue	799	145
♡	Red	321	9046
	Black*	310	403
	*Outline letters and numbers in black (one strand).		

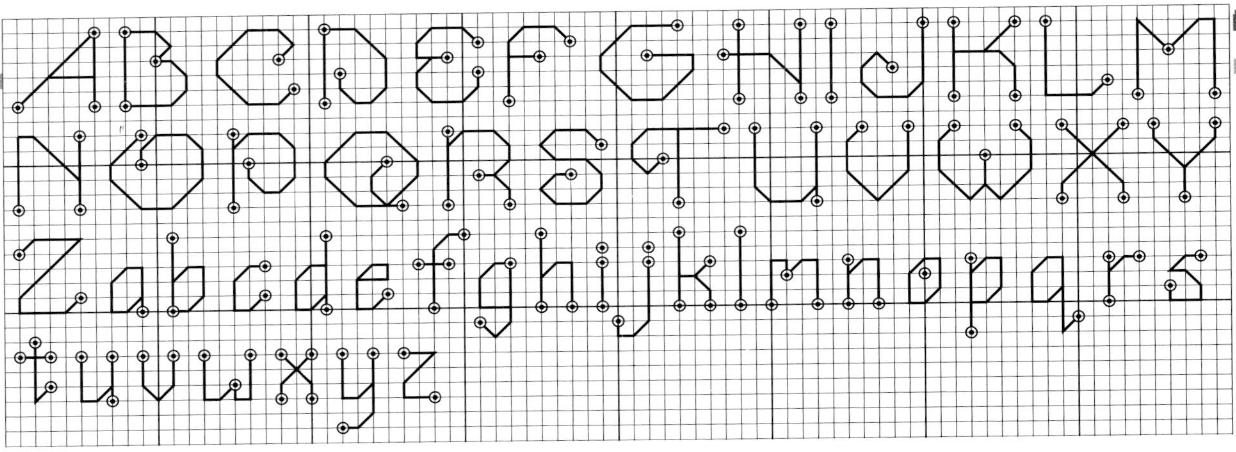

Kids' Dot Alphabet

⊙ French knots in colors of your choice.

Use the floss colors of your choice.

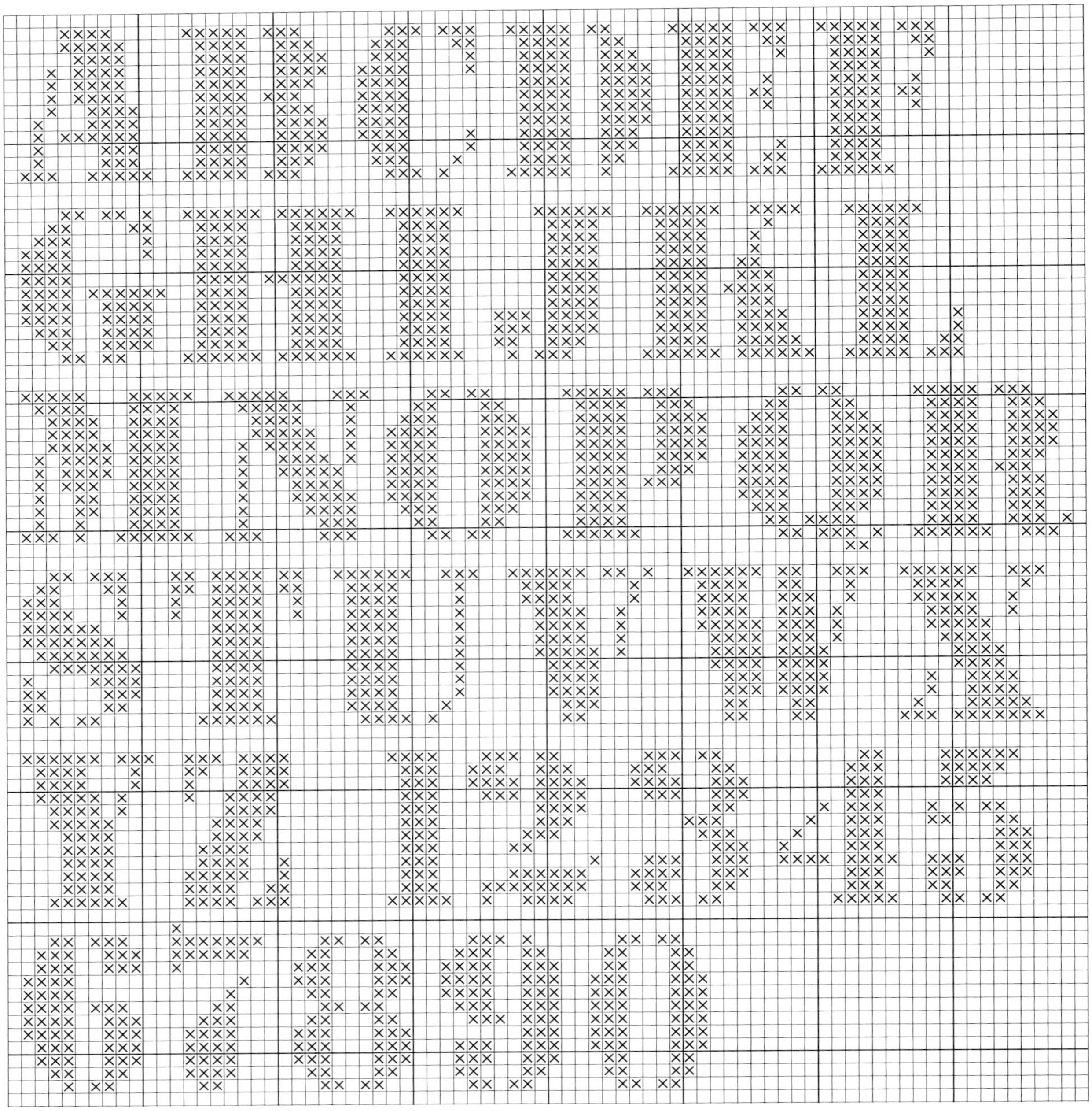

Kids' Stencil Alphabet

Use the floss colors of your choice.

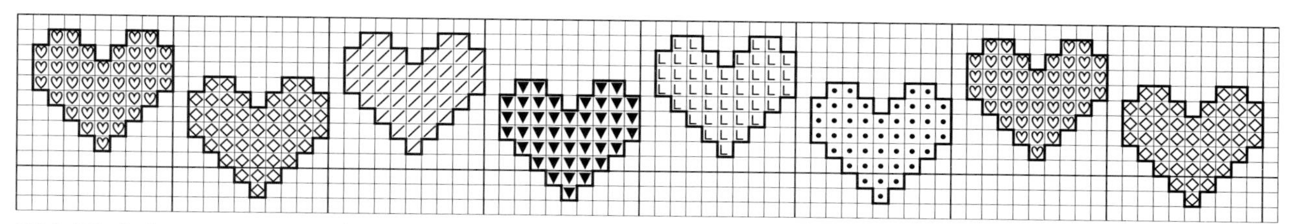

Kids' Rainbow Heart Border

Ideas for Use

Use the Heart Border all around a pillow and stitch a name in the center.

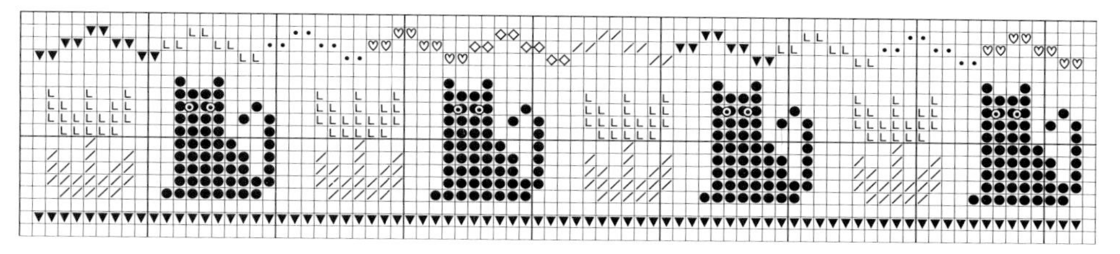

Ideas for Use

The Cat Border can be cross-stitched on the top of overalls using waste canvas.

Kids' Cats and Flowers Border

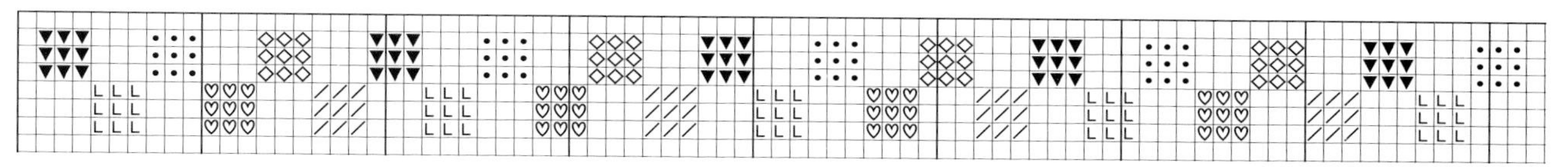

Kids' Checkerboard Border

Ideas for Use

The Checkerboard Border can be stitched with any of the alphabets to add interest to a mug, towel, tote, or sampler.

Kids' Paper Doll Border

Ideas for Use

This Paper Doll Border would be cute surrounding a mug, across a towel, or on a T-shirt (using waste canvas).

Floss for Borders

Symbol	Color name	DMC#	Anchor#
•	Light pink	605	60
●	Dark pink	603	57
◇	Yellow	742	303
L	Lavender	211	342
/	Green	911	205
V	Light blue	794	175
▼	Medium blue	799	145
♡	Red	321	904
■	Black*	310	403

*Backstitch in black (one strand).

Animal Alphabets

Old Noah would have been impressed with this captivating collection of alphabetized animals. All are stitched on a delightful, quilted wall hanging that is embellished with festive ribbons. That's just the beginning of our ark full of creative projects. A T-shirt sporting a child's initial, name, or fanciful Noah's ark motif is sure to become a favorite. And what better way to remind little ones to wash their hands than to give them their own personalized towel.

Quilted Animal Wall Hanging

USE ANIMAL ALPHABET ON PAGES 218–223

Materials

Aida fabric: 14 count, white, 11x17½ inches
Cotton print fabric: 1 piece, 1½x19½ inches (lining); 2 strips, each 2x17½ inches; 2 strips, each 2x13½ inches; 3 strips, each 4x6 inches
Batting: ¼ inch thick, 13x18 inches
Satin ribbon: Pink, ¾ inch wide, 72 inches; lavender, ½ inch wide, 72 inches; aqua, ¾ inch wide, 72 inches; yellow, ¾ inch wide, 40 inches
Wooden dowel: ½x15 inches, painted white
Knobs: 2, size to fit dowel

Stitch

Follow cross-stitch instructions given in Cross-Stitch Basics.

Finish

Cut the cotton print fabric into strips of the sizes indicated above.

Lay a 2x17½ inch strip on each long edge of the cross-stitched piece with right sides together. Stitch strips to cross-stitched fabric with a ¼ inch seam allowance. Unfold and press open.

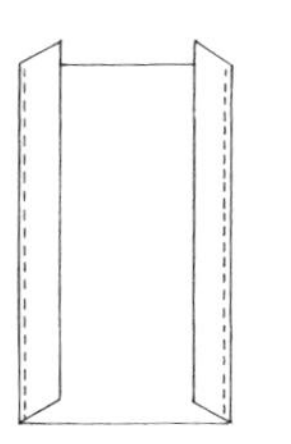

Lay a 2x13½ inch strip at the top and bottom of cross-stitched fabric with right sides together. Stitch strips to cross-stitched fabric with a ¼ inch allowance. Unfold and press open.

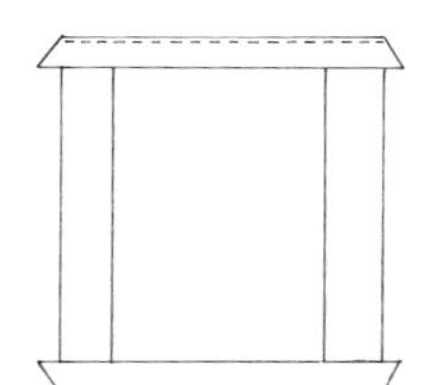

Lay batting on your work surface. Lay cross-stitched piece and lining, right sides together, on top of batting. Sew around edge with ¼ inch seam allowance, leaving top edge open. Clip corners and cut batting ¼ inch at the top. Turn right side out.

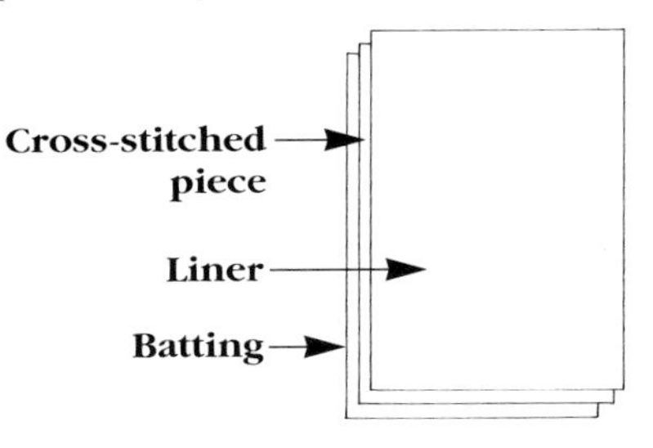

To quilt, sew running stitches with one strand of blue violet floss (#341) between letters (there are three spaces between letters), sewing through batting and lining.

For hangers, fold each of the three 4x6 inch strips in half lengthwise, and sew down long unfinished edges with a ¼ inch seam allowance. Turn right side out and press flat with seam in back.

Fold in ¼ inch of top edges; press. Fold hangers in half and tuck into opened top about ¼ inch. Topstitch with hangers in place.

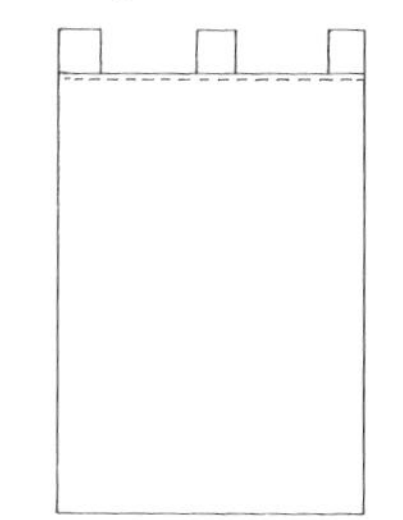

Slip banner over dowel and embellish with ribbons (see photo for placement).

Towel

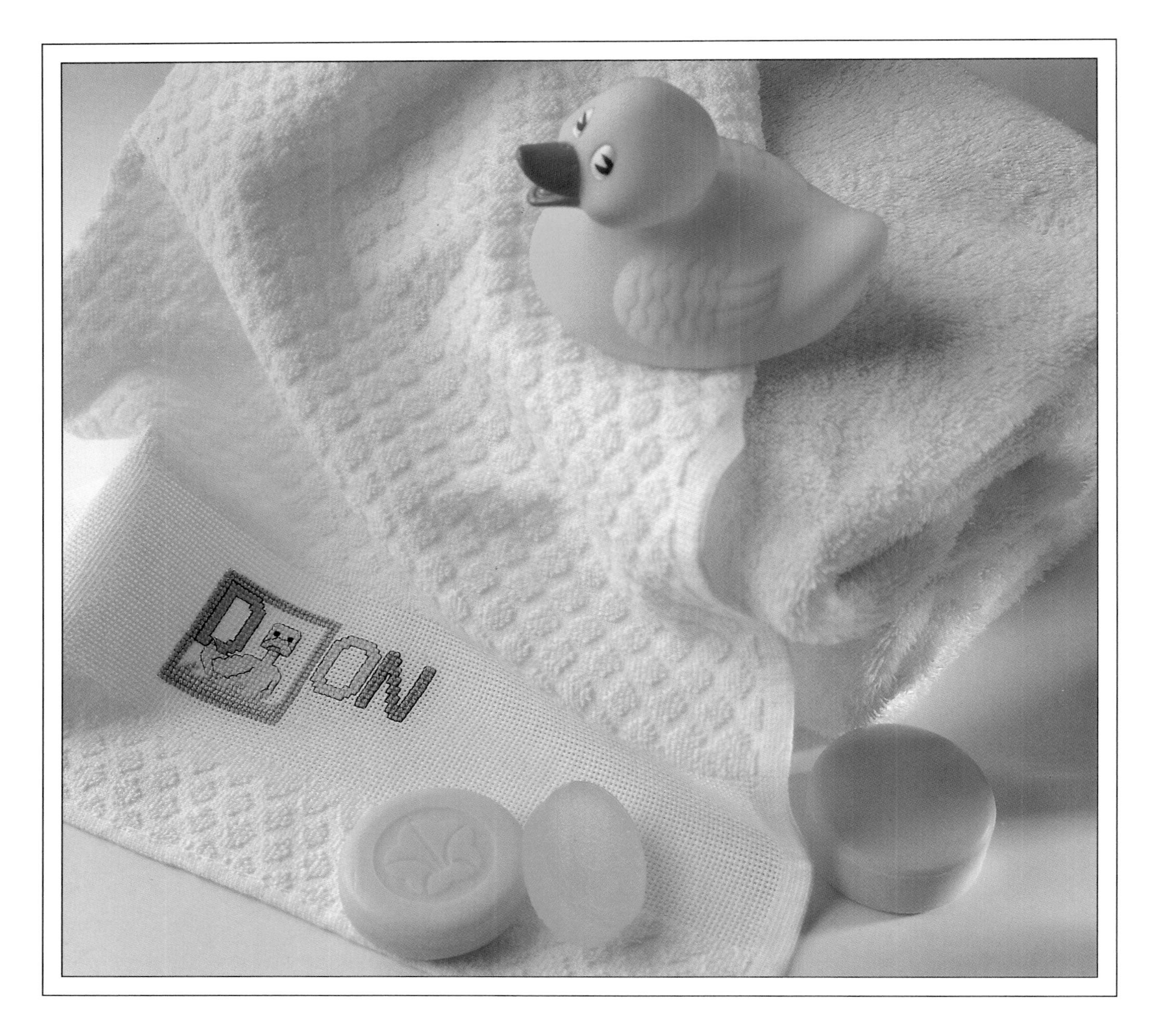

USE LETTERS FROM ANIMAL ALPHABET ON PAGES 218–223 TO SPELL THE NAME OF YOUR CHOICE

Materials

Towel: Premade, white Estate Cross-Stitch, 14 count (Charles Craft #TT6626-6750)

Stitch

Follow instructions for cross-stitching given in Cross-Stitch Basics.

Finish

The premade towel requires no finishing.

Mug

USE THE LETTER OF YOUR CHOICE FROM ANIMAL ALPHABET ON PAGES 218–223

Materials

Mug: Stitch-A-Mug (Crafter's Pride #30100W), with vinyl Aida insert
Satin ribbon: Purple, ⅛ inch wide, 20 inches

Stitch

Follow instructions for cross-stitching given in Cross-Stitch Basics.

Finish

After stitching, cut ribbon in half and glue on (see photo for placement). Insert vinyl Aida into mug according to manufacturer's instructions.

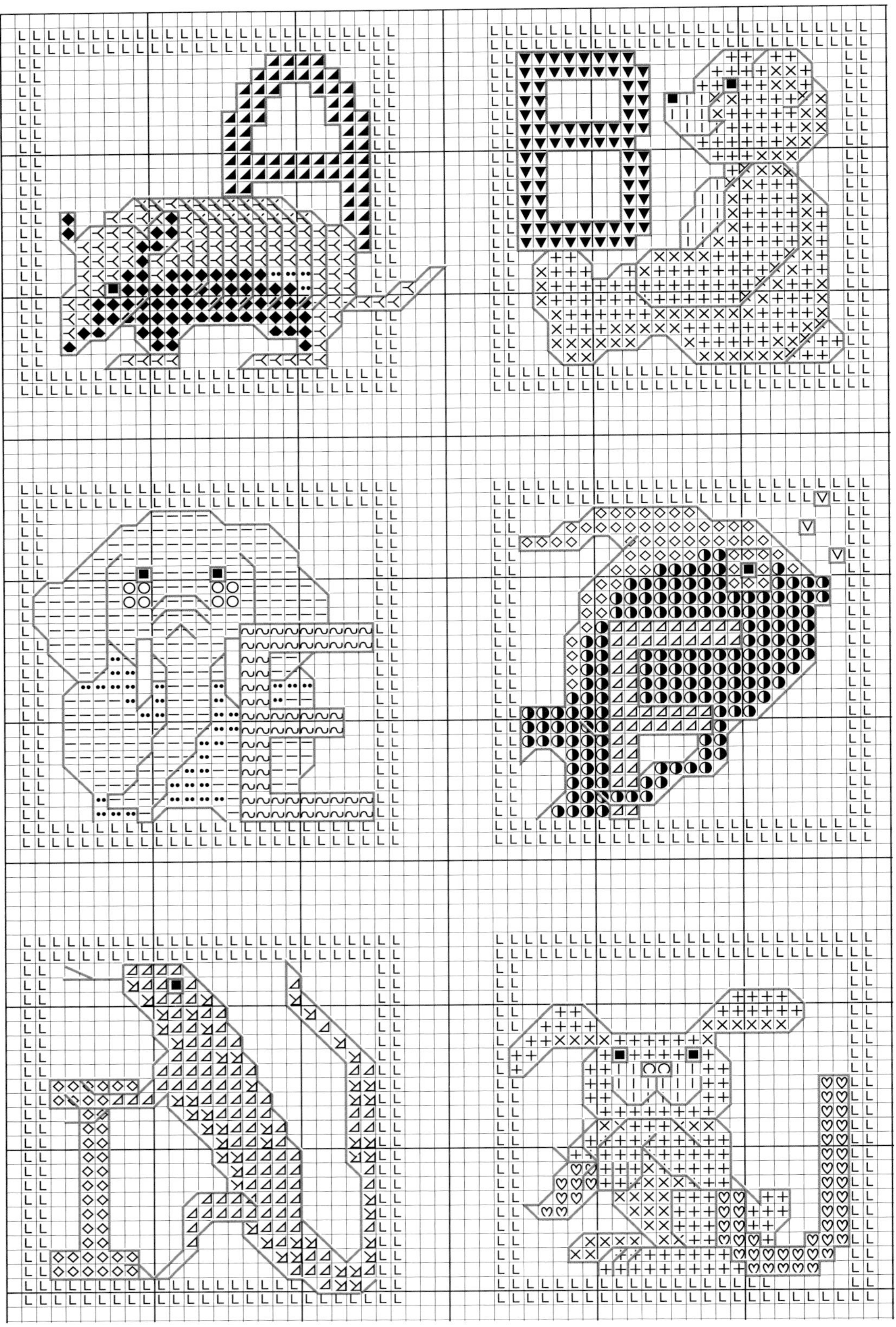

Animal Alphabet

The floss chart is on pages 222–223.

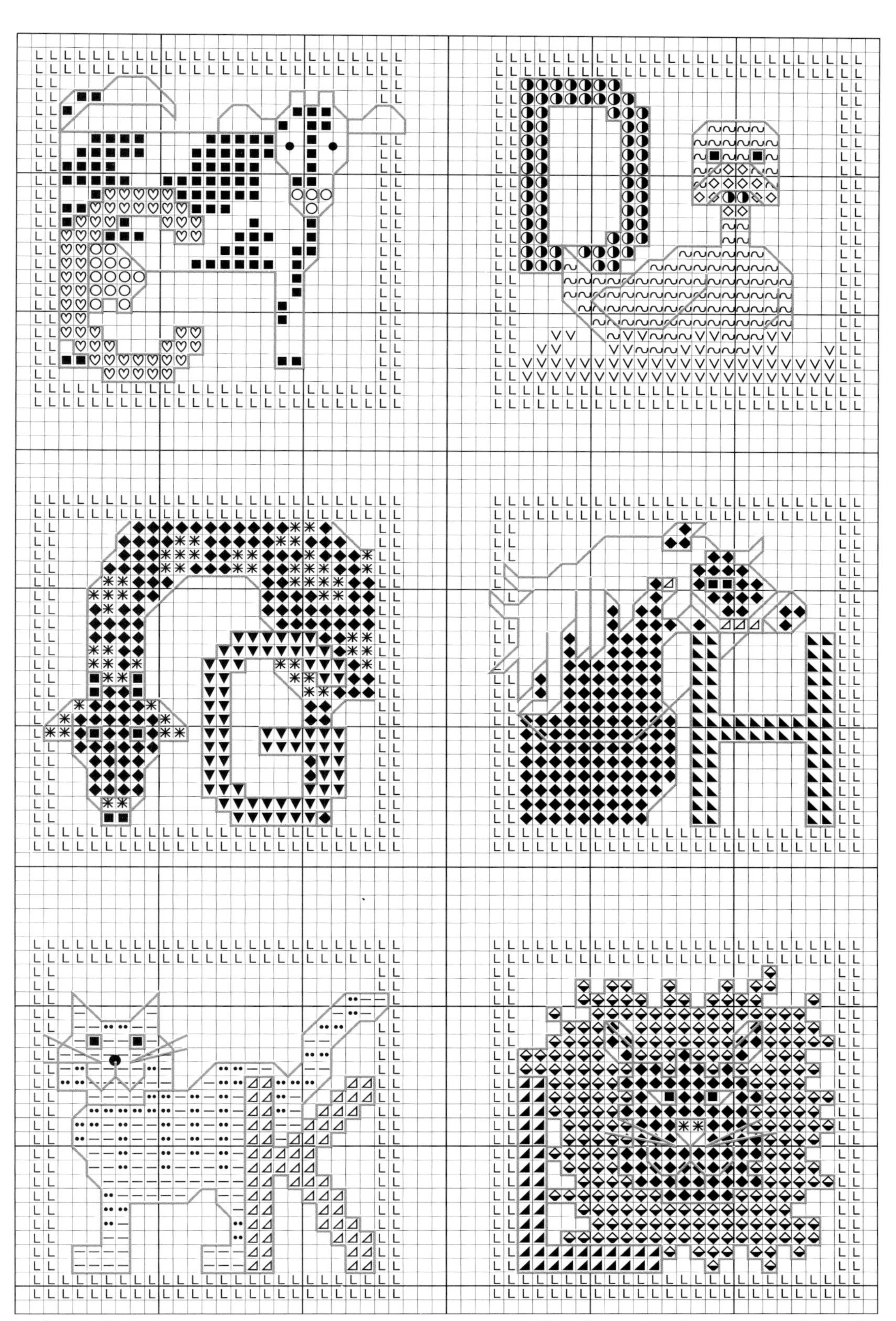

Animal Alphabet

The floss chart is on pages 222–223.

(continued)

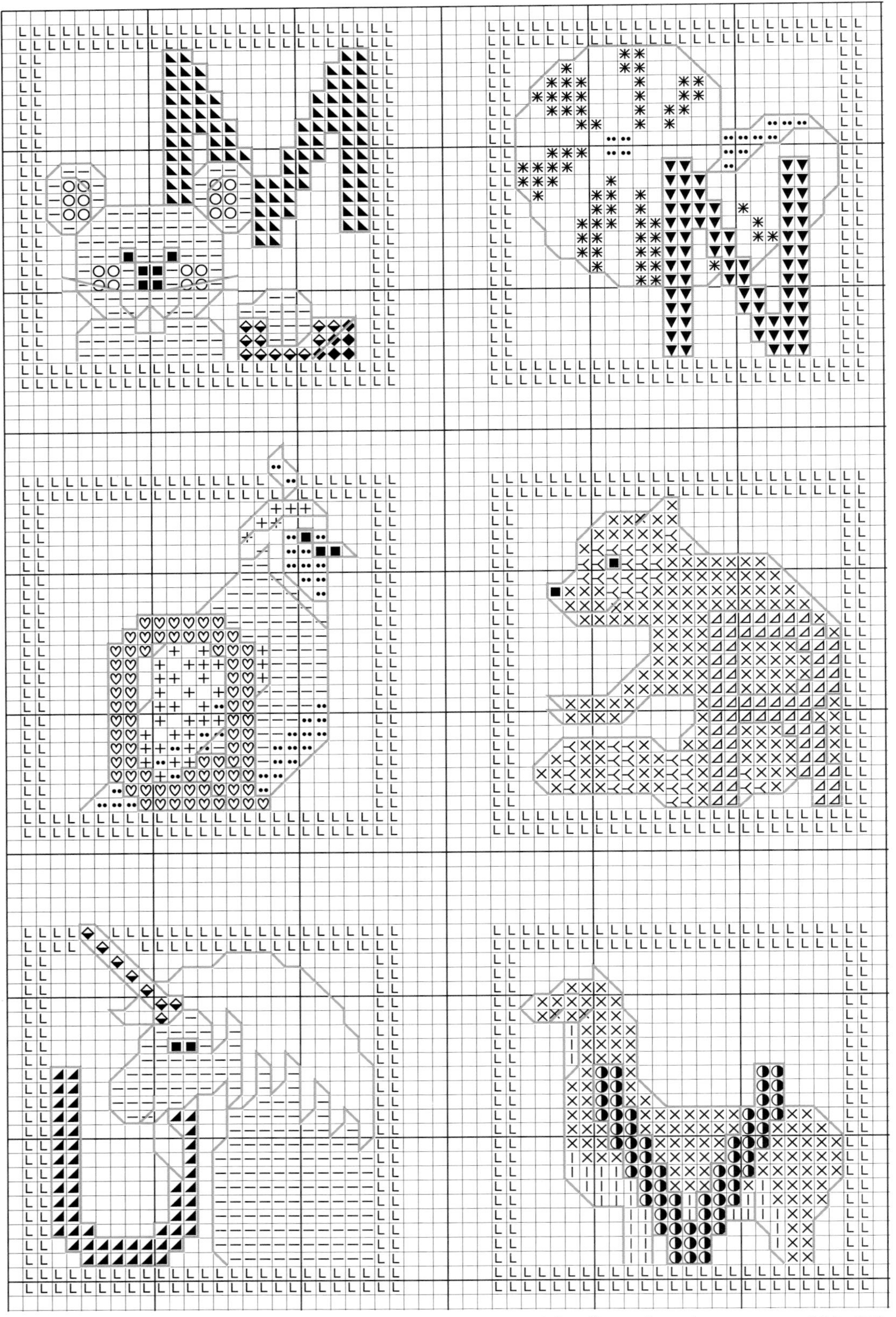

Animal Alphabet

The floss chart is on pages 222–223.

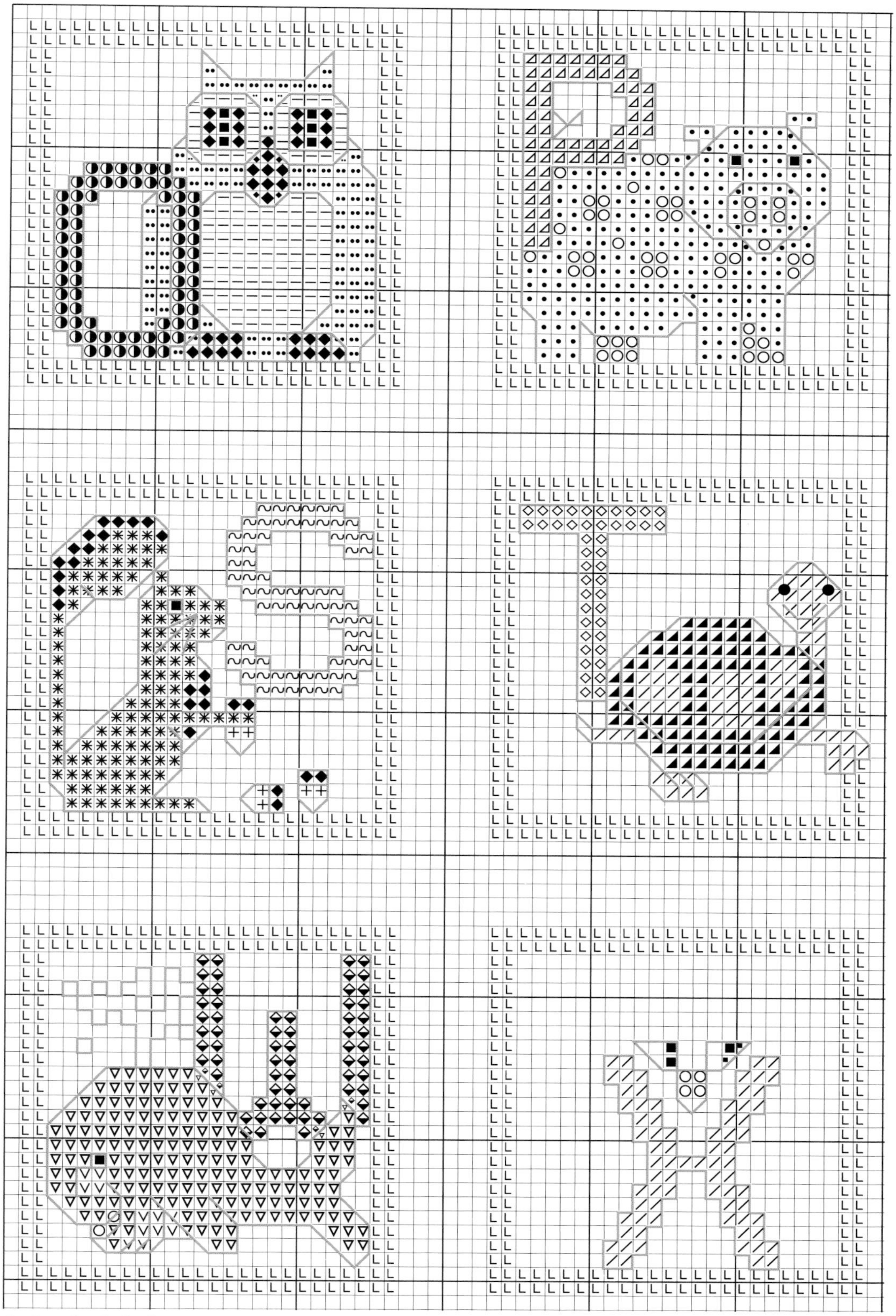

Animal Alphabet

The floss chart is on pages 222–223.

(continued)

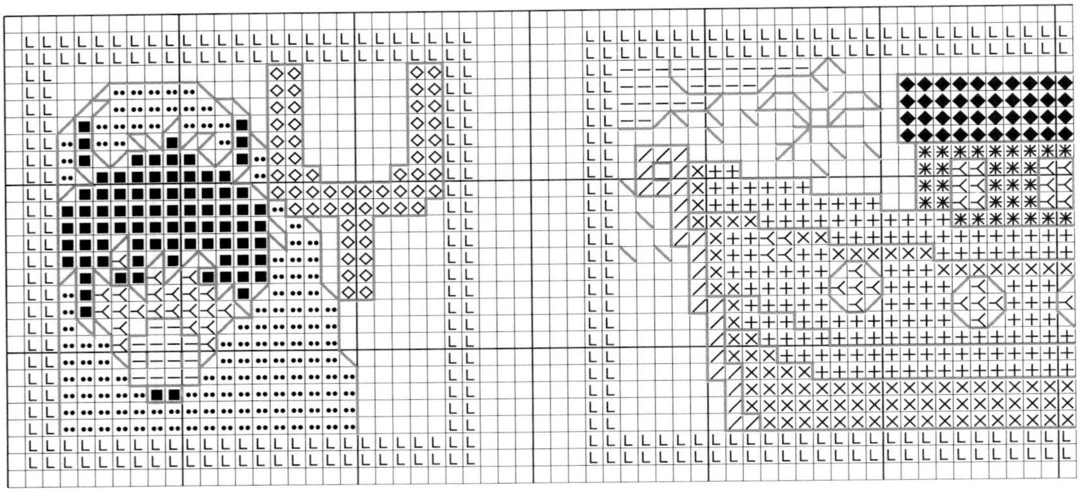

Animal Alphabet

Floss

Symbol	Color name	DMC#	Anchor#
•	Very light salmon	3713	1020
○	Light salmon	761	1021
∾	Dark golden yellow	726	295
◇	Light tangerine	742	303
⬙	Medium wheat straw	676	891
◆	Dark wheat straw	729	890
◑	Medium orange spice	721	324
⊻	Medium brown gray	3022	393
–	Beaver gray*****	648	900
••	Medium beaver gray	646	8581
≺	Dark beaver gray	645	273
|	Light drab brown	613	831
+	Medium drab brown	612	832
×	Dark drab brown	611	898
✳	Very ultra dark topaz	435	1046
L	Light blue violet	341	117
◣	Medium violet	552	99

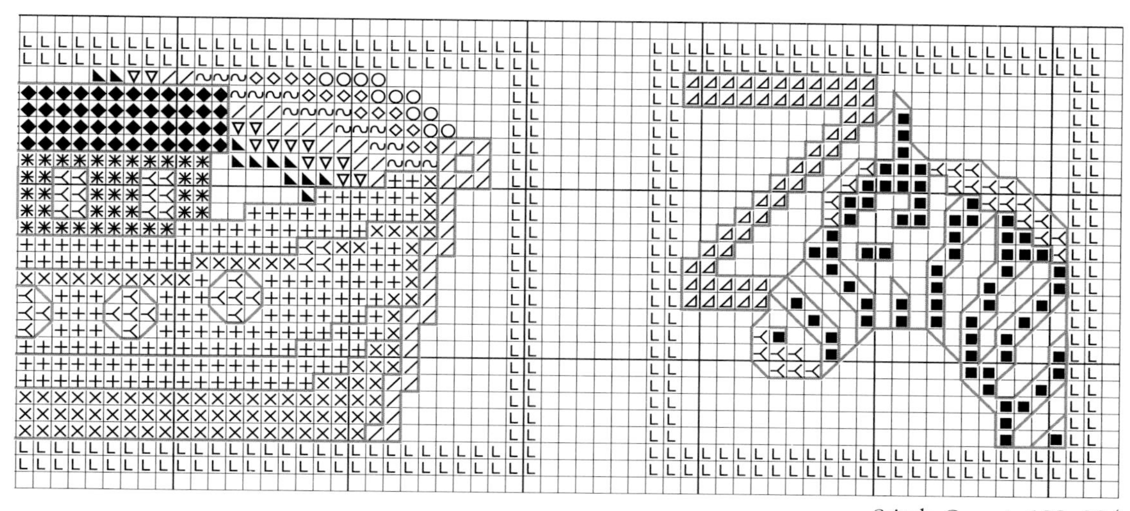

Stitch Count: 128x224

Symbol	Color name	DMC#	Anchor#
⁄	Parrot green	907	255
◿	Dark aquamarine**	992	187
◢	Dark emerald green***	910	229
V	Light blue	827	160
▽	Medium blue	826	161
▼	Dark blue****	825	162
♡	Christmas red	321	9046
■	Black*	310	403

*Backstitch everything in black, except where otherwise indicated (one strand).
*Stitch black French knots where indicated (C, K, S, T, and Ark).
**Backstitch rein on H in dark aquamarine (one strand).
***Backstitch strawberry leaf on J and olive branch on Ark in dark emerald green (one strand).
****Backstitch waterspout on W in dark blue (one strand).
*****Backstitch raindrops in beaver gray (one strand).

T-Dress

USE NOAH'S ARK FROM ANIMAL ALPHABET ON PAGES 222–223

Materials

Waste canvas: 8.5 count, 4x8 inches
T-dress with ruffle
Chenille needle: Size #24
Fabric glue
Satin ribbon: ⅜ inch wide, approximately 44 inches

Stitch

Follow instructions for cross-stitching using waste canvas given in Cross-Stitch Basics.

Finish

Glue or sew ribbon around waist of dress.

T-shirt

USE LETTER FROM ANIMAL ALPHABET ON PAGES 218–223

Materials

Child's T-shirt
Waste canvas: 8.5 count, 5x5 inches
Chenille needle: Size #24

Stitch and Finish

Follow instructions for cross-stitching using waste canvas given in Cross-Stitch Basics.

"Save the Animals" Tote Bag

USE SAVE THE ANIMALS SPOT ALPHABET ON PAGE 227

Materials

Tote bag: White, 13x14 inches
Waste canvas: 8.5 count, 6x10 inches
Chenille needle: Size #24
Fabric glue
Satin ribbon: Aqua, ⅓ inch wide, 28 inches; lavender, ¼ inch wide, 28 inches; brown, 2⅛ inches wide, 28 inches

Stitch

Follow instructions for cross-stitching using waste canvas given in Cross-Stitch Basics.

Finish

With fabric glue, add ribbon above and below design.

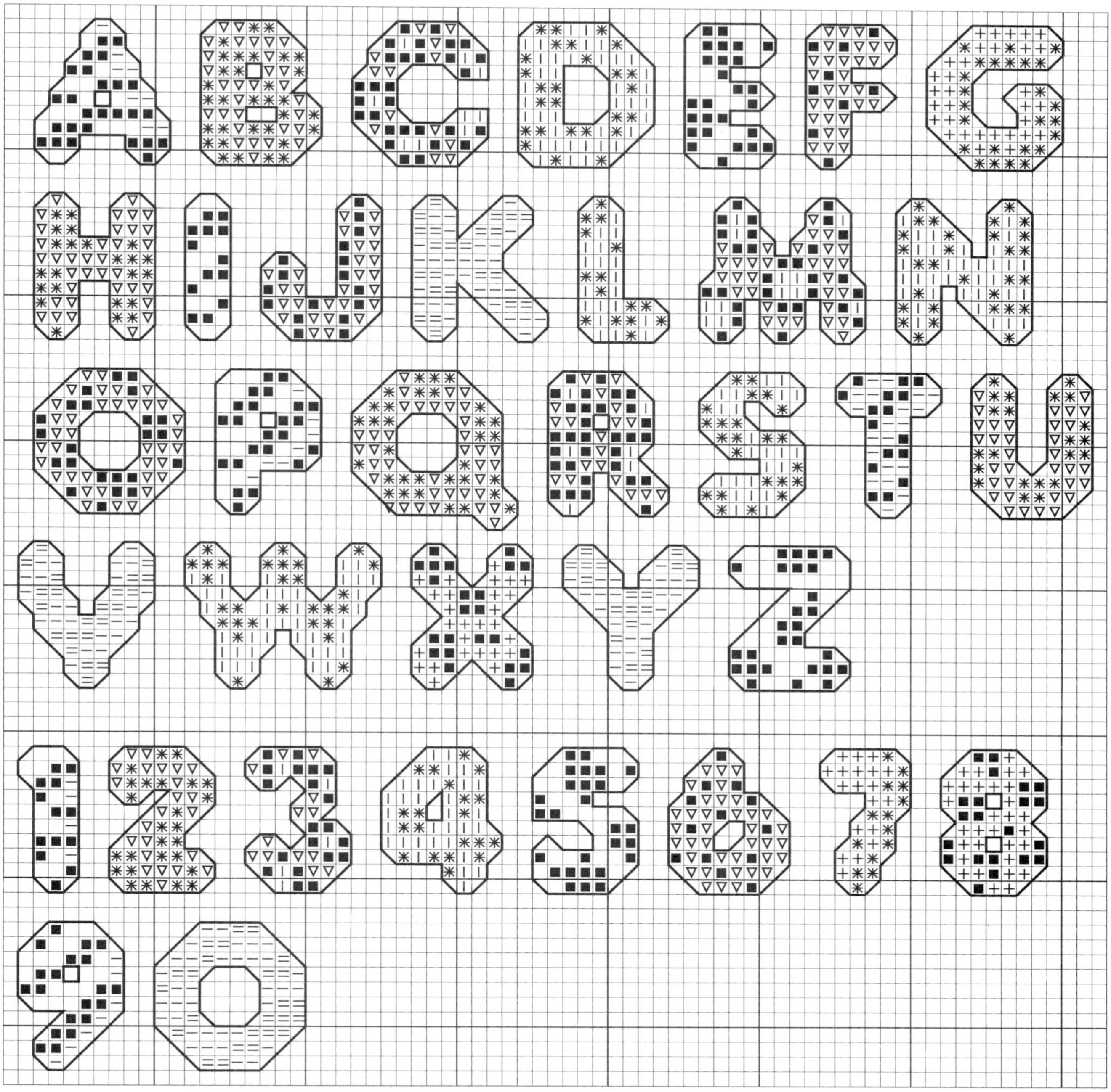

Save the Animals Spot Alphabet

Floss

Symbol	Color name	DMC#	Anchor#
—	Light gray	415	398
=	Dark gray	414	235
▽	Gold	783	307
|	Beige	738	361
+	Light brown	435	1046
✳	Dark brown	433	358
■	Black*	310	403
	*Backstitch letters in black (two strands).		

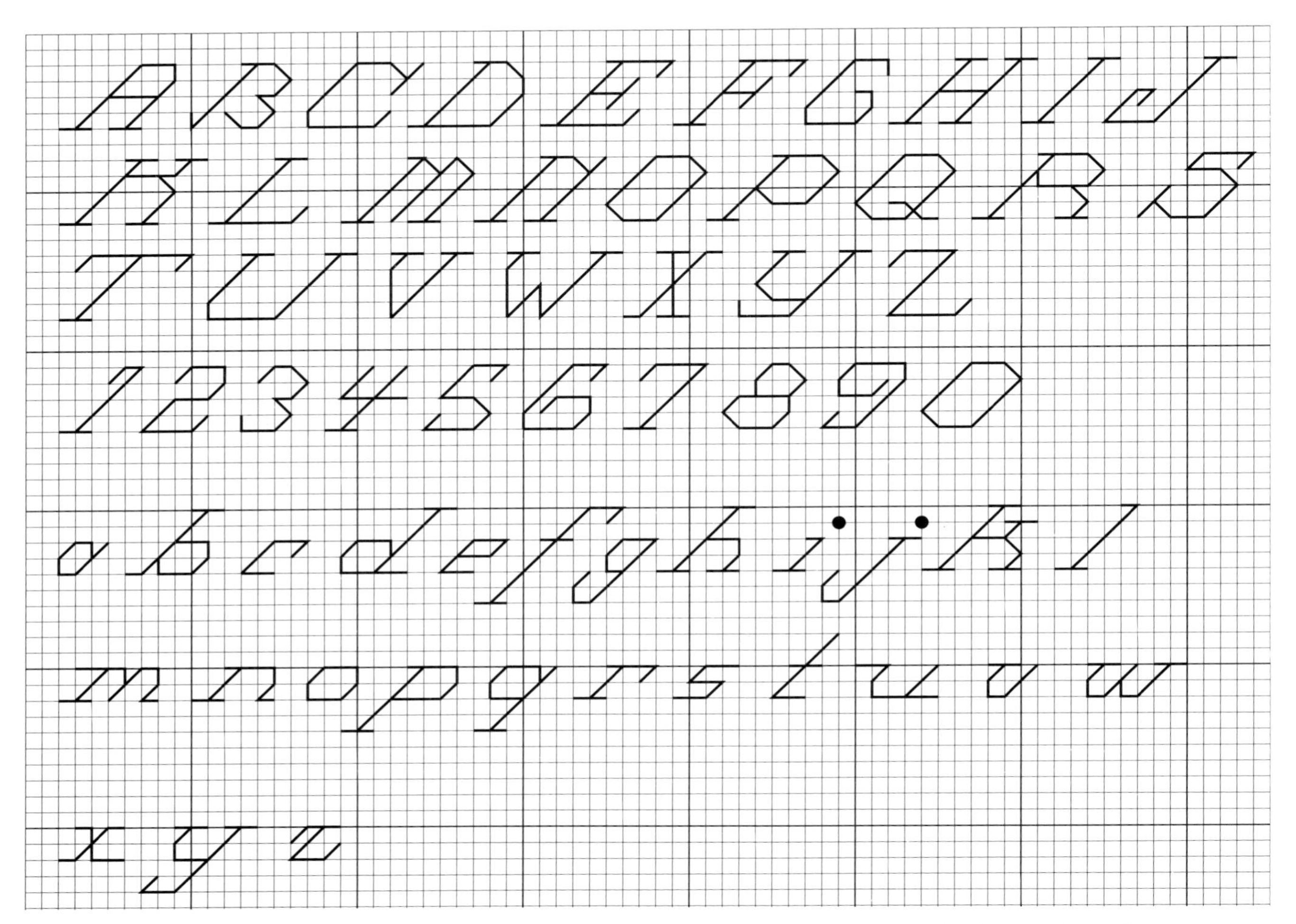

Animal Italic Alphabet

Use the floss colors of your choice.

Ideas for Use

Use the Animal Italic Alphabet to stitch a favorite saying about animals. Add one of the animal borders on pages 236–237 to make a charming animal sampler.

Ideas for Use

Using the Animal Zoo Alphabet, stitch "I love animals" on a T-shirt (using waste canvas). Give it as a gift to your favorite animal lover.

Animal Zoo Alphabet

Use the floss colors of your choice.

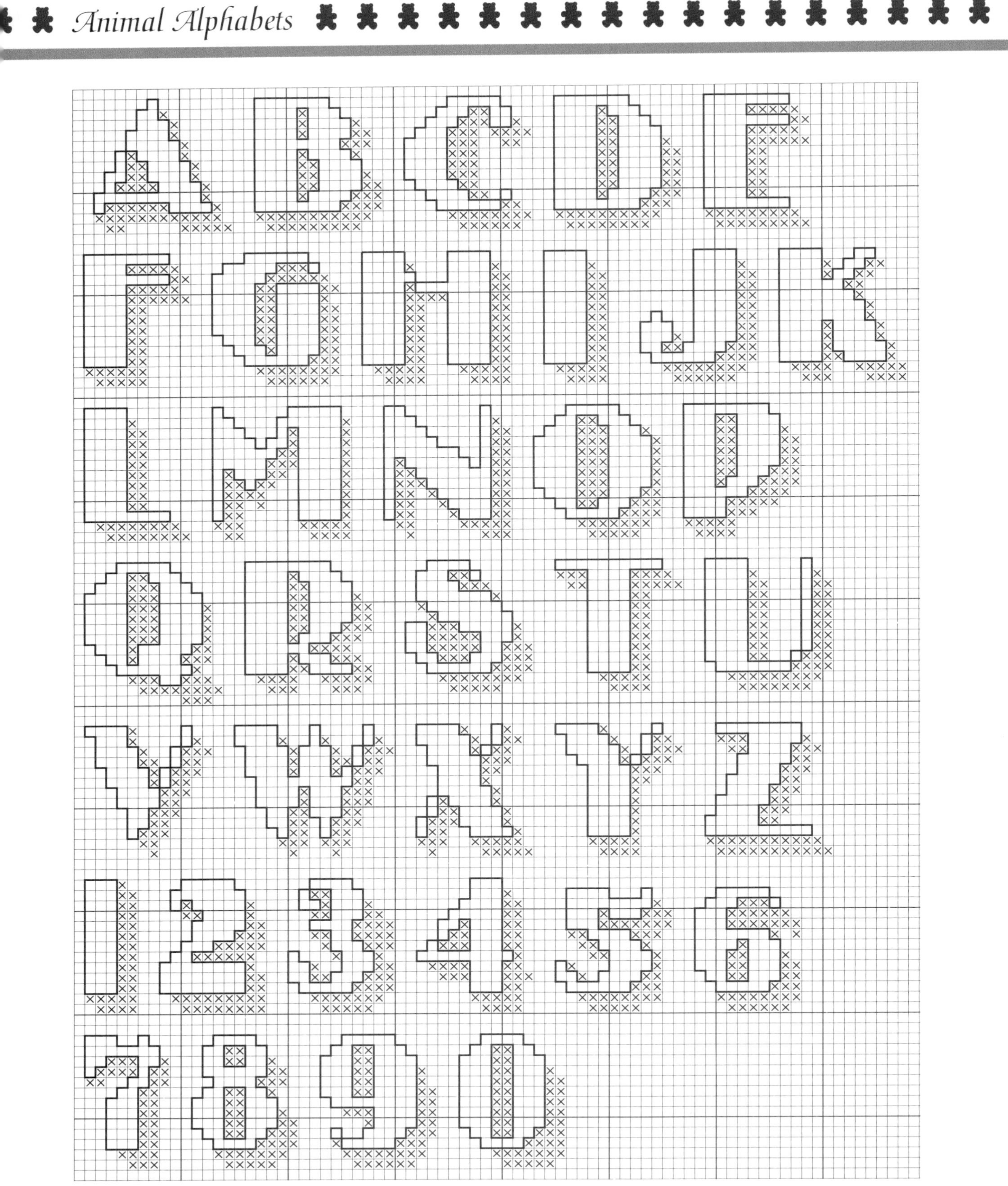

Animal Shaded Alphabet

Use the floss colors of your choice.

Ideas for Use

Stitch your child's name on a towel using this alphabet. Add one of the animal borders on pages 236–237.

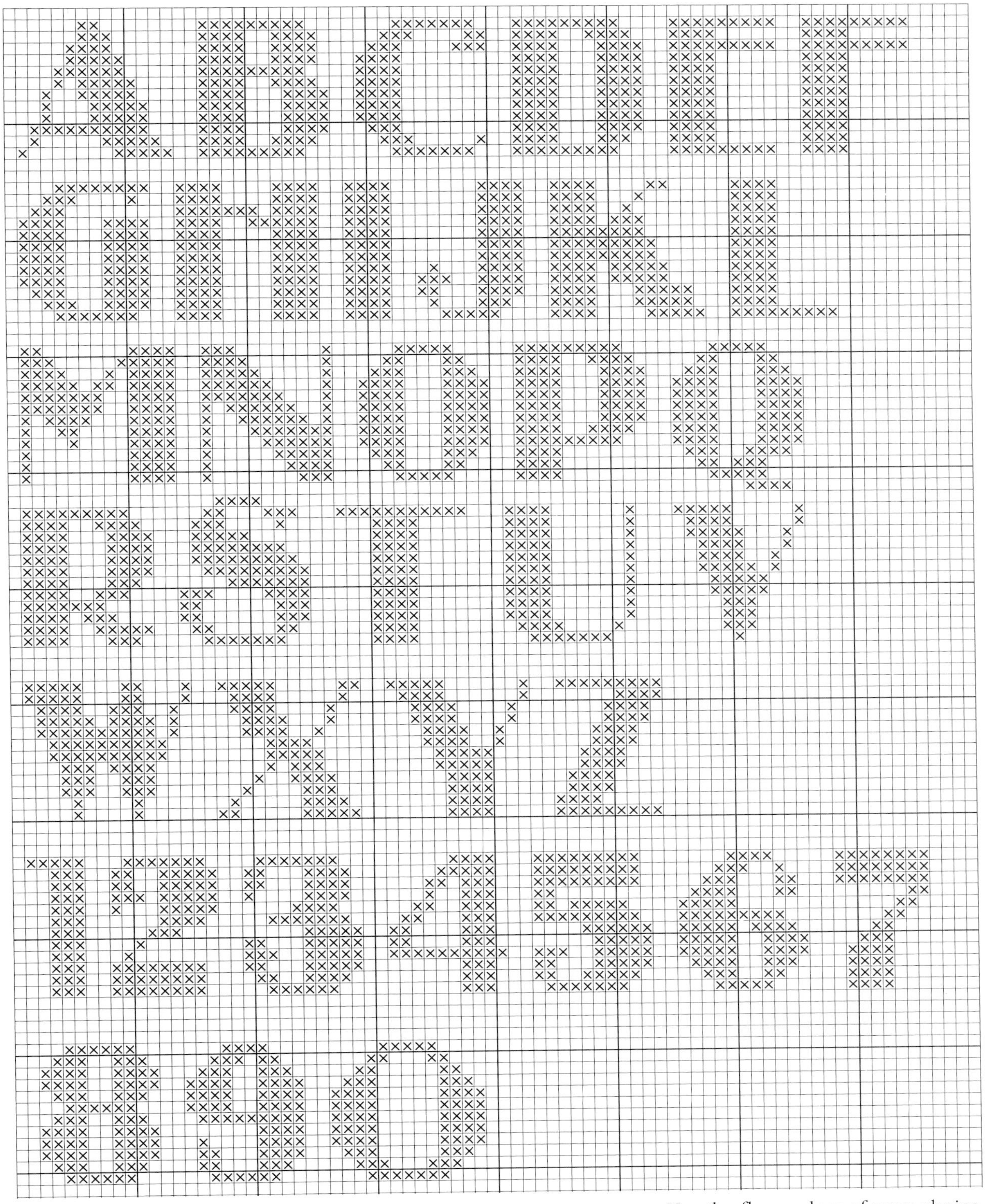

Animal Safari Alphabet

Use the floss colors of your choice.

Ideas for Use

Stitch your dog's name on a strip of cross-stitch fabric, hem, and add a buckle for a quick-and-easy dog collar.

Cats Alphabet

Use the floss colors of your choice.

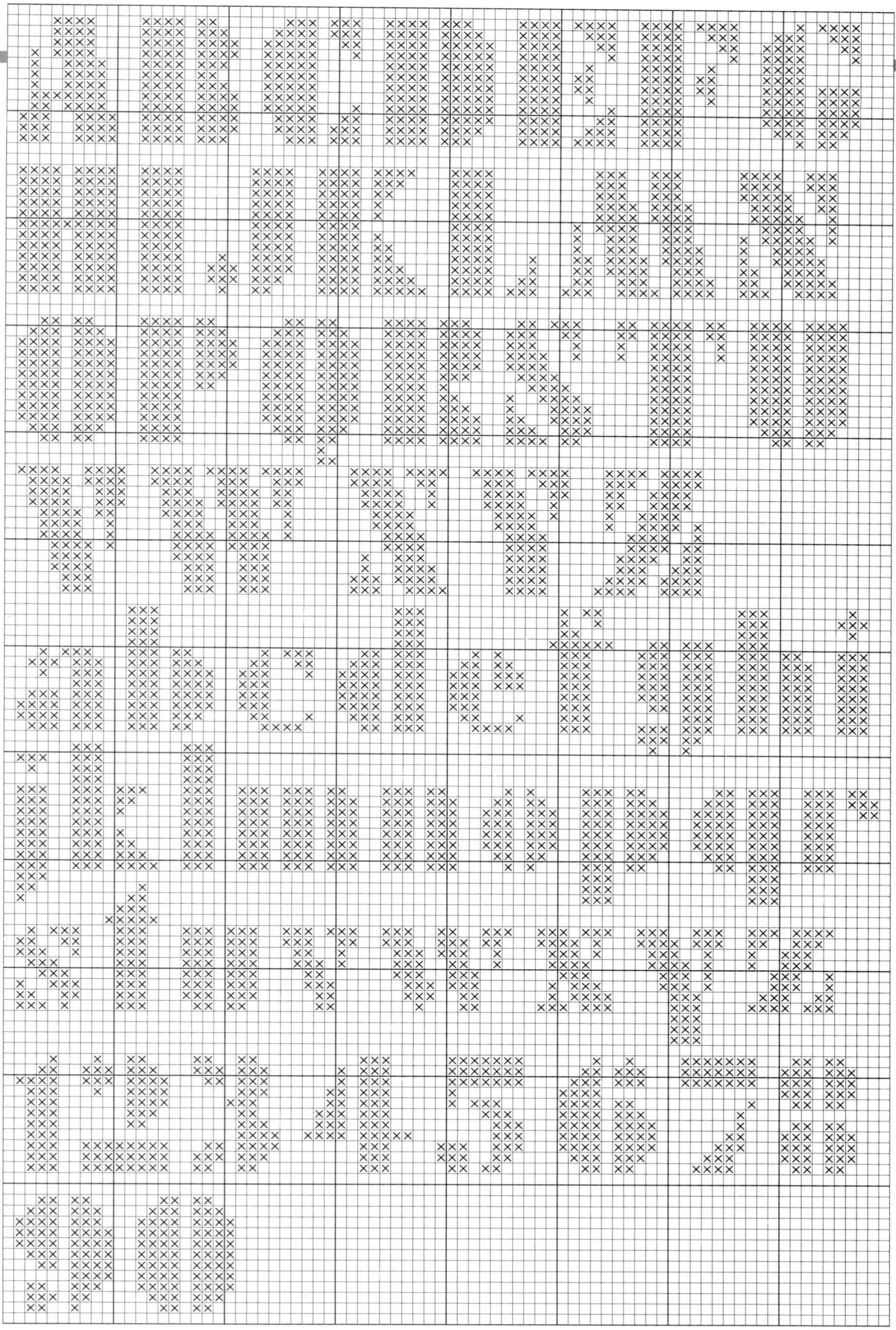

Animal Stencil Alphabet

Use the floss colors of your choice.

Ideas for Use

Stitch a child's name on a tote bag or back pack. Add the child's graduation year for even more personalization.

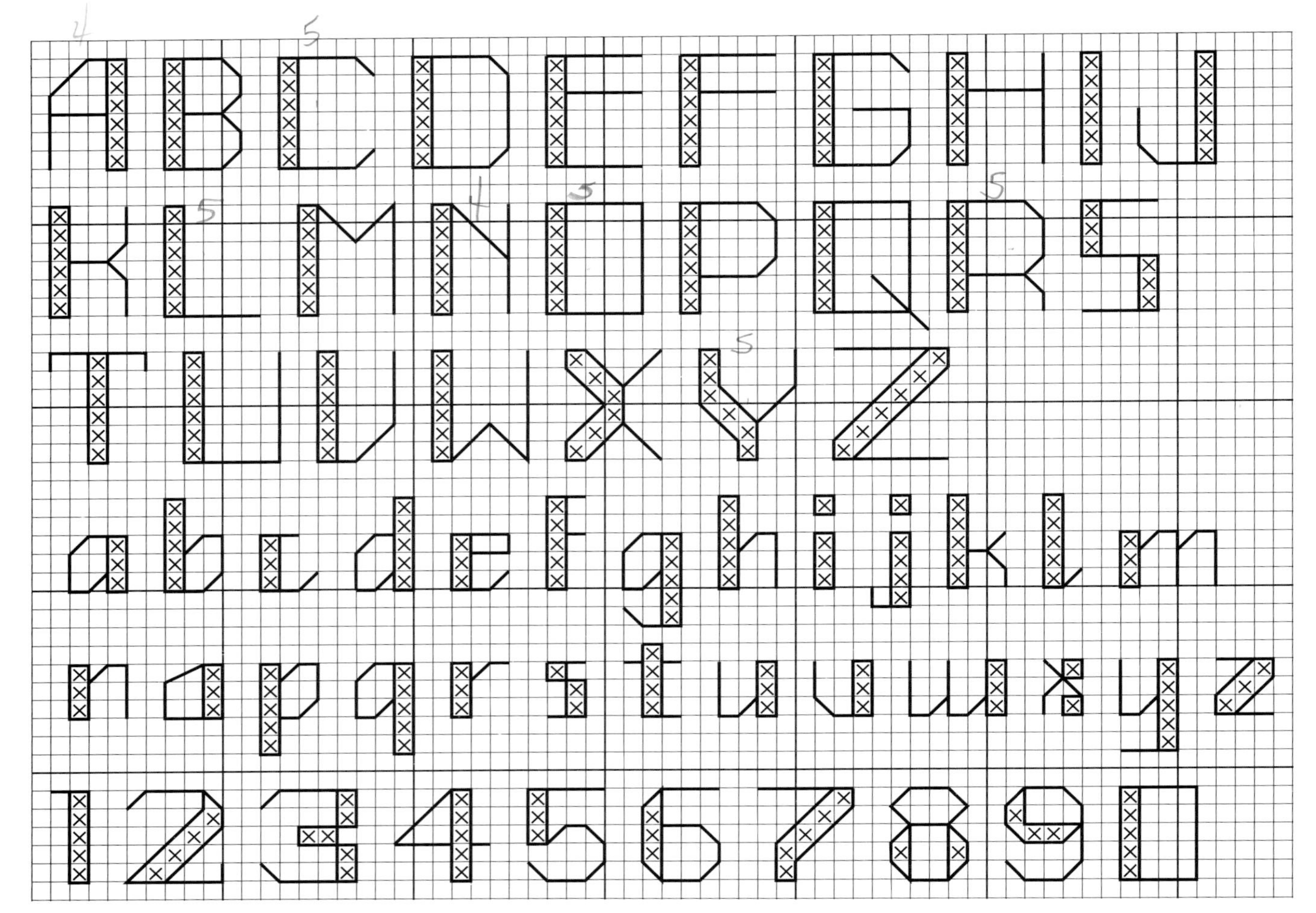

Animal Critter Alphabet

Use the floss colors of your choice.

Ideas for Use

Use this alphabet to spell out a name and match it with the Mouse Border on page 236 for a towel and tote combination.

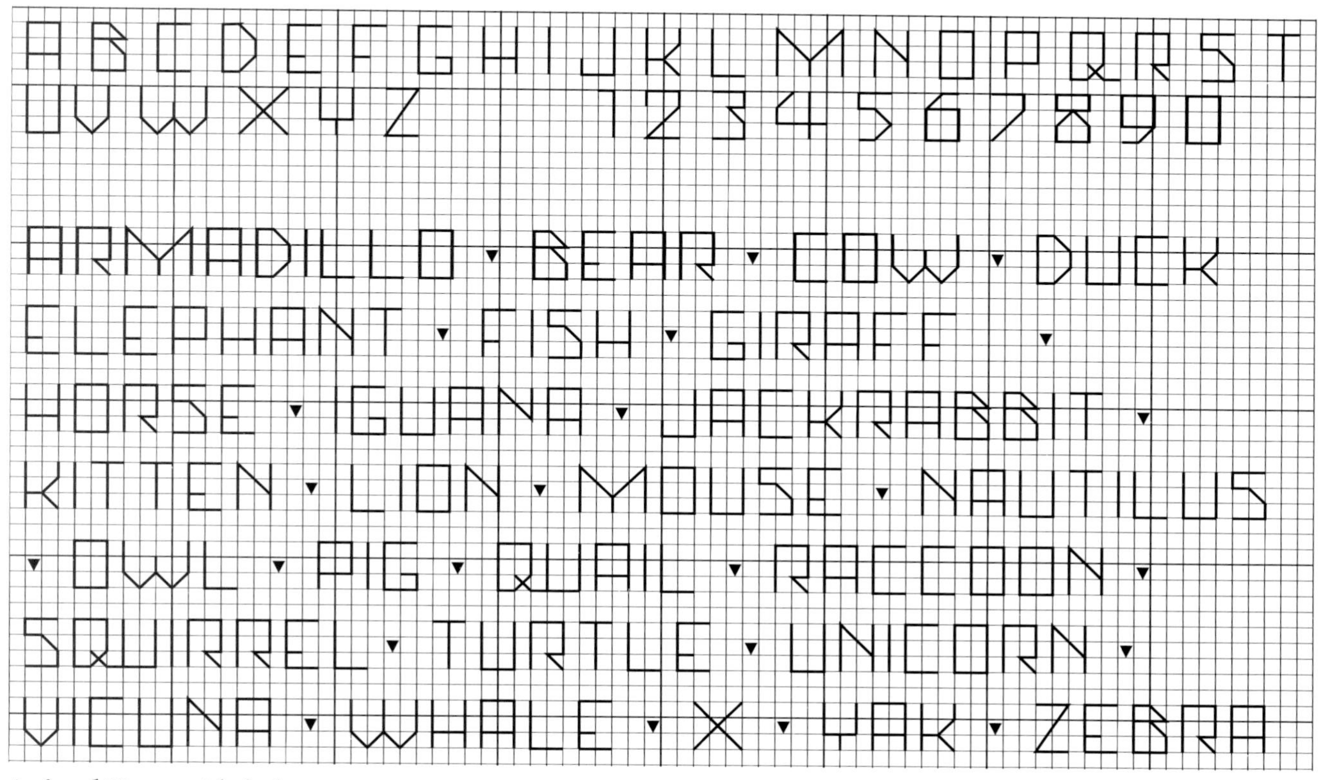

Animal Names Alphabet

Use the floss colors of your choice.

Ideas for Use

These animal names can be used in combination with the letters from the Animal Alphabet on pages 218–223.

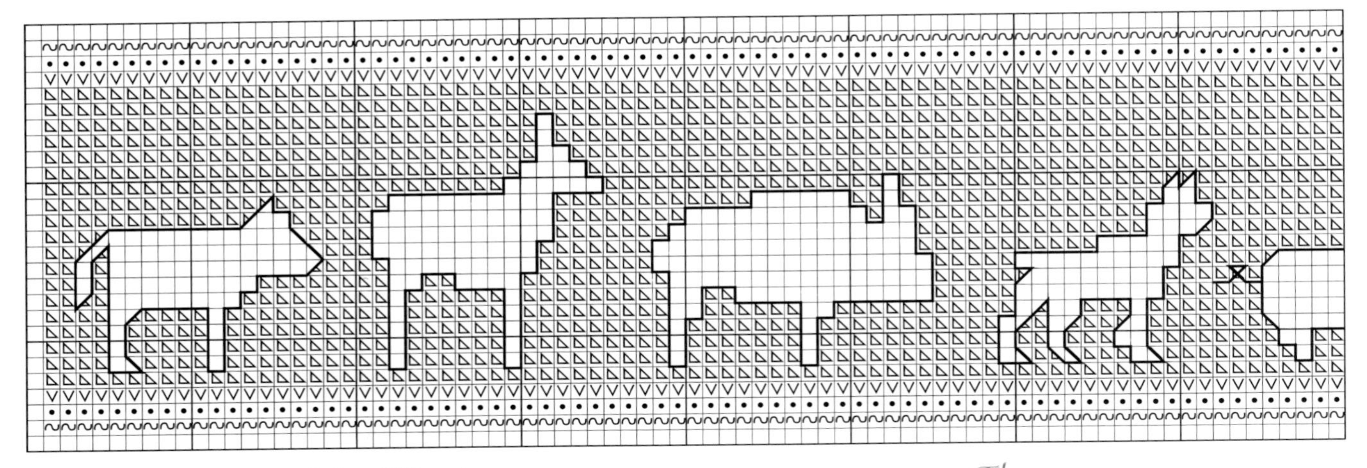

All Creatures Great and Small Border

Floss

Symbol	Color name	DMC#	Anchor#
•	Very light salmon	3713	1020
○	Light salmon	761	1021
∾	Dark golden yellow	726	295
◇	Light tangerine	742	303
—	Beaver gray	648	900
L	Light blue violet	341	117
◺	Light violet	340	118
◣	Medium violet	552	99
⊿	Dark aquamarine	992	187
V	Light blue	827	160
▼	Dark blue	825	162
■	Black*	310	403
	*Backstitch where indicated in black (one strand).		

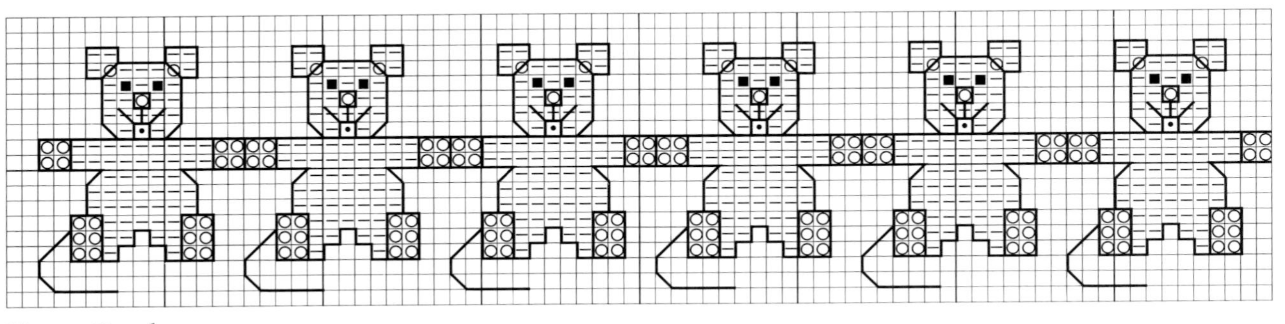

Mouse Border

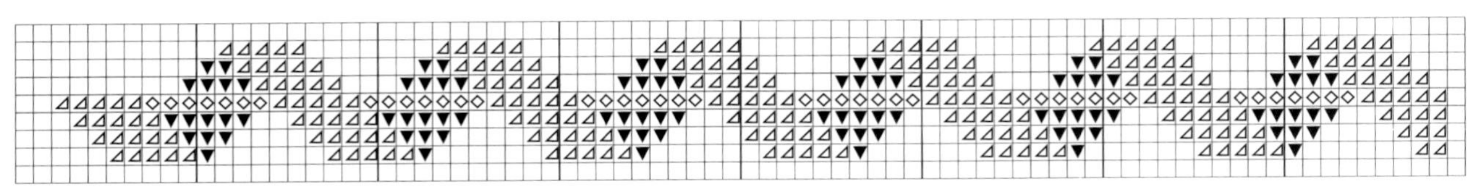

Ribbon Border

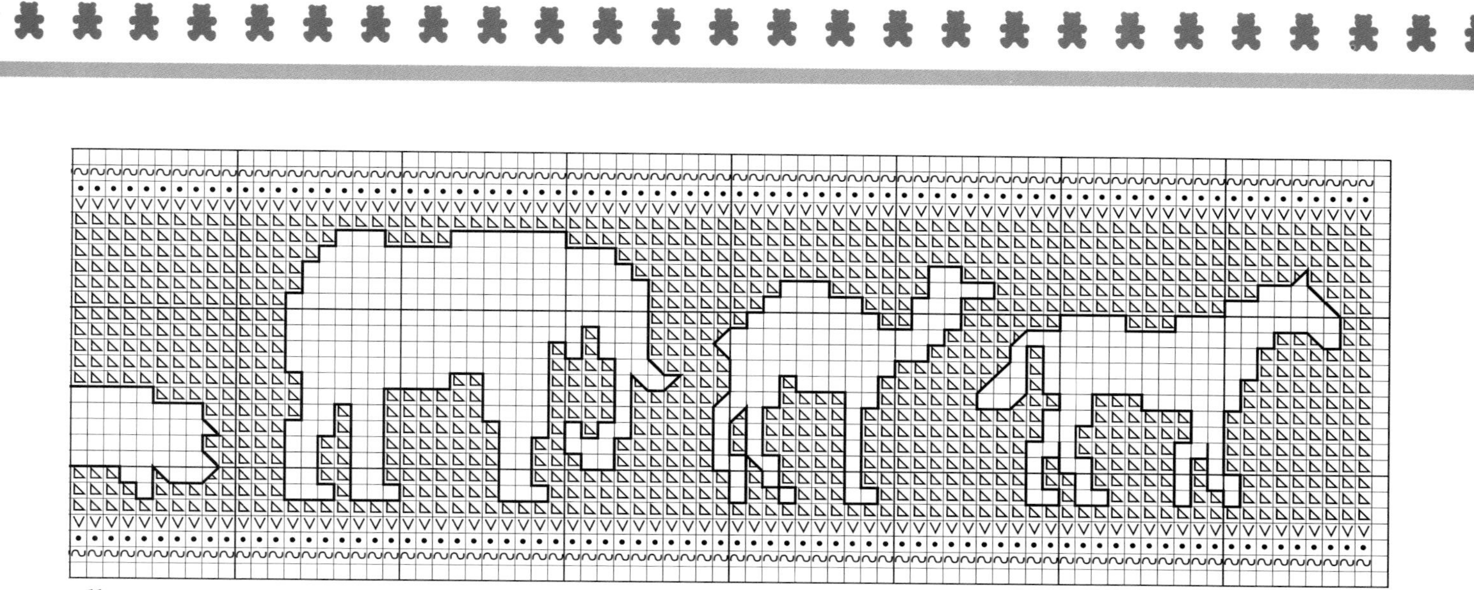

All Creatures Great and Small Border *(continued)*

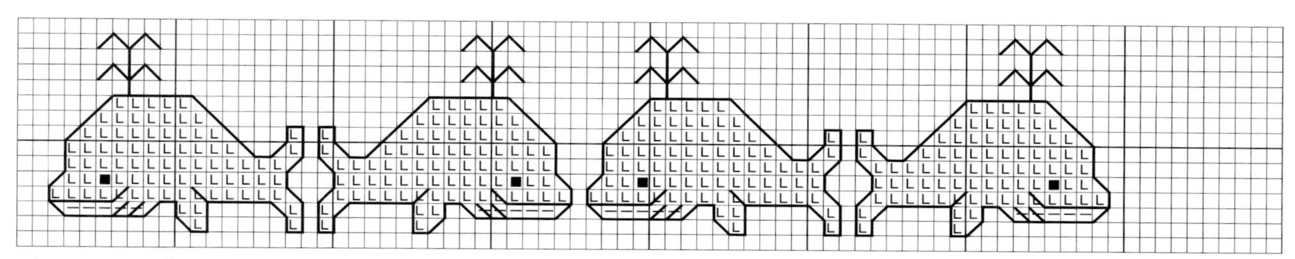

Shamu Border

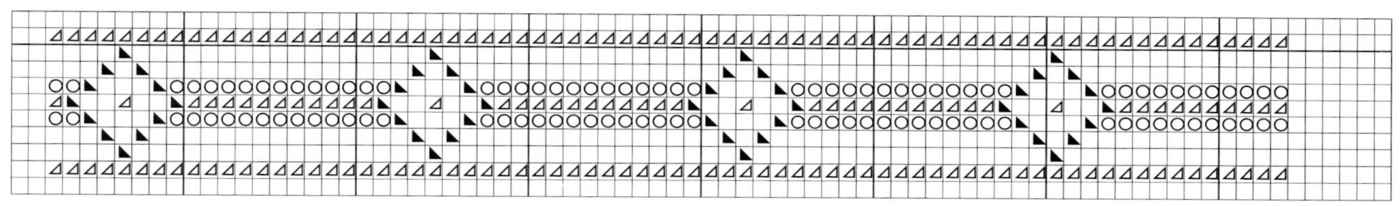

Diamonds Border

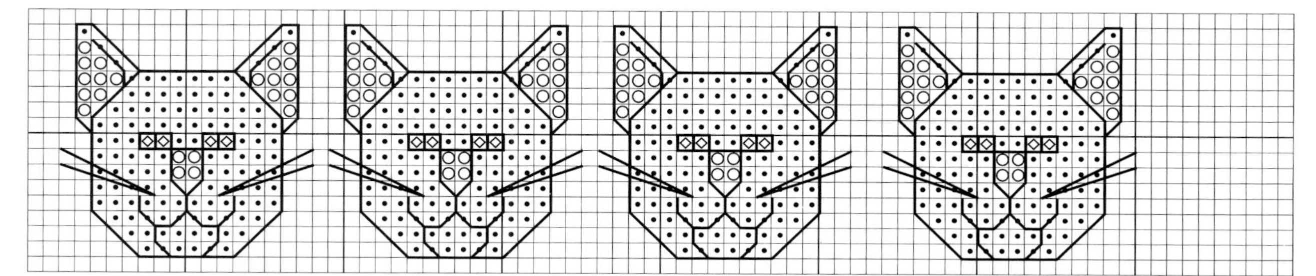

Cat Face Border

"Dog On Ice" Border

Special Occasion Alphabets

Life is full of special occasions and gift-giving times. This reference sampler and alphabet is as clever as it is useful. Choose the illustration for your occasion from the 24 on the sampler; match it to the appropriate charted salutation (or chart your own saying). Borders will help add the finishing touch to your special thoughtful gift. And don't forget to personalize your cross-stitch design with names and dates.

IT'S A GIRL
25TH
SWEET 16
Congratulations Good Luck
Happy Birthday Welcome
For my Dad To the Grad
ABCDEF
GHIJKL
MNOPQ
RSTUV
WXYZ12
34567890
teacher I love you
50TH
IT'S A GIRL
AMY
December 15
1993
50TH
Congratulations

Special Occasion Framed Piece

USE SPECIAL OCCASION ALPHABET ON PAGES 242–243

Materials

Aida fabric: 14 count, white, 15x15 inches

Stitch

Follow instructions for cross-stitching given in Cross-Stitch Basics.

Finish

We had this piece professionally framed with a double mat that matches the floss colors.

Ideas for Use

This Special Occasion Alphabet with symbols can be mixed and matched in literally hundreds of different ways for gift-giving all through the year. In this chapter we give you examples of its versatility. Use your imagination to combine the elements to fit your particular special occasions.

Wedding Shower Gift Tag

USE UMBRELLA AND GIFTS FROM SPECIAL OCCASION ALPHABET ON PAGE 242

Materials

Perforated paper: White, 3x3 inches (Yarn Tree Designs, Inc.)
Satin ribbon: Pink, ⅛ inch wide, 6 inches; lavender, ⅛ inch wide, 12 inches
Paper: 2x4 inch, white card stock
Hole punch
Craft glue

Stitch

Follow instructions for cross-stitching on perforated paper given in Cross-Stitch Basics.

Finish

Fold 2x4 inch paper in half. Cut stitched piece of perforated paper to 1½x1½ inches. Glue stitched paper onto the center front of the card stock paper. Glue pink ribbon around edges, then lavender. Punch hole in back of tag and thread with ribbon. Tie to top of a gift.

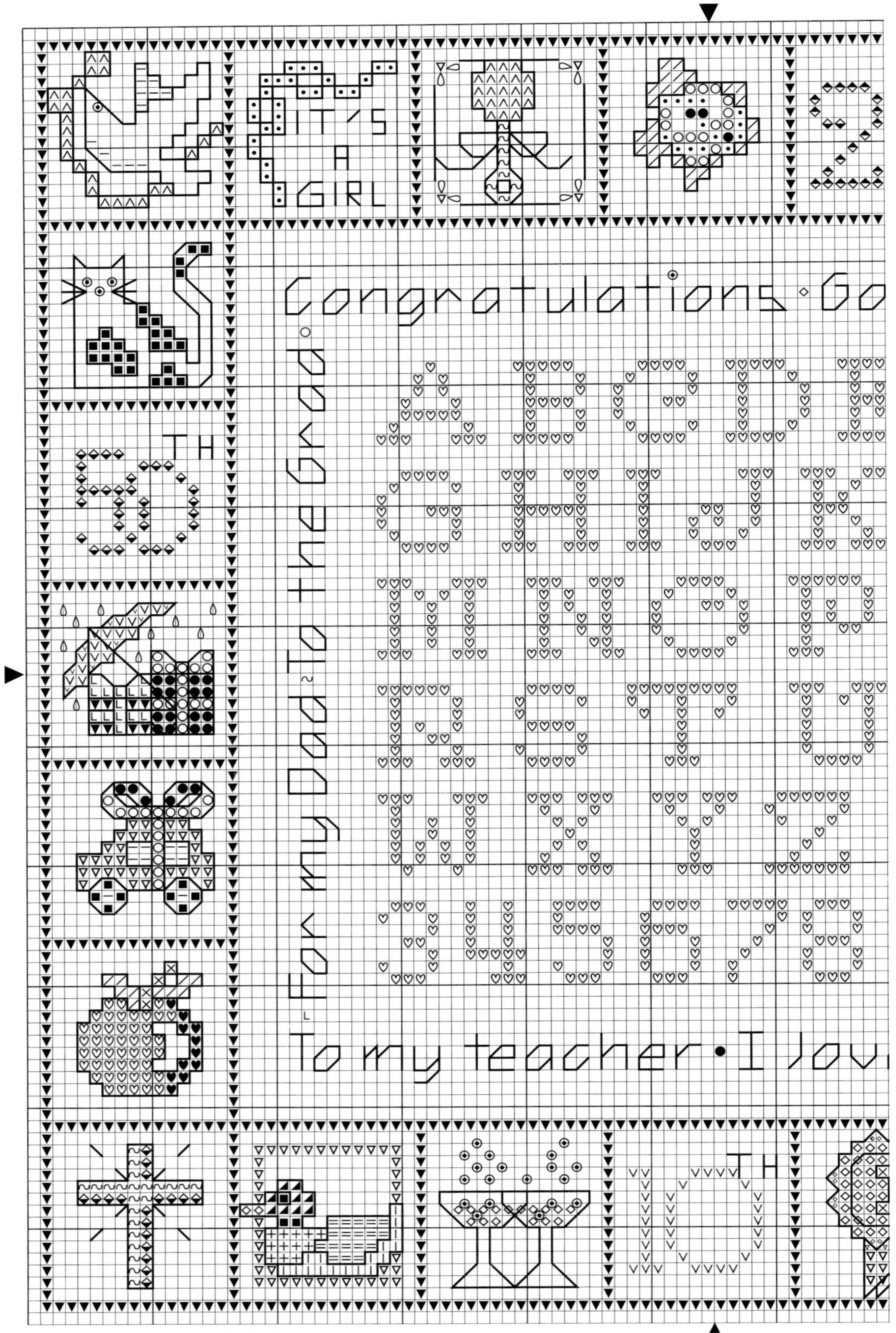

Special Occasion Alphabet

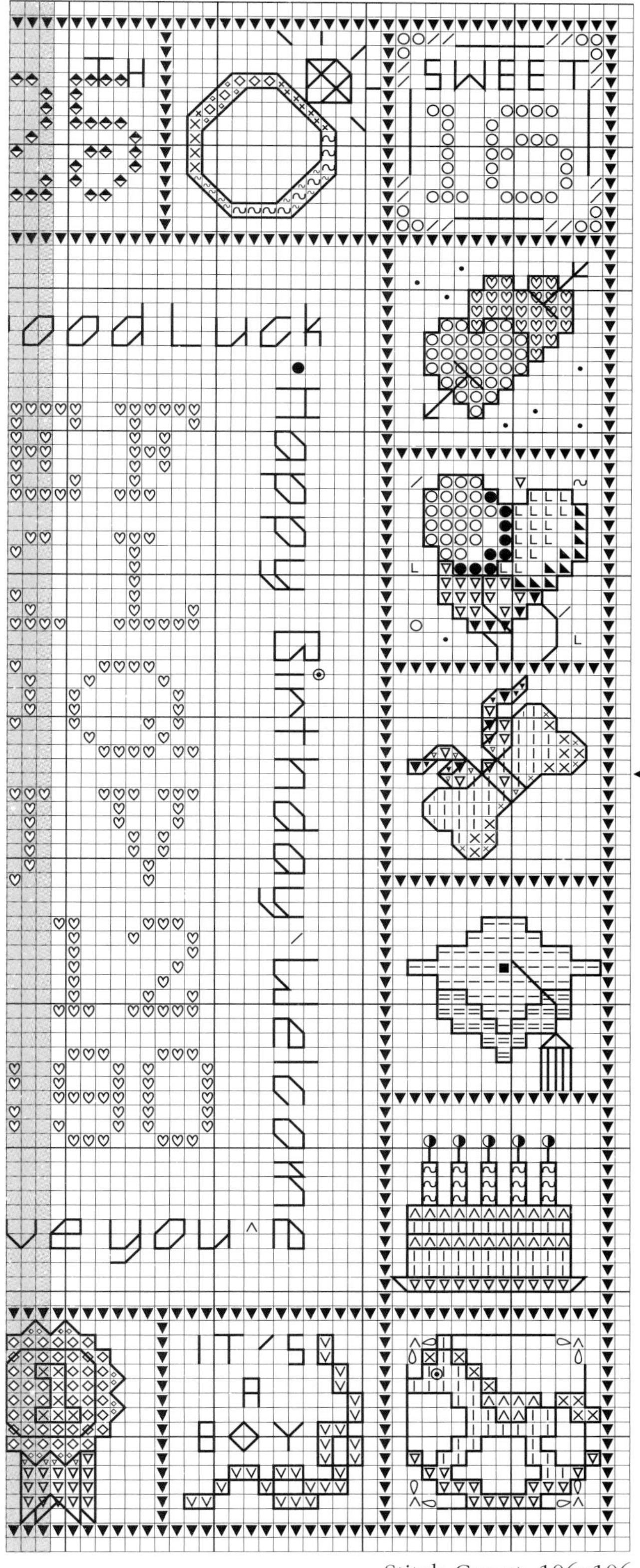

Stitch Count: 106x106

Floss

Symbol	Color name	DMC#	Anchor#
•	Light pink	818	23
○	Medium pink[2]	3688	66
●	Dark pink[3]	3687	68
∾	Yellow	745	292
◇	Gold[4]	783	307
+	Rust	355	1014
◑	Orange	742	303
–	Light gray[5]	415	398
=	Dark gray	414	235
|	Beige	437	362
×	Brown	435	1046
L	Light lavender	210	108
◣	Purple	208	110
/	Medium green[6]	320	215
◢	Dark green	890	218
V	Light blue[7]	827	160
▽	Medium blue[8]	793	176
▼	Dark blue[9]	792	941
Λ	Peach[1]	353	8
♡	Light red	816	1005
♥	Dark red	814	45
■	Black[12]	310	403
⬘	Metallic Silver[10] plus light gray	Art. 285	762
⬙	Metallic gold[11] plus gold	Art. 282	363
⬯	Lazy daisy		

[1] Backstitch borders around rattle in peach (one strand).
[2] Backstitch letters on "Sweet 16" in medium pink (one strand).
[3] Backstitch bow on "It's a girl" in dark pink (one strand) and letters in dark pink (two strands).
[4] Stitch gold French knots for champagne bubbles.
[5] Backstitch champagne glasses in light gray (one strand).
[6] Stitch medium green lazy daisies for leaves on borders of rattle and rocking horse (two strands).
[7] Stitch light blue lazy daisies for raindrops on shower gifts (two strands).
[8] Backstitch borders around "Sweet 16" and rocking horse and bow on rattle in medium blue (one strand).
[9] Backstitch "It's a boy" in dark blue (one strand).
[10] Mix one strand of metallic silver with two strands of light gray. Backstitch diamond in metallic silver (two strands).
[11] Mix one strand of metallic gold with two strands of gold. Backstitch rays on cross in metallic gold (two strands).
[12] Stitch black French knots for nose and eyes on cats, bird, and horse. Backstitch everything else in black (one strand).

Wedding Sampler

USE SPECIAL OCCASION WEDDING BORDER BELOW WITH INITIAL FROM SPECIAL OCCASION BLOCK ALPHABET ON PAGE 256 AND LETTERS FROM SPECIAL OCCASION BACKSTITCH ALPHABET ON PAGE 252

Materials

Aida fabric: white, 14 count, 7x7 inches

Stitch

Follow cross-stitching instructions given in Cross-Stitch Basics.

Finish

We had this professionally framed.

Ideas for Use

This is an example of one of the things you can do with the borders and alphabets in this chapter. This same border, with a color change, could also be used for Christmas.

Floss

Symbol	Color name	DMC#	Anchor#
◇	Gold	783	307
L	Lavender	210	108
^	Light peach	353	8
▲	Dark peach*	352	10
▽	Medium blue	793	176
▼	Dark blue	792	941
	Black*	310	403

*Backstitch heart in dark peach (one strand).
**Backstitch bells and bows in black (one strand).

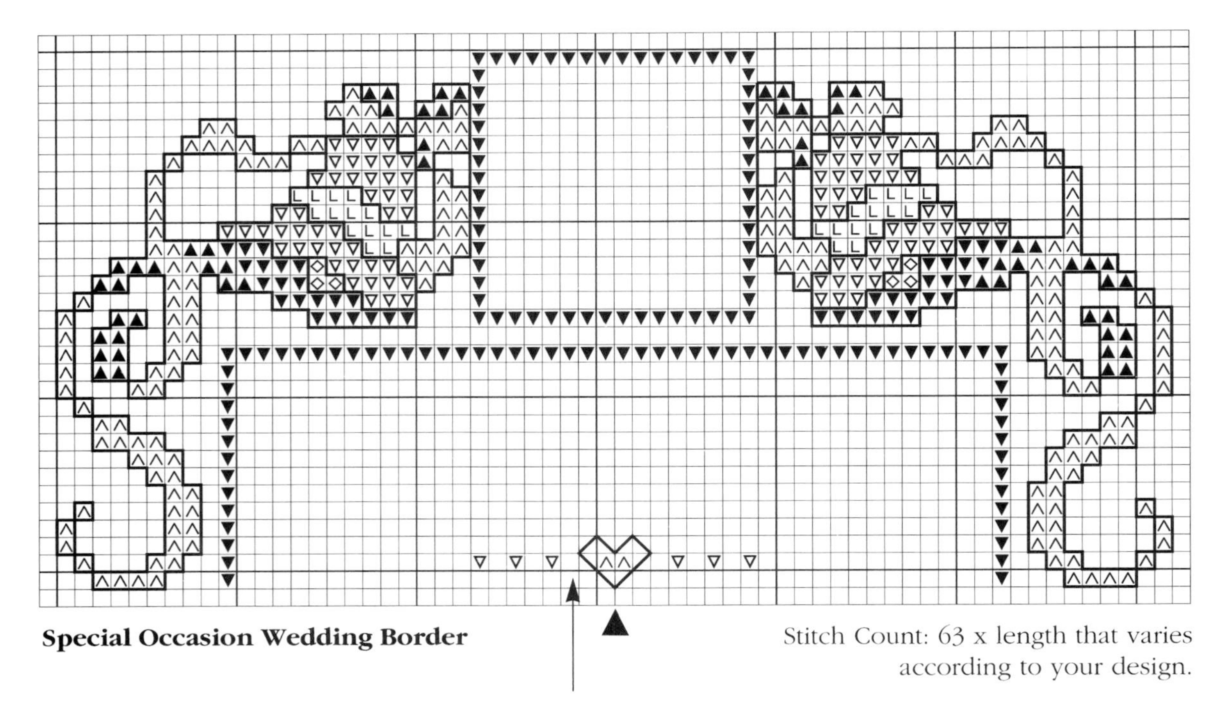

Special Occasion Wedding Border

Stitch Count: 63 x length that varies according to your design.

Use this small heart border to separate date and names. (Extend it to fit your project.)

Wed this day
June 5, 1993
Jane and Jim
Brown

"It's a Girl" Photo Album

USE SPECIAL OCCASION ROSES BORDER ON PAGE 247, SYMBOL FROM SPECIAL OCCASION ALPHABET ON PAGE 242, AND LETTERS FROM SPECIAL OCCASION BACKSTITCH ALPHABET ON PAGE 252

Materials

Photo album: 4½x6 inches
Aida fabric: White, 14 count, 5½x6 inches or to fit album
Fabric: Pink solid cotton, 6¼x11½ inches (plus enough to cover poster board on inside lining covers)
Cardboard: Heavyweight, 3½x4 inches
Poster board: Lightweight, 2 pieces, each 4x5½ inches
Lace: White eyelet, 1x36 inches
Rattail cord: Pink, 16 inches
Satin ribbon: Pink, ¾ inch wide, 28 inches; dusty green, ¾ inch wide, 28 inches
Craft glue

Stitch

Follow instructions for cross-stitching given in Cross-Stitch Basics.

Finish

After cross-stitching, follow the finishing instructions for covering photo albums and padded shapes given in General Project Instructions. The following are additional instructions for this album:

Cover the album with pink fabric. Glue eyelet lace on the inside of the covers and spine, extending it out about ¾ inch.

Before gluing the inner linings, cut two 28-inch lengths of pink satin ribbon and two 28-inch lengths of green satin ribbon; glue the ends of one pink and one green ribbon inside the center edge of each album cover to act as ties. Cover the glued ribbon ends with the fabric-covered lining boards.

Following the illustration in General Project Instructions, cover the heavy cardboard (3½x4 inches) with the batting. Place the cross-stitched fabric over the batting. Put glue around the edges of the back of the board, and fold the cross-stitched fabric into the glue, mitering corners. Glue this covered shape to the front of the album. Add rattail cord to cover where the shape meets the album cover.

Other symbols that you might want to use with this border include "It's a boy," "Sweet 16," dove and ribbon, rose, rocking horse, shower gifts, and wedding ring.

Floss

Symbol	Color name	DMC#	Anchor#
•	Light pink	818	23
○	Medium pink	3688	66
●	Dark pink*	3687	68
/	Light green	368	214
◿	Medium green	320	215

*Backstitch tiny bow in dark pink (one strand). Backstitch letters in "It's a girl" in dark pink (two strands).
Stitch the name and date in the floss colors of your choice (two strands).

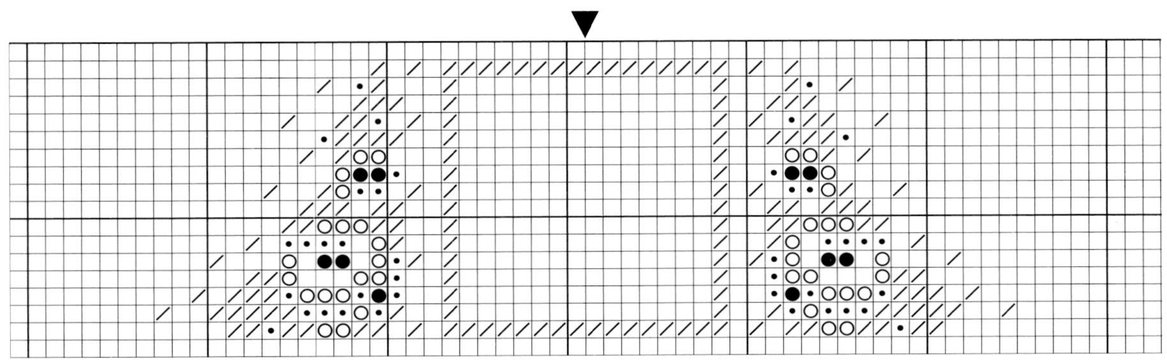

Special Occasion Roses Border
(Add a stitched border to this border to fit your project.)

Stitch Count: 16x48
(border element only)

50th Wedding Anniversary Card

USE SPECIAL OCCASION SCROLL BORDER BELOW AND SYMBOL AND LETTERS FROM SPECIAL OCCASION ALPHABET ON PAGE 242

Materials

White perforated paper: 3¼x2 inches
Blank card with color border: 3¾x5¼ inches
Silk ribbon: Blue, ⅛ inch wide, 10¾ inches
Small gold stars
Craft glue

Stitch

Follow the instructions for cross-stitching on perforated paper given in Cross-Stitch Basics.

Finish

After stitching, glue the perforated paper to the card. Glue the ribbon around the edge. Glue on stars.

Floss

Symbol	Color name	DMC	Anchor
◇	Gold	783	307
▼	Blue	792	941
	Black*	310	403

*Stitch "Congratulations" in black (two strands).

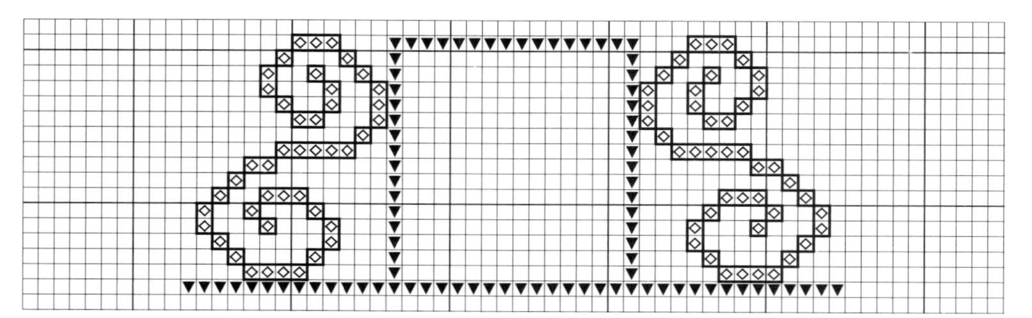

Special Occasion Scroll Border
(Add a stitched border to this border to fit your project.)

Stitch Count: 42x33
(border element only)

Father's Change Container

USE MALLARD DUCK FROM SPECIAL OCCASION ALPHABET ON PAGE 242

Materials

Caned container: 4⅜ inches diameter by 3½ inches deep
Satin ribbon: Brown or rust, ⅛ inch wide, 28 inches
Tapestry needle: Size #20
Craft glue

Stitch

Stitch using all six strands of the floss. Use two strands for backstitch. Count to the center of the lid, and mark lightly with a pen. Start stitching here. Follow cross-stitching instructions given in Cross-Stitch Basics.

Finish

After stitching, glue ribbon around edge of lid and bottom of container.

UNIVERSITY

Graduation Frame

USE SPECIAL OCCASION IVY BORDER BELOW AND GRADUATION CAP FROM SPECIAL OCCASION ALPHABET ON PAGES 242–243

Materials

Aida fabric: 14 count, white, 7x9 inches
Photo frame: 5x7 inch, with oval cutout, or heavyweight cardboard, 10x14 inches.
Fabric: Coordinating cotton fabric to cover the backing and easel.
Batting: 5x7 inches
Rattail cord: Dark blue, 1 yard
Craft glue

Stitch

Follow instructions for cross-stitching given in Cross-Stitch Basics.

Finish

Follow instructions for making and covering a 5x7-inch frame with an oval opening given in General Project Instructions.

If making your own frame, cut two 5x7 inch pieces from the heavyweight cardboard. Trace the oval pattern on this page onto one of the 5x7 inch pieces; cut out oval. Trace the frame stand pattern on this page onto the remaining cardboard piece; cut out frame stand.

Glue rattail cord around oval's outside and inside edges before assembling front and back of frame.

Oval Graduation Photo Frame
Full-Size Pattern

Floss

Symbol	Color name	DMC#	Anchor#
▼	Blue	792	941
/	Medium green	320	215
	Dark green*	890	218
	*Backstitch ivy vine in dark green (two strands).		

Top

Graduation Photo Frame Stand
Full-Size Pattern

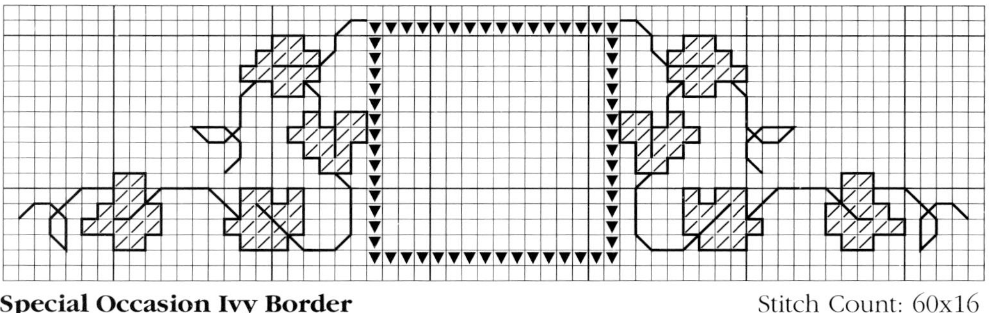

Special Occasion Ivy Border
(Add a stitched border to this border to fit your project.)

Stitch Count: 60x16

"For My Bible" Bookmark

USE CROSS FROM SPECIAL OCCASION ALPHABET ON PAGE 242 AND LETTERS FROM SPECIAL OCCASION BACKSTITCH ALPHABET BELOW

Materials

Perforated paper: White, 14 count, 2x5 inches
Ribbon: Grosgrain, blue, 1x9 inches
White paper
Craft glue

Stitch

Follow instructions for stitching on perforated paper given in Cross-Stitch Basics. Stitch the square and cross at top of the perforated paper. One row below this, stitch an open rectangle 16x38 stitches. Stitch "For My Bible" centered in this rectangle.

Finish

After cross-stitching, glue perforated paper to white paper; cut to 1¼x4⅛ inches. Glue one end of ribbon to back of white paper at the top; make a 1-inch loop, allowing entire length of ribbon to lay behind bookmark. Glue ribbon to paper. Cut ribbon so 1 inch extends from bottom of bookmark. Cut an inverted V into the ribbon (see photo for approximate size).

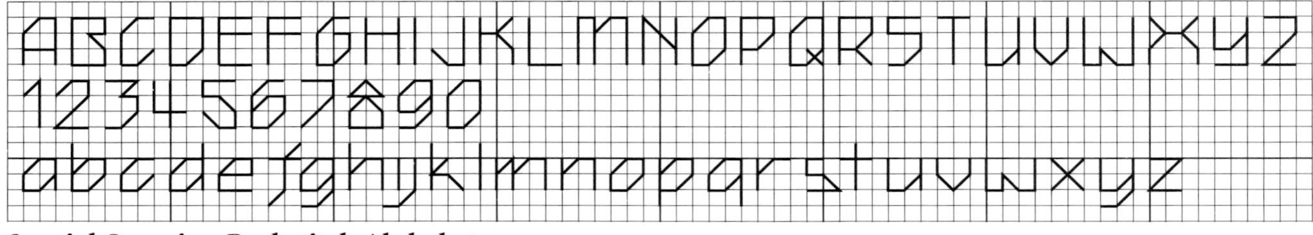

Special Occasion Backstitch Alphabet

Sleep Pillow

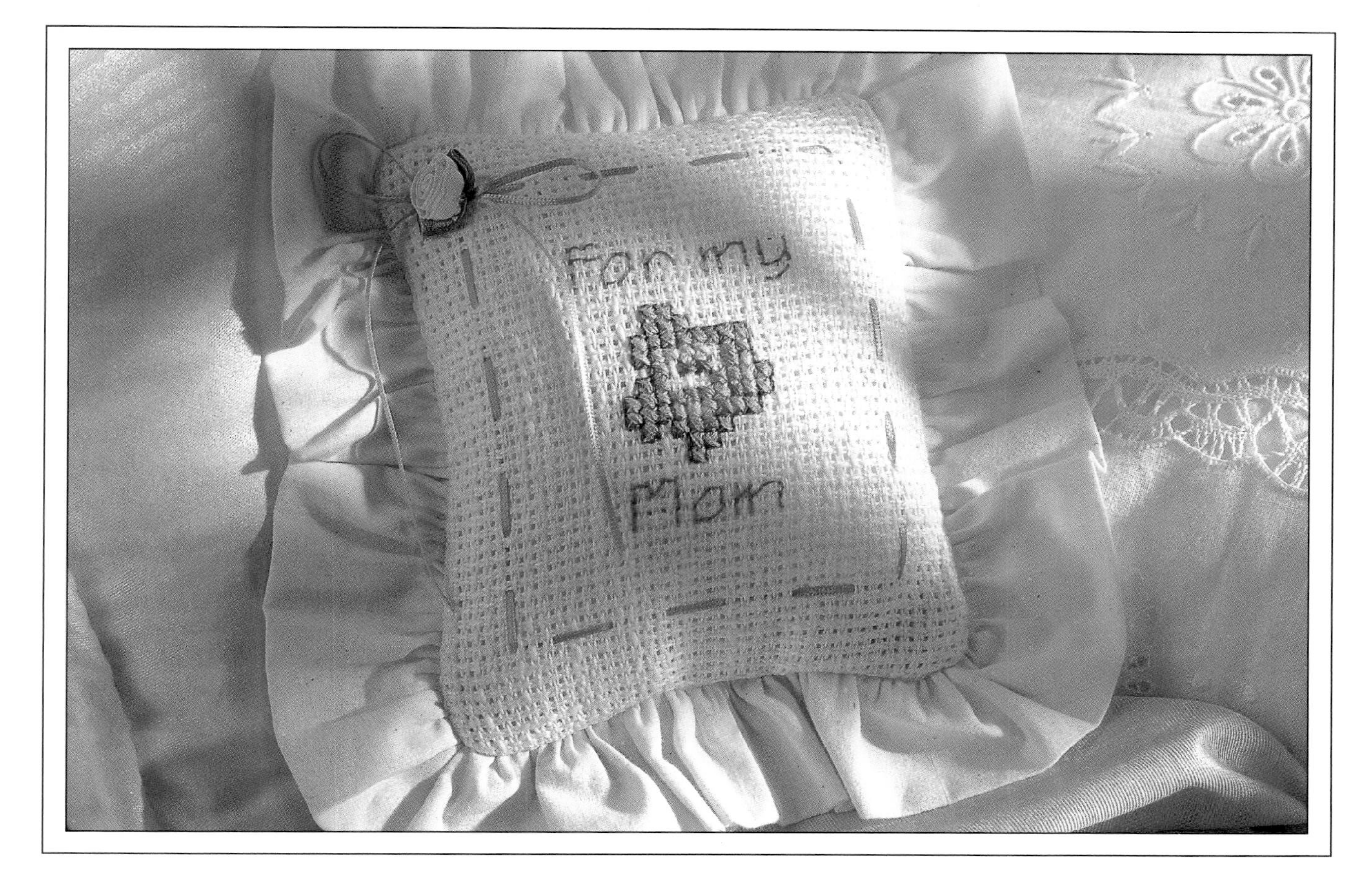

USE ROSE DESIGN FROM SPECIAL OCCASION ALPHABET ON PAGE 242 AND LETTERS FROM SPECIAL OCCASION BACKSTITCH ALPHABET ON PAGE 252

Materials

Pillow: Premade with 7-count fabric, cream, 5x6 inches with 1½-inch ruffle (Adam Originals)
Pillow stuffing
Satin ribbon: Pink, 1/16 inch wide, 44 inches
Pink ribbon rose
Muslin: 2 pieces, each 4x4 inches
Potpourri (lavender blend is recommended)
Tapestry needle: Size #20

Stitch

Reach inside the premade pillow back to cross-stitch the design. Follow the instructions for cross-stitching given in Cross-Stitch Basics. Use all six strands of floss for stitching; use two strands for back-stitching.

Finish

Thread a tapestry needle with the pink ribbon. Stitch around the edge of the design (see photo for placement). Leave 14 inches of ribbon as a tail in the upper left-hand corner. Tie a bow in the corner, and trim the bow with pink ribbon rose.

After stitching, insert stuffing into pillow. To make a potpourri pillow, place the two pieces of muslin together. Baste three edges, turn inside out, fill with potpourri, and stitch up fourth edge. Slip the potpourri pillow into the cross-stitched pillow.

Birthday Place Mat

USE SPECIAL OCCASION BIRTHDAY CANDLE ALPHABET ON PAGE 255

Materials

Anne cloth: White, 14x20 inches including 1-inch-wide fringe (Leisure Arts)

Stitch

Follow the instructions for cross-stitching over two threads given in Cross-Stitch Basics.

Finish

After cross-stitching the design, machine-stitch right next to decorative bars. (If desired, zigzag-stitch over two threads.) For fringe, carefully pull out threads right up to machine stitching.

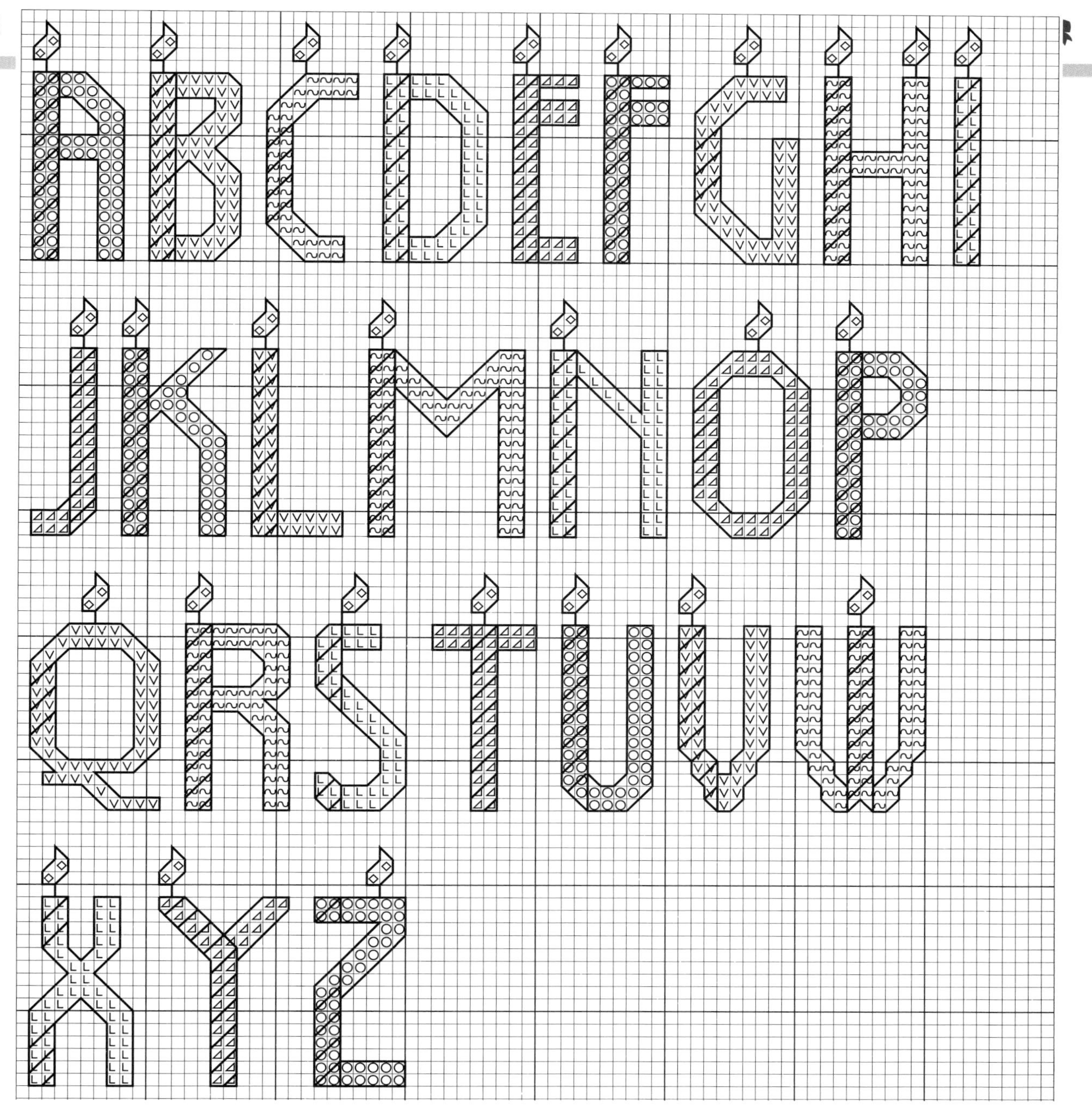

Special Occasion
Birthday Candle Alphabet

Floss

Symbol	*Color name*	*DMC#*	*Anchor#*
○	Medium pink	3688	66
	Dark pink**	3687	68
∾	Yellow	745	292
	Gold**	783	307
L	Lavender	211	342
	Dark lavender**	208	110
◿	Medium green	320	215
	Dark green**	890	218
V	Medium blue	793	176
	Dark blue**	792	941
	Black*	310	403

*Backstitch flames in black (two strands).
**Backstitch candle letters in the next darker shade (two strands).

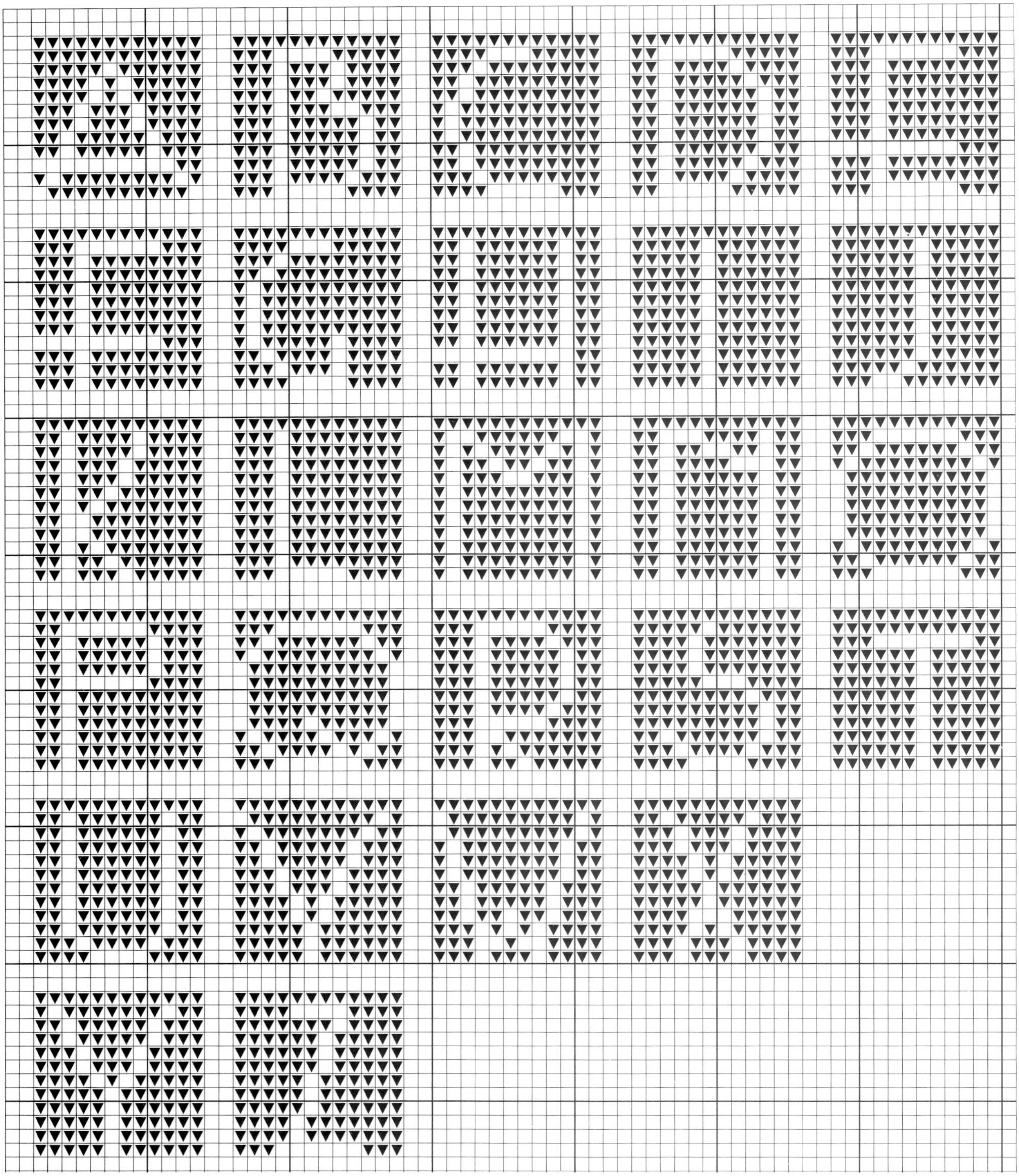

Special Occasion Block Alphabet
(These letters fit into the squares on all of the borders.)

Floss

Symbol	Color name	DMC#	Anchor#
▼	Dark blue	792	941
	(Or use the floss color of your choice.)		

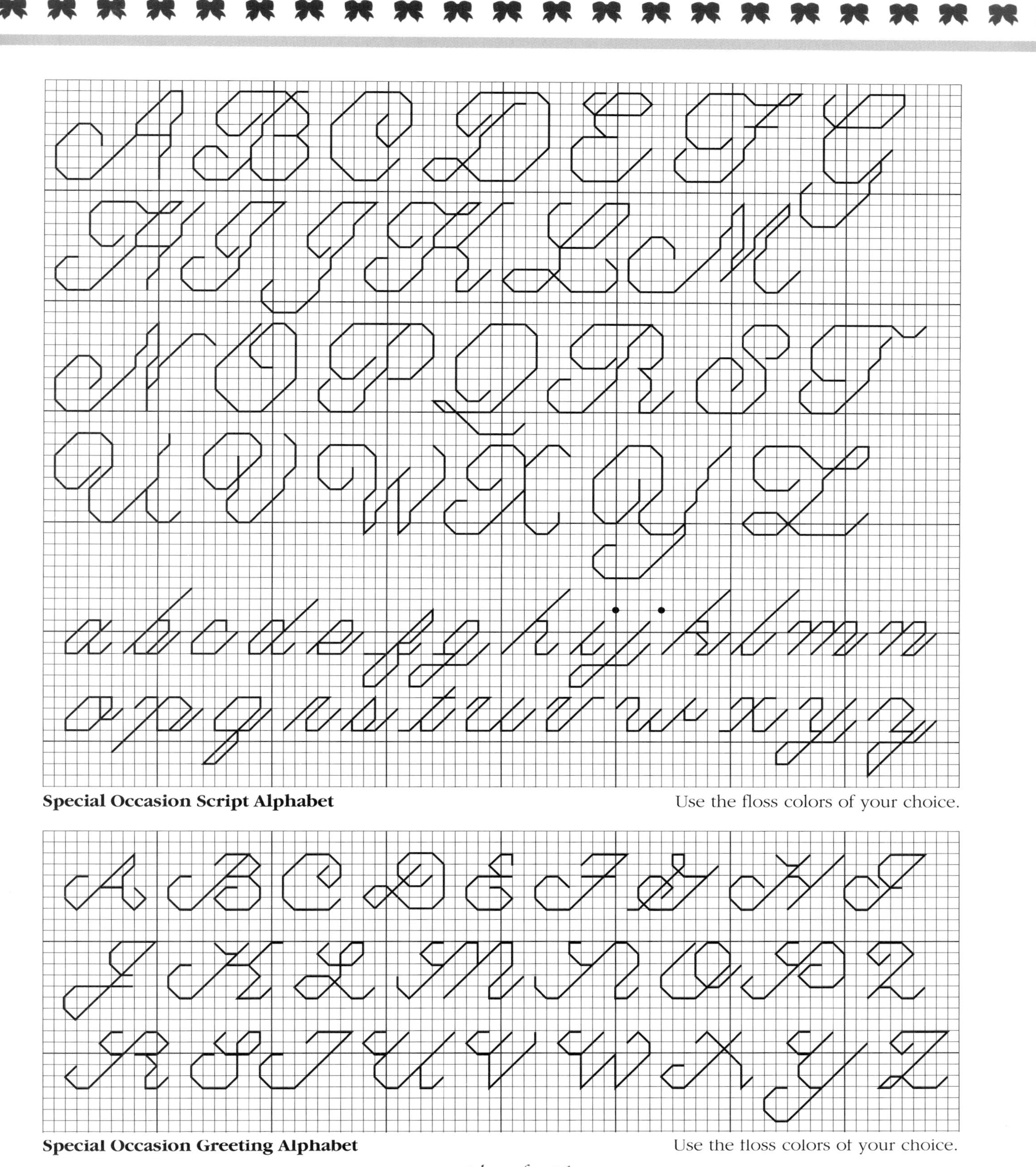

Special Occasion Script Alphabet

Use the floss colors of your choice.

Special Occasion Greeting Alphabet

Use the floss colors of your choice.

Ideas for Use

Both of these alphabets are very versatile and could be used with any of the symbols in the Special Occasion Alphabet on page 242–243 to form your own samplers and greeting cards.

Special Occasion Festival Alphabet (uppercase)

Use the floss colors of your choice.

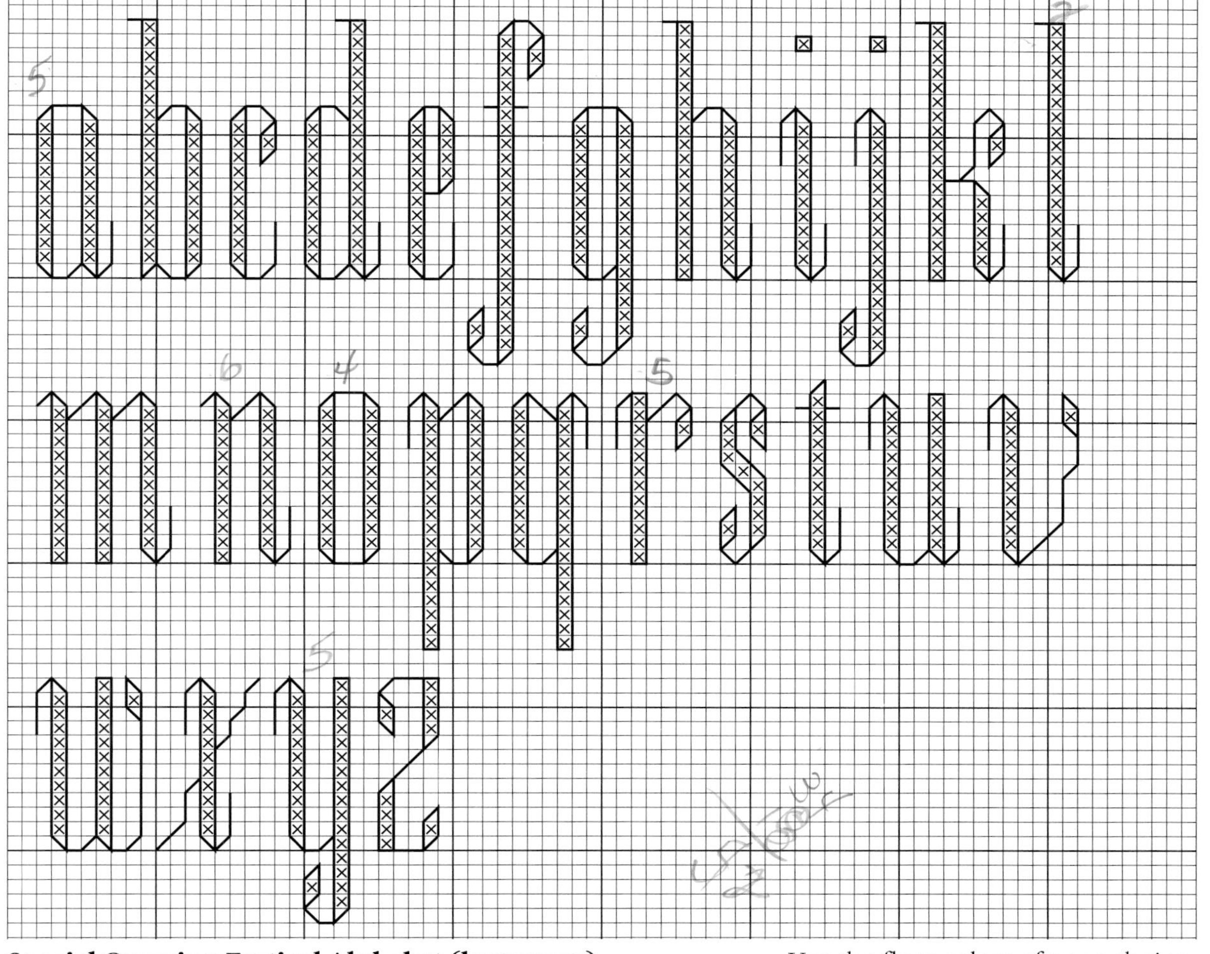

Special Occasion Festival Alphabet (lowercase) Use the floss colors of your choice.

Ideas for Use

This elegant alphabet would be very nice for monogramming guest towels or pillowcases for a wedding present. Cross-stitch the same initials on perforated paper to make the gift tag.

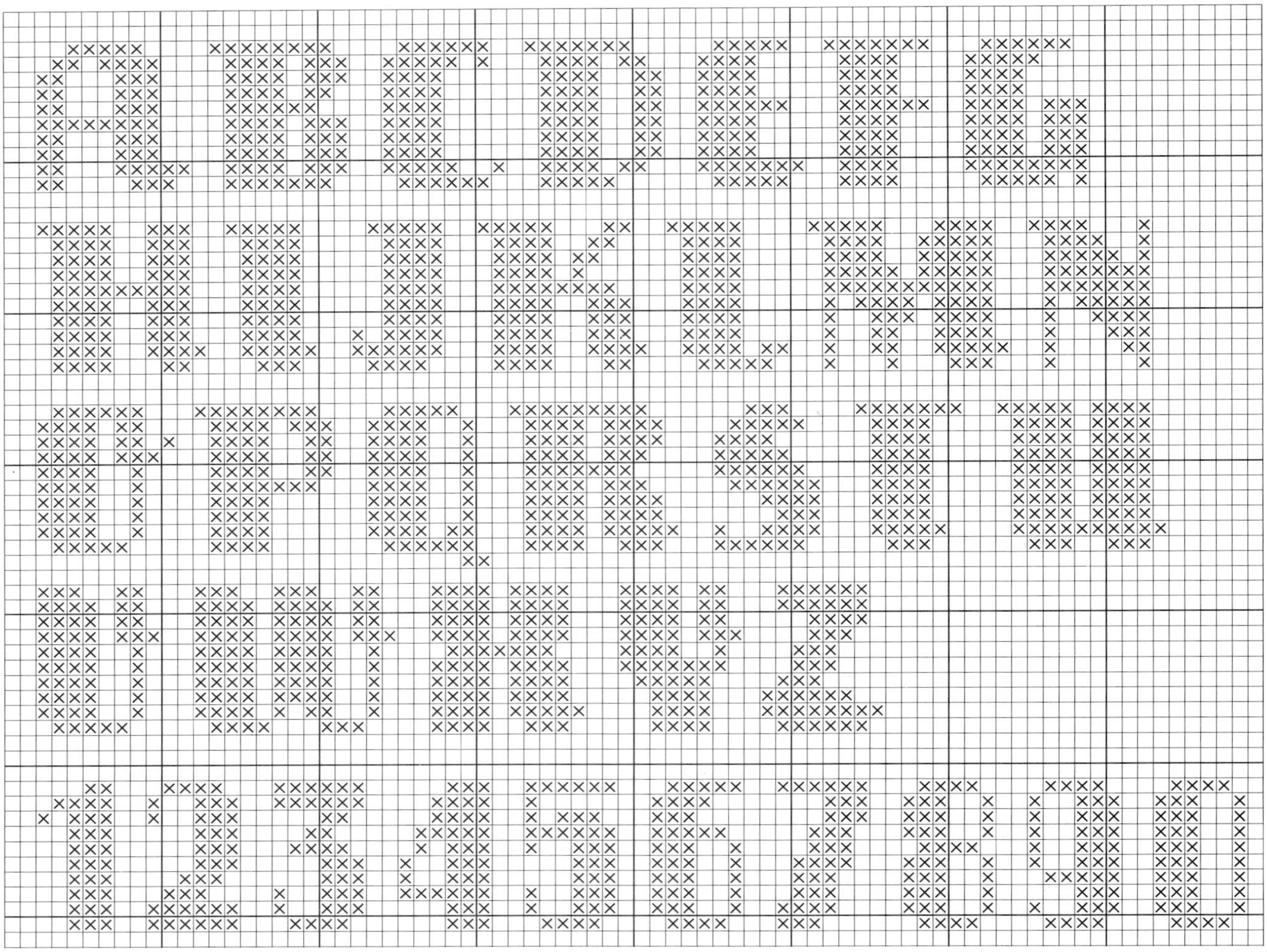

Special Occasion Best Wishes Alphabet

Use the floss colors of your choice.

Ideas for Use

This Best Wishes Alphabet would be cute for cross-stitching children's gifts and greeting cards. Try cross-stitching each vertical row of the letters in a different rainbow color.

Ideas for Use

The letters from the Formal Alphabet would be nice for monograms. Cross-stitch two to three initials with a pair of symbols from the Special Occasion Alphabet on pages 242–243 on either side.

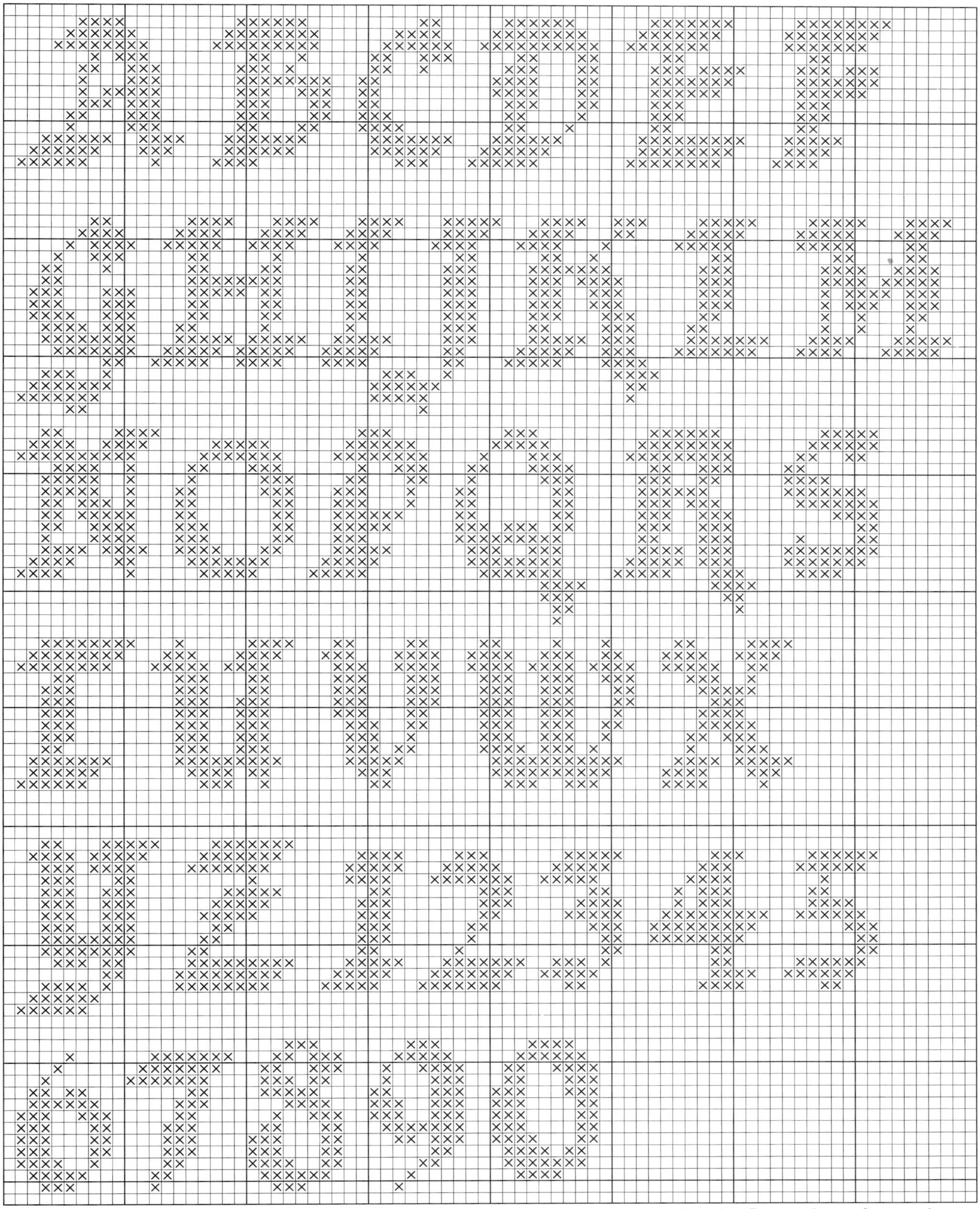

Special Occasion Formal Alphabet

Use the floss colors of your choice.

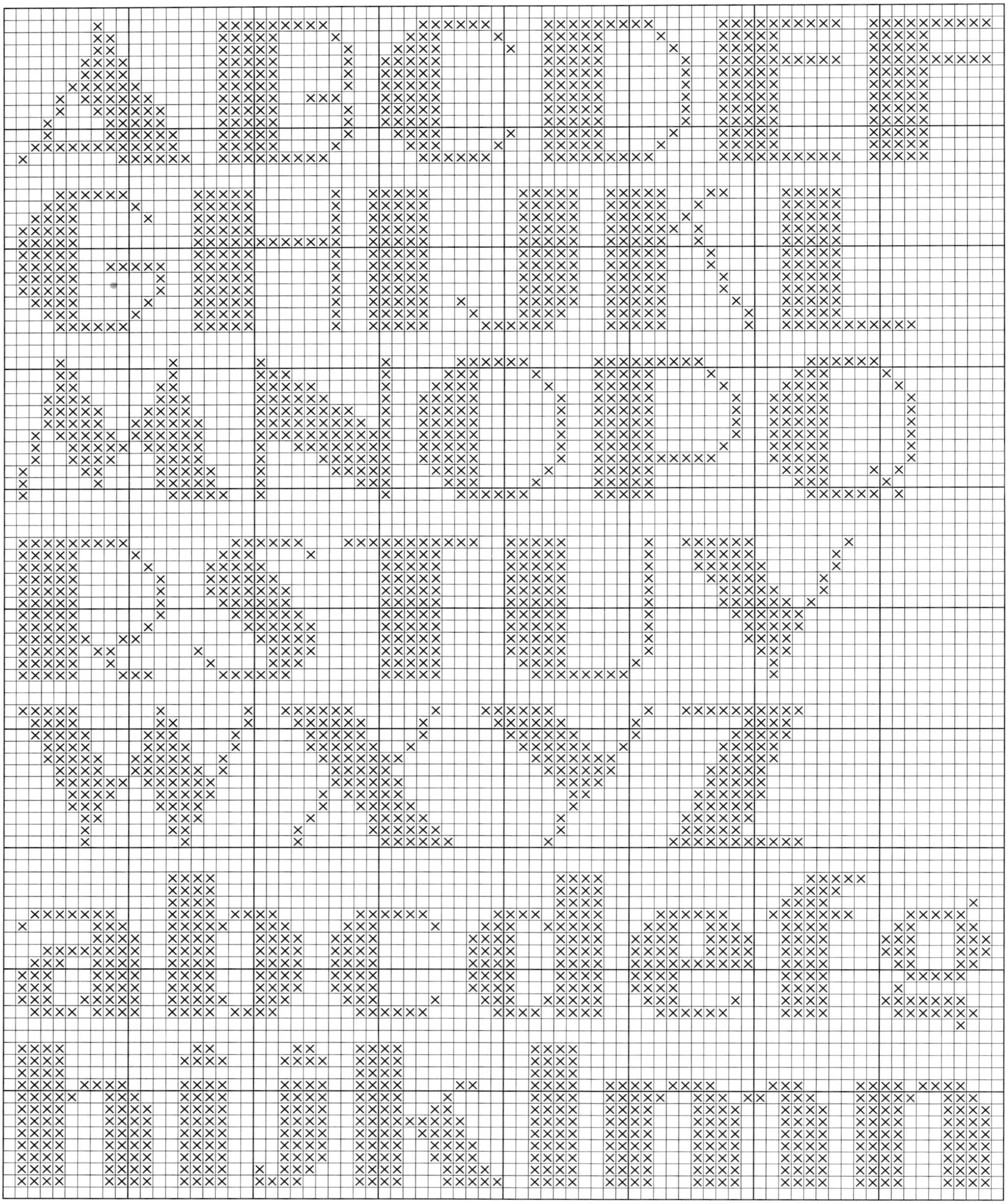

Special Occasion Salutation Alphabet

Use the floss colors of your choice.

Ideas for Use

Stitch a baby's name and birth date along with several of the baby symbols from the Special Occasion Alphabet on pages 242–243 to make a birth sampler.

Special Occasion Salutation Alphabet *(continued)*

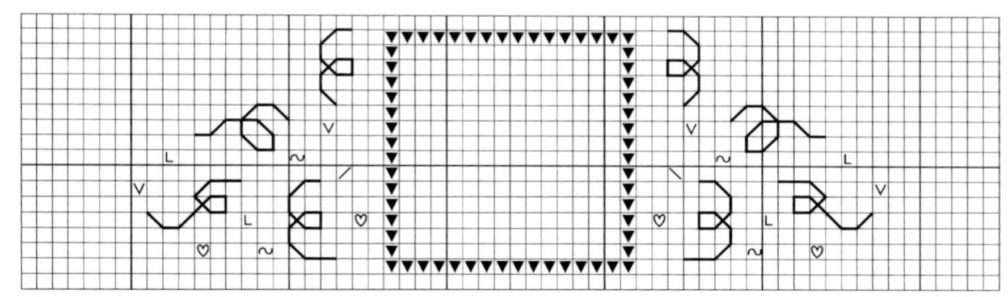

Special Occasion Party Border

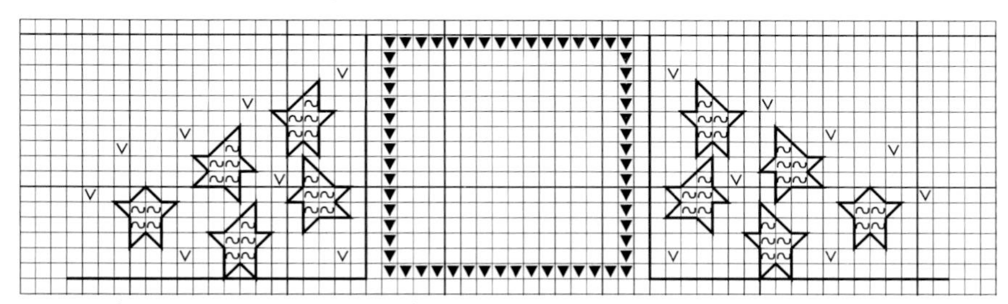

Special Occasion Stars Border

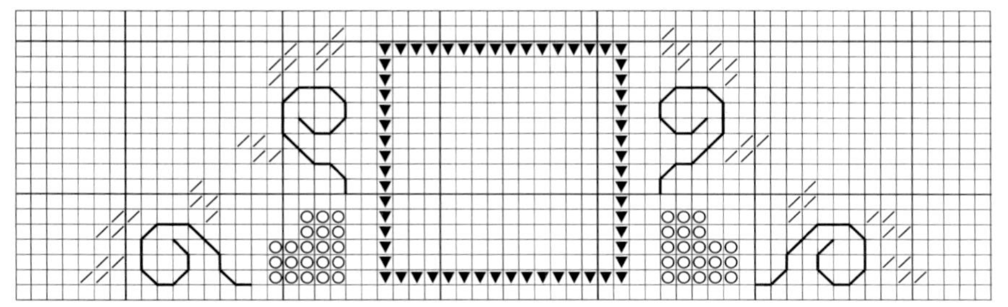

Special Occasion Love Border

Floss

Symbol	Color name	DMC	Anchor
V	Light blue	827	160
▼	Dark blue**	792	941
/	Medium green***	320	215
∾	Yellow	745	292
	Gold*	783	307
L	Light lavender	210	108
♡	Red	816	1005
O	Medium pink	3688	66

Backstitch confetti in Party Border in a variety of colors (two strands).
*Backstitch stars in the Stars Border in gold (two strands).
**Backstitch lines in the Stars Border in dark blue (two strands).
***Backstitch vines in the Love Border in medium green (two strands).

Ideas for Use

The Party Border in combination with a symbol from the Special Occasion Alphabet on pages 242–243 is perfect for any celebration.

Glue a photo in the center square of the Stars Border to reward your special "star."

Use the Love Border anytime you want to send a heartfelt message.

Holiday Alphabets

This chapter is actually five chapters in one. Alphabets and borders are included for Valentine's Day, Easter, Halloween, Thanksgiving, and Christmas. Mix and match the holiday designs for exciting home decorations and wearable items you can give as gifts or use to adorn your own home.

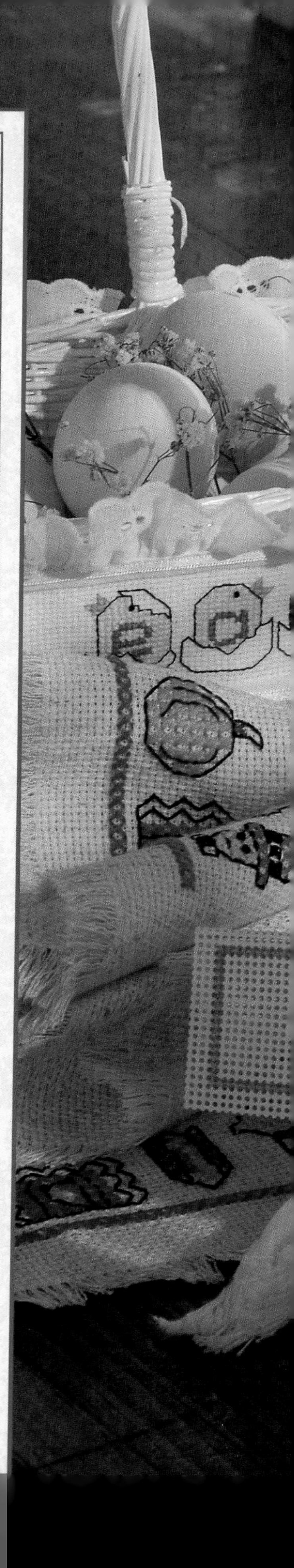

Joe + Ann
Tristan

Intertwining hearts and letters spell happiness for your Valentine. Shades of reds and pinks cast the blush of love on everyone with gifts and decorations made using the Valentine Alphabet. You can stitch a jar top for your true love, and fill the jar with candies. A basket encircled with a Valentine message makes a perfect centerpiece filled with flowers. This versatile alphabet is great for designing unique cards and gift tags, too.

Valentine Basket and Guest Towel

Valentine Basket

USE VALENTINE HEART ALPHABET BELOW

Materials

Ribband®: White with red edge, 18 count, ¾x10 inches or to fit basket (The Finish Line)
Basket: White, 5x7x3 inches
Ribbon: Red, wire edged, ½ inch wide, 24 inches
Lace: White, gathered eyelet, 1x24 inches
Hot glue gun and glue
Craft glue

Stitch

Follow the instructions for cross-stitching given in Cross-Stitch Basics.

Finish

Measurements are for a basket of the dimensions given above; adjust as necessary for smaller or larger baskets. After cross-stitching the design on Ribband®, glue lace to backside with fabric glue. Apply hot glue to back of band and press firmly in place around basket.

Floss

Symbol	Color name	DMC	Anchor
•	Pink	894	27
L	Light lavender	211	342
	Red*	321	9046
	*Backstitch letters in red (two strands). Alternate the colors of the hearts as you like. Backstitch hearts in the same color in which they are stitched (one strand).		

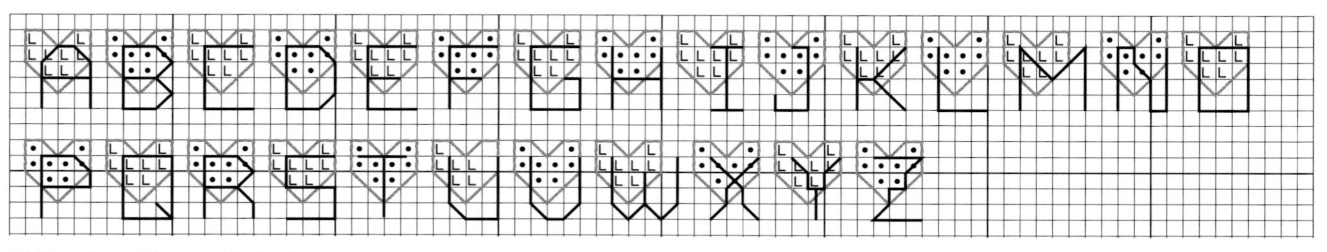

Valentine Heart Alphabet

Valentine Guest Towel

USE VALENTINE BORDER BELOW

Materials

Towel: Premade, fingertip towel, white, 14 count (Charles Craft #PT-6681)

Stitch

Follow the instructions for cross-stitching given in Cross-Stitch Basics.

Finish

Premade towel requires no finishing.

Floss

Symbol	Color name	DMC	Anchor
•	Pink	894	27
∿	Yellow	745	300
+	Brown*	434	310
L	Light lavender	211	342
◣	Dark lavender	209	109
/	Green	504	1042
∧	Peach	353	8
V	Light blue	747	158
▽	Medium blue	518	1039
♡	Red**	321	9046

*Backstitch arrow in heart in brown (one strand).
**Backstitch red and pink heart in red (two strands).
Backstitch other hearts in the same color in which they are stitched (two strands).

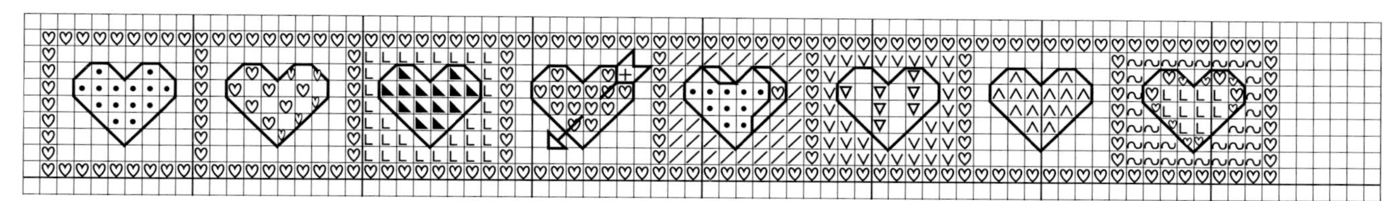

Valentine Border

Repeat border as needed.

Valentine Trinket Box

USE VALENTINE LACY HEART AND VALENTINE SCRIPT ALPHABET ON PAGE 271

Materials

Perforated paper: White, 4x4 inches, 14 count (Yarn Tree Designs, Inc.)
Ribbon: Red, wire edged, ½ inch wide, 12 inches
Gold charm: Heart (Creative Beginnings)
Braid: Pink, 12 inches
Pearls: 12-inch strand
Chipwood box: Oval, 4x2 inches
Valentine fabric: ¼ yard
Craft glue

Stitch

Follow the instructions for cross-stitching on perforated paper given in Cross-Stitch Basics.

Finish

Cut out heart shape one row from design as pictured. Cover chipwood box with Valentine fabric using craft glue. Trim with braid and pearls. Tie ribbon in bow and glue onto box. Crimp ends of ribbon. Glue cross-stitched heart onto bow. Hot-glue or stitch charm onto cross-stitched heart (see photo for placement).

Floss

Symbol	Color name	DMC	Anchor
••	White	Snow white	2
•	Pink	894	27
♡	Red**	321	9046
	Black*	310	403

*Backstitch lace in black (one strand).
*Backstitch names (or initials, if names are too long) in black (two strands).
**Backstitch heart in red (one strand).

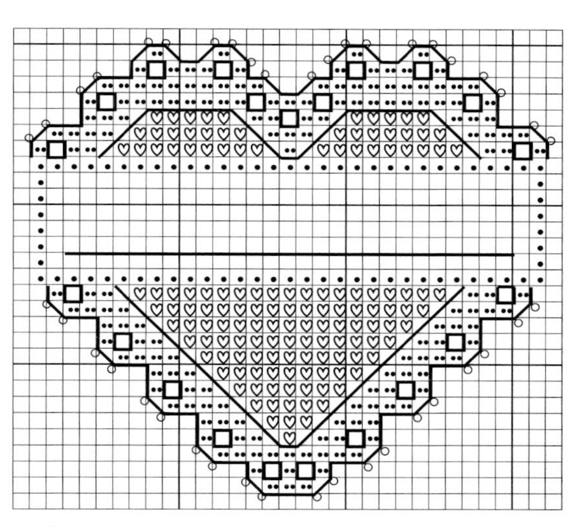

Valentine Lacy Heart

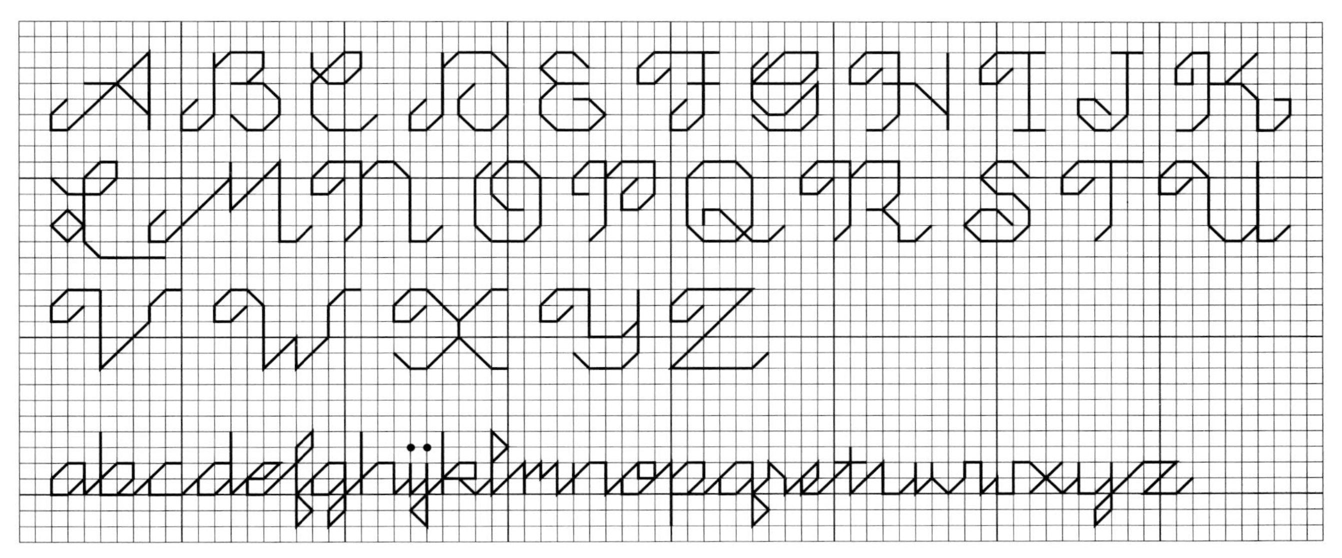

Valentine Script Alphabet

Valentine Candy Jar

USE VALENTINE TINY HEART BELOW AND VALENTINE SCRIPT ALPHABET ON PAGE 271

Materials

Aida fabric: White, 14 count, 6x6 inches
Lace: White, Cluny, 1x24 inches
Ribbon: Red, feather edged, ½ inch wide, 20 inches
Fabric glue

Stitch

Follow cross-stitch instructions given in Cross-Stitch Basics.

Valentine Tiny Heart

Finishing

Pin circle pattern on this page to fabric; cut out. Fold edges under ⅛ inch and hem by sewing or gluing. Add lace. Put candy (or a small gift) in jar and cover with the jar top. Tie ribbon around it tightly.

Candy Jar Top
Full-Size Pattern

Floss

Symbol	*Color name*	*DMC*	*Anchor*
▽	Red*	321	9046
♡	Black**	310	403
	Gray***	415	398

*Backstitch heart in red (one strand).
**Backstitch "Love" in black (two strands).
***Backstitch lace in gray (one strand).

Ideas for Use

Use this Valentine Alphabet along with the Valentine Heart Alphabet on page 268.

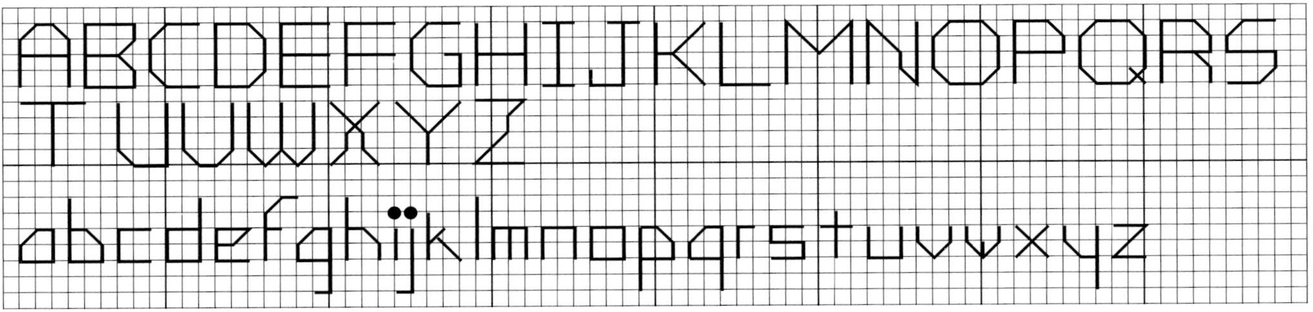

Valentine Alphabet

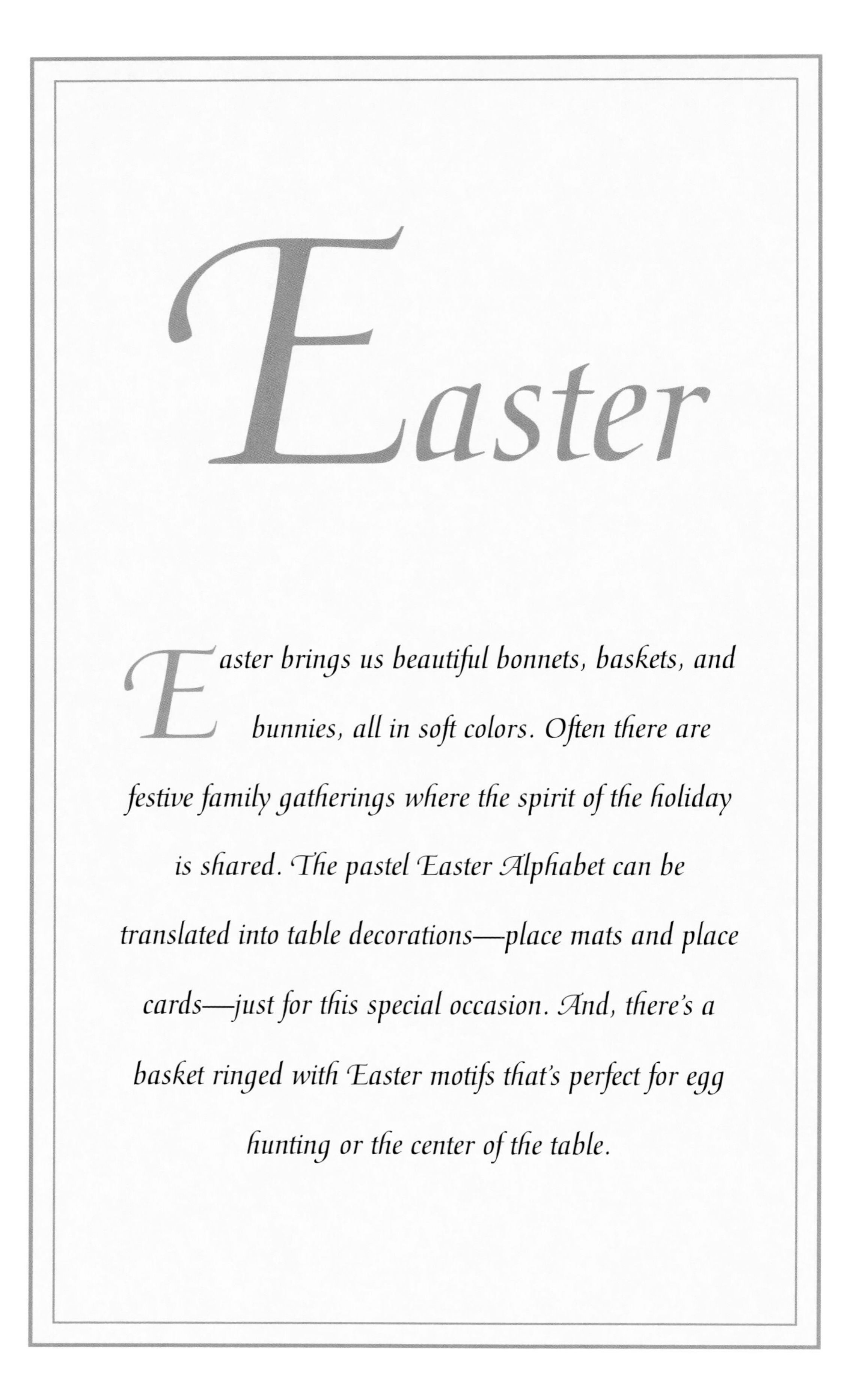

Easter

Easter brings us beautiful bonnets, baskets, and bunnies, all in soft colors. Often there are festive family gatherings where the spirit of the holiday is shared. The pastel Easter Alphabet can be translated into table decorations—place mats and place cards—just for this special occasion. And, there's a basket ringed with Easter motifs that's perfect for egg hunting or the center of the table.

Easter Basket

Easter Basket

USE LETTERS FROM EASTER ALPHABET ON PAGE 277

Materials

Ribband®: White, 18 count, 2x30 inches or to fit basket
Basket: 5x8x3 inches
Satin ribbon: Yellow, ⅛ inch wide, 57 inches
Lace: White, gathered eyelet, 1x57 inches
Craft glue
Hot glue gun and glue

Stitch

Follow instructions for cross-stitching given in Cross-Stitch Basics.

Finish

Measurements are for a basket of the dimensions given above; adjust as necessary for smaller or larger baskets. After cross-stitching design on Ribband®, apply hot glue to the entire back of the band. Press firmly in place around basket. Start and end at the back of the basket. Glue lace onto backside of Ribband® at top and bottom edge. Glue ribbon to lace (see photo for placement).

Floss

Symbol	Color name	DMC	Anchor
✱	Medium pink***	3688	66
∾	Yellow	745	292
◑	Orange**	742	303
	Black*	310	403

*Backstitch everything in black, except where otherwise indicated (one strand). Stitch black French knots for eyes.
**Backstitch beaks in orange (one strand).
***Backstitch letters in medium pink (two strands).

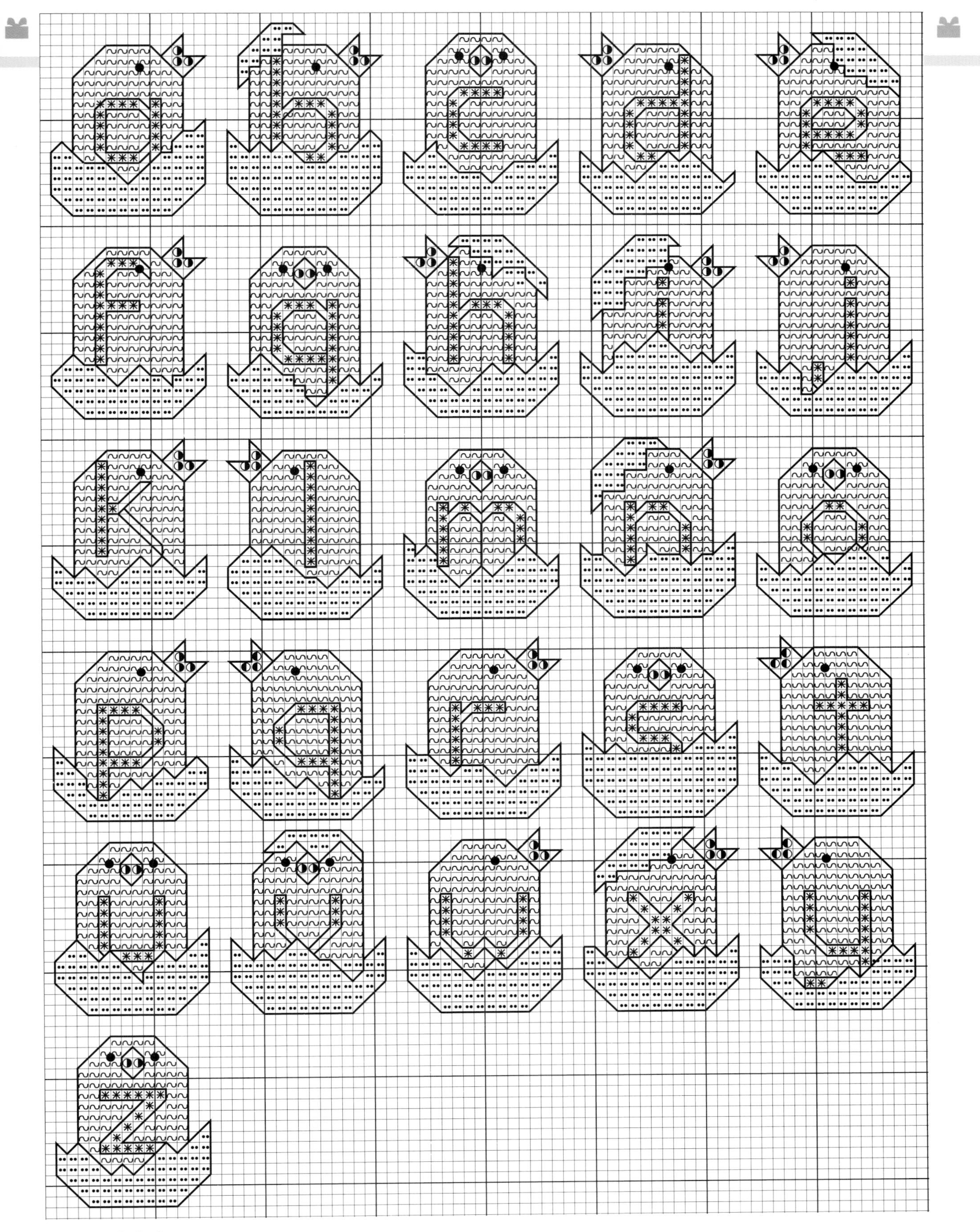

Easter Alphabet

Easter Place Mats

USE EASTER BUNNY AND WATER LILY BORDER ON PAGE 279

Materials

Place Mats: Premade, white, 14 count, Royal Classic (Charles Craft #RC4851-6750)

Stitch

Follow instructions for cross-stitching over two threads given in Cross-Stitch Basics. Stitch the border about 1 inch from the edge of the place mat around all sides.

Easter Place Card

USE EASTER BUNNY AND WATER LILY BORDER ON PAGE 279 AND VALENTINE SCRIPT ALPHABET ON PAGE 271

Materials

Perforated paper: White, 14 count, 4½x3 inches (Yarn Tree Designs, Inc.)

Stitch

Follow instructions for cross-stitching on perforated paper given in Cross-Stitch Basics.

Finish

If necessary, cut paper 4½x3 inches. Fold in half lengthwise. Find center and start stitching center of name at this point. Stitch one of the pictures from the border on both sides of name. Add a border of cross-stitches in light green about two spaces in from all edges.

Easter Bunny and Water Lily Border

Floss

Symbol	*Color name*	*DMC*	*Anchor*
•	Light pink	818	23
○	Medium pink**	3688	66
∾	Yellow	745	292
◇	Gold	743	302
◑	Orange	742	303
L	Light lavender	211	342
◣	Dark lavender	209	109
∧	Peach	353	8
∨	Light blue	809	130
▽	Medium blue	799	145
▼	Dark blue	797	148
/	Light green	504	1042
◢	Dark green***	502	877
—	Light gray	415	398
	Dark gray*	414	235
	Black	310	403

*Backstitch bunny in dark gray (two strands).
**Backstitch bunny ears in medium pink (two strands). Stitch medium pink French knots for eyes and nose.
***Backstitch leaves in dark green (two strands).
****Backstitch Easter eggs in black (one strand).
Backstitch flowers in same color as they are stitched (two strands).

Ideas for Use

The Easter Bunny Border would look cute stitched on the hat band of a little girls Easter bonnet. To complete an outfit, stitch the Easter Eggs Border around the top of her socks.

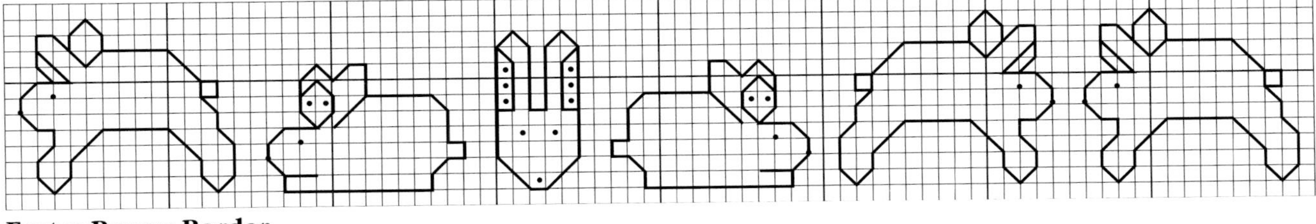

Easter Bunny Border

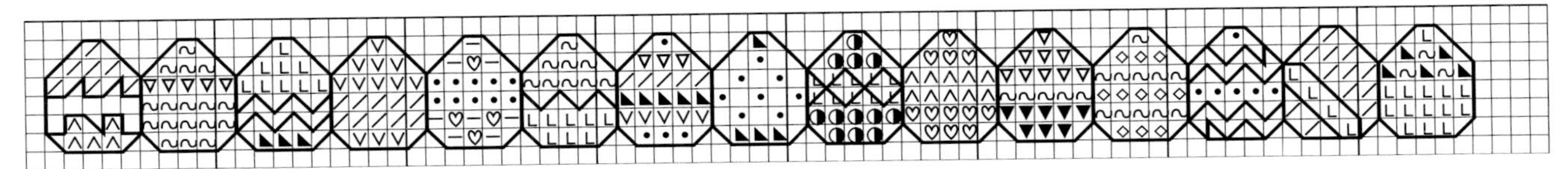

Easter Eggs Border

Halloween

Spooky ghosts and scary spiders creep out of our Halloween Alphabet to inspire you to create sinister gifts and haunting home decorations. The kids will love their very own trick-or-treat bags specially stitched by you. Or, use the bag as a centerpiece filled with twigs and cobwebs. Decorate a table near the door with a basket full of treats. A T-shirt becomes an instant costume when stitched with these "boo-tiful" designs. It's just the thing to delight all your little Halloween goblins.

Halloween Trick-or-Treat Bag, Basket and T-Dress

Halloween Trick-or-Treat Bag

USE HALLOWEEN GHOSTS AND SPIDERS BORDER ON PAGE 283

Materials

Bag: Premade, 7 count, Klostern (Adam Originals)
Tapestry needle: Size 20

Stitch

Follow instructions for cross-stitching given in Cross-Stitch Basics. Start stitching about ¾ inch from the bottom at the center of the bag. Repeat the border all the way around.

Finish

Premade bag requires no finishing.

Halloween Basket

USE LETTERS FROM HALLOWEEN ALPHABET ON PAGE 283

Materials

Aida fabric: 14 count, Fiddler's cloth, 2x14 inches or to fit basket
Basket: Black with handle, approximately 8½x3x5 inches
Ribbon: Orange Krinkle, 64 inches (Hirshberg/Schutz, Inc.)
Hot glue gun and glue

Stitch

Follow instructions for cross-stitching given in Cross-Stitch Basics.

Finish

Measurements are for a basket of the dimensions given above; adjust as necessary for smaller or larger baskets. After cross-stitching the design, apply glue to the back of the band. Press firmly in place around basket. Start and end band at the back of the basket. Add Orange Krinkle ribbon (see photo on page 281 for placement).

Halloween T-Dress

USE HALLOWEEN ALPHABET ON PAGE 283

Materials

T-dress: Black, child's size
Waste canvas: 8.5 count, 7x9 inches

Stitch and Finish

Follow cross-stitching and finishing instructions for using waste canvas given in Cross-Stitch Basics.

Floss for T-Dress

Symbol	Color name	DMC	Anchor
■	Orange*	971	316
••	White**	Snow white	2
—	Gray***	414	235
	Black****	310	403

*Backstitch letters in orange (two strands).
**Backstitch skull and ghosts in white (two strands).
***Backstitch cats, spiders and spiderwebs in gray (two strands).
****Backstitch eyes and mouth of skull in black (two strands). Stitch black French knots for eyes.

Floss for Bag and Basket

Symbol	Color name	DMC	Anchor
••	White	Snow white	2
∾	Dark yellow	742	303
◑	Orange	971	316
I	Beige	437	362
◢	Green	890	218
■	Black*	310	403
—	Gray	414	235

*Backstitch everything in black (one strand).

Halloween Trick-or-Treat Bag
*Stitch black French knots for ghost's eyes and for spiders.
*Backstitch in black around all images, on pumpkin faces, and for spider webs.

Halloween Basket
*Backstitch in black around eyes (one strand).
*Stitch black French knots for cat's eyes and for spiders, where indicated.

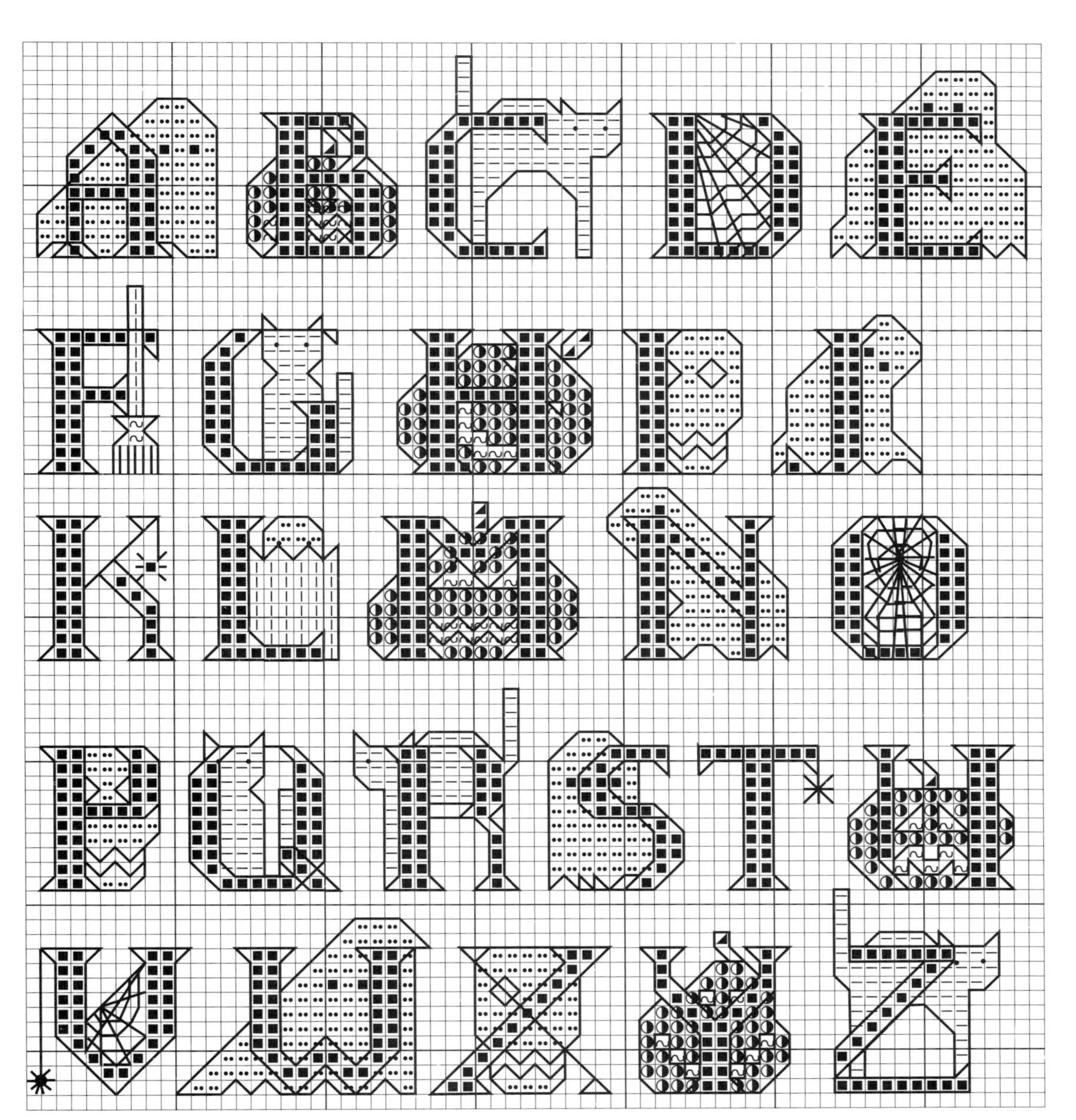

Halloween Alphabet

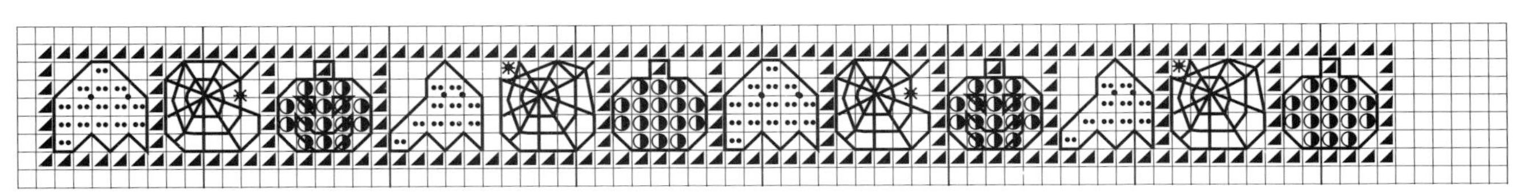

Halloween Ghosts and Spiders Border

Thanksgiving

At Thanksgiving we pause to give thanks for our many blessings, which are symbolized by the bountiful Thanksgiving dinner. What better time to decorate the holiday table and show each of our guests how much we care. Our table features a basket for the centerpiece, matching place mats and napkins, and a place card for each guest. Other possible ways of using this alphabet include personalized coasters, a framed sampler, and guest towels.

Thanksgiving Basket

Thanksgiving Basket

USE LETTERS FROM THANKSGIVING ALPHABET BELOW

Materials

Ribband®: Ivory with tan edge, 18 count, 1½x29 inches or to fit basket (The Finish Line)
Basket: 5x9x4
Hot glue gun and glue

Stitch

Follow instructions for cross-stitching given in Cross-Stitch Basics.

Finish

Hot-glue band around basket, overlapping slightly in back. Glue the edges down.

Floss

Symbol	Color name	DMC	Anchor
<	Light orange	977	1002
◑	Dark orange	971	316
+	Beige	437	362
×	Brown	434	310
–	Dark gray	414	235
/	Light green	911	205
◢	Dark green***	319	218
∧	Peach	353	8
♡	Red**	321	9046
■	Black****	310	403
	White*	Snow white	2

*Backstitch square on middle of Pilgrim's hat with white (two strands).
**Backstitch turkey's wattle in red (two strands).
***Backstitch letters in dark green (one strand).
****Backstitch everything else in black (one strand). Stitch black French knots for the eyes.

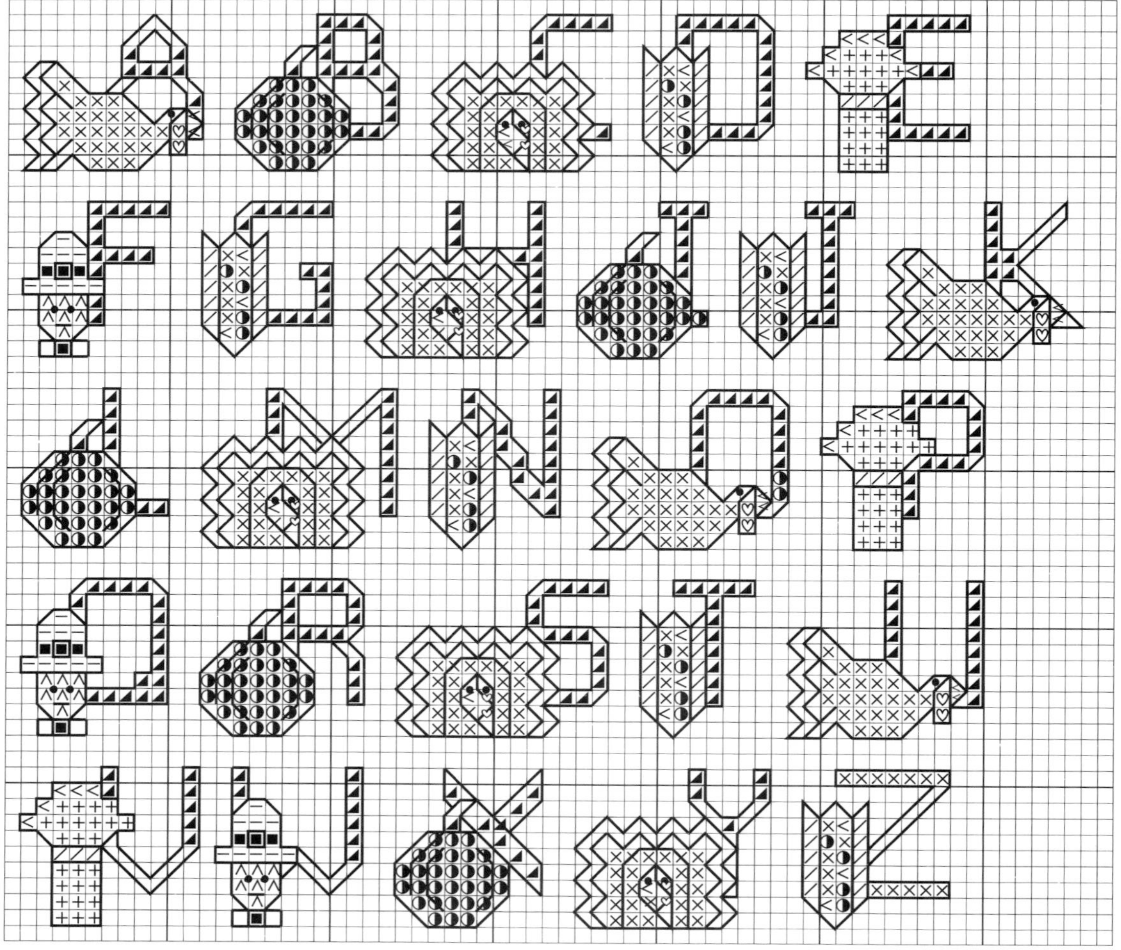

Thanksgiving Alphabet

Thanksgiving Place Mats, Napkins, and Place Cards

Thanksgiving Place Mats

USE THANKSGIVING BORDER BELOW

Materials

Place mats: Premade, 14 count (Charles Craft #RC4851-5451), oatmeal

Stitch

Follow instructions for cross-stitching over two threads given in Cross-Stitch Basics. Stitch the border about 1 inch from the edge of the place mat on bottom and right side only.

Finish

Premade place mats require no finishing.

Thanksgiving Napkins

USE THANKSGIVING BORDER BELOW

Materials

Napkins: Premade, 14 count (Charles Craft #RD4852-5451), oatmeal

Stitch

Follow instructions for cross-stitching over two threads given in Cross-Stitch Basics. Start stitching about 1 inch up from bottom at center of place mat.

Finish

Premade napkins require no finishing.

Thanksgiving Place Cards

USE THANKSGIVING BORDER BELOW AND VALENTINE SCRIPT ALPHABET ON PAGE 271

Materials

Perforated paper: Brown, 14 count (Yarn Tree Designs, Inc.), 4½x3 inches.

Stitch

Follow instructions for cross-stitching on perforated paper given in Cross-Stitch Basics.

Finishing

If necessary, cut paper to 4½x3 inches. Fold in half lengthwise. Find center and start cross-stitching center of name at this point. Cross-stitch one of the pictures from the border on each side of name. Add a border of cross-stitches in dark green about two spaces in from all edges.

Floss

Symbol	Color name	DMC	Anchor
<	Light orange	977	1002
◑	Dark orange	971	316
+	Beige	437	362
×	Brown	434	310
–	Dark gray	414	235
/	Light green	911	205
◢	Dark green	319	218
∧	Peach	353	8
♡	Red**	321	9046
■	Black***	310	403
	White*	Snow white	2

*Backstitch square on middle of Pilgrim's hat with white (two strands).
**Backstitch turkey's wattle in red (two strands).
***Backstitch everything else in black (one strand). Stitch French knots for the eyes.

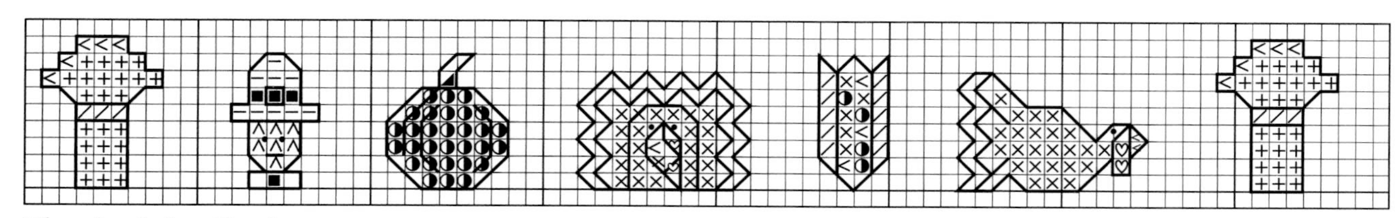

Thanksgiving Border

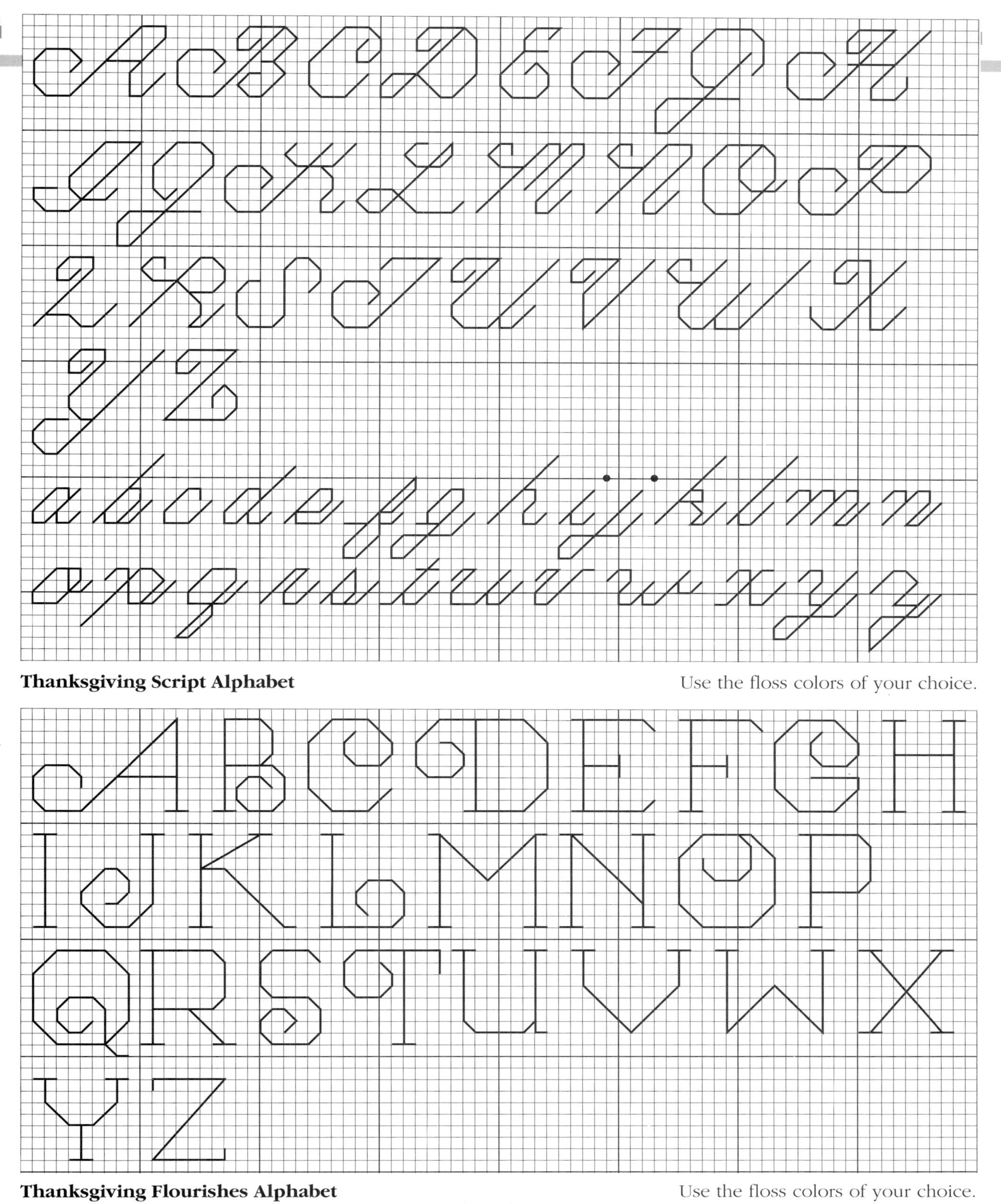

Thanksgiving Script Alphabet

Use the floss colors of your choice.

Thanksgiving Flourishes Alphabet

Use the floss colors of your choice.

Ideas for Use

Use the lowercase Script Alphabet letters with letters from the Thanksgiving Alphabet on page 286 to make a Thanksgiving sampler.

Send a Thanksgiving greeting stitched on perforated paper using the Flourishes Alphabet along with some of the pictures from the Thanksgiving Border on page 288.

Christmas

Remember the awe you felt each time you came upon a gloriously trimmed tree towering over dozens of packages tied with endless swirls of ribbons? Our ribbon-bedecked Christmas Alphabet recalls that thrill. It's a versatile design that lends itself to so many projects. For example, the individual elements of the larger Christmas banner can be used to create candle trims, Christmas stockings, and special tree ornaments. And you can stitch matching place mats and napkins that are perfect for Christmas entertaining.

ABC
DEFGH
XYZ

Christmas Alphabet Bell Pull

USE CHRISTMAS ALPHABET ON PAGES 296–297

Materials

Aida fabric: White, 14 count, 10x18 inches
Cotton fabric: Red Christmas plaid, ¾ yard
Batting: 12x25 inches
Cord: Red, 2 yards; gold, 1½ yards
Tassel: Red, 3 inch
Large Christmas jingle bell
Dowel: ½x16 inches (painted green)
Ribbon: Red, ½ inch wide, 2 pieces, each 1 yard; green ⅛ inch wide, 2 pieces, each 1 yard

Stitch

Follow instructions for cross-stitching given in Cross-Stitch Basics.

Finish

Cut a piece of plaid fabric 25½x13 inches. Fold it in half lengthwise. Measure up 7 inches from bottom of an unfolded edge. Draw a line with a ruler from this point to the corner of the folded edge (see diagram A). Cut along

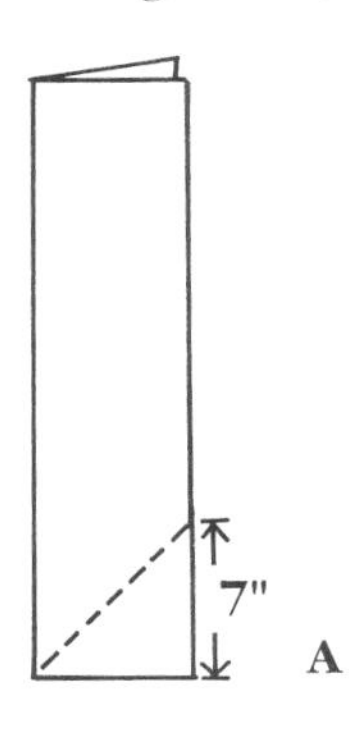

this line, keeping lines of plaid straight. This will be your liner fabric.

Cut a piece of plaid fabric 7x13 inches. Using the previously cut piece of fabric as a pattern (see diagram B), cut this fabric in a triangle (always be aware of the lines of the plaid).

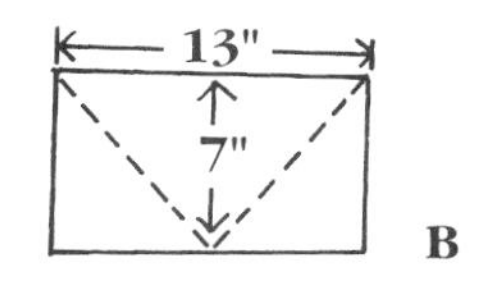

Cut two strips of plaid fabric 18¼x3 inches each and one strip 13x3 inches.

Lay an 18¼x3-inch strip on each long edge of the cross-stitched piece with right sides together (see diagram C). Stitch together with a ¼ inch seam allowance.

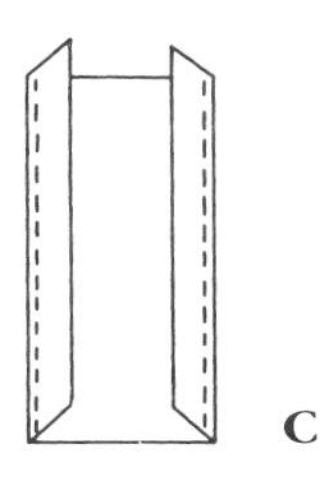

Unfold and lay the 13x3 inch strip at the top of cross-stitched piece with right sides together. Stitch together with a ¼-inch seam allowance (see diagram D).

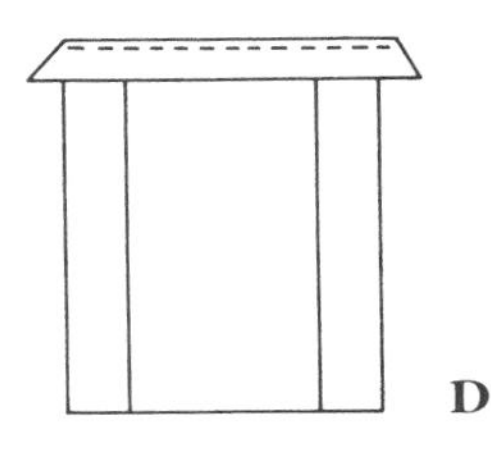

(continued)

Christmas Bell Pull

(continued)

Lay the triangular piece of plaid fabric on top of the stitched piece at the bottom with right sides together (see diagram E). Stitch together with a ¼ inch seam allowance. Unfold and press flat.

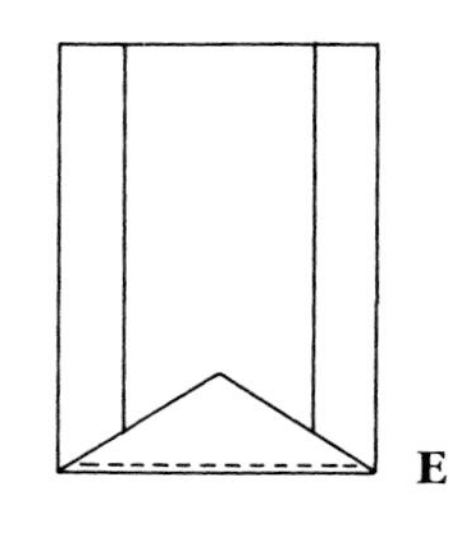

Cut a piece of batting the same size and shape as the liner fabric. Lay the batting on your work surface. Lay the cross-stitched piece on top of the batting with the right side up. Place the liner fabric on top of the cross-stitched piece with the right side down (see diagram F). Sew together with a ¼ inch seam allowance, leaving top open. Turn right side out.

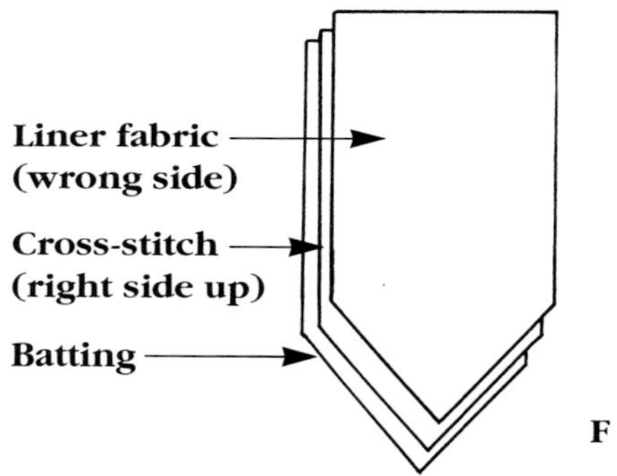

For hangers, cut three pieces of fabric 3x4 inches each. Fold each piece in half and sew each into a tube (see diagram G). Turn tubes right side out and press flat with seam in back (see diagram H). Tuck these hangers into top of bell pull

G

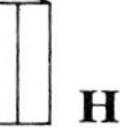

about ¼ inch. Turn top edges of bell pull under ¼ inch and topstitch with the hangers in place (see diagram I).

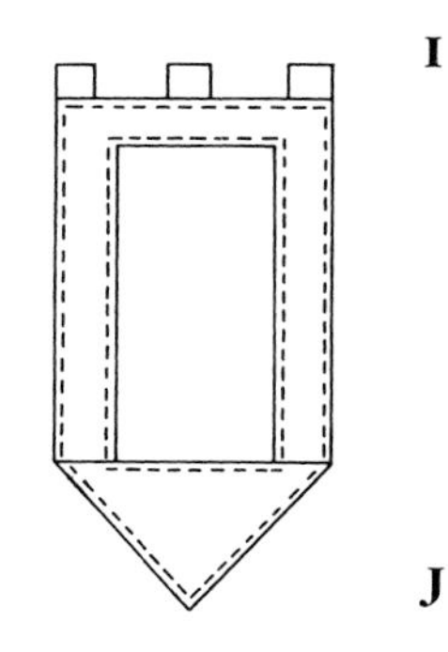

Topstitch all around edge of cross-stitched piece and around edge of bell pull (see diagram J).

Glue cords around edges and add a tassel and/or bell at the bottom.

Insert dowel through hangers and tie on ribbons (see photo for placement).

Christmas Pillow

USE CHRISTMAS ALPHABET ON PAGES 296–297 AND CHRISTMAS HOLLY BORDER ON PAGE 304

Materials

Pillow: Premade with 7 count, cream, Klostern fabric and a 2½-inch plaid ruffle (Adam Originals), 11x11 inches.
Pillow form: 11 inches square
Tapestry needle: Size 20

Stitch

Unzip the premade pillow and reach inside to cross-stitch the design. Follow the instructions for cross-stitching given in Cross-Stitch Basics. Use six strands of floss for cross-stitching and two strands for backstitching and French knots.

Finish

The premade pillow requires no finishing. Once stitching is completed, insert pillow form into pillow.

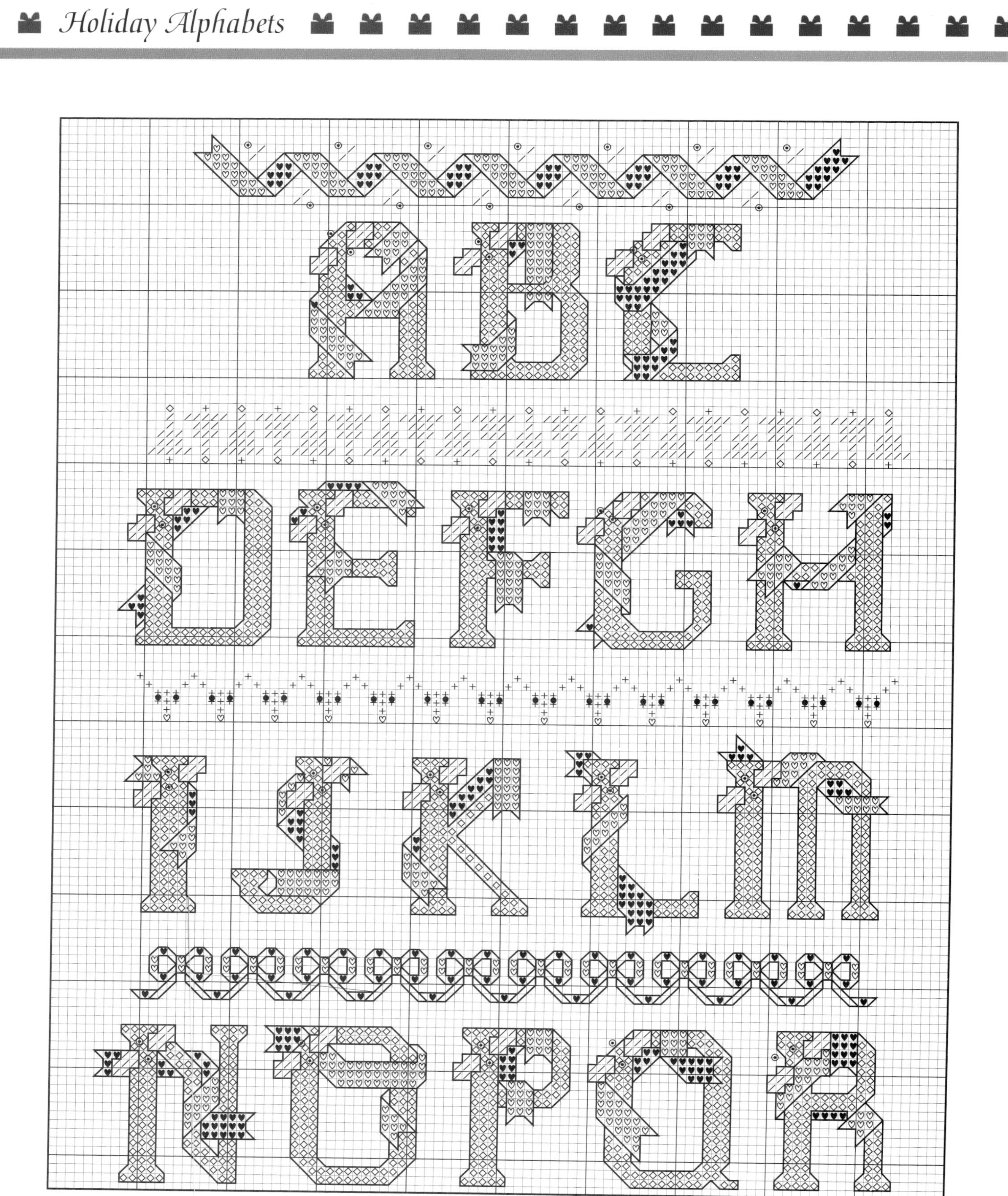

Christmas Alphabet

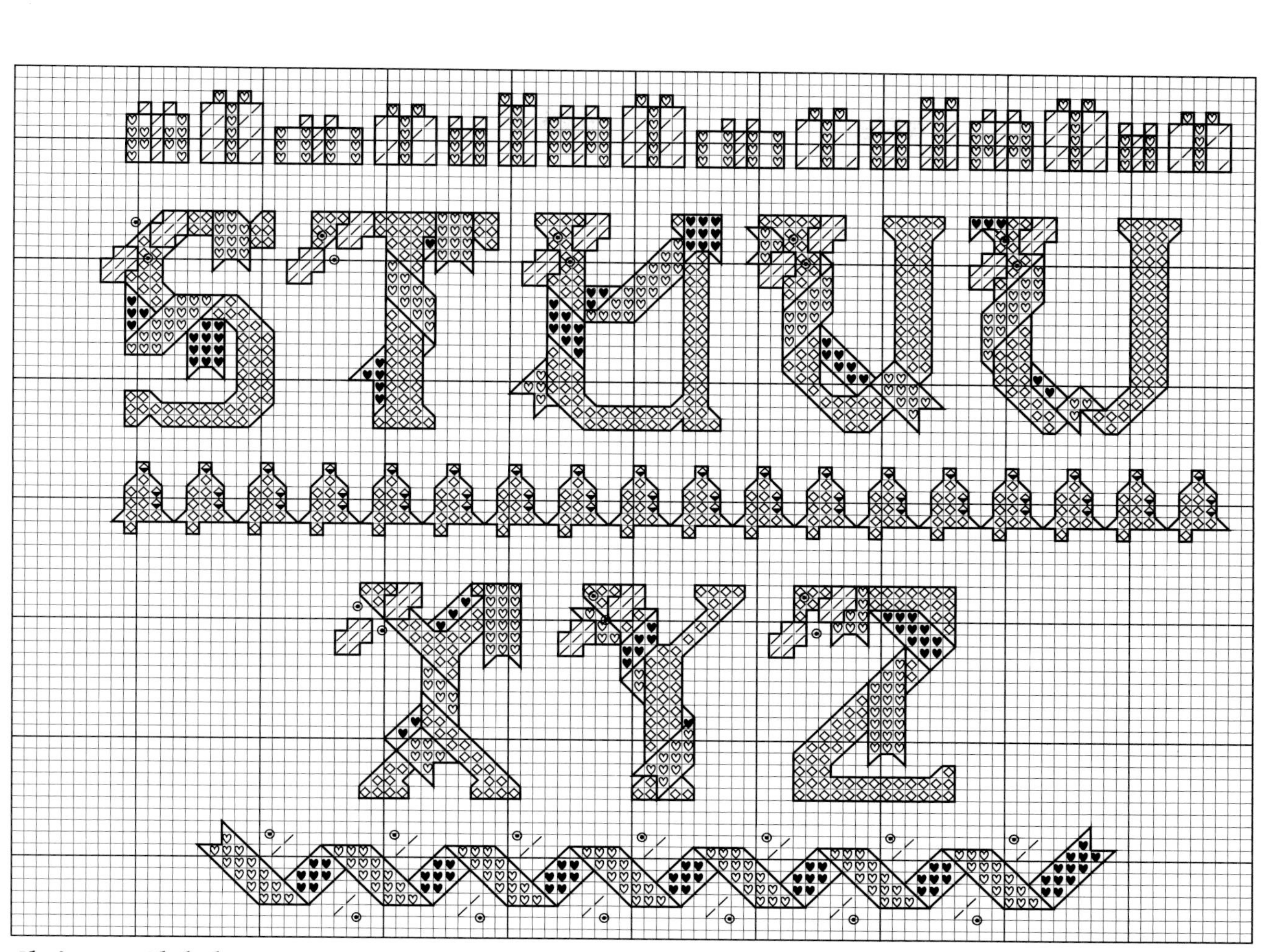

Christmas Alphabet

Floss

Symbol	*Color name*	*DMC*	*Anchor*
◇	Light gold	783	307
⬙	Dark gold	781	309
+	Brown	433	371
/	Green	700	228
♡	Light red	321	9046
♥	Dark red**	816	1005
	Black***	310	403
⦿	Light red French knots		
	Metallic gold*	Art. 282	363

*Optional: Mix one strand metallic gold floss with one strand light gold floss and stitch French knots for stars on Christmas Tree Border.
**Backstitch Christmas Bows Border in dark red (one strand).
***Backstitch everything else in black where indicated (one strand). Stitch black French knots for reindeer's eyes.

Christmas Basket

USE LETTERS FROM CHRISTMAS HOLIDAY ALPHABET ON PAGE 299 AND CHRISTMAS RIBBON BORDER ON PAGE 300

Materials

Ribband®: White with gold edge, 18 count, 1½x25 inches or to fit basket (The Finish Line)
Basket: 7 inches diameter, 3 inches deep
Hot glue gun and glue

Stitch

Follow instructions for cross-stitching given in Cross-Stitch Basics.

Finish

Measurements are for a basket of the dimensions given at left; adjust as necessary for smaller or larger baskets. After cross-stitching the design on Ribband®, glue the band to the basket using a hot glue gun. Press firmly in place around basket. Start and end at the back of the basket, overlapping slightly.

Use Christmas Ribbon Border on Page 300 and Christmas Holiday Alphabet Below

Materials

Stockings: Premade with 7 count, cream, Klostern fabric (Adam Originals)
Satin cord: Red, 1 yard
Tapestry needle: Size 20
Fabric glue

Stitch

The premade stocking is lined in muslin. You may stitch right through the lining and the cross-stitch fabric. Knot floss on back. Use six strands of floss for cross-stitching and two strands of floss for backstitching.

Finish

The premade stockings require no finishing. You may wish to add red cord for embellishment using fabric glue.

Christmas Stockings with Border

Use All of the Christmas Borders on Page 304

Materials

Stockings: Premade with 7 count, cream, Klostern fabric (Adam Originals)
Satin cord: Red, 1 yard
Tapestry needle: Size 20
Fabric glue

Stitch and Finish

This is a "sampler" that uses all of our different Christmas borders. Follow instructions at left for stitching and finishing. Try designing your own stocking using the borders and the Christmas Holiday Alphabet below for personalizing.

Floss

Symbol	Color name	DMC	Anchor
♡	Red*	321	9046
	*Backstitch lowercase e, r, s, and z in red (one strand)		

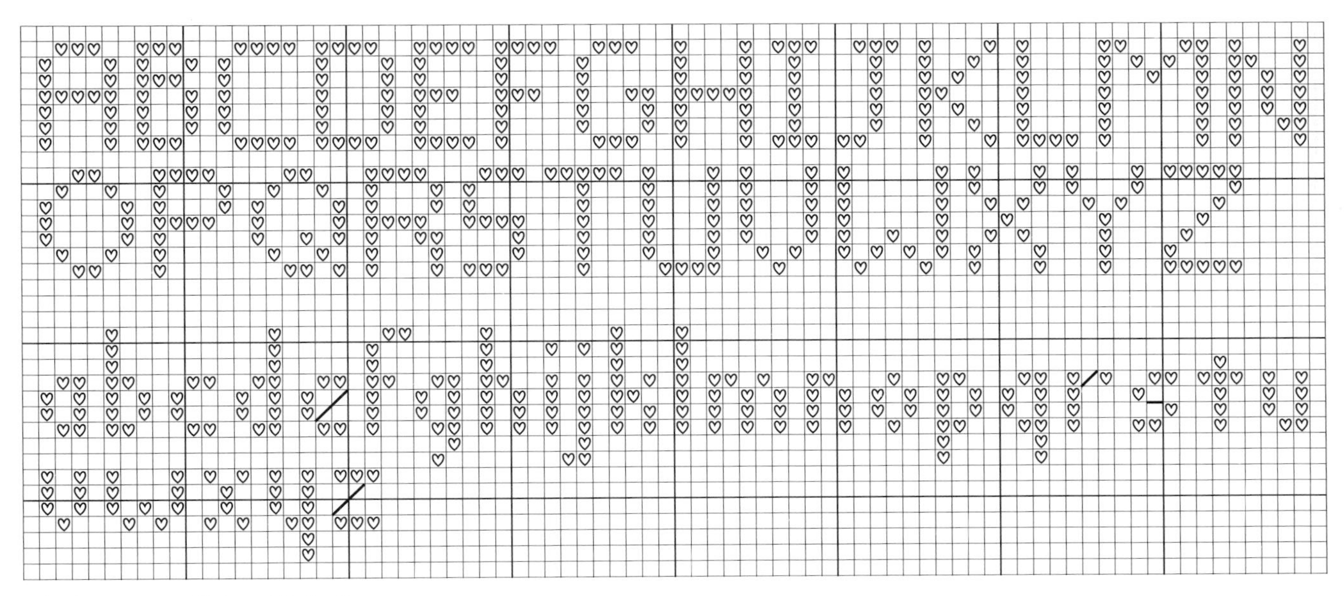

Christmas Holiday Alphabet

Christmas Napkins

USE CHRISTMAS RIBBON BORDER BELOW

Materials

Napkins: Premade, 15 inches square, white, Royal Classic (Charles Craft, #RC4852-6750)

Stitch

Follow cross-stitching instructions for stitching over two threads given in Cross-Stitch Basics. The design is cross-stitched ¾ inch in from edge of each napkin on the bottom and right-hand side. We stitched an extra holly and berry at the corner.

Finish

Premade napkins require no finishing.

Floss

Symbol	Color name	DMC	Anchor
/	Green	700	228
♡	Light red*	321	9046
♥	Dark red**	816	1005
⊙	Light red French knots		
	*Backstitch around light red areas in light red (two strands). **Backstitch around dark red areas in dark red (two strands).		

Christmas Place Mats

USE CHRISTMAS RIBBON BORDER BELOW

Materials

Place mats: Premade, 13x18 inches, white, Royal Classic (Charles Craft #RC 4851-6750)

Stitch

Follow cross-stitching instructions for stitching over two threads given in Cross-Stitch Basics. The design is cross-stitched ¾ inch in from the edge of each place mat on the bottom and right-hand side. We added an extra holly and berry at the corner.

Finish

Premade place mats require no finishing.

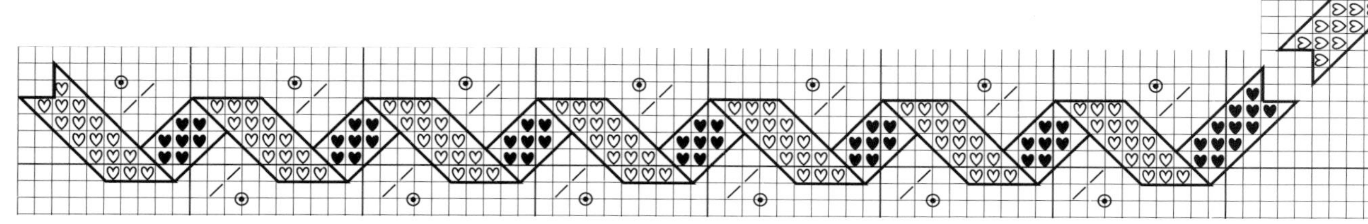

Christmas Ribbon Border

Candle Trims

USE CHRISTMAS TREE AND CHRISTMAS GIFTS BORDERS ON PAGE 304

Materials

Ribband®: 1½x14 inches, white with green edge, 18 count; 1½x14 inches, white with red edge, 18 count (The Finish Line)
Red candle
Green candle
Craft glue

Stitch

Follow the instructions for cross-stitching over two threads given in Cross-Stitching Basics.

Finish

After cross-stitching, trim Ribband® to fit candles. Place each piece around a candle, overlapping slightly in back. Glue edges tightly together.

Christmas Ornaments

USE CHRISTMAS GARLAND, REINDEER, HOLLY, AND ORNAMENT BORDERS ON PAGE 304

Materials

Aida fabric: 14 count, ivory, 4x5 inches per ornament
Stik 'N Puffs: 4 - 2½x2½ inch hearts, 4 - 2½x2½ inch rounds (BANAR DESIGNS, Inc.)
Cord: Red, 8 inches per ornament
Satin ribbon: Red, ½ inch wide, 6 inches per ornament
Tassels: Red, 2 inches, 4
Backing fabric: Christmas print, 4x4 inch per ornament
Craft glue
Floss: Red, 6 inches per ornament

Stitch

Follow instructions for cross-stitching given in Cross-Stitch Basics.

Finish

After stitching, cover Stik 'N Puffs following finishing instructions for Covering Padded Shapes in General Project Instructions. For each ornament, cover one Stik 'N Puff with a cross-stitched piece and the other with backing fabric. Before gluing the two shapes together, cut the 6-inch pieces of ribbon in half and wrap each piece around a covered Stik 'N Puff (see photo for placement) and into the adhesive on the back. Also stick a hanger (6 inches of red floss folded over) and a tassel into the adhesive. Glue the Stik 'N Puff pairs together, and glue cord around the edges.

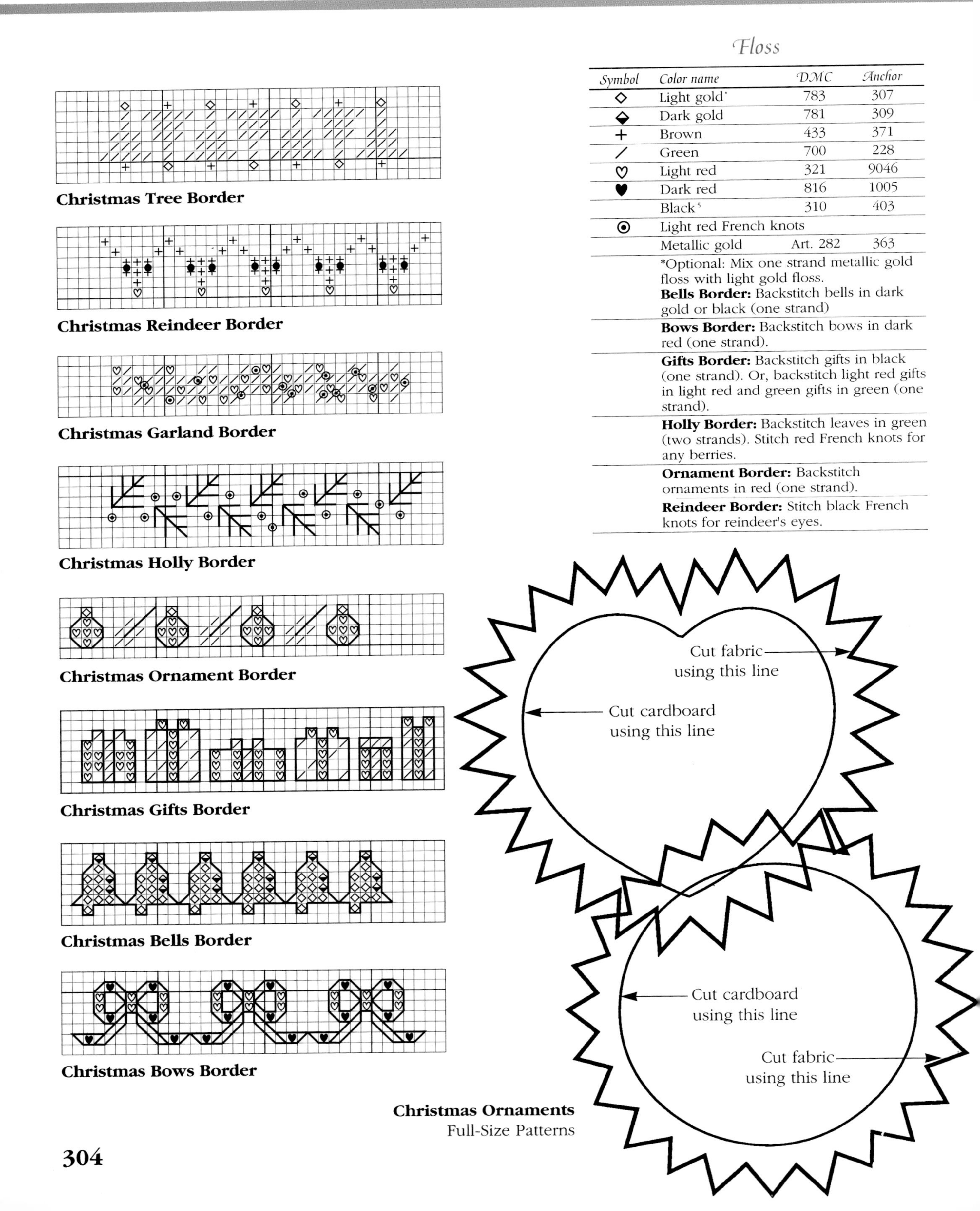

Christmas Tree Border

Christmas Reindeer Border

Christmas Garland Border

Christmas Holly Border

Christmas Ornament Border

Christmas Gifts Border

Christmas Bells Border

Christmas Bows Border

Floss

Symbol	Color name	DMC	Anchor
◇	Light gold*	783	307
◆	Dark gold	781	309
+	Brown	433	371
/	Green	700	228
♡	Light red	321	9046
♥	Dark red	816	1005
	Black[5]	310	403
⊙	Light red French knots		
	Metallic gold	Art. 282	363

*Optional: Mix one strand metallic gold floss with light gold floss.

Bells Border: Backstitch bells in dark gold or black (one strand)

Bows Border: Backstitch bows in dark red (one strand).

Gifts Border: Backstitch gifts in black (one strand). Or, backstitch light red gifts in light red and green gifts in green (one strand).

Holly Border: Backstitch leaves in green (two strands). Stitch red French knots for any berries.

Ornament Border: Backstitch ornaments in red (one strand).

Reindeer Border: Stitch black French knots for reindeer's eyes.

Christmas Ornaments
Full-Size Patterns

Joy To The World

Peace On Earth

Adeste Fideles

Season's Greetings

Merry Christmas

O Holy Night

May The Angels Sing

[illegible]

[illegible]

Christmas Phrases

Ideas for Use

Use these well-loved Christmas phrases for designing your own Christmas cards on perforated paper, Christmas samplers, stockings, or any other Christmas gifts. Combine them with any of the borders on pages 300 and 304.

Floss

Symbol	Color name	DMC	Anchor
♡	Red*	321	9046
	*Backstitch e, s, and r in red.		

Getting Started

Cross-stitching is needlework comprised mainly of X-shaped stitches that are formed by running threads through the holes in an even-weave fabric. This fabric is available in many types and colors, but all types have threads evenly spaced vertically and horizontally to form a grid-like pattern. The "count" given for the fabric indicates how many stitches can be made per inch on the fabric; stitching on a fabric with a count that is different from what is indicated in the directions will result in a smaller or larger stitching area. (See Using Charted Alphabets on page 310 for instructions on computing your stitching area.)

On the project charts, each symbol represents one cross-stitch, and there is a different symbol for each color of floss (see diagrams below). Backstitches

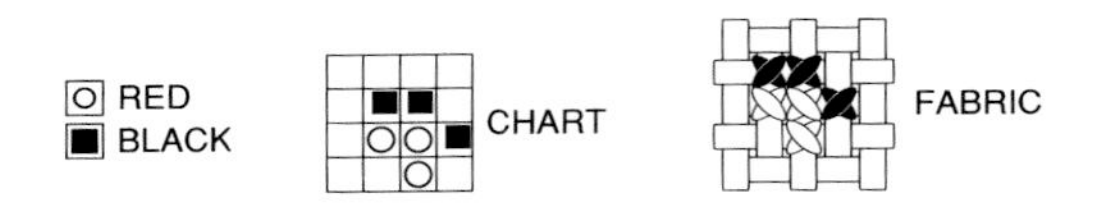

are represented by straight lines, with the floss color given on the color key for each alphabet. A key for the symbols, showing the color names and floss numbers for both DMC floss and Susan Bates' Anchor floss, is provided for each project; where applicable, Madeira floss is included. In alphabets done in only one color, an X is used to represent the cross-stitches; choose an appropriate color of floss to match the decor or favorite color of the recipient.

The horizontal and vertical center of the larger designs are marked with arrows on the chart. Find the center of your fabric by folding it in half in both directions and creasing the folds; unfold the fabric, and use a straight pin or running stitch to mark these center folds. Stitch the design in the center of the fabric, comparing the position of the stitches on the graph to the position on the fabric. (See additional information on centering your design on page 313.) When a project calls for perforated paper, do not fold to find the center, but measure along the sides with a ruler instead; tie a thread through the center hole on each side of the paper to mark it.

Materials

Fabrics

In this book, you will find projects featuring Aida and linen even-weave fabrics, premade fabric items with even-weave inserts, perforated paper with evenly punched holes, and plain fabrics stitched using waste canvas for its even-weave guidelines. Feel free to mix and match the fabrics with the projects you cross-stitch. Choose from the wide offerings of even-weave fabrics. There are variations in color, from black to white and all the colors in between; in count (holes per inch), from 7 per inch to almost 30 per inch; and in fiber content, from 100% linen or cotton to blends of natural and polyester fibers. Select fabrics that comfortably match your stitching style and project needs.

Some stitchers like to hold their fabric tight and straight in a stitchery frame or embroidery hoop; while this is optional for very small projects, it does make stitching easier in most cases.

General Materials Needed

Embroidery scissors
Sewing machine (for some projects)
Embroidery hoop (optional)
Iron
See individual projects for other necessary supplies

Floss and Special Threads

Floss is composed of six strands of thread. For cross-stitching, cut an 18-inch length; take the desired number of strands for stitching in one hand, hold the rest in the other hand, and pull it apart, letting the floss twist apart at the other end as you pull. Unless otherwise specified, cross-stitching is done with two strands; backstitching shapes is done with one strand, and backstitching letters is done with two strands.

Metallic floss may be used alone, but it has more impact when used with floss of a corresponding color. Use one strand of metallic gold floss and one strand of plain gold floss when metallic is specified on the color key. If you do not want to use metallic floss when it is called for on a chart, use a similar color of plain floss instead.

Quantities of floss needed may vary from project to project. Generally, one skein is enough for a project in this book. If a large quantity of one color of floss is used in a project you have designed, buy two skeins of the color or take a sample of the floss to the needlework store when buying more to be sure you have an exact match.

Needles

The details given for each project in this book indicate the type and size of needle used. For other projects, use the following guidelines in choosing needles. Tapestry needles, size 24 or 26, are used for most cross-stitching on even-weave fabrics or perforated paper. They have blunt points to move through the holes in the fabric or paper easily. Embroidery needles—those with sharp points—are best for cross-stitching using waste canvas on regular fabrics. If cross-stitching with glass beads, use a thin quilting needle (#11 size).

Embellishments

Charms, lace, ribbons, and buttons can be sewn or glued onto cross-stitched projects with washable fabric glue or craft glue.

Stitching

Begin a project by cross-stitching the center of the charted design in the center of the fabric. The most successful method of cross-stitching is to pass your needle entirely down through the fabric before bringing it through to the front again. This allows you to keep the floss even and does not distort the fabric.

Unless otherwise indicated, do not knot the floss; hold about a ½-inch tail of floss on the back of the fabric and cross-stitch over it with your first several cross-stitches to secure it. To end a thread, run the floss under several cross-stitches on the back to secure (see diagram below). Cut off excess.

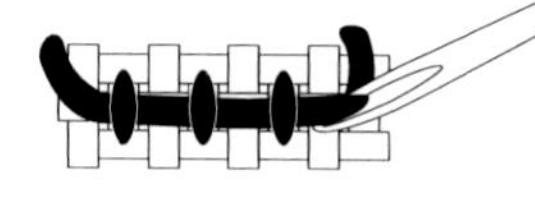

Most cross-stitching is stitched over one thread or square of the fabric, passing the needle from the back up through one hole, then down through the next diagonal hole.

Cross-Stitching over Two Threads

To make stitching more prominent, some designs are cross-stitched over two threads or squares of the fabric, passing the needle up through one hole, skipping the next diagonal hole, and going back down through the second diagonal hole.

The following instructions detail the basic stitches used to make the projects in this book.

Cross-stitch

Each individual cross-stitch is made up of two stitches that together form an X (see diagram at right). The bottom stitch is worked from lower left to upper right. The top stitch is worked from lower right to upper left.

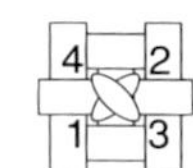

Do a row of bottom stitches first, working from left to right (see diagram at right).

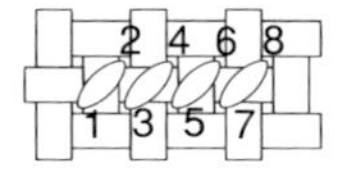

Complete the Xs by working the top stitches from right to left (see diagram at right).

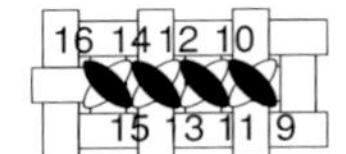

Backstitch

Backstitching is shown on the cross-stitch chart in heavy black lines. It is used to define shapes by forming a continuous line around them or to create lettering.

Backstitches can go diagonally across one or two squares of fabric or straight around the perimeter of a fabric square.

Do backstitching once the cross-stitching is complete.

The diagram below illustrates backstitching. The needle came up at 1; went down at 2, came up at 3, went down at 4 (the same hole as 1), came up at 5, and went down at 6 (the same hole as 3). In this manner, you travel twice as far on the back of the fabric as you do on the front, and you reuse holes.

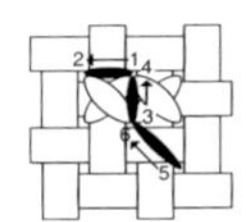

French Knot

French knots are shown as black dots on the chart; stitch these after all other stitching is completed.

Tie a knot in the end of the floss.

Bring the needle up from the back of fabric until the knot is against the fabric.

Pull the floss taut. With the needle close to the hole it came up through, wrap the floss around the needle two or three times (see diagram below).

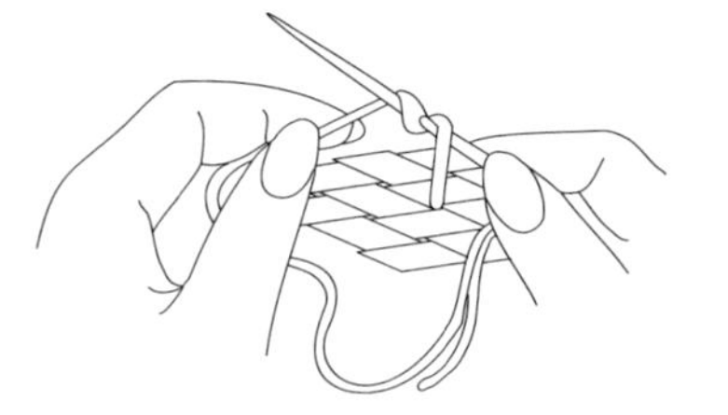

Hold the floss coming off the needle firmly near the hole, and push the needle through a new hole next to the first hole. Continue to hold the floss taut with one hand while pushing the needle through the hole with the other (see diagram top right).

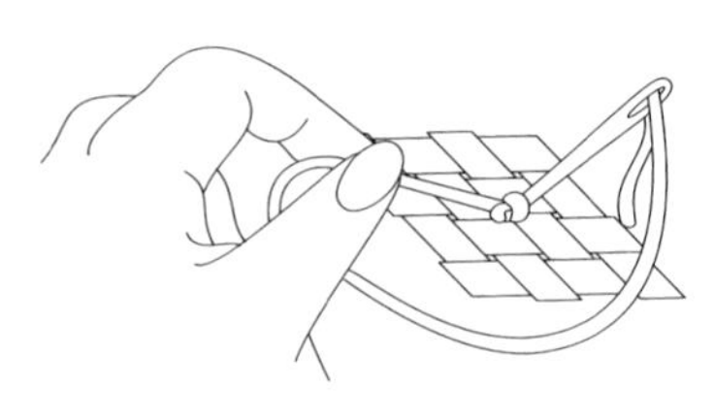

Pull the needle through to the back of the fabric until the tail of the floss is on the back side of the fabric; tie in a knot on back, and trim off excess.

Lazy Daisy Stitch

Bring the needle up from the back of the fabric.

Go back through the same hole, leaving a loop of floss on the top of the fabric.

Bring the needle up through a nearby hole, and position it inside the floss loop (see diagram at right). Pull the thread tight.

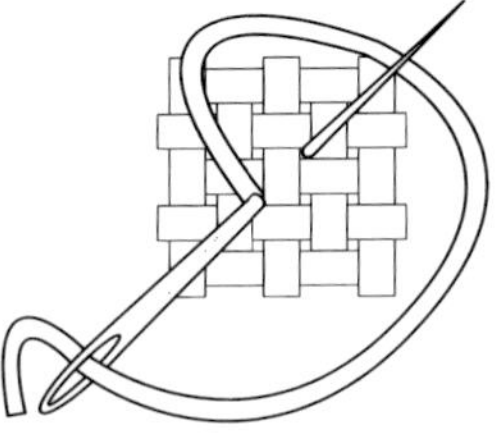

Pass the needle over the floss to the outside of the loop, and take it back down through the second hole (see diagram at right). Secure the thread on the back side when all stitches are complete.

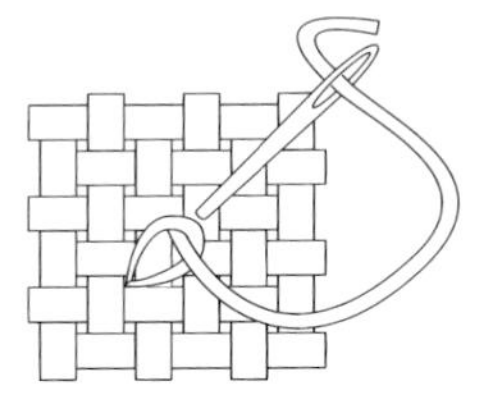

Correcting Mistakes

Everyone makes mistakes—especially in stitching. If you have used the wrong color or made a mistake in counting the placement of a stitch or stitches, first decide whether it is worth correcting. Some mistakes will go unnoticed, like the center of a flower being one square too small. But some errors, such as in symmetrical designs or letters, will need to be corrected. Identify the stitches you need to remove; use tiny scissors with sharp points or specially designed stitch-clipping scissors to cut the threads on the back side of the fabric. When the stitches are clipped, pull the remaining threads out of the fabric with tweezers and restitch.

Techniques with Special Materials

Perforated Paper

Cross-stitch on perforated paper just as you would on fabric, but be careful not to pull the floss too tightly or the paper may tear. Whenever you are cutting out shapes that have been cross-stitched on perforated paper, cut in the first empty hole outside the design. Cutting through a stitched hole may cause the stitching to become loose or frayed.

Glass Beads

When cross-stitching beads onto perforated paper or fabric, stitch all of them on the same angle, using a half cross-stitch. Use only one strand of floss to attach the beads; for best results, match the color of the floss to the color of the beads.

Use a No. 11 quilting needle or other sharp, thin embroidery needle.

Bring the needle up through the fabric or paper, through a bead, and down through the next diagonal hole, completing a half cross-stitch. Each bead may seem loose until you stitch the next one on.

Keep a few beads at a time in a small container such as a plastic lid. This makes them easier to thread onto the needle.

Start and finish the floss just as you do in traditional cross-stitching.

Waste Canvas

Waste canvas is a stiff grid of threads used as a guide when cross-stitching on fabrics that do not have an even weave. Follow these simple guidelines for using waste canvas.

Cut waste canvas to size specified in the project (about ½ inch larger on each side than the finished design will be).

To center the design on clothing, fold the garment in half lengthwise. Measure down this center fold to where you want the top of your design to be, and mark the location with a pin.

Measure to find the center of the canvas. Line the center of the canvas up with the center fold in the garment. Use the blue threads of the canvas as guidelines to place the canvas squarely on the garment. Pin it in place so the canvas is about ½ inch above where you want the design to start on the garment.

Baste around all edges of the waste canvas to hold it firmly in place or use Rescue tape, a double-sided tape especially for use on fabrics.

If desired, put the area in an embroidery hoop, making sure only the layer of the fabric you want to stitch is in the hoop.

Cross-stitch the design, using the large holes (not the small ones) where the threads of the waste canvas intersect. When working with waste canvas, you can knot the floss on the back when starting and ending a thread to make it more secure.

After stitching, remove the basting thread or Rescue tape, and trim the canvas close to the edge of the stitching, being careful not to cut the fabric.

Dampen the remaining canvas with a sponge or spray bottle of water to soften the fibers.

Pull out the horizontal and vertical threads of the canvas, one at a time, using tweezers.

Materials Needed for Working with Waste Canvas

Embroidery scissors
Tweezers
Rescue tape (optional)
Sponge or spray bottle
Embroidery or chenille needle

General Instructions for Cross-Stitching on an Anne Cloth Afghan

Find the center of the first square and mark it with a basting thread. Be sure you're working on the right side of the fabric. Check the decorative bars. The right side will appear more finished.

Start cross-stitching at the center of the design in the center of the first square of the fabric.

After cross-stitching is complete, cut off selvage edge.

For fringe, machine-stitch right next to decorative bars. (If desired, you can use zigzag-stitch over two threads.) Carefully pull out threads right up to machine stitching.

Helpful Hints

To make the back of your afghan neat and attractive:

Use the loop technique instead of tying knots to start new floss colors. For the loop technique, cut a piece of floss twice as long as what you need. Separate the floss into three sets of two strands each. Fold a set of floss in half, and thread cut ends through needle. Leave the loop at the opposite end. Stitch the first half of the first cross-stitch, bringing the needle up from the back, then down through loop on the back of the fabric; continue stitching.

Make your stitches as neat as possible. When going from one area to another, run the floss under a few stitches in the back. Don't run your floss in this manner more than a few stitches. If you need to carry the floss further, cut it and start again in the new area.

When you've finished cross-stitching with one color, run the floss under several stitches, and clip the ends close to the stitching. You may want to use a small amount of Fray Check on these ends.

Using Charted Alphabets

Introduction

Many of the projects in this book can be completed without any additional charting. If you have chosen one of those projects, you will not need the instructions in this section. However, one of the purposes of this book is to provide project ideas that call for you to chart a name or monogram and use it with a border. If you are even more adventurous, you may wish to combine several of the design elements, and maybe even a favorite phrase, into your own unique project. Follow the instructions below to become a "charting expert."

Materials for Charting

Gather the following materials for creating your own charts:

Pencil and eraser

Felt-tip pen (extra fine)

Chart paper and/or photocopies of the charted alphabet you choose (see Charting Methods *below*)

Calculator or paper for doing simple math

Choosing an Alphabet

The alphabets in this book are organized according to themes or styles. There are special occasion and holiday themes and Victorian, country, antique, and elegant styles. Some chapters are especially for children or babies and others feature floral and animal motifs. What you choose depends on your vision of the end result.

If you are creating a gift for a friend who decorates in a rustic style, you might want to choose something country. However, you may find that some of the animal designs would also be welcome in your friend's home. Some of the alphabets in each chapter are more generic and can be used in a variety of ways, including mixing and matching with other styles.

Experiment until you find the combination of letters and border designs that appeals to you and fits the style of your special project. And, by all means, don't forget to add your initials and the date to all your cross-stitching—it will be an heirloom someday.

To simply stitch a name or to sign your work, use the alphabets straight from the book; no charting is necessary. Simply count the squares in each letter, adding a space between each letter. Add these figures together and divide by two. This will give you the center of the name or initial. Then find the center of the fabric and start stitching the center of the name there. Or, place it wherever you want it to be in your design.

Charting Methods

Three basic methods can be used to create your own charts using the alphabets and borders in this book. You can trace the designs from this book onto transparent chart paper. You can hand-transfer the designs onto blank chart paper. Or, you can use photocopies of the charted designs to cut and paste a new chart. You may find a combination of these methods works best for complex designs.

Tracing Method

To use the tracing method, purchase transparent graph paper. Place the transparent graph over the design in the book, and use a pencil to trace the symbols and backstitching lines. When the chart is complete, go over the pencil symbols and lines with a felt-tip pen to make them more readable. Or, instead of tracing the symbols, you could fill in the squares with colored pencils or markers.

Hand-Transfer Method

Lay blank graph paper next to the charted design in the book. Copy all the symbols onto the corresponding squares on your graph paper using a pencil (or, fill in the squares with colored pencils). The graph paper can be folded to allow you to place it just beside or below the charted design you are copying. When the chart is complete, go over the pencil symbols and lines with a felt-tip pen to make them more readable.

Photocopy Method

You can also photocopy the chart you choose from the book, then cut and paste your variation together. Have copies made of the alphabet you want to use, and cut out the letters, leaving one or two blank squares around each. Tape or glue them on a piece of paper arranged in the design that you like. If you are using some letters several times, be sure you have plenty of photocopies made. For example, in Alexandra Allen, A is used four times, L three times, and E two times, so you'd need at least four copies. Form words first, then put the words together to form phrases.

Borders

Only small sections of most borders are given in this book. Repeat the design as necessary on your chart, making sure the repeat is fully represented, much as you would do with wallpaper. In the Kids chapter, for example, there is a border with children jumping rope, and the rope alternates in the up and down positions. Repeat the border with the rope in the correct position. Look at the photos of the various projects in this book to get ideas for various ways in which you can use borders.

You may wish to use a border design only on one side of a chart to give an attractive setting to a phrase or poem (see diagram A). Or, you can put rows

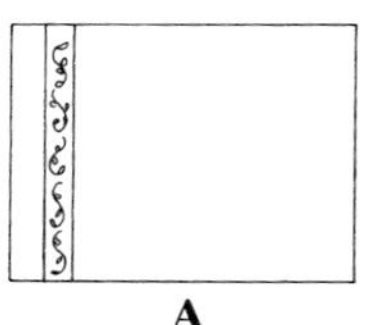

A

of border only above and below the design or phrase; be sure these border strips are identical (see diagram B).

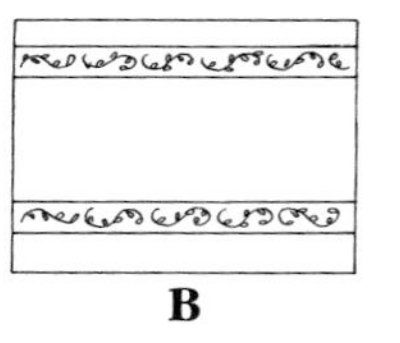

B

Some borders have special corner designs to use in combination with running edge designs to form rectangles. For those designs, start the border in the corner, repeat the running edge as many times as is needed to occupy the space enclosed; then add the next corner and repeat until all four sides are formed (see diagram C).

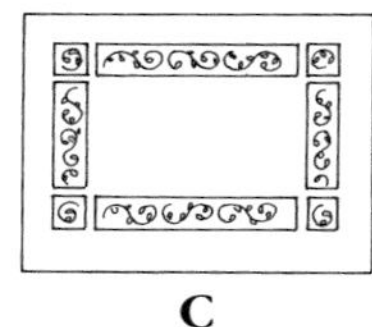

C

Borders without special corners may not occupy a rectangle evenly because there is no logical way to go around the corner. There are several ways to solve this problem. Run the border above and below the design area; fit the border sides within the top and bottom designs (see diagram D). Alternatively, you can

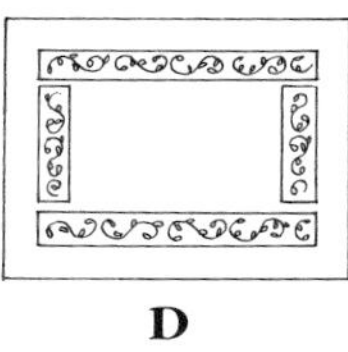

D

leave the corners blank, with the sides, top, and bottom of the border touching only at the inside corner edges (see diagram E).

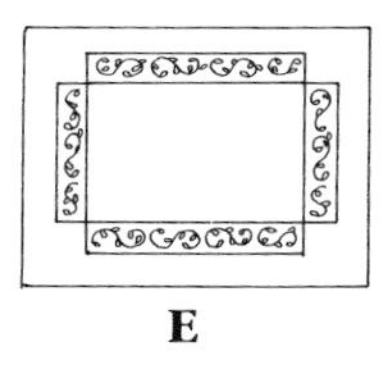

E

You may find your border is slightly larger or smaller than the exact size you desire due to the pattern of the border (you don't want half a flower, for instance). Just be sure you have enough space to enclose your letters or design within the border with one or two squares of fabric for spacing inside the border. Also, be sure you do not have a border so large that your cross-stitching doesn't fit in the area it's allotted (a pillow top, for instance).

Colors

In large charts, each square on the chart represents one cross-stitch and is marked with a unique symbol. These color symbols appear on the color key given with each chart. The same symbol does not necessarily represent the same color on different charts, so take care to use the specific color key for the chart you are working on. You may also want to substitute colors—

using shades of pink, instead of shades of blue, for instance. Less intricate alphabets merely use the X symbol for each cross-stitch and no color key is given. This allows you to choose your own floss colors.

Spacing

Spacing between charted letters should not be too large or too small. To achieve optimum spacing between letters, use whatever looks best to you and the following spacing guidelines.

When using smaller letters, you will probably need to leave one space or square of the fabric between letters and about three spaces between words. Sometimes, however, the letters look better overlapping, as in AVA (the tops of the V and the bottom of the A's are actually in the same row of holes on the fabric). The spacing between lines is often the same as the space between words, but it may vary according to the limitations of the space available, i.e., the frame or pillow size.

The larger the alphabet and the heavier (or more solid) the letters, the more space you need between the letters. The spacing between larger letters should be about ⅕ the width of the letters. If your spacing is too wide or too narrow, cut and paste the letters until you achieve the appropriate spacing; then stitch.

Centering

The arrows on the larger charts point to the center of the design. To find the center of your design, count the squares of the graph vertically and horizontally and divide each of those numbers by two. Begin stitching in the center. (For general information on centering, see page 306.)

To center lettering within a border, count the squares of the grid inside the border horizontally; then count the number of squares across the design or lettering you wish to place inside the border, and subtract. Divide by two and leave that number of squares on both sides of your design, between it and the border. Repeat for the vertical spacing. For example, if the inside, horizontal dimension of the border is 60 squares, and your design is 40 squares wide, the difference is 20; leave 10 blank squares on each side of your design to center it within the border. If the inside, vertical dimension of the border is 30 squares and the design is 15 squares from top to bottom, the difference is 15; leave 7 blank squares above the design and 8 squares below. (For numbers not divisible by 2, always leave the larger portion below the design or to the right of the design.)

Design

The elaborate letter alphabets, such as Floral Alphabet #1, are meant to be used as initials only or for the first letters of sayings or names. Use these fancy letters followed by some of the more simple lowercase letters when you want to spell out entire words or names.

Computing Finished Size

Once you have charted your design, you need to calculate the size of the finished design. This will help you choose the right count of fabric and help you determine if the chart needs further adjustment. Count the number of grid squares your design covers, both horizontally and vertically. If you have chosen a fabric, determine the count (how many squares there are in 1 inch); if you don't know, lay a ruler on the fabric, and count the number of squares in 1 inch. Then, divide the number of

(continued)

grid squares by the count of the fabric to find out how large the cross-stitched design will be. The following calculation for a sample chart, 33 by 96 grid squares, shows how large the cross-stitched design would be on various counts of fabric.

Grid squares Horizontally:	÷	Fabric count	=	Cross-stitched design width (approximately)
96	÷	11	=	8.7 inches
96	÷	14	=	6.9 inches
96	÷	18	=	5.3 inches

Grid squares Vertically:	÷	Fabric count	=	Cross-stitched design height (approximately)
33	÷	11	=	3 inches
33	÷	14	=	2.4 inches
33	÷	18	=	1.8 inches

You can see from the chart that as the count of the fabric increases, the amount of space the cross-stitched design covers decreases. So, if you are cross-stitching your design on a 2x8-inch bookmark, for instance, you would need to use 18-count material, making the cross-stitched design 1.8x5.3 inches; if you used another count of fabric, the design would be too large. If, on the other hand, you have an 8x10-inch frame, the 11-count fabric might be more appropriate; however, because the design would still only be 3 inches high, you might want to add a row of border above and below the design to fill in some of the excess space. Adjust your fabric count or your chart, whichever is appropriate.

Now, compute the size of your project, and get ready to stitch.

Grid squares	÷	Fabric count	=	Cross-stitched design size (approximately)
Vertically:	÷		=	
Horizontally:	÷		=	

Photo Albums

Materials

(See individual projects for amounts.)

Photo album: Ring-binder type
Fabric
Batting: 1-inch thick
Ruler
Felt-tip pen
Scissors
Thick, white glue
Poster board
Fabric-covered, padded shape (generally with stitching on it)
Lace, ribbon, rattail cord, or other decoration if desired)

Directions

(See diagrams for clarification.)

Note: Remove album pages while covering album; replace pages when glue is dry.

1. Place opened album on wrong side of fabric. Trace around the album with felt-tip pen. Add 1¾ inches all the way around, and cut out.

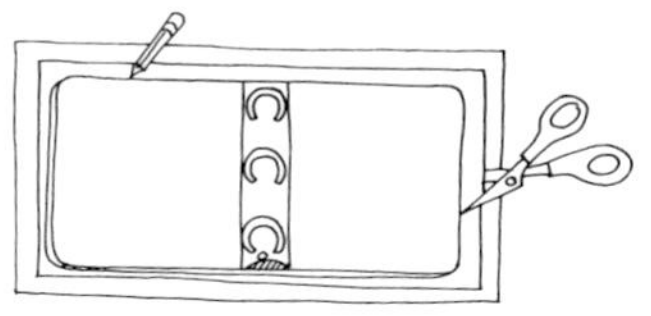

2. Place opened album on 1-inch-thick batting. Trace around it with felt-tip pen. Cut out on line.

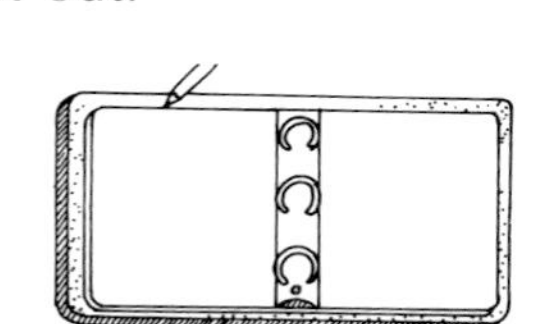

3. Cut two strips of fabric 1½ inches wide and ½ inch longer than the backbone of the album. Fold each end under ¼ inch and press folds to crease. Run thin line of glue down groove on each side of metal spine in center of album. Glue fabric strips down as close to metal spine as possible, or pry metal up slightly and slip fabric under edges. Then glue down remaining edges of fabric strip.

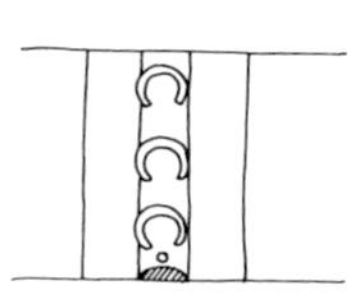

4. Lay fabric on your work surface with wrong side up; place batting in center. Place album on top of batting. Apply thin layer of glue to all corners of album cover. Pull fabric up and into glue at corners.

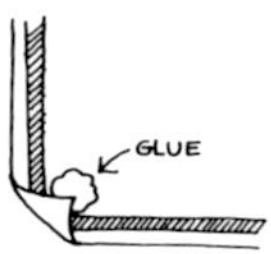

5. At bottom end of metal spine, cut two slits in fabric extending straight down from each edge of the spine. Fold fabric up at end of metal spine, and trim fabric to fit just under spine. Apply thin layer of glue along bottom edge of album. Fold fabric up into glue and smooth. At metal spine, fold fabric up into glue and, if possible, slip under the end of the metal; otherwise, fold fabric under and glue at end of spine.

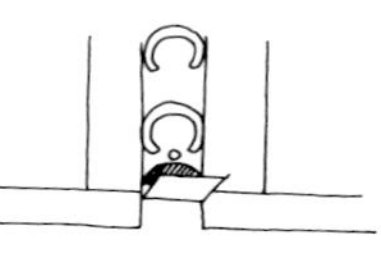

6. Repeat the previous step at the top edge of the album (turn the top edge of the album toward you to make it easier to work with). Pull the fabric taut so there are no wrinkles.

7. Apply glue to the side edges of the album. Fold fabric up into the glue.

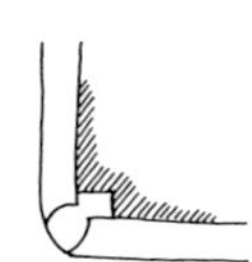

8. Apply thin layer of glue ¼ inch inside edges of album on top of just-glued fabric. Press lace into glue, starting and ending at center bottom of album.

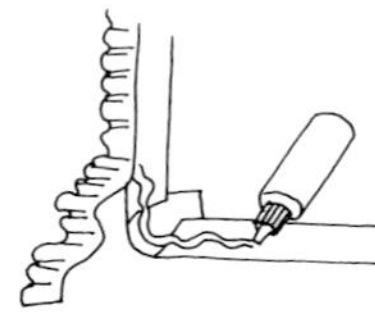

9. To round corners, pinch extra lace between your fingers and press into glue.

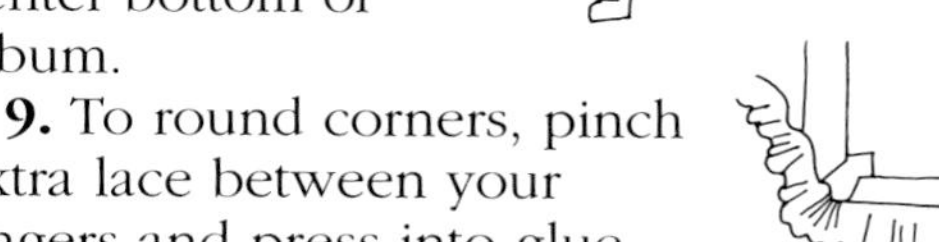

10. If you want ribbon ties on album, glue two or three lengths of ribbon to the center of each side of the album cover.

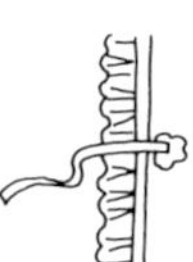

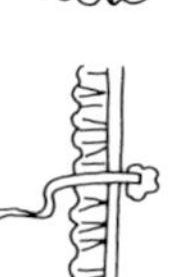

(continued)

Photo Albums

(continued)

11. Measure length and width of the inside covers of album. Cut two pieces of lightweight poster board this size. Cut two fabric pieces 1 inch larger than this size. Lay fabric pieces on your work surface with wrong sides up; place poster board pieces on top. Put glue around all edges of poster board; fold fabric up into glue, mitering corners (fold in from corners first, then sides). Put glue over the just-glued fabric. Turn over and place the covered poster board pieces, fabric sides up, on the inside of the album covers, covering the edges of any lace or ribbon already glued down.

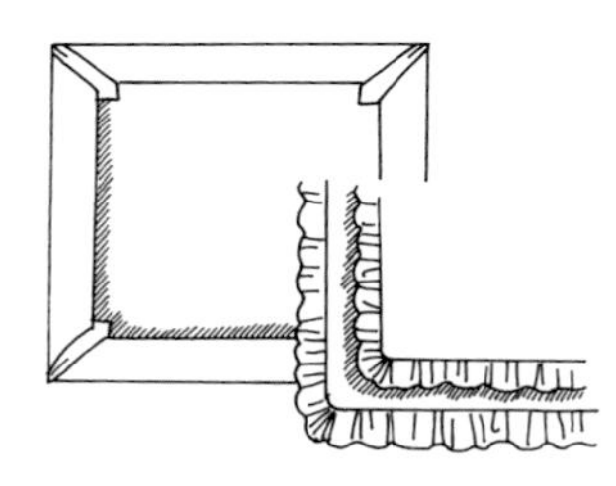

12. Make any covered shape or shapes called for in the instructions for your project (more complete instructions for padded shapes are given on page 318). If called for in your project, glue lace around the back of the shape.

13. Glue your covered shape(s) to the front of the album. If a more finished look is desired, add rattail cord to cover where the shape meets the album cover or the lace meets the edges.

Photo Frames

Materials

(See individual projects for amounts.)

Heavyweight cardboard: Such as 300-pound illustration board or precut photo frame with easel
Fabric: Cotton or cotton/polyester blend
Batting
Trims: Rattail cord, lace, or other as specified in project
Tracing paper
Thick, white glue
Scissors
Pencil
Felt-tip pen
Crafts knife, utility knife, or single-edged razor blade

Directions

(See diagrams for clarification.)

Note: Cover front, back, and easel of frame separately, then assemble.

1. Cut heavyweight cardboard using pattern specified in project; be sure to trace and cut both the inner and outer lines.

2. Hold the frame front up to a light, and place the cross-stitched fabric in front of it. Center the cross-stitched design over the cardboard, making sure no cross-stitching extends off the edge or into the center opening. Hold the fabric tightly in place on the cardboard and place on your work surface with cross-stitched design down, cardboard up; be sure the cardboard is aligned evenly with the threads of the fabric. With a pencil, trace around the cardboard on the fabric, both outside the edge and inside the center opening.

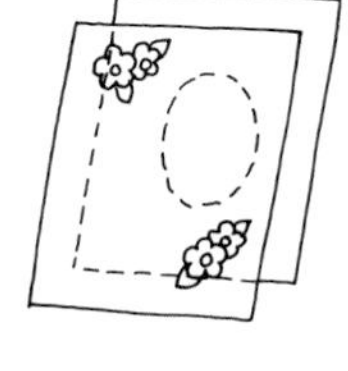

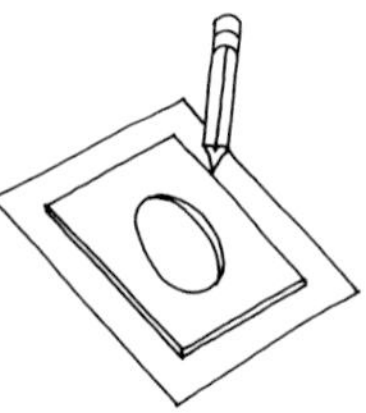

3. Remove cardboard, and trim fabric about ½ inch beyond the pencil marks (larger rectangle). Miter corners, cutting almost to pencil-marked corners.

4. Clip fabric every ½ inch on inside of center opening (in a sunburst shape) to within ⅛ inch of the pencil mark.

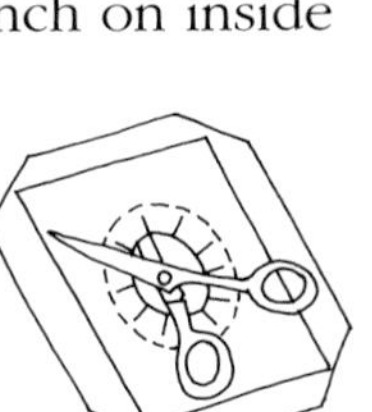

5. Place cardboard frame front on cotton batting and trace the shape, inside and out, with a felt-tip pen. Cut out and glue batting onto cardboard.

6. Place fabric on table, cross-stitched (or right) side down. Turn batting-covered cardboard upside down on fabric, lining it up with pencil marks on fabric.

7. Spread glue around outer edges of cardboard. Wrap fabric around outer cardboard edges and press into glue. Pull fabric as you work to keep it from wrinkling. Put a spot of glue in each corner, and work the corner fabric into it until it sticks, forming a neatly rounded corner; it will be moldable like clay. Press any loose threads into the glue.

8. Spread glue around the center opening. Pull fabric tightly into the opening, and press into glue. Pull any loose threads of fabric around to the back of the cardboard, and press into glue. Push and mold the fabric into the wet glue to make smooth edges (wash your hands several times as you work so fabric doesn't stick to your fingers). Look at the front of the fabric to make sure cuts in the fabric are not showing; if they are, keep pulling the fabric onto the back. If you want to add lace, do it at this time; spread glue near the edge of the back of the covered frame front, and lay lace around edge, pinching extra lace at the corners. Start and end lace at center bottom, overlapping ends slightly.

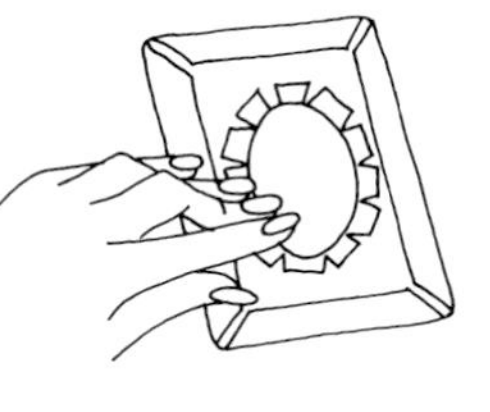

9. Cover the backing cardboard with fabric that coordinates with your cross-stitched design. Cut the backing cardboard, using the same pattern as the front, but not cutting out the center opening. Cut the fabric as you did in steps 2 and 3, and glue as in step 7, using a thin coat of glue so it won't soak through the fabric.

10. Spread a thin layer of glue on the front side of the backing cardboard that you have just covered (this area will show through the opening in the frame). Glue on a piece of fabric that is slightly larger than the opening.

11. Cut strips of cardboard ½ inch wide and as long as the two sides and bottom of your frame. Glue the strips in place on the cardboard backing to form a holder for your picture. If you wish, these strips also can be covered with fabric, at least on the outside edges and ends that will show.

12. When both front and back of frame are dry, glue them together, applying glue only to the cardboard strips around the edges.

13. Cut the easel out of cardboard (see pattern specified in your project). Score (cut slightly) horizontally with knife about 1 inch from the top (flat end). Place the easel on a scrap of fabric, and trace around it with pencil. Cut out a shape ½ inch larger than this tracing. Miter the corners of the fabric, and clip up to the points on the easel. Glue the fabric to the cardboard easel. Trace the easel shape with pencil onto another scrap of fabric, and cut it about ¼ inch smaller than the pencil mark. Glue this fabric to the back of the fabric-covered easel.

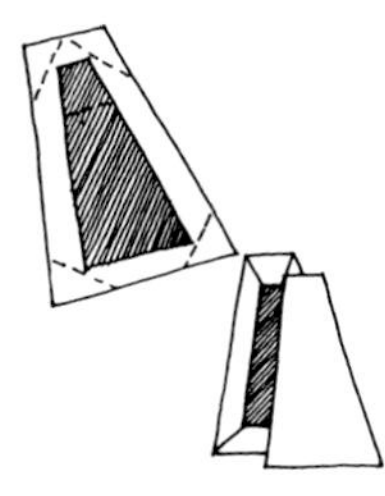

14. Glue easel to back of frame, positioning as shown at right.

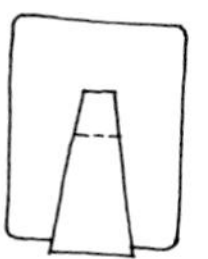

15. Add trims such as rattail cord around edges, if desired. Use the cord to cover the spacer strips if you didn't cover them with fabric. If you used lace, glue the cord where the stitched fabric meets the lace. Start gluing at bottom corner, and glue to very edge of top of frame so opening at top remains. Slide photo in position.

Padded Shapes

Materials

(See individual projects for amounts.)

Stick 'N Puffs precut, padded shapes with peel-and-stick back (or heavyweight cardboard, such as 300-pound illustration board, and batting to create your own)
Fabric: Cotton or cotton/polyester blend
Trims: Rattail cord, lace, or other as specified in project
Tracing paper
Thick, white glue
Scissors
Pencil

Directions

(See diagrams for clarification.)

1. If you are not using a Stik 'N Puff shape, cut heavyweight cardboard and batting using inner line of pattern or the size specified in project.

2. Pin the fabric pattern to the fabric, and cut out on the outer line; if no pattern is given, cut the fabric ¾ inch larger than the size specified in the project. If the fabric is cross-stitched, hold the pattern and fabric up to a light or window to center the cross-stitching in the pattern area.

3. Remove liner paper from Stik 'N Puff to expose sticky backing. If not using Stik 'N Puff, glue batting to cardboard.

4. Lay fabric on your work surface with right side down. Place Stik 'N Puff or batting-covered cardboard over fabric, cardboard side up. If not using a Stik 'N Puff shape, run a line of glue around edge of cardboard.

5. Press center of cardboard down to compress padding. Pull the fabric up around the padding, and press it into the adhesive or glue on the back of the cardboard. Look at the front of the fabric-covered shape; if there are any "points" showing on curved shapes, apply a drop of glue to the cardboard in back of the point, and work the fabric into the glue until the area is smooth.

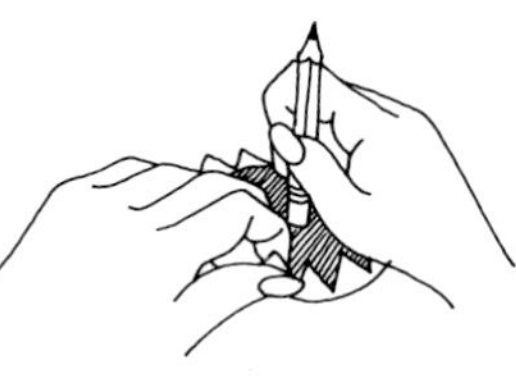

6. If using a square or rectangular shape, pull fabric sides up into adhesive. Apply a drop of glue to each corner, and smooth the fabric into the glue to seal the fabric to cardboard.

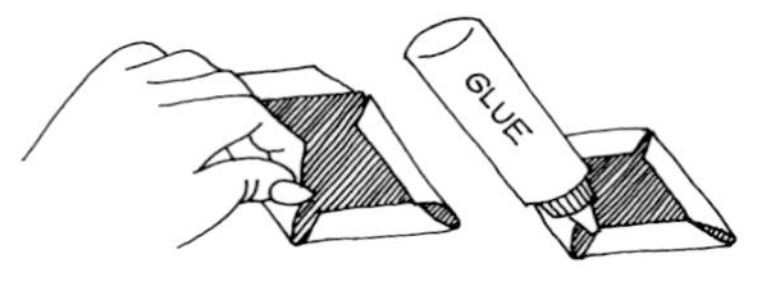

7. If the project calls for lace, run a line of glue about ⅛ inch in from the edge of the shape on the fabric on the back of the cardboard. Press the lace into the glue, pinching in extra at the corners to make an attractive turn.

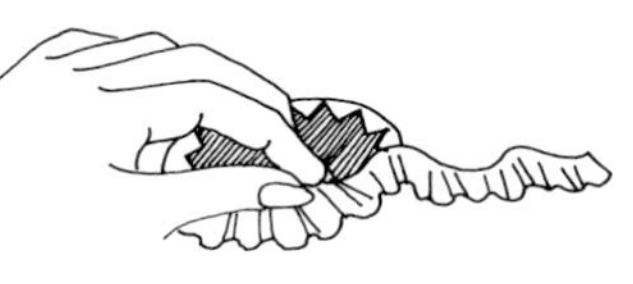

8. Glue the shape to an album or, for an ornament, glue two shapes back-to-back after adding a hanging cord at the top. Glue rattail cord around the ornament, if desired, to cover the area where the shapes meet; start and end behind the hanger cord.

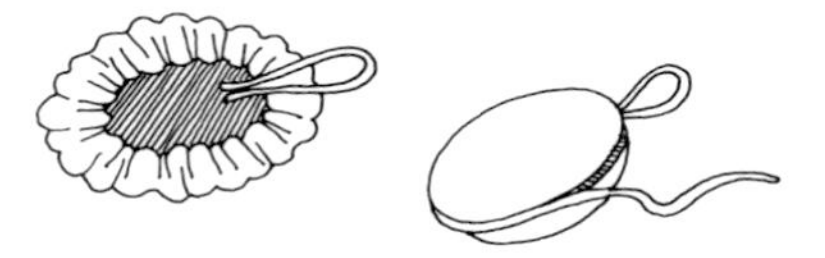

Making Tassels

Technique #1

Cut a rectangular piece of cardboard ½ inch longer than the desired length of the tassel. Cut a ¼-inch half-circle in each end of the cardboard. Wrap the fibers you have chosen around the cardboard lengthwise until you have the desired thickness. Slip one thread under cardboard at the top of the tassel (see diagrams below). Tie tightly.

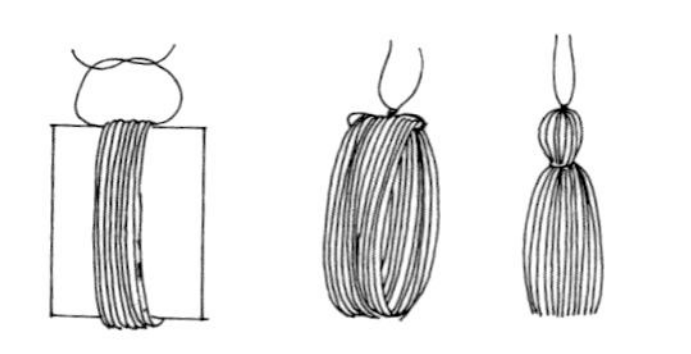

Technique #2

This gathering method works best when you are working with short pieces of fiber. Fibers should be double the desired length of tassel plus 3 inches (the extra 3 inches allows for trimming and fluff). Gather the fibers over a thin rod such as a piece of wire coat hanger, a chop stick, or a straw (see diagram A below). Fold the fibers over the rod. Tie one thread around the tassel approximately ⅓ of the way down to create the head of the tassel. If you wish the head to be bulkier, add a cotton ball or bead to the inside of the tassel head. Tie one thread around the tassel at the neck. Secure tightly (see diagram B below). Slip one thread through the head and tie at the top of the tassel. Remove the rod, trim, and fluff.

A

B

Making Monk's Cord

Monk's cord is twisted braid that resembles the cord monks wear around their robes. Easily handmade with any continuous yarn or fiber, monk's cord is a perfect way to customize your work. Select a color of yarn or fiber that is the same as one in your needlework or choose a complementary color.

Directions

1. For standard size monk's cord, calculate the length of yarn needed before twisting by multiplying the desired finished length by 7.
2. Fold the entire length in thirds, and tie a knot at each end.
3. The next three steps take two people. Insert a pencil in front of the knots at each end (see diagram A below). Stand facing one another. Keep the yarn taut at all times. Each person turns a pencil in a clockwise direction. Turn the pencils until the yarn is twisted so tightly that it begins to double back on itself just near the knot. *Keep yarn taut;* if not, it will kink.

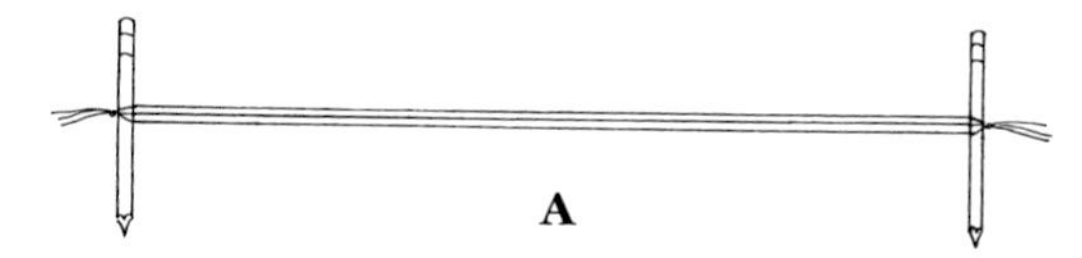

A

4. When twisting is complete, find the approximate center of the yarn. Have one person hold the center of the yarn while the other person pulls the two pencils together, always keeping the yarn taut (see diagram B at right).
5. After the pencils are joined, the center person can begin to let go a few inches at a time. The yarn will naturally twist itself (see diagram C at right).
6. Once the twisting has reached the pencils, remove the pencils and tie all ends in one knot.

To create a cord larger in circumference, begin with more strands than three. Try blending different yarns and fibers for a special look.

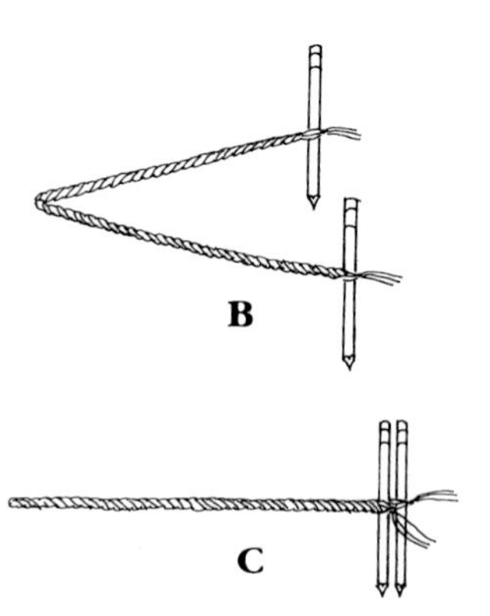

Sources

Look for the materials used in *Cross-Stitcher's Big Book of Alphabets and Borders* at your local needlework or craft shop. They were supplied by the following companies:

Cardboard Frames
Better Homes and Gardens® Book Club

Even-Weave Fabrics
Charles Craft
P.O. Box 1049
Laurinburg, NC 28352

Leisure Arts
P.O. Box 5595
Little Rock, AR 72215

MCG Textiles
5224 Bell Ct.
Chino, CA 91710

Wichelt
RR 1
Stoddard, WI 54658

Zweigart®
2 Riverview Dr.
Somerset, NJ 08873

Premade Linen Tote Bag
Janlynn
34 Front St.
Indian Orchard, MA 01151

Potpourri Bag and Vest
Hirschberg/Schutz & Co.
565 Green Ln.
Union, NJ 07083

Charms
Creative Beginnings
475 Morro Bay Blvd.
Morro Bay, CA 93442

Gold Locket
Thomas Collectibles
955 N. 400 West
North Salt Lake, UT 84054

Barrette
Wimpole St.
P.O. Box 395
West Bountiful, UT 84087

Premade Pillowcase
Designs for the Needle
2537 Madison
Kansas City, MO 64108

Round Button Drapery Tieback
Big Bold Button
Designs by Liz Turner Diehl, Inc.
385 W. Second Ave.
Eugene, OR 97401

Special Fibers from Elegant Chapter
Glissen Gloss™
Madeira Marketing Ltd.
600 E. 9th St.
Michigan City, IN 46360

Tissue Holder, Stitch-A-Mug, and Baby Cups
Crafter's Pride
from Daniel Enterprises

Mini Candle Screen and Clock
Wheatland Crafts
834 Scuffletown Rd.
Simpsonville, SC 29681

Perforated Paper
Yarn Tree Designs, Inc.
P.O. Box 724
Ames, IA 50010

Rescue Tape
Seams Great
12710 Via Felino
Del Mar, CA 92014

Ribband®
The Finish Line
P.O. Box 8515
Greenville, SC 29604
(Ribband® used by permission of the Finish Line)

Stik 'N Puffs (Padded Shapes)
BANAR DESIGNS, Inc.
P.O. Box 483
Fallbrook, CA 92088

Glass Beads
Mill Hill Glass Seed Beads
c/o Gay Bowles Sales
P.O. Box 1060
Janesville, WI 53547

Fabric Glue (washable)
Unique-Stitch
W.H. Collins
21 Leslie Ct.
Whippany, NY 07981